The Southern Past

A Clash of Race and Memory

W. Fitzhugh Brundage

The Belknap Press of Harvard University Press
Cambridge, Massachusetts ∾ London, England

First Harvard University Press paperback edition, 2008.

LIBRARY OF CONGRESS CATALOGING-IN-PUBLICATION DATA

Brundage, W. Fitzhugh (William Fitzhugh), 1959–
  The Southern past : a clash of race and memory / W. Fitzhugh Brundage
  p. cm.
  Includes bibliographical references (p.) and index.
  ISBN 978-0-674-01876-1 (cloth : alk. paper)
  ISBN 978-0-674-02721-3 (pbk.)
  1. Memory—Social aspects—Southern States. 2. Group identity—
Southern States. 3. Southern States—Civilization. 4. Southern
States—History. 5. Southern States—Race relations. I. Title.
F209.B78 2005
975'.01—dc22   2005041174

⁓

Quítame el pan, si quieres,
quítame el aire, pero
no me quites tu risa

Take the bread from me, if you want
take the air from me, but
do not take from me your laughter
                    —*Pablo Neruda*

Contents

ACKNOWLEDGMENTS   xi

Introduction   1

1 A Duty Peculiarly Fitting to Women   12

2 Celebrating Black Memory in the
  Postbellum South   55

3 Archiving White Memory   105

4 Black Remembrance in the Age
  of Jim Crow   138

5 Exhibiting Southernness in a
  New Century   183

6 Black Memorials and the
  Bulldozer Revolution   227

7 Contested History in the Sunbelt
  South   270

Conclusion   316

NOTES   345
INDEX   406

Illustrations

Members of the Oxford (Ga.) Women's
  Club dressed as wives of U.S. Presidents   23

Former slave and "Servant" Reunion
  organized by the UDC, Birmingham,
  Ala., 1931
     34

Edenton Tea Party dedication, North
  Carolina State Capitol   43

San Antonio (Tex.) Juneteenth Parade   56

Richmond (Va.) Emancipation Day crowd   66

Birmingham (Ala.) Knights of Pythias   74

Collections of the Alabama Department of
  Archives and History   109

Inside the Louisiana State Museum,
  New Orleans   116

Thomas Owen in his office at the Alabama
  Department of Archives and
  History, Montgomery   126

Suffolk (Va.) high school students   144

History Study Club at Tennessee State
   College in Nashville   151

Students in New Orleans studying
   black history   165

"Negro History" King and Queen,
   Lexington, Ky.   170

Black flower vendors on Charleston's
   streets, 1938   214

Charleston's Azalea Festival, 1938   220

John Avery Boys' Club, Durham, N.C.   229

John Merrick House, Durham   233

Protest march, Durham   249

White Rock Baptist Church, Durham   253

Westley Wallace ("W. W.") Law, civil
   rights and community activist   293

Exhibits at the Birmingham Civil Rights
   Institute   305

Natchez (Miss.) pilgrimage belles   323

Cast of "Southern Roads to Freedom,"
   Natchez, Miss.   325

Acknowledgments

FINDING THE WORDS TO ACKNOWLEDGE the small and large acts of generosity that have made this book possible seems an impossible undertaking. Yet I hope here to express my appreciation to at least some who have aided me during the many years I spent writing this book.

I owe a particular debt to scholars who pioneered the study of memory and civic culture. While writing this book I wore out the bindings and dog-eared the pages of books by David Blight, John Bodnar, Gaines Foster, David Glassberg, David Goldfield, Michael Kammen, Edward Linenthal, Mary Ryan, Michel-Rolph Trouliot, and Charles Reagan Wilson. My notes in this book cannot give a full measure of the inspiration that I have drawn from their writings.

I also have marveled at and benefited from the expertise and generosity of the staffs of the Alabama Department of Archives and History, Alabama State University Library, Arkansas History Commission, Auburn University, Birmingham Public Library, Daughters of the Republic of Texas Library, Duke University Library, Durham Public Library, Fisk University Library, Georgia Department of Archives and History, Georgia Historical Society,

Hampton University Library, Historic Natchez Foundation, Howard University Library, Library of Congress, Library of Virginia, Louisiana State University Library, Museum of the Confederacy, National Archives, National Humanities Center, North Carolina Department of Archives and History, South Carolina Department of Archives and History, South Carolina Historical Society, Tennessee State Library and Archives, University of Florida Library, University of Georgia Library, University of Louisiana at Lafayette Library, University of Mississippi Library, University of North Carolina Library, University of South Carolina Library, University of Tennessee Library, University of Virginia Library, Valentine Museum, Virginia Historical Society, Virginia State University Library, and Washington and Lee University Library. Without their help I could not have completed this book.

My research was generously funded by the American Council of Learned Societies, American Philosophical Society, National Humanities Center, Queen's University, Social Science Research Council of Canada, Virginia Historical Society, University of Florida, and University of North Carolina. Thanks to all who helped make this financial support possible.

To my friends and colleagues who have listened patiently and for too long as I learned about southerners and their contentious past, I offer my sincere appreciation. I look forward to returning the favor of enthusiasm and support that they gave to my work. David Blight and David Goldfield deserve special mention for their trenchant and enormously helpful comments on the completed manuscript.

Over the years, Bud Barnes, Frank Gallo, Kelly Minor, Andrew Moore, Leah Potter, Carey Shellman, Randall Stephens, and Bland Whitley proved to be tireless and skilled research assistants.

I could not have asked for better care and guidance from

Joyce Seltzer, Rachel Weinstein, and Julie Carlson at Harvard University Press. Julie did superb copyediting work, catching all manner of embarrassing errors. Rachel displayed uncommon patience with my queries as I worked to complete the manuscript. And Joyce's contributions to this book are so varied and important that I cannot imagine having written it without them. Whenever my ideas became muddled, Joyce reminded me what I was really trying to say and helped me to hone my argument. Most important, she transformed the work of writing this book into one of the most rewarding intellectual experiences of my life.

Introduction

In February 2000, the city council of Richmond, Virginia, voted to change the names of two bridges that link the north and south banks of the James River. Since then the J. E. B. Stuart and Thomas J. "Stonewall" Jackson bridges have carried the names of Samuel Tucker and Curtis Holt, two local notables in the civil rights movement. The council's decision outraged Jerry Baxley of the Southern Party of Virginia. "The Southern people are getting tired of being told they're not important," he fumed. He rebuked city officials for "taking away our heritage, our symbols." Three years later and a thousand miles away, Shelby Foote pondered the definition of southern art at the opening of a new museum in New Orleans. "I'm not aware that there is such a thing as southern art, at least not if you're defining it by technique," he explained. "If there's something distinct about it, it's subject matter and also inner heritage. All Southerners who try to express themselves in art," he announced, "are very much aware that they are party to a defeat, which is something most other Americans didn't feel until Vietnam." Baxley, a polemical provocateur, and Foote, a noted man of letters and interpreter of all things southern, define "southern" heritage similarly. Both presume that the Confederacy was the crucible of southern identity and that white heritage and southern identity are synonymous. The adjective "southern" apparently does not apply to African Americans who live south of the Mason-Dixon line. Moreover, by this definition, southerners have been unable to interpret the collapse of the Confederacy as anything other than a defeat.[1]

When southern identity is assumed to be interchangeable with white identity, much more than semantics are at stake. White claims to power, status, and collective identity are advanced at the same time that black claims are undercut. Baxley and Foote are hardly unusual in the cultural privilege they assign to whites. The logic of their comments rests on a presumption that the heritage of southern African Americans merits little recognition and has had scant influence on the region's culture. James K. Vardaman, an uncommonly zealous white supremacist and Mississippi's governor, made this claim at the dawn of the twentieth century. "The negro," according to him, had never built any monuments "to perpetuate in the memory of posterity the virtues of his ancestors." The black man, he proclaimed, had "never created for himself any civilization." Vardaman's strident claims are unlikely to be widely endorsed today. Yet the substance of his message still informs the commonplace use of "southern," which implies that southern heritage is the exclusive property of whites.[2]

In recent years headlines have announced heated controversies over the South's past: local discomfort in Laurens, South Carolina, about "The Redneck Shop" that also boasted it was the "World's Only Klan Museum"; the decision by the Virginia state legislature to retire the state song, "Carry Me Back to Old Virginia," because of its racist lyrics; a suit by a self-proclaimed white supremacist against the University of Mississippi for banning the

Confederate flag at football games; an attempt by blacks in Selma, Alabama, to topple a five-ton monument to Nathan Bedford Forrest, the founder of the Ku Klux Klan; and much-discussed campaigns to remove traces of the Confederate battle flag from various southern state flags. Some observers have been inclined to dismiss these contretemps as either an exotic southern variety of "political correctness" or an eccentric but harmless neo-Confederate revival. Actually, these controversies signal a profoundly important debate over the South's heritage, one that will continue to shape the region's public life for the foreseeable future. As Jerry Baxley well understood, much more is on the line than the names of a few bridges.[3]

To understand fully the significance of these controversies, we should pay attention to the history that southerners have valued, the elements of their past they have chosen to remember and forget, the ways that they have disseminated their past, and the uses to which their memories have been put. Southerners, white and black, men and women, obscure and famous, have used history to mold their deepest sense of self and articulate their aspirations for the region they call home. To understand the legacy of previous contests over the meaning of "southern," as well as the implications of ongoing debates over the South's past, is to sharpen our awareness of how competing histories divided southerners and how contests over the past eroded or strengthened public civility and democratic culture in the region. These questions remain as salient for southern public life and culture today as at any time in the past century and a half.

The notion that the South is a place saturated with history is so commonplace that it fuels the region's tourist industry and encourages the use of its exotic atmosphere in innumerable films and novels. This apparently tangible presence of the southern past is not happenstance; it is the consequence of more than a century of labor, investment, and design by individuals and groups who have imagined themselves as "southerners." These custodians of southern heritage have displayed the seemingly universal human impulse to keep memory alive and vibrant.

Scholars have adopted the conceit of "historical memory" to describe the amorphous and varied activities that southerners and others have employed to recall the past. No longer can we presume the existence of fixed images of the past that we retrieve intact through acts of memory. Instead, older notions of memory as a passive process of storing and retrieving objective recollections of lived experiences have recently given way to an understanding of memory as an active, ongoing process of ordering the past. Similarly, collective or historical memory is not simply the articulation of some shared subconscious, but rather the product of intentional creation. It consists of those common remembrances that identify "a group, giving it a sense of its past and defining its aspirations for the future."[4] Collective remembering forges identity, justifies privilege, and sustains cultural norms. For individuals and groups alike, memory provides a genealogy of social identity.

Collective memory, then, should not be mistaken for an "objective" record of the past. English dramatist Harold Pinter warns, "The past is what you remember, imagine you remember, convince yourself you remember, or pretend to remember."[5] Historical memory, in sum, transmits selective knowledge about the past. Yet in order for a historical narrative to acquire cultural authority, it must appear believable to its audience. Because groups care whether their historical narrative is "true" or "false," they establish standards of credibility against which they test it. Those standards, however, may vary greatly over time and from group to group, from society to society. In addition, whether provoked by slowly changing circumstances or sudden controversy, groups periodically apply new tests of credibility to differentiate what happened from what is said to have happened. The two-century-old controversy surrounding Thomas Jefferson's alleged paternity of slave children exemplifies this process. Until recently, defenders of Jefferson's reputation and many white professional historians dismissed as spurious rumors from black oral history that the author of the Declaration of Independence had fathered children by his slave Sally Hemings. Some, pointing to Jefferson's writings, concluded that an interracial relationship would have been inconsistent with Jefferson's character. Only when DNA testing apparently confirmed black lore did many scholars revise their conclusions. Throughout the long-running debate, groups fashioned and tested the credibility of their interpretations of Jefferson's relationship with Sally Hemings in particular ways at different times.[6]

Campaigns to remember the past by exorcizing parts of it have occurred in many times and places. Within collective memories a dialectic exists between the willfully recalled and deliberately forgotten. Shortly after the murder of Caesar, for instance, Cicero declared in the Roman Senate that all memory of the previous tumult should be erased. In Restoration France during the early nineteenth century, civil officials, following orders from Paris, adopted an explicit policy of "forgetting" the previous twenty-five years of revolutionary history. More recently, Austrians of Kurt Waldheim's generation recounted a past in which they were innocent victims of, rather than willing participants in, Nazi aggression. And in Colfax, Louisiana, the state Department of Commerce and Industry erected a monument commemorating a "riot" that "marked the end of carpetbag misrule in the South," but which might more appropriately have been described as a pogrom that claimed the lives of between fifty and 150 blacks.[7]

Groups secure broad recognition of their identities by colonizing public spaces with their version of their past. Like the Richmond City Council that previously named important civic facilities after Confederate icons and now recognizes civil rights activists, architects of historical memory display a keen appreciation of public space and understand that it is imbued with social meaning, and especially collective memory. By insinuating their memory into public space, groups exert the cultural authority, express the collective solidarity, and achieve a measure of the permanence that they often crave. To infuse objects and places with commemorative significance is to combat the transitory nature of memories and underscore the connectedness of the past and present. Historical memory thus becomes inextricably bound together with both public space and culture.[8]

Physical space is central to southern historical memory and identity. The public sphere—that figurative social space located between the home and the state—was claimed by white and black southerners as their own and as the appropriate venue to transform their private concerns into issues of general interest.[9] As the tangible, physical context for political debate and social action, public space serves as the most important arena for struggles over public power, resources, and values. The ability to occupy, use, and control one's physical surroundings is an essential measure of both personal freedom and collective power. Because access to public space entails claims of reciprocity and propinquity with other members of the "public," it is a fundamental marker of public identity. Historically access to the public sphere has required "social permission." Involvement is dependent on a sense among participants that they are equally implicated in public affairs and addressed by their discussion. Unwelcome participants can be ignored, thereby transforming the public sphere into a forum for exclusion as often as inclusion. In either case, public space serves to reproduce social relations that define some members of a society as worthy of access to public life and others as unworthy.[10]

Struggles over the control of space have been formative for both black and white southern culture. The breadth and tenacity of the historical memory that occupies public space serves as one measure of who has exerted power there. Elites, whether in Russia, India, or the southern United States, have been preoccupied with making "themselves the master[s] of memory and forgetfulness."[11] It is in the contests over the commemorative content of public space, such as the controversy over renaming the bridges in Richmond, that we can most clearly see how representations of history have been used as instruments of power. The civic landscape of the South looks the way it does because of both persistent inequality etched and erected in public spaces and dogged efforts to revise the same terrain. The enduring presence of white memory in the South's public spaces and black resistance to it, in short, is a central theme of the southern past.

The creation of historical memory in the public spaces of the South has harnessed the energies of all manner of groups. Because of the prevailing narrow conception of state obligations in the South, citizens necessarily looked to self-appointed groups in the public sphere to meet needs that officials were either unable or indisposed to address. The creation of influential historical narratives was as likely to take place outside of academia as within it; as custodians of the past, southern politicians, antiquarians, artists, and writers have exercised at least as much influence as have scholars.[12]

From bumper stickers and T-shirts we learn that "The South Will Rise Again," perhaps tempting us to conclude that some historical memory is impervious to change. But, as Eudora Welty observes, "memory is a living thing—it too is in transit." The identity of a group goes hand in hand with the continuous creation of its sense of the past. No enduring social memory can be static. Whenever a tradition is articulated, it must be given a meaning appropriate to the historical context in which it is invoked. Changes in the social and political circumstances of groups propel the evolution of the recalled past. Because power is central to the propagation of a version of history, changes in the relative power that groups enjoy invariably has consequences for what and how they remember. The recent controversy over the naming of bridges in Richmond is illustrative. When the Richmond City Council first named the bridges across the James, it was inconceivable that white councilors during the era of Jim Crow, let alone activists who challenged white supremacy, would name them after African Americans. Decades later, after the political empowerment of blacks and white flight to the suburbs, the now majority-black city council is sympathetic to calls to commemorate Richmond's black heritage. The name change thus is symbolic of recent transformations in the relative political power of whites and blacks in Richmond.[13]

This book traces historical memory in the South from the first Emancipation Day ceremonies in Norfolk, Virginia, in 1864 to the present-day controversies over the naming of bridges in Richmond and high schools in New Orleans. Its chronological focus reflects my interest in competing black and white historical narratives and their fate in the public sphere. My choice to begin this account at the close of the Civil War is not intended to endorse Shelby Foote's suggestion that the defeat of the southern rebellion is the defining theme of southern historical memory. The defeat of the Confederacy, of course, was a traumatic experience for white southerners. But of more profound importance for the historical memory of the South was the destruction of slavery and the freed people's acquisition of citizenship. If the war had ended before President Abraham Lincoln had issued the Emancipation Proclamation the future of southern slavery would have been unclear, but immediate abolition of the institution was unlikely. White southerners would have had to assuage their battered honor, but they would not have faced an immediate challenge to their power from their slaves. Because the war did not end in 1862 and instead became a war of liberation, however, the ignominy of defeat at Appomattox was magnified by the possibility of a virtual revolution in southern institutions and culture. From our vantage point, we recognize that Reconstruction was an "unfinished" revolution. But whites and blacks in the postbellum South could imagine various futures for their region and labored tirelessly to prevent some of them and secure others. The instability and uncertainty of the postwar era, at least as much as the unmistakable reality of Confederate defeat, was a formative influence on southern historical memory after 1865.

The postbellum South was not a tabula rasa on which blacks and whites could sketch their futures without regard to the past. Through law and custom, the slaveholding elites of the antebellum South had fashioned a public culture that was rigorously exclusionary. Civic rituals and public spaces gradually had become more democratic, participatory, and egalitarian (at least for white men) during the first half of the nineteenth century as more and more groups were incorporated into the "citizenry." But this expansion of southern public culture had clear limits. White women struggled to secure an honorific and circumscribed role in political life. Black men and women, whether free or enslaved, had virtually no acknowledged voice in the arena of public opinion. Public ceremonies and various associations celebrated the historical roots of the hallowed ideals of liberty and democracy that were enjoyed only by some white southerners. Rather than invoke an abstract, universal definition of humanity or citizens' rights, the recalled past that figured in the civic life of the antebellum South made the prerogatives of race, gender, and class appear to be a natural and inviolable part of history. There was no prospect of a democratic, biracial civic sphere in the South prior to the Civil War.

With the end of slavery, southern African Americans' relationship to the past changed as profoundly as did that of southern whites. If former slaves joined the ranks of the free with little more than their freedom, they also gained the capacity to celebrate their history and to participate in civic life in ways that had been impossible during slavery. Their nascent commemorative practices posed an unmistakable challenge to white understandings of the past. Indeed, the contest over the meaning of southern history after 1865 was waged not just between the North and the South, but also between white and black southerners. When white southerners set about codifying their heroic narrative and filling the civic landscape with monuments to it, they were conscious that the rituals of black memory represented a form of cultural resistance. For a century after the Civil War, whites ensured that public spaces conspicuously excluded any recognition of the recalled past of blacks. African Americans created their own understanding of the past, but whereas white memory filled public spaces and made universal claims, the black countermemory was either ignored by whites or was largely invisible to them. Not until the 1960s did blacks command the political power necessary to insist on a more inclusive historical memory for the South. Only then did they acquire the necessary leverage to displace white ideas about the past that had the cultural authority of tradition and habit.

Contestation over southern history for most of the past century and a half seldom took the form of knock-down, drag-out public confrontations. Such battles did happen occasionally, but usually only within the white or black community. While African Americans did challenge the competing memory of whites, they usually were unable to provoke any overt white response. Whites could not acknowledge acts of dissent without at the same time admitting the depth of black opposition to their power. Keen to preserve the "smooth surface" of their ephemeral power, southern whites urgently wanted to keep the social fact of black resistance out of public sight. Whites' responses to the black memory during much of the period since the Civil War, consequently, were oblique. Only at the very end of the twentieth century did the contests between whites and blacks over the South's past become volatile and distinctly public. Nonetheless, black and white southerners have been locked in an ongoing struggle over the past since at least the Civil War.[14]

Many pressing concerns about personal and regional identity, social interaction, and the exercise of power in the American South depend on an understanding of how the recalled past has been woven into southern life and institutions. This claim, on the face of it, may appear prosaic. After all, William Faulkner, C. Vann Woodward, and many other commentators have emphasized the power that memory exerts on the contemporary South. But to date we have explored, and haphazardly at that, only a small fraction of the South's remembered pasts. Rather than treat contested memory as an element of history that becomes salient only at moments of crisis or dislocation, we instead should acknowledge it as a central and enduring feature of the history that shapes daily lived experience, whether in Alabama, Mexico, or Ukraine.

During this book's lengthy period of development, the cultural landscape in the South has changed with a speed that I had not anticipated. Recently, black and white southerners have demonstrated that history need not be, as historian J. H. Plumb contended, exclusively destructive.[15] The proliferation of heterogeneous groups vying to interpret the South's past is one measure of the scope and health of the region's civic life. Robust debate has produced a more sophisticated appreciation of the region's heritage, one that will hasten the day when the South offers a truly inclusive public life. It is no longer premature to anticipate a future for the region in which the invocation of heritage will advance emancipatory rather than reactionary goals.

∾ 1

A Duty Peculiarly Fitting
to Women

WHEN THE RAIN CLOUDS THAT HUNG over Pensacola on the morning of June 17, 1891, parted, a throng of ten thousand spectators from across Florida and Alabama attributed it to a divine favor on "the most glorious day that the old city has ever seen." Vying for places along the city's streets, multitudes gathered to witness the unveiling ceremony for a thirty-four-foot shaft crowned with an eight-foot, musket-bearing Confederate soldier. Engraved on the four faces of the Virginia granite column were inscriptions immortalizing recently deceased Jefferson Davis, two prominent local Confederates, and the "Unknown Heroes of the Southern Confederacy." At the front of a parade of thousands were city officials, the state's governor, a float festooned with fifteen young women representing the states of the Confederacy, and carriages bearing the women of the Ladies' Confederate Monument Association, who had raised the money for the ceremonies and monument. Among the marchers were militia companies, members of the United Confederate Veterans (UCV), as well as the rank and file of assorted voluntary associations, fire companies, and white schoolchildren. The occasion, a newspaper boasted, was "a grand scene—grander by far indeed, than pen might adequately picture."[1]

The dedication of the monument concluded a year-long campaign by the Pensacola Ladies' Confederate Monument Association. An earlier effort to erect a memorial had foundered. Nine years later, Col. William D. Chipley, a local notable, took up the cause, publishing a circular in which he entreated local white women to launch a new monument drive. Chipley's wife and several other prominent women answered the call by organizing the monument association. By November 1890 they had awarded a contract to sculptor J. F. Manning of Washington, D.C. While he created the monument, the women solicited contributions by hosting benefit suppers, auctions, musical shows, elocution performances, lectures, and sporting events. In April 1891, with less than two months to spare before the scheduled unveiling, the association finally raised the $5,000 needed to pay for the monument. The dedication provided an opportunity to celebrate the collective sacrifice not only of Confederates, living and dead, but also of those who had made the monument possible. The privileged position of the members of the Ladies' Confederate Monument Association in the ceremonies made evident the prestige accorded them. With good cause, accounts of the monument's origins stressed that "Woman's hand and heart and deathless love" had "raised this object lesson in stone."[2]

Public commemorations across the South during the late nineteenth century were commonplace and not devoted exclusively to the Civil War. Less than a year before the founding of the Pensacola Ladies' Confederate Monument Association, a group of Nashville white women formed the Ladies' Hermitage Association to protest plans to use President Andrew Jackson's home as a facility for indigent Confederate veterans. When polite supplication failed to sway the legislature, the women organized opposition to the plan and forced a compromise. In April 1889 the state conditionally conveyed the Hermitage to the association, which, for all practical purposes, assumed responsibility for operating the shrine. In the same year a group of women, outraged by the threatened auction of Mary Washington's grave, organized the Mary Washington Monument Association in Fredericksburg, Virginia. Five years later, association members hosted President Grover Cleveland, the chief justice of the U.S. Supreme Court, the governor of Virginia, and other notable public figures. And in Texas, the Daughters of the Republic of Texas, organized in 1891, seemingly found their mission when in 1905 they assumed responsibility for the languishing Alamo, the famed shrine to the martyrs of the 1836 Texas Revolution. Across the region, white southerners sought to valorize their past by erecting countless monuments, staging parades, preserving historic homes, surveying cemeteries, chartering organizations, naming streets, unveiling plaques, and establishing parks.

This coordinated fashioning of a public past in Fredericksburg, Nashville, Pensacola, San Antonio, and across the South was a cultural development of profound importance to the region. When white southerners joined in the commemorative enthusiasm that gripped the nation during the late nineteenth century, they did so in a manner that sharpened their sense that they had a past and destiny apart from the rest of the nation. Through their activities, white southerners calibrated their allegiance to and their place in the restored Union. Even commemorations such as the Mary Washington monument or the Hermitage, which evoked a sense of national allegiance, displayed regional shadings.

This movement to craft a white public memory especially engrossed elite white women, who donned the mantle of "guardians of the past" to a degree without precedence in the region's history. By shaping the forms and methods used to evoke the past, organized white women established historical representations that endured long into the twentieth century. Their legacy included the creation of both a landscape thick with monuments and an infrastructure for the dissemination of a collective historical memory—at a time when few other groups were able to do either.[3]

These women architects of white historical memory, by both explaining and mystifying the historical roots of white supremacy and elite power in the South, performed a conspicuous civic function at a time of heightened concern about the perpetuation of the region's social and political hierarchies. Although denied the franchise, organized white women looked to history as a means to shape the South. Southern white women understood how power can make some historical narratives possible and silence others. Because the collective memory promoted by white women came to be viewed as authoritative tradition, it became an instrument of power.

Within the boundaries imposed by the prevailing beliefs of the era, the meaning of the history of the white South was open to multiple readings that in turn allowed white women to use it for varied purposes. For many white women, their gendered identities could not be separated from their ties to the past—not just their personal, familial past, but also the collective "History" of the South. Unsettled by the transformations of the New South, elite white women found in history a resource with which to fashion new selves without sundering links to the old. Historical activism also provided an antidote to exaggerated assertions of men's role in human progress. By giving meaning to the past, by crafting public memory, white women claimed for themselves the work of recording and narrating the progress of civilization, thereby laying claim to a new source of cultural authority.

Three years after the dedication of the Pensacola monument, the Virginia novelist Thomas Nelson Page complained that white southerners were "indifferent to all transmission of their memorial." At first glance, Page's appeal to white southerners to defend themselves before the bar of history appears curious. His plea, after all, coincided with an accelerating glorification of the Confederacy and the white southern past. Yet Page's despair about "the want of a history of the southern people" was not groundless. He implicitly contrasted his fellow southerners with their contemporaries elsewhere, especially Europe, and lamented the comparative paucity of their accomplishments.[4]

Page's lament reflected the divergence of American commemorative traditions, and Southern practices especially, from the conventions that prevailed elsewhere. In nineteenth-century France, for example, the national state used its administrative apparatus to affect everything from the market for art and museum holdings to civic rituals. Agents of the French government failed in many instances to impose their dictates, but their influence, felt through patronage and funding, swayed the strategies of cultural arbiters even in the hinterland. The same was true in Britain. The monarchies of Queen Victoria, Edward VII, and George V assiduously cultivated ceremonial splendor with the aim of inspiring allegiance to the Crown and the empire even at a time when royal power was in decline. Although regional identities endured and even appeared to strengthen in late nineteenth-century Britain, both state aid and royal patronage tethered these provincial expressions of memory to a larger national and imperial project. Even in Germany, where civic associations remained instrumental in promoting national monuments and celebrations through the 1870s, the reign of William II at the end of the century was marked by ostentatious public works, monuments, and rituals in which the emperor himself played a prominent role. Private organizations retained a place in articulating images of the German past, but the active role of the imperial state in selecting, popularizing, and institutionalizing a particular fund of historical knowledge was unmistakable. By actively influencing, directing, or subsuming most campaigns by the bourgeoisie and others to define public memory, European states strove to organize their citizenries into cohesive modern societies.[5]

With no meaningful tradition of royal cultural patronage inherited from the colonial era, Americans during the nineteenth century forged only a very weak link between the national government and national culture. Here, the tradition of limited government extended to the realm of public culture, where cultural voluntarism, rather than state intervention, prevailed. The nation's skeletal administrative structure and the dispersed authority inherent in U.S. federalism offered few resources with which to craft a national cultural policy, much less historical memory.[6] Campaigns to shape public memory, even by the most elastic definition of the term, rarely were topics of discussion within U.S. administrative corridors and legislative chambers. Even the most striking and enduring invented tradition of the late nineteenth century—the Pledge of Allegiance—was instigated by earnest grassroots activism; the federal government gave nothing more than its tacit approval to the campaign to promote this paean to the republic.[7] Likewise, none of the administrators of the nation's scattered and mundane museums (excluding the Smithsonian Institution) dared to rely on the generosity of government officials for funding. The appalling condition of most states' records confirmed officials' apathetic attitude about the preservation of the past. Only tireless pestering could pry funds from state coffers sufficient to subsidize the myriad monuments, statues, and other manifestations of memory that began to clutter the U.S. landscape in the late nineteenth century. In Florida, for instance, at a time when state disbursements grew from $1.5 million to nearly $4 million per annum, the largest single appropriation for historical commemoration between 1900 and 1915 was $14,654 for the Women of the Confederacy monument in Jacksonville. The sum total of state contributions for this and similar projects during this period was less than $50,000.[8]

Throughout the nineteenth century, state governments abjured responsibility over historical memory because it fell within that area of the public realm where their authority ended and the traditional authority of home and church began. It was precisely in this cultural space that voluntary associations held sway. Well before mid-century, the tradition of private citizens mingling informally, and independently from the state, to discuss public matters had given way to voluntary associations that served as self-proclaimed intermediaries between the state and a broader and ill-defined constituency, the so-called public. Because public authorities and ruling elites embraced a narrow conception of state obligations, citizens looked to voluntary associations to meet needs that public officials were either unable or indisposed to address. These conditions inspired increasingly ambitious voluntary organizations to shoulder ever larger roles within the public realm during the late nineteenth century.

That voluntary associations would assume the lead in matters historical was a given after the Civil War. Less clear was which groups would assume leadership of the project. Also uncertain were the respective roles that white women and men would play. The fault line of gender that cleaved life in the Gilded Age United States extended to the voluntary organizations that exerted the greatest influence over southern public culture. Although southern white men and women may have been united by their historical activism, they still divided themselves into organizations on the basis of gender. Their distinct groups vied, in a good-natured competition, to revere their region's past.

Confederate veterans were conspicuous among the southern white men who manifested interest in their region's past. Within a few years of Appomattox, local benevolent associations with ties to veterans proliferated across Dixie. Groups such as the Oglethorpe (Ga.) Light Infantry Association, the Northeast Mississippi Confederate Veteran Association, and the Charleston Light Dragoons Monumental Association were small, closely knit organizations that performed both memorial and charitable work within their immediate communities. By 1869 former Confederate officers in New Orleans, who harbored larger ambitions, had launched the Southern Historical Society. A year later, Confederate veterans eager to memorialize Robert E. Lee founded the Association of the Army of Northern Virginia. These organizations devoted themselves principally to compiling Confederate records, publishing justifications for the Confederacy, and excusing the South's defeat. Neither managed to mobilize more than a small fraction of the veterans in the region, let alone secure a mass following. Only gradually did local veterans' groups affiliate into larger associations, and not until 1889, with the founding of the United Confederate Veterans in New Orleans, did a truly regional organization committed to memorializing the Confederacy emerge. The simultaneous spread across the South of national patriotic and hereditary organizations such as the Sons of the American Revolution (SAR), as well as the founding of local historical societies, underscored the ambition of southern white men to shape the historical record of the region.[9]

Men's organizations typically offered only subordinate affiliations for interested women. Indeed, the Daughters of the American Revolution (DAR) traced its origins to the decision of the Sons of the American Revolution to bar women from their society. In October 1890, the Daughters convened their first official meeting, with no more than a handful of women present, but all vowing to "Perpetuate the memory and spirit of the women and men of the Revolutionary period." In just five years, the new organization boasted a membership that exceeded the combined membership of both the SAR and its friendly rival, the Sons of the Revolution. The rapid eclipse of the SAR by the DAR demonstrated the newfound influence wielded by women's historical associations.[10]

By the dawn of the twentieth century, men's voluntary organizations could not easily ignore that their white female counterparts had emerged as the preeminent custodians of "liberal culture," including matters historical. But white men did not hand over the authority to craft public memory so much as white women seized it. As Earl Barnes explained in the *Atlantic Monthly* in 1912, "It is not through the generosity of men that liberal culture has come into the possession of women; they have carried it by storm and have compelled capitulation." Two decades earlier, Joel Chandler Harris, one of the South's most popular and historically conscious writers, had already perceived the ambitions of southern womanhood. "There is no question and no movement of real importance in which she is not interested," he concluded. Beyond these general acknowledgments of women's activism, many commentators identified organized women as peculiarly adept custodians of the past. After a Virginia woman publicly deplored the neglect of Jamestown, a male letter writer to the *New York Times* in 1902 asked, "Why is it we [men] are not more interested in the preservation of links with the past? If I am not mistaken, women are more inspired with this spirit than men. In fact, we are indebted to their noble work for most of what has been accomplished." It was this presumption about women that had prompted Colonel Chipley's appeal to the white women of Pensacola to assume the leadership of the Confederate monument campaign.[11]

The Sons of the American Revolution and similar groups were, with few exceptions, junior partners to women's organizations. Even the influence of the UCV was ephemeral. It exerted considerable influence over white memory between 1890 and 1910; at its peak, more than 1,500 local "camps" of the organization dotted the South and perhaps as many as eighty thousand veterans filled their ranks. In addition, the official organ of the group, the *Confederate Veteran,* carried its message to an estimated fifty thousand readers. But the lifespan of the UCV was only as long as that of its members and it lost influence rapidly after 1910. The Sons of the Confederacy, a spin-off organization, faltered from its inception. The *Confederate Veteran* survived the withering of the UCV only because the United Daughters of the Confederacy (UDC) adopted the journal as its official periodical.[12]

Southern white men may have venerated the hallowed sacrifice of their ancestors, but they lacked enthusiasm for historical projects. A letter writer to the *Richmond Times-Dispatch* noted with regret, "I know of at least four counties in which the good women have started a movement for monuments and have failed and abandoned the scheme because of cold water thrown on them by men." Perhaps because defeat loomed so large in the southern past, the sons of the Confederate generation looked elsewhere for less ambiguous sources of male power and status. Athletic, political, and financial exploits, not cultivation of the past, were the preferred means through which fin-de-siècle men defined themselves. Matters of history evidently did not motivate white men to join fraternal societies. Jonathan M. Woodson admitted as much. In a 1904 letter he described his puzzlement at a woman friend who proudly wore the badge of the Colonial Dames. Although he had the requisite pedigree to join the Society of Cincinnati, a society of male descendants of Revolutionary-era officers, he had no interest in such "evanescent" honors, which he dismissed as "trivial." Almost certainly, Woodson and other southern white men who shared his view of patriotic and hereditary societies did not fully recognize the potential cultural power implicit in giving meaning to the past. That power became evident only over time through the energetic activism and cultural innovations of white women.[13]

The consolidation of white women's custodianship of memory in part was a consequence of the organizational revolution under way among southern women during the late nineteenth century. Just as voting and participation in the rituals of partisan politics were an essential part of contemporary male public identity, club activities had become for many women an equally important component of their public selves. So ubiquitous was the tireless and invasive clubwoman that she became a popular figure of ridicule. Dismissive stereotypes of armies of busybody women who demanded deference from men bespoke a real fear among many contemporaries about the expansion of white women's cultural influence within the public sphere.

Hints of white women's future organizational influence emerged even before the collapse of the Confederacy. Few southern towns lacked a Ladies' Aid Society during the Civil War. Organized Confederate women raised money for war supplies, tended the wounded, and oversaw the burial of the dead. A dra-

Members of the Oxford (Georgia) Women's Club celebrated women's roles in history by dressing as the wives of U.S. Presidents, ca. 1920. (Vanishing Georgia Collection, Georgia Department of Archives and History)

matic proliferation of women's literary associations and social reform groups occurred after the war, especially during the 1880s and 1890s. The rapidly swelling ranks of these societies were ideally positioned to become crafters of public culture, and of collective memory in particular. Organized like corporations with boards of directors and trustees who supervised squads of members, these voluntary associations exerted influence out of proportion to their size. Moreover, the overlapping memberships that were routine among women in civic, philanthropic, and hereditary associations facilitated the pursuit of missions that extended well beyond those implied by the names of many women's organizations. From the Caxtons Club of Pensacola and the Wednesday Club in Galveston to the Every Saturday History Class in Atlanta, women's groups maintained an active interest in local history. Virtually all state federations of women's clubs took up historical issues.[14]

The ranks of women with an organized interest in history were bolstered by women who joined "patriotic" and "hereditary" societies. The number of such organizations devoted to filiopietism and history reached comical proportions and assured steady employment for genealogists who compiled (or manufactured, as some skeptics suggested) the requisite documentation for membership. Two prominent but not atypical club women, Ida Caldwell McFadden of Texas and Mrs. Chalmers Meek Williamson of Mississippi, were, between the two of them, members of the UDC, DAR, Association for the Preservation of Virginia Antiquities (APVA), Daughters of the Pilgrims, Daughters of the War of 1812, Daughters of Colonial Governors, Daughters of the Founders and Patriots of America, Scions of the Cavaliers, Order of the First Families of Virginia, Order of the Knights of the Golden Shoe Society, Order of the Crown of America, Descendants of the Barons of Runnemede, and Colonial Dames of America.[15]

The rise of white women's associations demonstrated the continuing potency of the ideology of public service that many women embraced. Inherited ideals of "republican motherhood" and the cult of domesticity had long accorded women an important role in the transmission of culture within the home. Common wisdom held that selfless, disinterested, and virtuous women promoted harmony, morality, and discipline in the domestic sphere. By contrast, men, driven by selfishness and ambition, pursued their self-interest in the public realm. These ideals, in their most rudimentary form, charged mothers with instilling in their sons civic virtue and a love for the Republic. But even before the Civil War, notions about women's civic duty had been revised.

Rather than insist on the strictest boundaries of domesticity, proponents of women's activism claimed that women had a duty to infuse the public sphere with their moral beneficence.

Women's groups preserved the image of womanhood as guardian of the nation's soul but transformed its ideological association with individual mothers into a social image of organized women bonded together as mothers of the nation. Beyond extending women's moral domain from inside the home to the broader public realm, women's groups also demanded that women, in their own right, have a voice in the public sphere. Using voluntary associations, legislative petitions, publications, and their presence at public rallies and meetings, elite white women became important actors in politics and in reform campaigns of the antebellum South. The exigencies of the Civil War and Reconstruction encouraged even further expansion of women's organizational energies. The New South, now an increasingly complex society confronted by urbanization and industrialization, demanded yet broader forms of feminine public influence. Clubwomen challenged notions of privatized domesticity and, in pursuit of self-improvement and in the name of collective uplift, staked out increasingly expansive public goals. Arguably, women's "patriotic" activities in the seven decades after the Civil War were a logical extension of their traditional roles as educators and moral stewards of the nation's children. They were, in part, another manifestation of moral housekeeping writ large.[16]

Victorian conventions of mourning also assigned to women prominent roles in public remembrance. After Appomattox, white women often transformed their wartime soldiers' aid societies into memorial associations devoted to commemorating the Confederate dead. The Soldiers' Aid Society of Columbus, Georgia, for instance, begat the postbellum Columbus Ladies' Memorial Association. The first task undertaken by this group and many others was the creation of a Confederate cemetery. Beyond seeing to the proper burial of the Confederate dead, white women created rituals of remembrance. The pathos of widows gave rise to Confederate Memorial Day, which allegedly originated in Columbus, Georgia, in 1866 after a soldier's widow circulated an open letter to southern women calling on them to decorate the humble graves of the Confederate dead at least once a year. The appeal found wide support, and by 1870 local memorial observances had been knit into a regionwide holiday. For countless white women in the late nineteenth-century South, Confederate Memorial Day was the year's most important public event. They devoted months to recruiting the participation of schoolchildren, writing and distributing flyers, meeting with public officials, publishing articles in local newspapers, inviting orators, cleaning cemeteries, and tending to the minutia inherent in any public occasion. On the day itself, women performed the central ritual—the decoration of the graves. They also marched along the parade routes and sometimes even spoke to the gathered crowds—still controversial and symbolically powerful poses for women to take in public.[17]

Men sometimes bankrolled these activities, but women led them. They did so because memorialization and mourning belonged to the realm of sentiment that white men deemed and white women accepted as "peculiarly fitting to women." Speaking at the 1875 unveiling of the Confederate monument in Augusta, Georgia, Gen. C. A. Evans explained, "It was not man's privilege but woman's to raise these monuments throughout the land." With the hierarchical order of the South shaken by war, many elite white women, fearful of social chaos, committed themselves to reestablishing antebellum class and racial divisions. The participation of white women in the burgeoning Confederate celebration was a salve for their psychic wounds as well as those of Confederate veterans; women's memorial associations in large part reassured white men of their manliness and authority, and of feminine deference.[18]

Yet when white women scripted, oversaw, and participated in the memorialization of the Confederate dead, they expanded the boundaries that confined their behavior and authority. Throughout the antebellum period, mourning customs had narrowly confined women's conduct and dictated the most minute details of their dress. But at the same time, convention allowed and encouraged women to demonstrate their grief openly. So great were the region's losses during the Civil War that white women revised the restrictive customs they had maintained. United in mourning, white women redirected their networks of voluntary associations to perform tasks that government either could not or chose not to perform. Whereas the Union dead were assured a burial in national cemeteries established by the federal government, the Confederate dead often rested in unmarked graves, sometimes far from home. Ladies' memorial associations across the South retrieved the bodies of tens of thousands of fallen Confederates and returned them to Dixie. Once the remains were properly interred, ladies' associations tended the graves because local and state governments in the South lacked the resources to assume these tasks. Moreover, grieving white women could mourn and pay homage to the Confederate dead without arousing Northerners' fears of treason.[19]

While older notions of womanly public service and mourning explain the historical activism of the war generation, at the century's close a contentious debate over the role of white women as agents of civilization spurred a new generation to embrace the role of guardians of the past. Instead of casually perpetuating inherited cultural traditions, fin-de-siècle white women instead experimented with civic rituals and roles specific to their own times, needs, and possibilities. Much remained unresolved about the reconciliation of white women's conspicuous activism with the ongoing effort to perpetuate a patriarchal order in the South. Disfranchisement, legal segregation, economic discrimination, and white violence all worked to bolster the power of white men in the region. Yet a lingering mistrust of white men and an uneasiness with dependence on them encouraged white women to enhance their own power and sense of self. Even as many white women validated white male authority, they did so without renouncing their own claim to power—their role as partners in the millennial progress of the white race.[20]

Ideas about gender, race, civilization, and history were practically inseparable in the language and debates of the day. Civilization, as used by late nineteenth-century U.S. citizens and western Europeans, referred to a precisely calibrated stage of human development achieved when societies evolved beyond savagery and barbarism. Civilization itself was considered by many whites to be virtually a racial trait that only Anglo-Saxons and some other whites shared. Gender roles were one measure of civilization. The greater the gender differentiation in society, the reasoning went, the more refined the civilization. Consequently, the elaborate code of conduct that divided the idealized lives of white men and women into distinct realms was intrinsic to an advanced civilization. The perceived absence of such clearly defined gender roles among African Americans and other nonwhites purportedly demonstrated their limited evolutionary progress.[21]

This significance attached to whiteness and masculinity left ambiguous the contributions of white women to civilization. The logic of some ideas about civilization suggested that Anglo-Saxon men alone had the racial genius for self-government and the manly capacity of self-control that made the highest levels of social development possible. Accordingly, the story of human progress was a record of the power and beneficence of white men. Women, as vessels of civilization, arguably furthered human evolution chiefly as wives and mothers. And even this contribution was possible only because of the support and protection provided by white men, a point underscored by the white-hot debate about lynching and the defense of southern white womanhood during the 1890s. As women expanded the scope of their cultural custodianship, then, they confronted an ascendant, stridently masculine conception of civilization that represented an implicit attack on their female cultural authority.

That white women sought to forge a link between civilization and their gender and race helps to explain the projects they undertook as well as the rhetoric they used to justify them. Invocations of civilization littered the minutes, speeches, and publications of women's groups. Evelyn E. Moffitt of Raleigh, North Carolina, for instance, used the occasion of a Daughters of the Revolution (DR) meeting in 1911 to situate women in the saga of human evolution. "For two thousand years," she explained, "woman has gradually moved upward in the scale of civilization and now she is at the zenith of her power." With men protecting her and extending to her "such rights as reason and justice demand," modern woman had become an "independent agent" free to advocate "the uplift and betterment of humanity." Although Moffitt acknowledged women's dependence on "the chivalry of man," she nevertheless distinguished women as independent agents in the advancement of civilization. Some women made even larger claims. Inspired no doubt by the patriotic fervor that accompanied American participation in World War I, Sallie Southall Cotten, in a speech before a UDC chapter, proclaimed that "Civilization and religion are menaced and organized womanhood will strive to save both."[22]

Women backed up these claims by pointing to the historical

record. Mary Hilliard Hinton used the North Carolina exhibit that she organized for the Jamestown Tercentennial Exposition in 1907 to highlight the "Lost Colony" of Roanoke as the birthplace of Virginia Dare, the first "infant child of pure Caucasian blood"—a milestone that "proclaimed the birth of the white race in the Western Hemisphere." Sallie Southall Cotten joined with Hinton in elevating Virginia Dare as a paragon of historical womanhood. To commemorate "the advent of the white woman in America," she announced, was to inspire "woman, who now as then, continues to bring blessing to the land, and is recognized as a factor in all development." Hinton and many other white clubwomen dedicated themselves to recovering, recording, and emulating the heroic deeds of Dare and other unheralded predecessors. White women recast the familiar narratives of male valor so as to find vicarious honor for themselves. In 1896 DAR member Ellen Douglas Baxter insisted that "we must not forget" that women "made it possible for men to accomplish the grand results which history attributes to them alone." The dedication of the Edenton Tea Party memorial in the North Carolina Capitol in 1908 provided Evelyn E. Moffitt with an opportunity to vent her frustration over the inattention to white women's historical contributions. "This daring and heroic stand, so interesting and ever so fascinating[—]the wonder is that it has not held a place on the page of every revolutionary history. But has not this been the case in America that the lives of the generality of women are not deemed to be important enough to trace along side the histories of their distinguished sons!" White women even refused to concede the Confederate spotlight entirely to men. Speaking before a 1900 Confederate reunion, Lizzie Pollard announced on behalf of Confederate women, "Many of us are veterans, veterans as much as the gray, battle scarred old soldiers, tho' we bided at home. Are we not veterans as well as they?"[23]

White women activists remained committed to the ideology of civilization even while they revised it. When Ellen Douglas Baxter urged the women of the DAR to recall the deeds of revolutionary women, she did so in hopes that modern women would emulate their "same sense of duty," "quiet submission to the will of [their] husbands," and "long suffering, patience, and endurance." According to Mrs. Patrick Matthew of the DR, Penelope Baker, organizer of the Edenton Tea Party, represented "a leader and teacher of loyal womanhood, wife, mother, and with these elements of Christian love and obedience she became a jewel among her sex, a womanly woman of strength and vigor." Few white women looked to history to find inspiration for overturning the prevailing idea of civilization; instead their concern revolved around women's relation to it. Most clubwomen occupied a middle ground between feminists such as Charlotte Perkins Gilman who claimed that one's gender should not affect one's contribution to civilization and antifeminists who countered that women could advance civilization only as wives and mothers. Instead, history seemed to offer a useable past in which white women had remained "womanly" even as they, along with white men, pulled civilization forward.[24]

White women simultaneously affirmed the links between inherent racial attributes and civilization. The extraordinary emphasis placed on Anglo-Saxon heritage, manifest in the racial romanticism surrounding whites living in mountainous areas, the lore surrounding Virginia Dare, the punctilious vetting of genealogy, and the erasure of Hispanic participation in the Texas Revolution, reflected not only the logic of white supremacy in the South but also much larger, national concerns about the effects of immigration and apparent "race suicide" (that is, declining birthrates) of "old stock" Americans. When fused, these racial anxieties could generate language seemingly most appropriate to European imperial ambitions, as in the case of Sarah B. C. Morgan's 1902 report to the UDC. Active as an educational reformer and in the Georgia Federation of Women's Clubs, Morgan proclaimed that the preservation of Georgia's historic relics would not only bring "honor and glory" to the state but also "prove the brightest jewel in the diadem that crowns the Anglo-Saxon race the master work of creation."[25]

These and similar appeals by organized white women provided crucial ideological ballast for white supremacy by rooting the contemporary racial hierarchy in a seemingly ordained historical narrative. In autobiographies, essays on contemporary issues, nostalgic recollections published in the *Confederate Veteran,* and historical novels, white women contributed mightily to the moonlight-and-magnolia imagery of the old South. Even before academic historians at Johns Hopkins, Columbia, and elsewhere produced their "proslavery" historiography of the South, white women rendered idyllic the institution of slavery. Taken together, their writings and other representations of slavery and antebellum life achieved a kind of classic purity; the setting might vary from Revolution to the Civil War, but women populated their accounts with idealized renderings of dashing and honorable white planters, beautiful and refined plantation mistresses, content black mammies, and armies of loyal and innately ignorant slaves.[26]

To these fictional renderings of the Old South, organized southern white women added pageants of nostalgia. When, for instance, members of a Texas UDC chapter contemplated "Slavery Days" fifty years after the Emancipation Proclamation, they did so with unabashed fondness. In addition to performing music evocative of the Old South, such as "Swing Low, Sweet Chariot," "My Kentucky Home," "Old Black Joe," and "Uncle Ned," the daughters heard readings from Joel Chandler Harris, a sketch on "The Pickanines in the Quarter," and a paean to the "Black Mammy and her White Chillun." Other clubwomen went so far as to appropriate black dialect, dress, and alleged mannerisms to glorify slavery and the social order that it made possible. Cordelia Powell Odenheimer of Virginia won over audiences at fundraisers by wearing black face, singing "old darkey hymns," dancing the "Juba," and performing "Old Mammy" monologues. The glorification of the loving and faithful black mammy by white clubwomen was particularly conspicuous, reaching its zenith during the 1920s when the UDC proposed, and Congress considered, a national monument to black mammies on the Washington Mall. The corollary of this representation of slavery was that Reconstruction was rendered as a bacchanalia of corruption and barbarism that ended only when the Ku Klux Klan and white vigilantism restored white rule and, by extension, civilization.[27]

Behind this memory of domestic harmony and black subservience lurked anxieties about the brittle state of southern race relations, the domestic authority of white women, and traditions of interracial intimacy in an age of segregation. The representations of black mammies and carefree slaves suppressed those concerns by extolling the memory of slavery as a golden age of race relations when love and "familial" duty bound the races together. By shaping the imagery of slavery and of black slaves, white women fixed the cultural legacy of slavery, virtually expurgating alternative representations of slavery as brutal or immoral.

In the historic sites under the dominion of white women, the black past was acknowledged only when it seemed to validate the preferred white narrative. In 1889, when the Ladies' Hermitage Association assumed control of Andrew Jackson's home and opened it as a shrine, they became the de facto employers of Alfred Jackson, a former slave of Andrew Jackson's who lived his

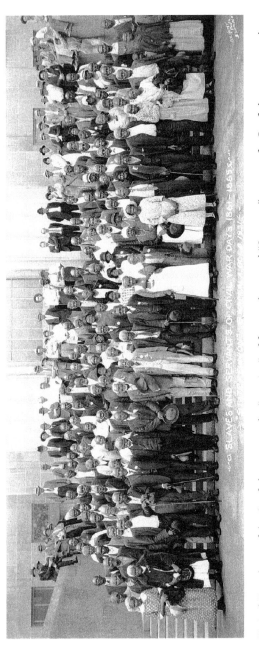

United Daughters of the Confederacy staged a "reunion" of former slaves and "Servants" as part of a Confederate veterans' reunion in Birmingham, Alabama, October 8, 1931. (OVHFF14.44SI, Birmingham Public Library)

entire life at the Hermitage. The association mined Alfred's intimate knowledge of the house, the personalities who visited it, and the possessions that filled it. His recollections informed everything from the placement of furniture to the presentation of the site's history. Indeed, Alfred became a favored guide at the site, a task he performed for dignitaries ranging from military heroes to ex-presidents. What meaning Alfred intended his memories to convey is unclear. We can only wonder the extent to which Alfred's position—an aged former slave who was dependent on his storytelling and white audiences for his livelihood—influenced his voiced memory. Whatever his intent, the Ladies' Association heard in his yarns a soothing chronicle in which General Jackson was noble, slavery benign, and white privilege unquestioned. Alfred's "loyalty to General Jackson, his exaltation of his fame, and his devotion to his memory approached the sublime," gushed a member of the Ladies' Hermitage Association. His humor deflected potentially contentious questions, as when, for example, a white visitor asked him if General Jackson had ever tried to sell him. "Did any of your folks ever try to sell you, madam?" he parried. "Uncle Alfred," as he was known by whites, was "so quaint, so original, and so pronounced a type that visitors, as well as the Association of ladies, overlooked his shortcomings and regarded his story as a product of the old plantation days, of which Uncle Alfred was a most interesting exponent." When Alfred died, the Association buried him near his former master's grave at the Hermitage. His epitaph—"A Faithful Servant"—reduced his life to terms that white visitors could readily understand and accept.[28]

This commitment to white power and civilization encouraged a distinctively nationalist version of history as well. The DAR offered a history of the Revolutionary War and the nation's founding from which sectional flashpoints were expunged. But if the DAR sought to provide a common ground for women who identified with either the Union or the Confederacy, the organization nonetheless limited its ranks to Anglo-Saxon womanhood and extolled Anglo-Saxon civilization. Local chapters and the national organization alike celebrated the contributions of the white South in building the nation and worked to rehabilitate the wounded pride of white southerners. On the occasion of the Jamestown Exposition, a DAR leader reminded the nation that "if the rosary of patriotism should be counted," the South's role in the building of the republic could not be underestimated: "First in settlement, first, with Massachusetts beside her, in resistance to tyranny through the fiery eloquence of Patrick Henry and Richard Henry Lee; first through Thomas Jefferson in the Declaration of Independence; first through James Madison, in framing the Constitution." In 1912, the DAR even invited the UDC to conduct its formal ceremonies at Washington's Independence Hall, the DAR's most hallowed symbol, when the southern women held their first convention outside of the former Confederacy. With Confederate flags flying next to the American flag, and to the sounds of the U.S. Marine Band playing "Dixie" and "The Star-Spangled Banner," UDC and DAR members mingled in a festival of nationalism that simultaneously promoted the restoration of white southern pride and sanctioned white supremacy.[29]

The cultivation of a refined sense of class status was another corollary of white women's embrace of Anglo-Saxon civilization and the South's privileged place in it. The finely honed elitism of most women's societies is evident in their very names. Membership in them evinced an unmistakable claim by birthright to cultural dominion over the remembered past. The elaborate vetting of ancestry required to join hereditary societies (which also bespoke notions about the links among blood, race, and civilization), as well as the ever-popular Martha Washington tea parties and colonial balls, precisely apportioned roles among participants according to the groups' standards of birth, wealth, and social station. Although claiming to speak in the name of the broader "public," white women's voluntary associations operated in a less-than-democratic public arena where those groups with the deepest pockets and the closest ties to elites had the greatest likelihood of imposing their sense of the past on the civic landscape. The Ladies' Memorial Association of Athens, Georgia, for example, was led by Laura Cobb Rutherford, the sister of two prominent secessionists and the wife of a professor at the University of Georgia. Among the organization's other officers were her sister-in-law and the wife of a prominent state legislator. The officers of the Ladies' Confederate Monument Association of Pensacola included Angela S. Mallory, whose husband was memorialized on the monument, Ann Elizabeth Billups Chipley, whose husband had originally proposed the monument, and the wives of leading businessmen. Women club members presumed to speak for a broader "public" across the region, even though the membership of that public, as these representatives conceived of it, was effectively limited to elite, urban whites.[30]

This orientation was evident in the stridently elitist narratives of history authored by most white women's clubs. Along with preserving historic sites, the Association for the Preservation of Virginia Antiquities (APVA), for example, incorporated veneration of bloodlines and elite white culture into its mission. The Virginia past, when distilled by the APVA, sanctioned the continuing leadership of the state by a purportedly disinterested elite. Such invented traditions as the APVA-sponsored annual pilgrimages to Jamestown were intended to instill respect and awe for the state's dutiful white leaders, who had founded the nation, established representative government, and purportedly provided steadfast public service. The unmistakable lessons of this past were deference to white social betters, reverence for established institutions, and fidelity to tradition.[31]

By invoking the past, different groups of white women

sought to depict certain visions of the region's future as disloyal to its heritage. Some white women, gripped by doubts about modernity, cast the meaning of the southern past in explicitly antimaterialist and antimodernist terms. Hostility to innovation was evident in those women's historical associations, reform groups, and literary societies, which criticized fast-paced change, selfish individualism, and excessive materialism. In 1897, Rosa Woodbury, a Georgia educator, alerted UDC members that without women's activism the South might become "fossilized by gross materialism." Five years later, President Belle Bryan of the APVA warned members not to be swayed from their "pure and lofty ideals" by the prevailing climate of "sordid aggrandizement and selfish pleasures." Mary Hilliard Hinton of North Carolina repeated a similar mantra when she chided those of her contemporaries who deemed monuments and tablets "an utterly useless expenditure of money." To the contrary, she answered, reminders of the past safeguarded progress by "preventing the vandalic [sic] supremacy of materialism." At the onset of World War I, she was still complaining about "this age of perpetual unrest and dangerous commercialism." These jeremiads against progress evinced a widely held concern that men would abandon the past in their headlong pursuit of the future. These fears convinced the women that it was their duty to defend the "lost civilization" of the Old South and to soothe the corrosive effects of modernity.[32]

Tradition was the watchword for many white women who opposed woman suffrage. Opponents to black woman suffrage in North Carolina appropriated the cultural power of the first Caucasian child born in North America when they beseeched "in the name of Virginia Dare, that North Carolina remain white" at the polls and repudiated woman suffrage. Mary Hilliard Hinton, who assumed a prominent role in the antisuffrage movement in her native North Carolina, asserted that women in the colonial era had demonstrated that they did not need the vote in order to exert public influence. Moreover, to heed "the song of the suffrage siren" would be to renounce the "cause bought by the blood of your fathers and tears of your mothers." She saw nothing incongruous in using the *North Carolina Booklet,* a historical journal that she edited for two decades, to eulogize Revolutionary-era women and to denounce woman suffrage. Invoking the memory of the Lost Cause, a delegate to the 1911 UDC national convention proclaimed that "No daughter will be a suffragette." Similarly, Mildred Rutherford, the historian of the UDC, warned the Georgia legislature that "The women who are working for this measure are striking at a principle for which our fathers fought during the Civil War." Josephine Pearson and Nina Packard, leaders of the opposition to the Nineteenth Amendment in Tennessee, literally wrapped their cause in the Stars and Bars in 1919 by posing for a publicity photo with an aged Confederate veteran and an outstretched Confederate battle flag.[33]

The civilizationist ideology and the historical memory that it informed, however, could also generate demands that defy any antimodernist (or even reactionary) label. Many white women club activists yoked the Confederate memory to myriad social causes including child labor reform, prohibition, and educational reform. For Janet Henderson Weaver Randolph, commemoration and public activism were so intertwined as to be indistinguishable. Besides being a founder of the Richmond chapter of the UDC and an active member of the Confederate Memorial Literary Society (CMLS), which operated the Confederate "White House" in Richmond, Randolph was a indefatigable campaigner for relief for impoverished widows and children of Confederate soldiers. She prodded the UDC to create permanent relief committees and beseeched her club sisters to attend to the needs of "poor, blind, and helpless" Confederate women wherever they were found. And despite her "impeccable devotion to Virginia traditions," she jousted with opponents of women's education at the University of Virginia, promoted various charitable organizations active in the black community, and championed programs for working white and black women undertaken by the Richmond YWCA. Rebecca Latimer Felton, in an address before the Georgia division of the UDC, urged her audience to devote themselves to more than "decoration days" and pensions for elderly Confederate veterans. "To my mind," she announced, "the grandest monument that Georgia women could raise in memory of the [Confederate] dead" would be institutions that provided equal educational opportunities for women. Sarah B. C. Morgan connected the causes of the American Revolution and the Civil War to her campaign to expand women's educational opportunities when she mobilized the Georgia DAR and Colonial Dames to petition the trustees of the University of Georgia to allow women's admission to the school.[34] Although many women historical activists were prominent in the antisuffrage movement, so too were many conspicuous in the suffrage campaign. Some of the suffragists had become convinced by their study of history that granting the ballot to women would secure white political hegemony and elevate southern civilization.

Other white suffragists refused to allow southern traditions to be hijacked by the antisuffragists. Southern suffragists, as a rule, did not invoke white supremacy as the principal justification for extending the right to vote to women. Instead they contended that the vote was a natural right, that it would make women both better mothers and more effective reformers. When Virginia suffragist leader Lucy Randolph Mason demanded the ballot as a natural right, she skillfully affiliated her ancestors, including John Marshall and George Mason, with the cause. For her and other suffragists, their sense of themselves as prospective political participants rested to a considerable degree on a cultural authority rooted in the southern past. The "white-gloved" respectability that these women derived from their ancestry and their membership in patriotic, hereditary, and historical societies countered antisuffragists' assertions that woman suffrage was both a foreign and a radical abomination. Even while Susan Pringle Frost of South Carolina tirelessly promoted historical preservation in her hometown of Charleston, South Carolina, by appealing to sacred southern traditions, she was a dedicated suffragist and member of the National Woman's Party. And Jane Y. McCallum's zealous suffrage activism in Texas was only matched by her lifelong dedication to the Colonial Dames. Suffrage, for these women activists, was a continuation of the rich reform tradition of southern women, not a repudiation of regional heritage.[35]

However divided white women activists may have been over suffrage and other contemporary debates, they shared a conviction that it was both their place and their right to nurture the memories of their class and people. That they were surprisingly successful at renovating the public spaces of the South to reflect their image of history was the result of the vision, resources, and talents they devoted to being "guardians of the past." Their stamp on civic life in the New South was both conspicuous and subtle. It shaped the civic spaces of the region's cities and towns, now increasingly important to the New South, as well as the lessons those spaces taught. Likewise, the manner in which organized white women conducted themselves in public life dictated how public discussions over the region's past were waged and resolved. And, more often than not, it was white women's fund-raising acumen that determined what in the South's white past was commemorated.

Women well understood the importance of the historical representations with which they filled public spaces. Their activities, after all, took place in an environment in which gender distinctions were conspicuous and at a time of intensifying racial segregation. Historical sites, like all public places, had to be situated within the region's spatial grid of gender and race.[36]

In commemorating the past, clubwomen created historic spaces that welcomed other white women. By doing so, they seemingly rendered ambiguous or contradictory the exact boundaries between white male and female public spaces. The shift over time in where monuments were erected by women is revealing. The white women located the earliest Confederate memorials in cemeteries, where women had an accepted place and role. By the end of the century, their preferred location for monuments was in courthouse squares and other prominent public spaces, such as the Pensacola park, situated on a bluff overlooking the downtown. This migration of monuments symbolized the new authority that women's groups exerted over the official, political landscape. In such instances, as when Hinton and the North Carolina DR erected a commemorative marker to the heroines of the Edenton Tea Party in the North Carolina Capitol, women intruded their presence into spaces previously associated exclusively with male power.[37]

Other sites established the historic domain of women—at least as understood at the time—as worthy of both historical recognition and preservation. The campaign to save George Washington's Mount Vernon, waged during the 1850s by the Mount Vernon Ladies' Association (MVLA), established the precedent for the "house museum" movement at the century's close. In Virginia, the APVA saw itself as continuing the work of the MVLA and pointed with pride to its restoration of Mary Ball Washington's home as a shrine in Fredericksburg. Women's associations in

Daughters of the Republic celebrated the contributions of women to the American Revolution by dedicating a plaque commemorating the Edenton Tea Party in the North Carolina State Capitol, 1908. (*North Carolina Booklet,* 8 [April 1909]: 264.)

Atlanta, Charleston, and Tampa, to name only a few of many examples, quickly embraced historic preservation as part of their mission and acquired historic house shrines. In the process of preserving these homes, women indulged their fascination with the evolution of domestic spaces. They shifted the focus on the Revolutionary era away from male exploits on the battlefield and in politics and toward "spinning wheels and balls," thereby incorporating feminine material culture into the recorded past. On occasion, the women's devotion to preservation clashed with that of some of their erstwhile allies and patrons. When Colonel Crenshaw of the male advisory board of the Confederate Memorial Literary Society in Richmond recommended the removal of unsightly outbuildings at the White House of the Confederacy, he aroused the ire of Kate Pleasants Minor. Rejecting the need to render the historic dwelling "up to date," she insisted on the importance of preserving intact the "environment" surrounding the mansion. For Minor and the women who erupted in applause in support of her position, the enduring significance of the outbuildings outweighed any offense they might have posed to modern sensibilities. Although in this instance Minor's expansive vision of preservation did not prevail, elsewhere women with similar attitudes enjoyed greater success.[38]

By the turn of the century, no historic home was complete without a colonial kitchen, spinning wheel, or other tropes of bygone domesticity. Simultaneously, the commercialization of the past—manifest in everything from colonial revival architecture to the mania for antiques, decorative arts, and historical kitsch of all kinds—made historical icons of the feminine sphere available to women shoppers. To connect the duties and rituals of the domestic world with glories of the past, to celebrate the prosaic, was to magnify the role of women in the creation of the nation. Integrating women's values with the commemorated past satisfied white women's need to feel included rather than separated, important rather than insignificant.[39]

When white women set about transforming the public spaces of the New South, they employed time-honored techniques to win support for their commemorative activities. Since the early nineteenth century, women had used associations to exert power lodged not in political or religious institutions but in the mandate of "public opinion." The commemoration of past valor and sacrifice meshed easily with the belief held by many women that public life should be conducted according to moral convictions. Women, to a greater degree than men in the nineteenth century, endorsed the idea that popular suasion, and, when appropriate, government influence, could and should be used to shape citizens' behavior.[40]

Sallie Southall Cotten's unflagging efforts to establish the Virginia Dare Association during the 1890s typified the innumerable techniques that organized women used to generate "public" support for commemorative activities. Born of a genteel but financially insecure family in antebellum Virginia, Cotten changed along with the New South. While serving as one of the "Lady Managers" of the 1893 Chicago Exposition, she came to appreciate the excitement and potential power of organized women. She later confided, "I do so enjoy meeting intelligent women—who think and act—and are not satisfied to be puppets in this world of action." The "action" that absorbed her attention at the Chicago fair was the celebration of the history of her adopted state, North Carolina, and above all the legendary life of Virginia Dare of the Roanoke Colony. After the fair, she continued her campaign to memorialize the girl heroine. She blanketed North Carolina with flyers announcing the founding of the Virginia Dare Association. In private letters soliciting support, Cotten outlined her plans to excite public enthusiasm. She promised plenty of offices in the organization to occupy the interest of chapter members and proposed that the chapters hold monthly meetings in order "to keep up an interest so that we will be ready to act at all times." The essential task, Cotten insisted, was the maintenance of "a *strict list*" of all members, "so we know our strength when it comes to *memorializing Congress.*" A robust association was a prerequisite for an ambitious campaign to secure endorsements from state and national teachers' organizations for a federally funded women's college, which would serve as the true monument to Virginia Dare. Cotten's plan eventually ran afoul of the politics of education in North Carolina, but it nevertheless demonstrated the methods used by self-appointed leaders who summoned the citizenry to provide support for their preconceived commemorative projects. Suasion, as Cotten well understood, was an essential attribute in campaigns that relied on voluntarism.[41]

Activist women adopted stronger methods when aroused by perceived threats to their aspirations. Both the UDC and the

DAR, for instance, carefully monitored the presentation of history in southern classrooms. They encouraged "patriotic" sentiments among students by providing teaching materials and awarding prizes to student essays on topics dear to the organizations, especially those that celebrated the role of the South in the American Revolution and defended the Lost Cause. They crusaded for the teaching of the "true history" of slavery and the sectional strife of the nineteenth century by censoring school texts and intimidating textbook publishers. Mrs. W. C. H. Merchant bragged to a 1904 UDC meeting that "owing to the efforts and influence of the United Daughters" every southern state had adopted texts sympathetic to the Lost Cause. Voluntary associations in the New South often became the arbiters of public opinion, above all with regard to the Confederate tradition.[42]

The full measure of the power of southern white women became evident in several contentious battles on southern campuses. In 1911, Enoch M. Banks, a young history professor at the University of Florida, six years out of graduate school at Columbia, recklessly announced that "in the calm light of history" secession was contrary to the national interest and that "the North was relatively in the right while the South was relatively in the wrong." Ever vigilant to defend secession, members of the UDC, reinforced by members of the United Confederate Veterans, berated the university for employing a historian who was "not fitted to teach true and unprejudiced history." In little more than a month the uproar compelled Banks to resign. Eager to appease the custodians of the Confederate tradition, both Governor Albert W. Gilchrist and University of Florida president Albert A. Murphree hailed the banishment of a historian with such "unsound views."[43]

A decade later, university officials at Washington and Lee University announced plans to refurbish their campus's Lee Chapel, where the body of Robert E. Lee was interred. They badly misjudged the response to the renovations. The Lexington Mary Custis Lee chapter of the UDC, which opponents described as a "little group of willful women," swiftly organized against the renovations of what they believed to be a sacred shrine. They repeatedly outflanked their opponents through adroit appeals to tradition and assertions of their dominion over the site, which arose out of a 1920 contract with the university to provide a custodian for the chapel and an endowment out of which to pay her. Confronted by the entrenched authority of university officials, the aroused women recognized their need to find a public forum better suited to their influence. As one woman activist explained, "It is of the greatest importance to enlist the support as far as possible of the Press, Alumni, & our public men. In other words, it should be *a public protest*." Eventually, President Henry Louis Smith acquiesced and left the Lee Chapel unchanged. In these and other examples, white women skillfully shifted the discussion from settings where their influence was necessarily limited to the broader public sphere where their artful use of publicity proved decisive.[44]

Despite their tenacity and acumen, women's groups periodically suffered defeats. In Richmond, the women of the Confederate Memorial Literary Society, who presided over the so-called White House of the Confederacy, could only sputter in rage when a major shrine to the Confederacy, the Battle Abbey, was not located at their site. In this instance, the women's influence was overmatched by weightier business and political interests, who gave the women the cold shoulder after courting their support for years. Likewise, Atlanta businessmen eager to promote local tourism and, more important, to profit from fund-raising opportunities, refused to stand idle while the UDC presided over the carving of the huge Confederate monument on the rock face of Stone

Mountain, Georgia. By 1924 they had elbowed the women aside and assumed control over the project (which they in turn failed to bring to completion). In Stone Mountain, as in Richmond, women activists fought to defend their jurisdiction over public memory. There and elsewhere, the broad goal of revering the region's white heroes and all things Confederate was as safe and unimpeachable a grounds for women's activism as was conceivable in the New South. Consequently, women's associations engaged in sometimes venomous disputes without undue risk of alienating public sentiment. Instead, it was their opponents who often found themselves perceived as unprincipled, insensitive, and unpatriotic.[45]

Beyond suasion, whether of the genteel or muscular variety, organized white women exerted their influence through their impressive fund-raising capacities. As long as voluntary contributions, in lieu of state subsidies, were essential to the funding of collective memory, the influence of women's organizations was secure. Few voluntary societies by themselves possessed the resources to sustain grandiose and unending projects, but by the mid-nineteenth century women's groups had devised all manner of fund-raising techniques, such as charitable balls, fairs, and bazaars, that lightened the collective purses of their communities and raised prodigious sums of money. Clubwomen harnessed their own increasingly important role as consumers to philanthropic ends by fashioning crafts and other goods for sale to other public-spirited women. They also tapped the wealth of their husbands and any other likely male contributors. (We can only speculate about why men were such willing contributors to campaigns, but perhaps male donors looked to these causes as an opportunity to cleanse wealth acquired in the hurly-burly world of commerce by associating it with the unsullied public service of women.) During the fund-raising campaign in Pensacola, for example, women secured the local opera house and a public dining room for free, then hosted a public lecture for one thousand attendees and organized a dinner for five hundred. Women's groups in Richmond hosted four bazaars over a span of three decades that raised nearly $108,000 for Confederate monuments in Hollywood Cemetery and along Monument Avenue. Fund-raising extravaganzas on this scale required formidable organizational skills and demonstrated the financial prowess requisite for the increasingly ambitious philanthropic activities undertaken by women.[46]

The crucial contributions of the Ladies' Confederate Monument Association in Pensacola were duplicated in countless communities. In this regard, the success of the UDC and the comparative failure of the UCV to raise money for the Jefferson Davis Memorial in Richmond, Virginia, are telling. Calls for a memorial to the Confederate president arose after his death in 1889. In 1896 the UCV launched a campaign to build a costly marble shrine in the Confederate capitol. But as of 1899 they had raised only $20,000 of the $210,000 their plans required. With fund-raising stalled, the UCV grudgingly turned the project over to the UDC. During the following eight years, the UDC revised the plans in favor of a less expensive and grandiose monument and methodically raised money. Eventually they collected $70,000, a sum sufficient to complete the monument that now stands. The unveiling of the monument in 1907 was a striking testimony to the capabilities of the UDC and confirmed the organizational limits of the UCV.[47]

The influence that organized white women exerted over public memory in the South declined gradually after World War I. The historical connections that white women drew among race, gender, and "civilization" lost their persuasive power at a time when psychology, consumerism, and modernist culture were eroding nineteenth-century ideals of masculine and feminine behavior. A growing enthusiasm for raw masculinity, which became increasingly evident in the popular culture of the 1910s and 1920s, rendered irrelevant older formulations of male power that rested on advanced civilization. Social scientists also challenged assumptions of innate racial attributes and cultural potentials. The exaggerated importance attached to ancestry, which had flowed logically from the Victorian conflation of civilization with blood, now appeared hopelessly old-fashioned. As a result, the celebration of heroic Anglo-Saxon history lost both its urgency and patina of modernity.[48]

The transformation of women's public roles also had consequences for white women's historical activities. During the 1920s, the meaning of the past for women began to change. The extension of the right to vote to women and the new emphasis on "individualism and self-realization" threatened older norms of selfless service. "At the deepest level," explains Ellen DuBois, "the ratification of the Nineteenth Amendment undermined the consensus about what women's path through history signified." Just when women called into question the purpose and structure of the organized women's movement, so too did some question the purpose of women's historical groups. The DAR, for instance, underwent a dramatic transformation during World War I, emerging as one of the shrillest voices of antiradical and anticommunist nationalism. The organization purged itself of members who were sympathetic to social reforms that previously had been tolerated or even endorsed. The scope and membership of other women's historical groups shrank as well. If women's clubs in Atlanta are representative, club members during the 1930s were less socially prominent, less cohesive, and less active in the full array of women's associations. By then, the UDC, DAR, Colonial

Dames, and other historical associations were no longer at the center of the network of women's voluntary associations and failed to harness to their causes the energies of the largest portion of clubwomen.[49]

The most profound challenge to the role of white women as arbiters of white memory came not so much from opposition to their campaigns but from these campaigns' success. The erosion of the women's influence followed from their own efforts to coax the state to assume a larger role in historical matters. In important ways, the gradual expansion of state authority over the region's heritage, and the resultant waning of women's authority, mirrored the contemporaneous extension of state services and the consequent abating of women's leadership over social welfare. Many women championed a more activist government because myriad public issues demanded the application of resources and power that only the state possessed. Yet clubwomen were eager to retain their influence over public history. To the satisfaction of many women activists, effective partnerships between the state and private women's organizations emerged during the early twentieth century. Women's associations threw their organizational brawn behind campaigns to create a state-subsidized infrastructure of archives and museums in the region. Hereditary and patriotic women's groups viewed such state archives as long-needed shrines of public memory. More important, women, who had resolutely insisted on the relevance of historical awareness for civic life, were eager to introduce historical activities into the business of the state.[50]

The struggle to establish a historical commission in Texas underscored the effectiveness of women's voluntary associations in rousing the state to assume new responsibilities over public culture. Three consecutive sessions of the legislature had rejected bills to establish a state historical commission sponsored by the

Texas State Historical Association. Simultaneously the newly founded State Federation of Women's Clubs, which promoted public libraries throughout the state, failed to secure legislation to create a state library commission. Finally in 1909, the historical association and the state federation joined forces and cajoled the legislature to launch the Texas Library and Historical Commission. Clubwomen understandably concluded that, as Emily Benbury Haywood of North Carolina put it, they, along with "historians," were "co-guardians" of the nation's "glorious past."[51]

In the wake of the accelerating institutionalization of public history in the South came professional opportunities and authority attractive to male professional historians. Intent on establishing respectable professional institutions across the region and eager to enhance their insecure status, these scholars labored to create institutions that would cultivate competence and consolidate their professional authority over the past. Initially, professional historians desperately needed allies to create public institutions that could promote modern civic culture in the South. As the success in Texas demonstrated, the public constituencies beyond the tiny academic community in the South, such as women's organizations, had an interest in archives and museums. But given the aims of professional historians and the prestige they hoped to garner, they could not easily tolerate rivals. Women's voluntary associations (and other nonspecialist individuals and groups) had a place in recalling the southern past as long as they remained adjuncts who deferred when necessary to trained (male) specialists. They were welcome to contribute as fund-raisers, to provide essential secretarial skills, and to direct the social activities of historical societies. But women enthusiasts who continued to display unwelcome ambition to participate in the serious business of crafting history were politely reprimanded.

Yet even after the commemorative impulse in the South waned

and the energy of organized women was directed elsewhere, the fifty-year legacy of white women's guardianship of public memory in the South remained. The useable history that white women fashioned acquired considerable cultural power because it addressed pressing social and political issues of the day in the New South. When white women collected, organized, and propagated a remembered past, they dictated the shape of those contemporary public debates that were rooted in history, such as those over racial segregation, the disfranchisement of black men, and inequitable funding for black and white education. To collect relics, preserve sites, and build monuments was to establish the "facts" of southern history that subsequent narratives had to take into account.

For good and ill, the accomplishments of white women guardians of the past, from the modest monument in Pensacola to the enormous Jefferson Davis statue in Richmond, Virginia, from historical markers on the Natchez Trace in Mississippi to the UDC shrine in Charleston, South Carolina, linger on the southern landscape. This imprint left on the region's public spaces should be understood as part of a broader, national struggle by women to shape, even redefine, civic spaces in the late nineteenth and early twentieth centuries. Manipulation of the physical environment by organized women ranged from campaigns for city beautification and playground construction to crusades against poverty and prostitution. Where middle-class and elite women were successful, they created spaces that enhanced women's cultural authority, and sometimes their economic opportunities. But whereas the activities of some women outside the South, and even within the region, fostered alliances that bridged class and racial chasms, southern white women's commemorative work impeded such possibilities. The cultural spaces nurtured by members of the UDC, DAR, and similar groups accrued authority to women who were like them. They succeeded in their goal of filling the civic spaces of the South with monuments glorifying the Confederacy and other episodes of white heroism for "unborn generations." Indeed, with school texts parroting a pro-Confederate rendering of the past and with monuments in every town square, we might well ask what more white women in the South could have achieved. Their activities created enduring obstacles to the production of alternative renderings of southern history and, by extension, alternative visions of the southern future.[52]

2

Celebrating Black Memory in the Postbellum South

On June 19, 1883, an eighteen-gun salute on the plaza in front of the Alamo in San Antonio, Texas, signaled the start of the annual Juneteenth observance. Since the end of the Civil War, blacks in Texas had celebrated the date in 1865 when General Gordon Granger arrived in Galveston and read General Order No. 3, informing Texans that the Emancipation Proclamation henceforth ended slavery in Texas. The 1883 festivities in San Antonio, which marked the twentieth anniversary of the Emancipation Proclamation, were the most elaborate to date. After the artillery fusillade, the grand marshal of the festivities led a long promenade that included a marching band, two militia companies, a baseball team, a volunteer fire company, teachers and students from the city's black school, a float featuring young girls costumed as "Columbia and the States of the Union," and decorated carriages bearing ministers and distinguished locals. Eventually the paraders snaked their way through the streets of the

A Juneteenth Parade passes by the hallowed ground of the Alamo Plaza in San Antonio, Texas, ca. 1890s. (Daughters of the Republic of Texas Library, San Antonio)

city to a park, where J. R. Carnes, a noted minister, read the Emancipation Proclamation and the Fourteenth and Fifteenth Amendments. James Newcomb, a prominent black politician, news-paperman, and businessman, then spoke on "The Progress of the Colored Race from Slavery and the Benefits Derived from Emancipation." The tight marching of the black troops, the gusto of the marching band, the pomp of the volunteer fire company, the respect accorded to the marchers, and the oratory made for a cathartic, communal celebration of freedom.[1]

Fifty-six years later, thousands of blacks flocked to Fort Worth, Texas, for Juneteenth celebrations there. In a now familiar tradition, excited crowds followed a parade through the downtown streets before dispersing to picnic grounds and churches to enjoy food, music, and entertainment. The festivities underscored to generations of blacks born long after slavery the continuity between their present circumstances and their race's past. Beyond reminding audiences about past traumas and accomplishments, the presence of fifty-five former slaves as guests of honor at the local Prince Hall Masonic Mosque made the reality of bondage, if only temporarily and symbolically, a living history.[2]

The celebrations in San Antonio, Fort Worth, and elsewhere demonstrated the dedication of blacks to acknowledge and ennoble what writer and activist James Weldon Johnson called their "gloomy past." With the end of slavery, southern African Americans not only joined the ranks of the free but also gained the capacity to celebrate their history in ways that had been impossible during slavery. Blacks eagerly grasped this opportunity and worked during the half century after the war to establish a commemorative tradition that made sense of the past and accorded them a central role in it.[3]

When contemplating the conditions that blacks faced, Alexander Crummell, a prominent black activist and minister, stressed that historical consciousness was critical to any struggle for equality in the United States. His race's progress, he prophesied, would rest on the shoulders of "intelligent men and women" who were capable of "the clear induction of historic facts and their application to new circumstances." Their claims to equality and full access to American life had to be grounded in history no less than in timeless principles. Appeals to natural law or the tenets of Christianity would not dislodge whites' presumptions about innate black inferiority or the folly of assimilating blacks into American civilization. The link, then, between the past and the contemporary ambitions of blacks was simple and direct: as long as the place of blacks in the nation's history went unrecognized, blacks would remain relegated to the margins of American life.[4]

Pervasive racism reinforced blacks' impulse to fashion a re-demptive past. Whites continually reminded blacks of their separateness. Along with commonplace slights and discrimination, blacks had to withstand the viciously racist cultural milieu of the late nineteenth-century United States. Beginning during the antebellum era and reaching a climax at the century's close, U.S. popular culture projected crippling images of African Americans. The inescapable affront of white racism provoked blacks to give collective voice to the trauma they endured. As Dr. L. B. Capehart observed during the 1908 Emancipation Day exercises at Shaw University in Raleigh, North Carolina, white prejudice "is one of the means of making us distinctly a race with a common cause, a common purpose, and a common interest." United by their experiences as outcasts and by a collective resentment of their oppression, blacks yearned for an ennobling historical memory. The simple human drive for self-worth demanded as much.[5]

In the wake of emancipation, a truly public culture emerged in which virtually all segments of southern society—white and black—had some prospect of voicing their concerns and claims. Blacks had reason to be optimistic about the potential of raising black consciousness at a time when the public sphere was, in principle, open to them to an unprecedented degree. The dramatic changes in the public demeanor and fashions of freed people that so shocked and outraged many white southerners demonstrated how blacks turned all manner of public expression into acts of simultaneous liberation and self-creation.

But whereas white southern women and their allies could and did marshal a full array of cultural forms to give voice to their collective memory, blacks had to make do with comparatively meager resources. Even so, blacks defiantly insisted on the public expression of their memory, and in their robust ceremonial life, blacks most fully revealed their collective historical imagination. As the *Richmond Whig* acknowledged in 1872, southern blacks "have a genius for display" and "we may expect them to get up pageants that will rival any undertakings by whites." Public ceremonies, which became the preeminent forum in which blacks displayed their recalled past, enabled vast numbers of blacks to learn, invent, and practice a common language of memory.[6]

When white southerners systematically set about codifying their heroic narrative and filling the civic landscape with monuments to it, they were conscious of a challenge from not only northern counternarratives, but also southern blacks. The resentment that southern whites vented every Fourth of July, the mocking derision that they showered on black commemorative spectacles, and the frequency of legal and extralegal harassment directed against black revelers leave little doubt that whites understood that the rituals of black remembrance represented a form of cultural resistance. For all the efforts of southern whites, especially white women, to enshrine their historical understanding of slavery, the Civil War, and black capacities, black celebrations made manifest a forceful and enduring understanding of their own. Postbellum blacks, no less than whites, appreciated the power that flowed from the recalled past.

೧๏

Public celebrations emerged as the principal expression of black memory because of the harsh realities of the New South. Although former slaves scrambled to acquire the ability to read and write, illiteracy remained pervasive until at least the end of the century and limited opportunities to use the printed word to promote racial uplift and disseminate black memory. The experience of William Still demonstrates the difficulty that black authors had reaching audiences in the southern hinterland. A self-educated son of slaves and a former abolitionist, Still launched an ambitious marketing campaign for his stirring account of slave escapes, *The*

Underground Rail Road, in 1872. Despite soliciting the support of black leaders and organizing southern canvassers who sold his book for generous commissions, he failed to garner even modest sales. His experience underscored that among an impoverished people in a poor region where public libraries were rare until after the turn of the century (and even then seldom tolerated black patrons), the community of black book buyers was small.[7]

Black leaders acknowledged the impediments to any campaign to instill a sense of collective history among newly literate and illiterate blacks during the 1870s. Andrew Chambers, an earnest African Methodist Episcopal (AME) minister in Arkansas, warned that cultivators of black memory might confront widespread indifference or concerns about squandering scarce resources on something as intangible as historical commemoration. Nonetheless, he was adamant that there was a desperate need to direct "our illiterate race" toward "loftier institutions." "Visual displays," he insisted, were needed to "arouse the masses."[8]

Instead of the imposing monuments of stone and marble that Chambers had in mind, public observances like the 1883 San Antonio Juneteenth ceremonies better suited the ambitions and resources of black communities in the New South. Such celebrations demanded neither literacy nor large sums of money, and, most important, they ensured that the black sense of the past was accessible to more than just literate, elite African Americans: the events had a unique capacity to involve the breadth of the black community, from the college-trained preacher to the illiterate day laborer, from the battle-scarred veteran to the impressionable schoolchild. Blacks understood that by entering public spaces and performing communal pageants, they were incorporating black history into the region's civic culture, thereby ending their historical exclusion from "ceremonial citizenship."[9]

By the end of the nineteenth century, the calendar was filled with at least a half-dozen major holidays and countless smaller occasions during which southern African Americans celebrated their heroes and hallowed events. Some of these ceremonies evolved from older traditions that antedated emancipation. In the antebellum North, African Americans had perpetuated a lively tradition of Election Day and other festivals, characterized by good-natured revelry, mockery of white hypocrisy, and open discussion of black aspirations. Southern blacks almost certainly knew of these traditions. After the abolition of slavery in the British West Indies in August 1835, blacks in a few southern communities celebrated the anniversary of the event as a milestone in the gradual progress of universal freedom. And despite the intentions of antebellum white southerners to exclude blacks from any conspicuous participation in civic occasions, black musicians, performers, waiters, and spectators found ways to make themselves part of them. In this manner, blacks acquired a refined sense of the language and the rituals associated with public celebrations in the United States.[10]

The calendar of postbellum commemorative rituals included traditional celebrations that southern blacks appropriated as their own. They used Washington's birthday to highlight the irony that their ancestors had fought beside Washington to found a nation that subsequently had rejected them. They virtually laid claim to Independence Day, which most white southerners refused to celebrate until the Spanish-American War revived their patriotic ardor. Before then, black southerners celebrated the nation's founding in the face of unmistakable white hostility. Voicing the resentment of many whites, the *Atlanta Constitution* grumbled that "Darktown has a sort of idea that the Fourth of July belongs to it [because] . . . every man, woman, and pickaninny believes the abolition of slavery and the Fourth of July are in some way mixed up." White indignation notwithstanding, blacks understood that if the Declaration of Independence was to be a resounding appeal to liberty and equality, the Fourth of July, its anniversary, was the appropriate occasion to present their unfulfilled claims to equality. Blacks also celebrated holidays that commemorated the Civil War. To the extent that Lincoln's birthday was celebrated in the South it was by African Americans, who were keen to link their own history to that of their martyred liberator. And in 1865 the eager participation of blacks in Charleston, South Carolina, and elsewhere helped to establish Decoration (Memorial) Day in late May as the preeminent commemoration of military valor and sacrifice.[11]

Blacks invented their own commemorative festivals as well. New Year's Day, previously "the most bitter day of the year" because of its associations with slave auctions traditionally held on that day, now provided an occasion to commemorate, "with acclamations of the wildest joy and expressions of ecstasy," Lincoln's Emancipation Proclamation. Blacks added Frederick Douglass's February birthday to their calendar of holidays after the beloved abolitionist's death in 1895. Some blacks also championed the observation of Ratification Day every March 30, to celebrate the adoption of the Fifteenth Amendment and the Constitutional guarantee of suffrage.[12]

Religious anniversaries, too, punctuated the black commemorative calendar. Perhaps the most widely celebrated denominational holiday was the birthday of Richard Allen, the founder of the AME Church. Initially adopted by the AME Church in 1876 as a way to arouse black interest in the nation's centennial, Allen Day had become by the late 1880s an enduring region-wide celebration. Although it and similar anniversaries were affairs exclusive to specific denominations, they were nevertheless important milestones of collective achievement for black communities. Even members of competing churches and organizations took pride in ceremonies honoring the founding and subsequent triumphs of their rivals' churches. Black residents of Savannah, Georgia, for example, were reminded annually of their religious heritage by a cycle of anniversaries. Every January the First Bryan and the First African Baptist churches competed to defend their claim to be the nation's oldest and preeminent black Baptist church. On the occasion of the 127th anniversary, both churches, adorned with lavish decorations, welcomed congregants and invited guests from throughout Georgia and neighboring states to elaborate ceremonies and banquets. Wherever black churches prospered, comparable local traditions of commemoration developed.[13]

These "private" exercises spilled out into public spaces. The nineteenth anniversary of the founding of the Covington, Virginia, chapter of the Order of Good Samaritans in July 1896 typified the expansive ceremonies that such groups staged. Men and women of the order, dressed in elaborate regalia, gathered at their hall and then, following a brass band, marched through the main streets of the small western Virginia mining town. Eventually the paraders reached the Covington Baptist Church, where officers of the order recounted the Good Samaritans' history and ministers blessed the occasion. Then the celebrants enjoyed a ceremonial feast and an evening of fellowship. Similar extravaganzas were commonplace in the region's larger cities, where, month after month, year after year, the rhythms of everyday life were enhanced by spectacular parades of flamboyantly garbed black marchers honoring their respective benevolent societies, churches, or voluntary associations.[14]

No black community, it seems, was too small to nourish an ambitious commemorative tradition. In Purcellville and Hamilton, two neighboring villages in northern Virginia, blacks organized the Loudoun County Emancipation Association, which planned and hosted an annual celebration every September 22 (the date when Lincoln had announced his provisional Emancipation Proclamation in 1862). The fact that the association had its own letterhead stationery was only one indication of its ambitions. Although both poor and obscure, the association nonetheless enlisted prominent figures, including W. Calvin Chase, the editor of the *Washington Bee* and a leading black journalist, to deliver its annual oration. So audacious were the association's directors that in 1922 they displayed no insecurity when they wrote, in labored script and ungrammatical prose, to Mary Church Terrell, one of the most respected black clubwomen of the era, asking her to deliver an address at upcoming Emancipation Day celebrations. That tiny communities like Purcellville and Hamilton would attempt such an impressive celebration was hardly exceptional. Two decades earlier, on April 3, 1906, Oak Union (a community so small it did not merit recognition on maps of Albemarle County, Virginia) celebrated "one of the greatest days of her history." Festivities began with a cavalcade of Civil War veterans who performed intricate maneuvers on horseback while riding through small settlements scattered across the countryside, continued with a service at a local Baptist church, and concluded with a feast.[15]

More impressive in magnitude and pomp were celebrations in the region's large cities. There, the size and comparative wealth of black communities made possible spectacles that attracted thousands of onlookers. In Vicksburg, Mississippi, huge crowds observed Fourth of July festivities, which included orations and "grand parades" of several hundred marchers and brass bands. Emancipation Day ceremonies in Norfolk, Virginia, routinely drew tens of thousands of black spectators, who watched parades that stretched for miles through the main streets of the city. In Beaufort, South Carolina, Decoration (Memorial) Day evolved into a similar region-wide celebration that drew visitors and black military units from across South Carolina and Georgia.[16]

These processions were intentionally staged against the backdrop of landmarks associated with commerce, politics, culture, and religion. In this way, blacks made the same claims to use prominent public spaces for public assembly that whites took for granted, thereby linking the ritual of procession with their own contemporary struggle for rights. The public spaces visited by paraders in Nashville, Tennessee, and Columbia, South Carolina, were representative of those favored by black memorialists. In 1892, blacks staged the climax of the Nashville Emancipation Day ceremonies in the chambers of the state capitol, one of the most conspicuous and venerated landmarks in the state. And even though the day's orators avoided overtly political topics, the setting itself made clear the connection that blacks drew among freedom, citizenship, and their inalienable political rights. The following year, an Emancipation Day procession of several hundred marchers gathered before the city's customhouse in the heart of the racially and ethnically heterogeneous waterfront district, then paraded down Broad Street, a major commercial thoroughfare, to the Public Square, Nashville's main business center. From there the celebrants marched on Line Street to the fashionable Spruce Street, where the procession ended at Saint John's Church. On the same day, blacks in "holiday attire," secret order regalia, and military uniforms gathered at the state capitol in Columbia, South Carolina. The "monster procession" proceeded along Main Street to the post office and then to the grounds of Allen University, where the day's formal ceremonies unfolded. At their conclusion, the parade reformed and filed back through the city's streets to the capitol grounds.[17]

During their celebrations, blacks tested the boundaries of racial etiquette that regulated public spaces. Segregation, whether de facto or de jure, became at these moments particularly irksome to many celebrants. As early as 1868, blacks in Nashville demanded that streetcar segregation be discontinued on the

Crowds of Emancipation Day marchers and spectators filled the streets of Richmond, Virginia, ca. 1905. (Detroit Publishing Company Photograph Collection, Library of Congress)

Fourth of July. The *Jacksonville Times-Union* recorded that during the July 4, 1886, celebrations "a large number of colored people" intermingled "indiscriminately" with white revelers, thereby generating "a good deal of comment." In other instances, blacks tweaked white sensibilities by making use of public spaces that were either traditionally off-limits to blacks or especially hallowed for whites. Blacks in Richmond, for example, pointedly included the grounds of the Virginia capitol in their celebrations. That the former capitol of the Confederacy would be the site for annual celebrations of the capture of Richmond and the defeat of southern independence was abhorrent to many whites. But black paraders continued to challenge white pride by marching through the parts of Richmond most associated with Confederate memories, and even incorporated the imposing Robert E. Lee statue on Monument Avenue, erected in 1890, into their ceremonial landscape. When the local black militias conducted their musters at the foot of the monument, they intended to associate themselves with the memory of a renowned military figure. But at the same time they reminded Richmond's whites of Lee's defeat at the hands of an army that included former slaves. In this and other instances, blacks skillfully used civic spaces charged with racially contested associations to extend and intensify the power of their own rituals.[18]

Whites could not easily ignore black holidays because black celebrants intruded themselves into public spaces and interfered with the routines of everyday life. In many communities, whites withdrew into their private domains on such days, temporarily ceding streets and parks to blacks. Alice Ravenel Huger Smith of Charleston, for example, recalled, "We were not allowed to go out much on the 'glorious Fourth,' for the negroes took it over as their day of revelry." A white Atlantan groused in 1884 that "since the war the 4th of July has been preeminently niggers' day in the South." In some communities, however, whites grudgingly tolerated, and even actively joined in, black celebrations. In east Texas, some white planters subsidized Juneteenth barbecues; in at least one community in western Tennessee, whites not only donated food for Emancipation Day celebrations, but even joined in the merriment. Emancipation Day revelers in Fredericksburg, Virginia, paraded through the town's streets, stopping at the homes of prominent white public officials and ringing a large "Liberty Bell" (which had been donated by local whites) until the occupants came out and saluted the celebration. In Savannah, Richmond, and several other southern cities, local school superintendents approved requests to close schools during Emancipation Day celebrations. So accommodating were the mayor of Lynchburg, Virginia, who approved parade permits, and white businessmen, who gave their black employees half-day holidays, that blacks made it an annual tradition to offer them "a vote of thanks" for these gestures. On occasion, white public officials, ranging from mayors to governors, even reviewed black parades.[19]

An undercurrent of white contempt, however, soured many celebrations. For example, as long as many whites in Texas trivialized Juneteenth as "coon day," they were unlikely to tolerate roads filled with boisterous blacks. Whites were especially suspicious of black celebrations during the immediate postwar years, when they seized upon flimsy pretexts to harass black celebrants. The white mayor of Oxford, North Carolina, for instance, banned future parades at the behest of several white businessmen who had complained that Emancipation Day processions interfered with commerce. March organizers countered by challenging the mayor's order in court. They emerged victorious when the North Carolina Supreme Court upheld their right to peaceable assembly. But elsewhere white officials enjoyed more success at thwarting blacks. In Atlanta, onerous regulation of black street vendors coincided with the revival of white enthusiasm for the Fourth of July. In 1904, city authorities refused to license the traditional street vendors who had served crowds of blacks each Independence Day. So stringent was the enforcement that the vendors' stalls disappeared, the crowds of blacks shrank noticeably, and, the *Atlanta Constitution* crowed, "In so far as the police regulations are concerned the Glorious Fourth in Atlanta was a glorious one in fact."[20]

Whites sometimes resorted to overt intimidation to stamp out black festivals. Memorial Day ceremonies at Andersonville, Georgia, the site of the notorious Confederate prisoner-of-war camp and a national cemetery, were especially obnoxious to white Georgians. The celebration of Union valor and victory by blacks at such a problematic Confederate site was so galling that local white authorities eventually intervened and suppressed the celebrations altogether. Beginning in 1902, the sheriff, bolstered by "a posse of hand picked men" and state militia, supervised thousands of black excursionists from southwest Georgia and Alabama who gathered annually at the national cemetery. Local authorities then pressured railroad companies to end special excursion rates for blacks. The effect of the police and military presence was unmistakable; white news accounts applauded when the military kept away "the disorderly colored element" and at the same time drew "the increased attendance of the white people." Within a few years, blacks had been virtually exiled from Memorial Day ceremonies at the site.[21]

Tensions over the use of public space during black celebrations sometimes flared into open violence. Even in Savannah and Norfolk, two cities noted for their comparatively benign race relations, friction over parade routes and crowd behavior provoked racial clashes. On several occasions in both cities, white streetcar operators came to blows with black marchers. Almost anywhere in the South, and especially on Memorial Day, black Civil War veterans attired in their uniforms ran the risk of being harassed, humiliated, and beaten by white ruffians. The likelihood of white violence increased when black militias were present. The so-called Hamburg riot in Edgefield County, South Carolina, in 1876 is one conspicuous example of black commemorative activities that became the flashpoint for white anxieties. On July 4, a local black militia muster obstructed the passage of two whites through the nearly all-black town. The perceived arrogance of the militia and its commanding officer, who was a former slave, Union veteran, and Republican politician, enraged whites. Four days later, white rifle clubs, without provocation, surrounded and slaughtered many of the black militiamen. The combination of the adoption of the Fourth of July as a black holiday, the brazen assertion by blacks of their right to use public space, and the demonstration of continuing military ambitions by former slaves and veterans was an intolerable provocation for many southern whites.[22]

Given the possibility of violence, many blacks were anxious to escape white hostility and segregation by securing spaces where they could conduct their celebrations without fear. As early as 1872, blacks in Houston raised money to purchase a ten-acre lot several miles from the city's downtown. Emancipation Park, as the site was known, became the focal point of Juneteenth ceremonies. In the same year, blacks in Nashville constructed an elaborate amphitheater and fairgrounds to host celebrations. In Mexia, Texas, blacks held their festivities in various locations near the town until 1898 when the Nineteenth of June Organization purchased land (now Booker T. Washington Park) on the banks of the Navasota River to serve as the permanent venue for commemorative observances. And in Fayette County, Tennessee, blacks established "the Colored People's Emancipation Park" as the setting for their celebrations. Although not dignified by commemorative sculpture or shrines, such spaces acquired enduring associations with the rituals of black memory.[23]

Even as blacks established their own sites of memory, they never surrendered their claims to public spaces. While segregation cordoned off more and more of black life within black neighborhoods, blacks continued to stage processions that demonstrated—to themselves and to whites—their civic spirit and version of history. Indeed, parades took on added significance in the age of segregation because they offered African Americans a unique opportunity to present complex self-portraits of their communities that were largely unmediated by white interference. The *Savannah Tribune,* on the eve of Memorial Day in 1918, explained the importance of processions for African Americans. Parades allowed all blacks, regardless of occupation or status, to come together in common cause. Beyond demonstrating the complexity and diversity of black communities, the sequence and orderliness of marchers contradicted white stereotypes of black primitiveness. "The vanguard of the race," the newspaper pledged, "will be there as well as the denizens of Negro ghettos, unlettered and unkept— the complete kaleidoscope of racial gamut, but all of common mind and bent upon a common goal." And why was such a display of "unanimity and solidarity" so important? Because, by participating in what the newspaper predicted would be a "mammoth parade," "every worthy colored man, woman, and child . . . would dedicate himself to the great causes of racial interest."[24]

For all the appearance of community solidarity, the ordering of black commemorative parades displayed an unmistakable hierarchy. The black community presented itself as a polyglot array of self-defined groups that asserted their collective claims on public space by participating in the procession. Processions, as homages to black civic culture, made manifest on the streets and byways of the South for all to see the relative prestige enjoyed by different black organizations and groups.

The privilege of occupying the front ranks of processions often went to black militia and military veterans of the Civil War, and later of the Spanish-American War and World War I. Parading veterans were a reminder of the blacks who had proved at Port Hudson, San Juan Hill, and in the trenches in Europe that battlefield heroics knew no color line. For onlookers, lines of Civil

War veterans connected the military acts of ordinary men with great deeds, including the destruction of slavery and the eventual achievement of political rights. Similarly, the presence of black militias, which had their origins during Reconstruction when Republican governments welcomed blacks into the formerly all-white state militias, testified to black men's ongoing sense of civic responsibility. Despite attacks by white terrorists during Reconstruction and persistent opposition by white legislators, black militias enjoyed exceptional status within their communities until the turn of the century, when white lawmakers used the rallying cry of white supremacy to abolish them.[25]

The representation of blacks as soldiers took on particular significance in an age when southern whites, especially organized white women, engaged in a frenzy of monument building to celebrate the common (white) soldier. This proliferation of soldier monuments "militarized" for the first time the U.S. landscape of civic patriotism. Black soldiers, however, were virtually invisible in this commemoration of war and soldiering; they won no place on the pedestal of civic recognition. Even in the North the typical common soldier monument advanced the primacy of the white male citizen by depicting the face of the nation as white. In the South, of course, the black soldier could not be represented without acknowledging the Union cause or the abolition of slavery. George Washington Williams, the pioneering black historian, lamented this symbolic lacuna. "The deathless deeds of the white soldier's valor," he observed, "are not only embalmed in song and story, but are carved in marble and bronze. But nowhere in all this free land is there a monument to brave Negro soldiers." Prompted by such concerns, black activists made several unsuccessful attempts to erect monuments to black soldiers. Yet by century's end only three monuments depicted blacks in military service, and none of them were located in the South.[26]

Because blacks were excluded from monumental representations of military valor, displays of military prowess by black militia during commemorative pageants acquired special significance. A company's stylish and correct showing on the parade ground reflected equally on the troops and their community. As the *Savannah Tribune* observed in 1897, the local black militia had "for over twenty years" borne "the burden of representing their people." Black militia, consequently, seized any opportunity to demonstrate their competence and to disprove white criticism that black soldiers were little more than overdressed and undertrained poseurs. News accounts regularly highlighted the young men's "excellent marching," "splendid soldiery," and "very soldier-like appearance." Well-dressed and precisely ordered black troops came to symbolize the ideal of black masculine leadership. [27]

The eventual abolition of black militia companies in the South threatened to rob black men of the opportunity to demonstrate their military and civic valor. Long-established black secret orders, however, quickly transformed themselves into quasi-military organizations complete with precision drill squads and elaborate faux-military uniforms. Angered by the disbandment of black militia in 1905, blacks in Savannah displayed renewed determination to stage holidays with appropriate fanfare. On Emancipation Day in 1906, for example, the "uniform ranks" of the Knights of Pythias escorted a mile-long parade through the principal streets of the city. The men in uniform may not have been in the militia, but the local black newspaper reported their maneuvers as though they were. The men, the newspaper bragged, "presented an excellent appearance" and "showed the great possibility of the race." Readers of news accounts of the Richmond Knights of Pythias Emancipation Day parade in 1898 might be excused for having presumed they were reading about a military drill. The description of the brigadier general's "glittering, heavily gold-

Knights of Pythias, like this lodge in Birmingham, Alabama, ca. 1920, often had prominent roles in black commemorative ceremonies. (829.1.32, Birmingham Public Library)

plated uniform," complete with a "silk-folding chapeau, heavily gold-plated epaulets, gold plated belt and sword, [and] a 14 foot long imported silk sash," earned the same extended notice that had previously been devoted to the attire of militiamen.[28]

In communities without militia, volunteer fire companies and labor organizations often occupied the front ranks of black civic festivities. Fire companies offered another avenue for displays of public service, while also contributing pomp and spectacle to the ceremonies. Following them were labor organizations and trade groups. The 1888 Emancipation Day cavalcade in Washington, D.C. included two floats of whitewashers and plasterers who advertised their trades with "yells which would do credit to Comanche Indians." During Emancipation Day in Jacksonville in 1892, the longshoremen's association, the printers' union, the carpenters' union, and a "Trade display" float joined the procession through the city's streets. A few even perpetuated ancient traditions associated with European celebrations by performing craft pageants in mock workshops. These street dramas linked outward displays of occupational pride with both the honored past and contemporary concerns. To insist on the variety and dignity of their labor at a time of systematic discrimination against black tradesmen and workers was to contest the stigma of being hewers of wood and drawers of water.[29]

At century's end, the parade lines were joined by business floats that advertised the wares and skills of black entrepreneurs. An enterprising black butcher in Jacksonville, for example, used the 1887 Fourth of July parade as an opportunity to sell "his fine fresh meats" from the back of his "well arranged float." Funeral home operators in Charleston used the 1917 Emancipation Day parade to introduce automobile hearses to the public. To some extent, the business floats reflected the commercialism that crept into all manner of public commemoration during the late nineteenth century. The commercial floats also testified to the efforts of black business organizations, such as the National Negro Business League, to inform the public of advances made by black businesses and to inspire community pride. Although critics ridiculed such organizations for their tub-thumping bluster, advertising stunts meshed well with the theme of communal uplift that was central to black celebrations. Each business float offered tangible confirmation of the black progress that orators tallied in their speeches.[30]

With banners that saluted Abraham Lincoln, abolitionists, and great blacks, organizers transformed parades into mobile living-history exhibits that traced the evolution of African Americans from slaves to proud and progressive citizens. Typical of such displays were three floats in the 1896 Emancipation Day parade in Savannah. On the first float, which bore the banner

"The Negro Before Emancipation," two blacks, clad in rags befitting slaves, sat on bales of cotton. The second float, which portrayed newly emancipated blacks in 1865, conveyed joyous young boys, presumably representing a youthful race with its future before it. The historical cavalcade concluded with a float crowded with well-dressed and dignified young men exemplifying modern blacks. With floats depicting slaves spinning cotton and singing "songs of slave days," the 1913 Knoxville Emancipation Day parade "was designed to represent the colored race from the days of '61 until 1913." A decade later, Emancipation Day organizers in Ocala, Florida, employed similar stagecraft to convey the speed and extent of black progress. Befitting the contemporary romance with the automobile, the procession included blacks in every mode of transportation from the ox and mule cart through bicycle and the horse buggy to late-model automobiles.[31]

No matter how purportedly inclusive, civic festivals spoke to the particular concerns of their organizers. The intricacies of the organizational networks required to arrange these well-attended ceremonies remain obscure, but the broad patterns are clear. During Reconstruction, the Republican Party played a prominent role in promoting black commemorations and its leaders usually occupied conspicuous places in them. But with the passage of time, explicitly partisan uses of commemoration waned. This evolution reflected in part the return to power of conservative white Democrats during the 1870s and the subsequent efforts of some white Republicans who, in the hopes of attracting white support, attempted to distance their party from its black base. Simultaneously many blacks recoiled from the exaggerated partisan tenor of some celebrations staged by white Republicans "for their own interest." According to Joseph T. Wilson, a black editor and community activist in Norfolk, Virginia, "a large number [of blacks] opposed the mixing of celebration with the personal politics of the white leaders, simply to enhance their individual interests."[32]

By the 1880s, black voluntary organizations, which were eager to extend their influence over black public life, had supplanted the Republican Party as organizers of commemorative events in most communities. Often, the most influential organization in a community, rather than a public committee, planned and oversaw local celebrations. The remarkable variety of black organizations was evident in the array of groups that oversaw festivities. In Ocala, Florida, and Scriven County, Georgia, the Knights of Pythias and the Odd Fellows of Captolo hosted Emancipation Day celebrations. In Darien, Georgia, the Golden Waves Debating Society planned the ceremonies for "freedom's natal day." In Woodville, Georgia, the local Law and Order League interpreted its mission, which was "to oppress crimes and better the moral condition of the village," so broadly that it too hosted the local Emancipation Day celebration in 1909.[33]

Many communities, intent on marshaling the broadest possible support, founded umbrella organizations to oversee commemorative planning. Emancipation Day associations proliferated across the New South to such an extent that communities lacking them risked condemnation for their apparent lack of race pride. Such organizations recruited members from voluntary societies, as well as ministers, politicians, and businessmen. They took pains to demonstrate that they were natural custodians of the common good. When inviting "all public spirited citizens" to attend a meeting to plan the 1917 celebration of Emancipation Day in Savannah, organizers stressed that their committee "was not an organization that belonged to a special set of men but was an organization which belongs to the entire citizenry."[34]

Sometimes rifts between groups staging celebrations resulted in competing ceremonies. Richmond was home to three rival organizations with a longstanding disagreement over the appropriate date for the city's Emancipation Day. And in Atlanta, the accelerating commercialization of leisure prompted competing impresarios to stage rival Fourth of July celebrations. Some of the disputes reflected tensions among black secular leaders and ministers who were loath to share their customary power with ambitious laypeople. Between 1892 and 1897 in San Antonio, for example, church-sponsored groups staged one Juneteenth celebration while black fraternal orders staged another. The same fault lines were evident in Rome, Georgia, in 1896 and Spartanburg, South Carolina, in 1903, where competing groups conducted separate celebrations. In Rome, the "younger element, including the secret orders," organized a large procession of the town's benevolent groups before retiring to the local opera house to listen to addresses on the respective histories of the orders. The town's ministers, who bridled at the prominence accorded the secret orders, hosted a more somber celebration in the city courthouse. The source of conflict between two Emancipation associations in Savannah in 1914 was the appropriateness of allowing floats advertising black businesses to join the Emancipation Day parade. The Chatham County Emancipation Association, which boasted many ministers among its executive committee, opposed compromising the occasion by accepting business floats. The Emancipation association, which recently had come under the influence of the local branch of the National Negro Business League, insisted that the ceremonies include commercial floats. Unable to resolve the dispute, the competing associations conducted separate parades on January 1, 1914.[35]

These tussles were as much about how the black community would be represented in commemorative events as about who would plan and preside over them. Of paramount importance to many planners was that the celebrations project an image of a respectable black community. Many black leaders accepted that securing the right to participate fully in U.S. society depended in large measure on African Americans refuting racial stereotypes and displaying proper comportment in public. In those spaces shared with whites, blacks had to be careful when asserting claims to status lest they provoke white retribution. Commemorative celebrations provided blacks with a conspicuous opportunity to display their mastery of public etiquette. Such concerns lay behind the counsel of the *Savannah Tribune* to "Let us remember that the world round about us is going to size us up by the character and the size of our demonstration on this [Emancipation] day and we can ill afford to be adjudged an indifferent people." This sense of representativeness, and the almost palpable feelings of obligation that flowed from it, were abiding features of the black quest for respectability that, in turn, shaped the conventions of respectable street drama. Elegant, well-ordered spectacles, during which participants were expected to comport themselves with decorum and modesty, were sine qua nons for public performances. Failure, whether manifest in an inept public speech or a flawed ceremony, would provide ammunition to those who maintained that blacks were inherently inferior. Black deportment, in sum, had clear political significance; debates over black fitness fused the issue of participation in public life with questions of individual and collective integrity.[36]

The obsession with respectability extended to black news accounts of the events. Black editors bounded the public stage so as to highlight only certain groups and behavior. Most accounts boasted that "nothing occurred to mar the joyfulness of the occasion," that the procession was "admirably conducted in all its details," and that "good feeling and rigid observance of the laws characterized the parade." One report stressed that the revelers had permitted "no rowdyism, . . . no cross or harsh words, . . . no intoxicants, . . . [and] no vulgar dances." When unseemly behavior was acknowledged, it was only to demonstrate that the participants had no tolerance for it. Reports of the 1891 Brewton, Alabama, Emancipation celebration, for example, boasted that "Everybody behaved well." The author of the account conceded that a drunkard had attempted to join the festivities, but saluted the officers who had preserved good order by sending him away.[37]

Black organizers in Brewton and elsewhere quarantined their celebrations from any associations with marginal subcultures. Above all, the festivities were never to degenerate into a lower-class revel like the John Canoe festival of coastal North Carolina. With origins in Africa, filtered through the West Indian and American slave experience, the John Canoe celebration incorporated rhythmic chanting, bell ringing, drumming, and outlandish costumes. Swaddled in an elaborate costume of rags and a grotesque white mask, John Canoe mocked white pretensions and even demanded concessions and civilities from whites that at other times would never have been extended to blacks. The high-spirited and cathartic festival, celebrated at the close of the Christmas holidays, contradicted the message of black respectability that was ascendant in the late nineteenth century. In the face of mounting white suspicion and the opposition of black clergy, who denounced the tradition as undignified and harmful to the good standing of the black community, the John Canoe festival gradually faded.[38]

Similar anxieties surfaced whenever the behavior of participants in black celebrations deviated from the conventions of Victorian respectability. Until 1890 "Surrender Day" celebrations each April 9 in Mecklenburg County, Virginia, provided the pretext for each celebrant "to make himself as uncouth looking as possible" by donning "strange fantastic costumes in which all the colors of the rainbow predominated." A group of aroused ministers and local notables, who had made repeated efforts "to break up this unworthy way of celebrating," finally in 1890 organized a committee that succeeded in staging ceremonies "in an orderly dignified manner." The undignified behavior of several marchers during Memorial Day exercises in Richmond in 1897 prompted John Mitchell Jr. of the *Richmond Planet* to rant against "this element of our race" that "prejudiced whites delight to hold up before the gaze of the world" that "make any self-respecting Afro-American blush with shame."[39]

At least one prominent black person concluded that parades and respectability could not be reconciled. During the 1880s W. Calvin Chase, the acerbic editor and publisher of the *Washington Bee,* grumbled that Emancipation Day was coarse and unbecoming. "We are not to be governed by the rabble and the mob," he wrote. "What the people desire is a respectable gathering." He subsequently declared that parades "are universally condemned" by "the more intelligent colored citizens" as "detrimental and disgraceful." Long before President William McKinley reviewed a purportedly rowdy and scruffy Emancipation Day parade in Washington D.C. in 1897, Chase had repudiated the tradition categorically: "Our freedom is made a mockery of by street parades."[40]

Many blacks apparently shared Chase's anxiety, but few matched his complete contempt for parades. Instead, most blacks concluded that commemorations could channel the crowds' enthusiasm into acceptable forms of expression. The challenge facing black celebrants was to muzzle impolite outbursts without suppressing appropriate revelry. Drinking and carousing were too deeply rooted in U.S. traditions of leisure to be suppressed entirely. Moreover, as early as the 1880s black organizers and entrepreneurs had begun proffering a wide array of amusements to the throngs of blacks released from work during holidays. Juneteenth, the Fourth of July, and other summer celebrations became occasions for elaborate amusements, including "ugly boy and pretty girl contests," greased pole competitions, bicycle races, band performances, picnics, baseball games, and dances. Attuned to contemporary tastes, black impresarios even catered to the popular romance with the American West by staging elaborate Wild West shows, complete with sham cavalry battles staged by blacks representing both Native Americans and U.S. soldiers. Such activities tamed the raucous spirit of celebrants with inoffensive (and lucrative) entertainment. Organizers also made sure that the growing popularity of competitive athletics in the early twentieth century augmented rather than challenged their ceremonies.[41]

That displays of black male athletic prowess would be incorporated into commemorative celebrations was consistent with the larger aim of organizers to use the exercises to publicly contradict white stereotypes of black manhood and womanhood. In particular, black male organizers were keen to refute emasculating images of black men in American popular culture. To combat the stigmatization of black manhood, black men like Theophilus G. Steward, a journalist, educator, and member of the AME Church, searched for evidence of "the production of a robust and chivalric manhood." Steward and others called for a strenuous but refined black masculinity to provide a "proper shelter for a pure and glorious womanhood." Through a vigorous assertion of their manhood, black men would elevate themselves and redeem the women of their race. Motivated by these anxieties, some blacks during the late nineteenth century began to reinterpret the whole history of the race in order to assert a longstanding link between heroism and black manhood.[42]

Commemorative ceremonies made explicit the perceived connection between proper gender roles and blacks' historical inheritance. A Fourth of July orator in Jacksonville in 1887 explained that freedom had given his audience "the right to make ourselves upright men and upright women." The struggle since Emancipation, he affirmed, had "shown that there are within us those qualities which make men and women." The speaker at the 1900 Emancipation Day in Ocala, Florida, voiced an urgent concern that "all Negro men and Negro women resolve today to be manly men and womanly women." Daniel Webster Davis, a celebrated Virginia orator much in demand as a speaker for commemorative celebrations, displayed little subtlety when he urged black women in his audiences "to be modest and retiring, [to] Stay in your proper places and let men seek you."[43]

Some of the ceremonial roles open to black women required not only a reserved, feminine demeanor but also tacit support for the ideals that black men professed—concerns principally associated with the male public sphere. Ceremonies often included the presentation of elaborate flags by solicitous black women to militia units. During the August 1876 militia muster in Savannah, members of the United Daughters of Lincoln gave to the troops a flamboyant silk flag depicting the Goddess of Liberty holding a sword in her right hand and scales containing the Emancipation Proclamation and the Civil Rights Bill in the other. In Charleston, South Carolina, the black militia carried silk regimental colors crafted by the local Ladies Volunteer Aid Association. In countless parades, costumed women posed as the female deity Liberty on tableaux mounted atop floats. By presenting liberty, the most prized human condition, as feminine, by personifying the Union with black womanhood, and by surrounding both with marching men in uniform, these ceremonies dramatized both feminine dependence and black men's role as defenders of home, freedom, and the values of the nation.[44]

Some black women balked at the preoccupation with black manliness and the subordinate role assigned to them within conventional views of racial progress. They warned that racial uplift was impossible without an improvement in the status of black women. Anna Julia Cooper and other skeptics tired of the marked propensity in black public life to celebrate the black man as the beacon of progress. But even this dissent was often couched in the rhetoric of female domesticity. Frances L. Williams, of the Emerson Industrial Home in Ocala, Florida, revealed both the limits and possibilities of this line of reasoning when she announced during an Emancipation Day address that black "women must be virtuous and self-respecting and on them hangs the destiny of her people." By insisting that black women were the moral conservators of the race and that family life was the engine of progress, black women expanded without overturning many of the prevailing notions of respectable femininity. In the process they encouraged the black women who during the late nineteenth century streamed into those women's voluntary associations that were engaged in racial uplift.[45]

The dynamism of black women's clubs ensured that black leaders anxious to mobilize the race during civic celebrations could not ignore organized black women. Moreover, black women, like white clubwomen, earned respect as fund-raisers and hostesses. As reluctant as some black male organizers seem to have been to promote black women's participation, they grudgingly acknowledged the Herculean backstage support often provided by women's groups. When planning the mammoth 1885 Emancipation Day ceremonies in Norfolk, Virginia, organizers tellingly elected women to the "Finance Soliciting Committee" and the "Committee on Decorations and Illuminations." (Equally noteworthy, the names of these women were left off the official program.) Likewise, the fifty members of the local Ladies Auxiliary, who prepared the food and banquet space for an estimated five thousand celebrants, made possible the fellowship and feasting that was the highlight of the 1898 Emancipation Day ceremonies in Roanoke, Virginia.[46]

Although the participation of black women as more than

spectators or as icons of femininity merited only cursory mention in news accounts, women's organizations regularly joined in celebrations. In Richmond, Virginia, during the late 1870s, black women even participated in a ceremonial militia company that paraded during festivities. Although they served no apparent military function, the women's drill company achieved military precision and marched to military commands. The drill team did not survive long, but their presence served as a harbinger for the growing number of women marchers at the end of the century. By then few parades failed to include women's mutual aid and community reform groups within their ranks. And where washerwomen's unions existed, they often joined the processions as well. Black women presented themselves as an organized force for racial progress that merited, even demanded, public recognition commensurate with that given their male counterparts.[47]

With each passing year after 1900, women's groups became increasingly assertive in the organization and celebration of holidays. The trend in Savannah, Georgia, may be representative for the region as a whole. There, organized black women first assumed a prominent role in those holidays that were in decline, such as Lincoln's birthday. During the 1910s, the Women's Relief Corps and local Girl Scouts joined with the shrinking membership of Civil War veterans' groups to perpetuate the annual celebration of the Great Emancipator. The same groups honored their ties of blood and obligation by staging Memorial Day marches. By the mid-1920s the number and size of women's mutual aid and cultural groups had increased until they comprised fully half of the participants in the city's Emancipation Day processions. Elsewhere, black women took advantage of circumstances that allowed them to expand their influence. World War I in particular offered opportunities to black women energized by wartime, who appealed to patriotism as a way of challenging male authority over even the most hallowed of black holidays. In Farmville, Virginia, for instance, the Mother's Council, under the leadership of Lula Coles, organized the 1919 Emancipation Day celebrations at the local AME church. Black women had assumed only circumscribed roles in previous celebrations, but they now performed all of the ceremonial duties. Coles and three other women delivered the day's orations, while another woman served as the "mistress" of ceremonies. Even if few other black celebrations came under the complete control of black women, the increased prominence of women that was evident in Savannah and Farmville persisted during the postwar years.[48]

Just as black women assumed growing roles in planning celebrations after the turn of the twentieth century, so too did they assume with increasing frequency a place behind the podium. During the 1890s a tradition developed in which women delivered brief speeches, recited poetry, performed patriotic songs, and read hallowed documents, such as the Emancipation Proclamation or Lincoln's Gettysburg Address. Men, meanwhile, delivered the day's main oration. Why women were accorded this honor is difficult to discern, but it may not be coincidental that the inclusion of women's voices in ceremonies occurred at a time when the grip of black ministers on the commemorative celebrations was loosening and secular and civic organizations were exerting increasing influence. Moreover black women, like their white counterparts, were eager to be seen as nurturers and conservers of memory.[49]

The black press seldom accorded these performances much space and consequently little can be reconstructed. The only surviving clues are the titles of the papers—"Lincoln" and "Freedom"—delivered by black women during the Emancipation Day celebrations in Ocala in 1891. How Miss E. E. Warner answered the question of "Why we as freedmen should cultivate friendly relations with the southern whites" during her 1893 Emancipation Day address in Jacksonville is unclear. We can only speculate about what Ellen Minor discussed in her address on "The Women of the Race" at Brunswick, Georgia, on January 1, 1895. That Ethel Wright touted the evidence of "The Progress of the Negro in America" during her Emancipation Day speech in Savannah in 1910 is apparent only because the *Savannah Tribune* reported that "Her rendition was perfect and the paper was teeming with salient points of race progress." Two years later, Miss V. O. Sherman spoke on "Our Fiftieth Anniversary" during the semicentennial of the Emancipation Proclamation, but news accounts remain mute about her conclusions. And we can only assume that Eugenia Taylor, a teacher, and Lucy Addison, a nurse, used their respective Emancipation Day speeches on "Our Schools" and "Our Hospitals" to proselytize on behalf of their professions and their importance for black progress.[50]

The constraints of middle-class Victorian decorum continued to circumscribe black women's roles in commemorations until at least World War I. With their emphasis on unity and respectable male stewardship of the black community, commemorative exercises were unlikely venues for a full airing of black women's broadest ambitions. Black male leaders remained unwilling to cede the public stage of commemorative ceremonies to women for most of the half century following emancipation, especially after disfranchisement effectively foreclosed black male participation in conventional politics. Beyond the limits imposed by male ambitions, the prevailing cultural definition of womanhood limited black women's participation in commemorative exercises. Women, considered innately moral beings, were thought to be ideally suited to serve as society's conscience. There was a cultural predilection for women to address moral issues and for men to acknowledge their role as society's moral guardians. But women were expected to prick society's conscience with a gentle and compassionate tone incompatible with the more strident proclamations of black progress and predictions of eventual vindication that were expected during commemorations. Such occasions seemed to call for jeremiads filled with harsh reproach and stern counsel. Black women could not easily impersonate stern clergymen, the embodiment of masculine, patriarchal attributes, without also assuming a singularly male public role. Historical celebrations, then, did not provide black women, as they did white women, the leverage to renegotiate their public roles or to assert new claims to cultural influence.[51]

Whether organized by black clubwomen or by ministers, and whether led by militia companies or by labor organizations, the parades that wound through the main thoroughfares of southern communities several times a year were vivid reminders that blacks refused to allow the South's public spaces to become the exclusive commemorative landscape of whites. Beyond challenging white control of civic space, the black festivals were virtual open-air classrooms in which blacks recalled their history. When aged black veterans donned their blue uniforms, fraternal societies marched in ceremonial attire, and black youths staged tableaux of slavery and liberty, they presented a record of black accomplishment that went otherwise unacknowledged in southern civic life.

When James Newcomb spoke on "The Progress of the Colored Race since Slavery and the Benefits Derived from Emancipation" in San Antonio in 1883, his oration was intended to expand the symbolism and deepen the meaning of the grand procession that preceded it. Speaking for a generation in transition from folk memory to a broader historical consciousness, Newcomb and his fellow orators helped turn the atomized memories of individuals into a collective past, one that could sustain black civic culture throughout the era of Jim Crow and counter the dominant white version of the southern past. In these speeches, which commonly lasted hours, black orators displayed little caution when they traced their contemporary grievances back through their long history of oppression at the hands of whites.[52]

Commemorative celebrations presented the saga of black history in surprisingly uniform ways. The stability of the genre in part reflected the ritualized context of the ceremonies. After formal openings, the celebrations typically continued with readings of such cherished texts as the Declaration of Independence and the Emancipation Proclamation. Next came recitations, often by schoolchildren, of appropriate poems and essays. The climax arrived when the day's principal speaker delivered the oration. These solemn rituals, performed again and again, year after year, were intended to be disciplined rehearsals of appropriate behavior.[53]

The powerful influence of black ministers contributed to the unvarying form and content of black celebrations. Contemporary notions of public decorum and masculine prerogatives gave men the most prominent roles on the podium. As black political fortunes waned during the late nineteenth century, black ministers and educators emerged as the public figures best qualified to serve as keynote orators. By employing familiar rhetorical and religious forms, ranging from conventional patriotic oratory and traditional Protestant jeremiads to analogies between blacks' contemporary circumstances and the plight of Jews in the Book of Exodus, these orators cast both the distant and recent past as scenes in a familiar spiritual drama. So compelling was this representation that its form, cadences, and message were taken up by lay and religious orators alike.

Repetition of form and argument also suited the needs of a people who had only limited means of telling their history and found uplift and comfort in familiar stories of their past. The aim of commemorative speakers was not to offer unorthodox or novel interpretations of the black historical experience but rather to apply their individual craft and inspiration to making relevant a codified genre. And to the degree that white renderings of the past remained constant, so too did expressions of black memory. Black orators, intent on refuting white historical narratives, necessarily repeated, over and over, their ripostes to the shibboleths of white supremacy.

To counter white versions of the southern past, African American orators had to call into question the notion of "civilization" that undergirded those lies. Like white women, black men, and to a lesser extent, black women, entered into the spirited debate about the capacity of various human societies to progress through stages of development to "civilization." With whites concluding that they stood at the apex of human development and blacks at the opposite end of the evolutionary continuum, the implications of the civilizationist ideology for black Americans were clear. In 1901, the *Jacksonville Times-Union* summarized orthodox white wisdom on the connection between race and civilization. "Civilization and culture and decency and learning," the newspaper explained, were "a spontaneous product growing out of the hard soil of experience and adversity." American blacks had made progress in acquiring the rudiments of civilization, the newspaper acknowledged, "But the Negro has had centuries of independence within which to show the metal that is in him—what has he done in Africa but evolve monsters that put our monkey ancestors to shame?" The lesson was obvious; the entitlements of civilization, such as "manhood suffrage," should not be extended to blacks. Such reckless generosity "where civilization comes into contact with the barbarian," the editorialist cautioned, was folly.[54]

Without fail, blacks used commemorative celebrations to rail against such white hubris. Orators often made a point of dismissing as ignorant the dominant image of Africa. Rather than a metaphor for barbarism, the continent, they insisted, had been the cradle of much that the world had come to define and salute as "Western civilization." Rather than assimilate blacks into white historical narratives that began with Greco-Roman civilization, black orators proudly reclaimed the grand heritage of ancient Egypt from whites who chose to identify it with Caucasians. "The Negro race in primitive ages," O. M. Steward of Richmond, Virginia, boasted in 1907, had enjoyed "a high degree of civilization and culture." He and others boasted that the technological and cultural innovations that made possible all subsequent civilization had emerged first in ancient Egypt and Africa. "The Egyptians," Professor Joseph L. Wiley teased during the 1900 Emancipation Day celebrations in Ocala, Florida, "found the Greeks wild and unclad, living in trees, subsisting on roots." This reclamation of ancient Egypt represented a crucial first step in correcting crippling white distortions of history.[55]

The principal concern of black commemorations was to present a useable history for blacks in America. The marvels of ancient Egypt, the decline of Africa, and the enslavement of Africans were less important than the divine purpose assigned blacks in the United States. Orators readily conceded that Africa had lapsed into isolation and had languished while Europe and North America had progressed. The explanation for the "fall" of Africans was simple. "It was sin; idolatry—forgetfulness of God," rather than innate inferiority. Rev. C. C. Summerville, speaking to an Asheville Emancipation Day crowd, speculated that Africans had been consigned to the "furnace of affliction" so that "they might mount up to the highest of true Christian civilization." Slavery, according to J. C. Lindsay of Savannah, had represented "years of preparation in which gradually the captive race

assimilated to a wonderful extent the civilization surrounding it
. . . [and] Barbarism gave way to enlightenment and Christianity."
The terrible suffering of slavery, then, had profound historical
value: it had been part of a providential design to transport their
pagan ancestors to North America, where they could assume their
momentous role within a Christian civilization.[56]

This providential interpretation of slavery placed the slave
experience at the center of black commemorations. Although individual blacks were not eager to reopen the scars left by their
enslavement, collectively they did not shy away from recalling it.
Indeed, commemorative ceremonies remembered the slave experience in various ways. During the 1890 Emancipation Day ceremonies in Montgomery, Alabama, a young black woman evoked
the trauma of slave auctions by reading "the farewell of a Virginia
slave mother to her daughters sold to Southern bondage." Elsewhere, choirs performed spirituals and work songs associated
with slavery. Organizers honored elderly slaves with conspicuous
roles in the ceremonies and by distributing to them contributions
donated by the audience. And although most commemorative
orations eschewed historical particulars and hovered above the
specifics of the carnage of slavery, they did so not to deny its importance. Rather, by lifting the slave experience to the level of an
abstraction they purged it of its sordidness and gave it a transcen-
dent significance.[57]

However restrained their presentation of slavery's horrors,
black commemorations left no doubt that the institution had been
inhuman and debased. Few orators parroted white depictions of
slavery as a benign enterprise sustained by black acceptance and
mutual affection between master and slave. Instead, black speakers followed Frederick Douglass's lead in denouncing romantic
renderings of slavery while contributing to "a constant recollection of the slavery of their race and of the wrongs it had brought

upon them." Fields Cook, a black freedman and activist in Rich-mond, announced during the 1866 Emancipation Day celebra-tions that "if any man supposed that slavery was the natural state of the negro," he was mistaken. "The fact of their assembling to celebrate their freedom proved it," Cook asserted. During the centennial of Abraham Lincoln's birth in 1909, Rev. R. R. Wright so poignantly evoked the suffering of slavery that, according to a local newspaper, "Tears could be seen stealing from the eyes of strong men and women." On other occasions audiences heard slavery described as "centuries filled with sorrow, anguish, and degradation," "the terrible and trying ordeal of human bondage," "the greatest of all villainies," and "the blackest crime that ever disgraced America's dignity."[58]

Blacks differed no less sharply with whites over the meaning of the Civil War. Southern whites, of course, strenuously de-fended secession and were acutely sensitive to any suggestion that the defense of slavery had motivated their failed rebellion. The black counternarrative was equally unambiguous. Over and over again, speakers insisted that the Civil War had been God's pun-ishment for slavery and that the plight of African Americans had been the catalyst for the nation's Armageddon. Rather than a tac-tical sleight of hand dictated by wartime exigencies (as white southerners claimed), the Emancipation Proclamation was a re-demptive act through which God had wrought national regenera-tion. A banner that hung from the speaker's platform during the 1866 Emancipation Day celebration in Richmond made this point by proclaiming that "this is the Lord's work, it is marvelous in our sight." Divine will, announced Rev. W. H. Dixon of Norfolk, had operated through human agency during the Civil War. God had answered "our fathers' and mothers' prayers" by whispering to Lincoln that "the Negro's emancipation was the country's only redemption." Rev. R. S. Williams told his audience in Columbia,

South Carolina, that Lincoln had "caught the approving eye of heaven and incurred the defeated murmurs of hell" when he issued his proclamation. By so explaining the mystery of slavery, black orators insisted that the divine providence of history had worked (and might work again in the future) to elevate the African peoples. Emancipation anticipated for some an even more profound, imminent, and millennial transformation in the status of black people.[59]

As important as providential design was, human agency, especially the exploits of black heroes, received recognition as well. Against the backdrop of the heightened patriotism of the late nineteenth century, African Americans reworked national icons and retold the nation's history so as to challenge claims that African Americans had played no role in the nation's progress. Rebutting white claims, black orators protested that they and their ancestors had always been shapers of history who deserved the nation's respect for their sacrifices. Rev. L. B. Maxwell assured his 1889 Emancipation Day audience, "There has not been a great movement in this country since the Negro has been on American soil—political or social—upon which he has had no influence." Crispus Attucks, Richard Allen, and Frederick Douglass, among others, were invoked as exemplars of black achievement and sacrifice.[60]

When the *Raleigh Baptist Searchlight* described the decorations of the local 1912 Emancipation Day ceremonies as "pre-eminently United States in appearance," it drew attention to the energetic and earnest patriotism that suffused the celebration. Black paraders and orators intended their fervent identification with the nation to contrast sharply with the resentful sectionalism of white southerners. On occasion blacks did acknowledge a regional allegiance. In 1912, Charles N. Hunter, a North Carolina educator and avid historian, admitted to his Raleigh audience that "I am a

Southerner." But his embrace of his southern identity, however heartfelt, was a rhetorical tactic that enabled him then to berate his region for its ill treatment of his race. Far more often, orators dwelled on their identity as U.S. citizens, acknowledging their southernness implicitly, if at all. Speaking to an Emancipation Day crowd in New Bern, North Carolina, Virgil A. Crawford declared that "Our love for our native land, these United States of America, shall never be excelled by any other class of people." A Jacksonville, Florida, orator whipped his audience into a paroxysm of patriotism when he announced, "In whatever capacity we may be called upon, whether as sturdy yeomanry upon whose shoulders rest the Government or whether in the front of battle, we will be found there doing our duty as good citizens of this great Government of ours."[61]

That the United States was a nation with a millennial destiny, and that blacks had an important role to play in it, was the central theme of the black commemorative tradition. The future of civilization in general and the black race in particular would be played out on this continent, where blacks already discerned ample evidence of their rapid ascent up the ladder of civilization. They viewed their history paradigmatically, as a parable of racial elevation. Whereas most whites presumed that centuries would be required to elevate blacks above abject barbarism, blacks pointed to the exceptional strides they had made since slavery. Surrounded by evidence of the progressive realization of God's purpose, their goal was to speed blacks along the path they were already destined to follow. Consequently, commemorative ceremonies, especially orations, became paeans to black "progress" and "achievement."[62]

Seemingly no Emancipation Day or Fourth of July celebration was complete without a speech that enumerated the race's progress. What may sound to modern ears like tedious recitations of arcane data about black schools, business investments, and property holdings were to black audiences a confirmation of their steady advance and refutation of "the odious charge that the Negro is lazy and shiftless." Rev. R. R. Wright's 1892 Emancipation Day address, for instance, detailed the impressive accumulation of wealth by former slaves. Similarly, an 1896 Juneteenth orator at Waco, Texas, regaled his audience with a long list of figures intended to establish that his race had "built a progressive history in industry, wealth, education, and morals."[63]

If the record of black accomplishment augured a promising future, the challenge of overcoming white oppression remained. Commemorative celebrations, especially orations, provided a forum in which to inveigh against white racism before the gathered black community. By criticizing white America, blacks claimed for themselves and their audiences a position of moral authority that made them, not whites, the true exemplars of civilization in the nation. Orators and their audiences compiled litanies of white transgressions. As Joseph T. Wilson observed during the 1885 Emancipation Day ceremonies in Norfolk, "Injustice and wrong seems to have been one of the principal sciences in the white man's civilization." Resolutions adopted at the 1890 Atlanta Emancipation Day ceremonies denounced anti-black violence in South Carolina and Georgia as "blots upon the face of civilization and outrages against humanity" that could be traced to the "cruelty, barbarity and lawlessness of white ruffians." Participants in the 1893 Emancipation Day exercises at Shaw University in Raleigh, North Carolina, resolved that whites, not blacks, threatened civilization. Racism, and the segregation that it justified, was "contrary to all that is true and ennobling,—but consistent to the will and wishes of poor, untutored, unintelligent, unmanly, and low down prejudiced white people, who are but serfs and parasites continually seeking to interfere with the rights of the Negro."[64]

Commemorative orators gave voice to enduring black political aspirations. At the same time that whites, ranging from UDC members to playwright Thomas Dixon, denounced the "dark record" of Reconstruction, black orators used commemorative celebrations to challenge the accomplishments and legacy of the postwar period. To explicitly defend Reconstruction in commemorative orations was an important political exercise that refuted white claims that "redemption" and the return of white rule had improved black fortunes. Rather than the tawdry corruption of democracy that white southerners (and increasingly northerners) recalled, Reconstruction remained for black orators a reminder that blacks could exercise power with courage, skill, vision, and compassion. Those who listened in 1917 to J. C. Lindsay lament that "the old wail is still heard that the period that followed emancipation was filled with mistakes" did not need to wait for W. E. B. Du Bois's revisionist account of Reconstruction for an antidote to white histories.[65] When Rev. W. H. Styles condemned lynching as barbaric during the observance of the anniversary of the Fifteenth Amendment in Blackshear, Georgia, he stressed that the political rights guaranteed by the Constitution offered the only reliable protection against white violence. Rev. J. J. Durham warned his Savannah audience in 1900 that any "attempts to deal with the Negro as something less than a citizen" would "cost this country more blood and treasure than it took to establish its independence." Through speeches and resolutions, orators and celebrants alike made strenuous demands for black political rights, denounced racism, and defended black citizenship on the grounds that blacks had surpassed all reasonable tests—of education, patriotism, and fortitude—they had faced. And audiences,

by giving their assent through resolutions adopted during celebrations, voiced concerns and opinions that were otherwise seldom
acknowledged in southern public life.[66]

Even while blacks lashed out at their oppression, they intended their formal commemorative exercises, like the orderly
parades that preceded them, to confirm black mastery of the etiquette of American public culture. This concern for respectability
(in all the myriad nineteenth-century meanings of the word) reflected a widely held anxiety that indecency, sloth, and sinfulness
might impede blacks from following their intended trajectory.
After describing blacks' proud history, God's lofty ambitions for
the race, and the enduring challenge of white bigotry, commemorative speakers routinely adopted the tone of Jeremiah of the Old
Testament and scolded their listeners for their lapses. They rebuked blacks who were slovenly in their appearance, who mim-
icked whites, or who committed crimes. Without integrity, sacrifice, and stamina, they warned, their audiences would never earn
white respect or lift the race out of its impoverished, vice-ridden
urban neighborhoods and ramshackle sharecroppers' cabins.[67]

As a fusion of recitals, memorials, protests, and jeremiads,
black commemorative ceremonies occupied a crucial role in the
evolution of black collective memory in the postbellum South. If
black orators at times seemed to parrot the dominant American
faith in a progressively unfolding historical drama, they did so not
because they necessarily identified with white values, but in order
to promote an African American collective identity. This strategy
of reversal—of appropriating purportedly American ideals and
turning them back on their oppressors—was fundamental to expressions of black public memory after the Civil War. Such inver-
sions of white presumptions about the past had especially strong
purchase at a time when blacks struggled to establish that the
large and central themes of the black experience were only

identifiable when traced through history. Commemorative exercises helped in this endeavor by serving as a visual and oral archive of black strivings and African American claims for justice.

The frequent and impressive public celebrations of black memory during the half century following the Civil War mobilized black communities to recall and reflect on the possible meanings of their past. Opportunities to participate in the crafting of collective memory were less restricted among southern African Americans than among whites, but organized groups and local elites in both communities took for granted their self-appointed stewardship of public festivities. Southern whites and blacks alike engaged in fashioning collective memories for their respective communities that rendered history as the record of the progressive evolution of human society; both assumed that their race had inherent capacities and a predestined future that could only be fulfilled, not evaded.

These similarities, however, could not mask profound differences between black and white memories. Southern white historical memory exalted white civilization, legitimated white power, and virtually excluded any admission of meaningful black agency in the region's past. White accounts seemed to insulate blacks from history. There was, in white history, no acknowledgment of true suffering or real accomplishments among blacks. They were without personal ancestry, their lives were small, and there was a great void in their past. And if southern whites grudgingly acknowledged the restoration of the union, they still embraced a willfully sectional historical identity. This jealous defense of sectional honor that was at the heart of the white southern memory had no parallel in black memory. Rather, most southern blacks, in rhapsodically nationalist terms, imagined a biracial America in which they would assume their place as equal and full citizens. To the same extent that white southerners insisted on their sectional identity, southern African Americans exalted their national ties. Likewise, blacks recounted a past in which black participation figured decisively in all of the nation's defining moments.

For many southern whites, the Civil War had broken the ribbon of time, severing the present from preceding eras. The predominant postwar white memory dwelled on loss—of battles, loved ones, a way of life, prestige, and power. When white southerners scrutinized the past, they found irrefutable evidence of their victimization. In contrast, the black record of the past recognized no comparable discontinuity. For blacks, the past was bound up in a present that was neither exotically different nor obsolete. Blacks did attach millennial significance to emancipation, but the trying adjustments to freedom and the enduring obstacle of white racism encouraged them to see history as an unresolved, ongoing process. And despite the searing experience of slavery and the disappointments of freedom, blacks found in their history cause for optimism. This purposeful memory encouraged southern African Americans to look to the future for the fulfillment of hopes that had been anticipated, inspired, and urged on by centuries of sacrifice. Or, as Emancipation Day orator Charles N. Hunter explained, "the past has its lessons . . . the present has its duties . . . the future has its rewards."[68]

Black celebrations disseminated a distinctive black translation of the civilizationist ideology deep into the southern hinterland. Black lumbermen in East Texas, black mill workers in Birmingham, Alabama, and self-sufficient black farmers in Glynn County, Georgia, almost certainly never heard the learned speeches or read the writings of Alexander Crummell and other black intellectuals at the forefront of advancing a black interpretation of the civilizationist ideology. Yet blacks in far-flung reaches of the

South who gathered to hear Lincoln Day orations, to cheer Emancipation Day processions, and to honor Memorial Day were exposed to expressions of the civilizationist ideology that meshed seamlessly with the more erudite renderings of black intellectuals. Year after year, common black folk in the South listened to and watched ceremonies that gave meaning to the whirlwind of black experience that extended from ancient Egypt to the present, all the while emphasizing black agency and destiny.

The evolution of southern white attitudes about the Union and their place in it directly affected black commemorative activities. For several decades after the Civil War, most white southerners refrained from or openly repudiated any observation of the Fourth of July. But the Spanish-American War reawakened frenetic nationalism even among former Confederates, and southern whites displayed renewed enthusiasm for the anniversary of national independence. Leading the efforts to revive white observance of the Fourth of July in many areas of the South were the Daughters of the American Revolution and other patriotic societies. In Atlanta, for instance, the DAR prodded public officials to stage large patriotic festivities and parades in public spaces that blacks previously had used without challenge. As a consequence, blacks and their festivities were pushed to the margins of the civic landscape. This reassertion of white cultural authority over many patriotic celebrations, in combination with segregation, exacerbated the contest over public spaces and the remembered past in it. Disfranchisement, which occurred across the South at this time, added to the political significance of public celebrations of black history. For blacks who could no longer vote or who had never voted, commemorative holidays provided a forum in which to act politically and to give voice to political aspirations that contradicted whites' presumption of a cowed black populace.[69]

The most important changes in the expression of black memory, however, were not brought about by white pressure, but rather by changes within the black community. By the second decade of the twentieth century, the role of black ministers in many commemorative celebrations had changed significantly. Ministers retained important roles as orators for and hosts of black celebrations. But typically the planning and formal control of the ceremonies passed into the hands of laypeople, including, increasingly, women. This transformation may give the mistaken impression that black memory was becoming secularized during the early twentieth century. But millennial Protestantism remained at the center of the celebrations' representation of the past. The change in leadership instead reflected the growing diversity within the black community and the proliferation of voluntary and social organizations eager to share some of the cultural authority previously exercised by black ministers.

An even more important change in black commemorative celebrations was the declining persuasiveness of the civilizationist ideology itself. World War I and its effects prompted blacks, like whites, to reconsider the presumptive supremacy of Anglo-European civilization. After witnessing Western Europe destroying its youth in the trenches of blood-soaked fields, black Americans could not easily subscribe to the belief that they should measure their progress against the standard of Western civilization. The revival of Pan-Africanism, dramatized by the 1919 Pan-African Congress that coincided with the Versailles Peace Conference, stirred hopes among blacks that the future of blacks, and even the world, would be settled in Africa. At the same time, Marcus Garvey's Universal Negro Improvement Association attracted hundreds of thousands of black men and women, including many in the U.S. South, to the cause of African redemption. By the 1920s interest in Africa had come to dominate African American intellectual life, as expressed in the "New Negro" movement to popular drama and even the new mass art form of cinema. This diverse cultural movement prompted blacks to reconsider Africa's legacy in America and their relationship to their ancestral continent. Taken together, the waning of the civilizationist ideology and the Pan-Africanist revival worked to glorify the primitive and to undermine the idea that African Americans should slavishly defer to the conventions of modern civilization. The presumption that the black masses were an uncouth child-race, striving to overcome the legacy of their barbarous ancestors and the peculiar institution while ascending the ladder of civilization, seemed obsolete. Indeed by the 1920s, with the scars and trauma of the past less glaring, black intellectuals and leaders evinced less and less embarrassment about the black common folk. As historian Wilson Jeremiah Moses has pointed out, "The black masses became acceptable to the black world—more than incidentally— at the same time that they were becoming more acceptable to the white." Once assumptions about Africa, black capacities, and white civilization all became subject to revision, the uses and meaning of the past were open to reinterpretation as well.[70]

These new currents of thought, as well as the rise of new black historical activists, including professional historians, would reshape black memory during the 1920s and 1930s. The Emancipation Day processions, Lincoln Day orations, fraternal society festivities, church anniversaries, and myriad other activities that made up the rituals of black collective memory would endure. The collective performance of black memory did not wane along with the civilizationist ideology. (Traces of that ideology would linger in black collective memory for years.) But unmistakable changes in the form and content of black collective memory took place.

Charles Carroll, the orator at the 1896 Juneteenth celebrations in Waco, Texas, brilliantly expressed the desperate need of blacks to fashion a useable past despite their understandable ambivalence about Africa, the United States, and their race's history. "We must not sink in despair," he entreated his audience. "We must not give up the high hope of our race, for who could determine our existence today had our forefathers ignored the hope of this generation." He refused to believe that the sacrifice of "brave Negro heroes" during the Civil War and the efforts of Frederick Douglass and other "redeeming fathers" had not eased the way for future blacks. Yes, blacks had been defrauded of the full meaning of citizenship "by every means human ingenuity can devise." But, Carroll promised, "as this race unfolds the canvas of time and recollection which represents it from bondage to freedom, it whispers consolation to generations unborn."[71] To find consolation in the black experience in the United States was to defy reality and insist on a hopeful future for the community. We might well wonder how southern African Americans would have survived the disappointments and hardships of the age had they not engaged in such an act of extraordinary social imagination.

3

Archiving White Memory

On December 7, 1898, former governor Thomas G. Jones stood on the lawn of the Alabama capitol grounds. Behind him stood a tall, gleaming monument honoring the Confederacy. Jones, a member of the newly revived Alabama Historical Society, used his speech dedicating the monument to urge his state to shoulder more responsibility for the preservation of its history. Only a day before, the legislature had debated a bill that proposed to establish a state historical commission and appropriate, for the first time, funds for ongoing historical activities. "Our duty," Jones implored, "is not ended with the unveiling of this monument." "Where," he asked "may [an] Alabamian find a roll of the men who made history and yet left no name on its pages?" Two days later, the state legislature answered Jones's appeal and formally established the Alabama Historical Commission. This modest initiative foreshadowed a region-wide expansion of state authority to promote the preservation and study of the past as an essential facet of official public life in the South.[1]

In the past, white voluntary groups had secured the imprimatur of state prestige by mobilizing the "public" behind campaigns for monuments like the one Jones dedicated. Otherwise the role of the state in shaping representations of the past was largely passive. Prior to 1900, nowhere in the South had any significant public funds been committed to the ongoing interpretation and dissemination of historical understanding. In the first decade of the twentieth century, however, a coalition of white hereditary societies and patriotic groups, historical enthusiasts, and professional historians urged that the state actively promote public appreciation of history by funding archives, museums, commissions, and public history programs. Within two decades, these campaigns had prodded every southern state, at least in principle, to expand state authority to include the collection, preservation, and presentation of remnants of the past.

The enthusiasm that some whites displayed for state-supported historical agencies was an extension of the political ambitions of white elites. It is inconceivable that white Democrats would have condoned public funding for such agencies during the three decades immediately after the Civil War when they faced robust challenges from white and black Republicans and Populists. To have done so might have enabled political insurgents to use state funds and offices to promote historical narratives that were anathema to the Democratic Party and its supporters. But by 1900, white Democrats had a firm grip on the region's politics and public institutions. They also had an acute need to establish the legitimacy of their recently secured power, in large part because their hegemony rested on coercion and anti-democratic constitutional manipulations. State historical agencies provided the means to present the southern past in a manner consonant with the needs and goals of this ascendant white elite. Through decisions about the appropriate focus of archives, museums, and historical agencies, white historians and their allies effectively removed competing groups and historical alternatives from the region's past. Although couched in terms of promoting civic spirit, this archival impulse in the South impeded any inclusive or democratic understanding of southern history. The region's archives and museums, reflecting the "highest stage" of white supremacy, were, for all practical purposes, for whites only.

In 1890, it would have been inconceivable that several southern states would be at the forefront in pioneering state-funded public history. The archival impulse and creation of "knowing institutions" came late to the American South. By the close of the nineteenth century, such enterprises had been long established in much of Europe and even in far-flung European colonies. But until then, almost no one in a position of authority in the South displayed any interest in preserving, organizing, and methodically studying historical documents. Instead, such remnants of the past were generally disposed of once they were no longer actively used. When the occupants of the Georgia State Capitol warmed themselves by burning discarded state records, for example, they felt satisfied that they had found a new use for seemingly worthless artifacts.

Traditions of record-keeping throughout the region were notoriously haphazard. In North Carolina, colonial and Revolutionary War records were stored in an abandoned outhouse near the state capitol. Everywhere obsolete documents were stuffed into convenient spaces until their accumulated mess demanded attention. A capitol janitor in Nashville won praise from state employees when he gathered up several cartloads of old records that "lay piled in masses on stone floors" and burned them. They, after all, were "wet and nasty and smelled bad." Autograph collectors defaced or made off with those documents that escaped his bonfire. Perhaps the bleakest portrait of negligence occurred in 1906 Florida, where Prof. David Y. Thomas recorded the efforts of a conscientious state official to recover state records from "the coal bin" and the "garret of the capitol building." The bulk of the documents were in a "wretched state of preservation." State legislators took notice only when a growing mountain of discarded state documents stored in the attic of the state capitol threatened to crash down through the ceiling of the legislative chambers. In such an environment, chance, rather than foresight, dictated which public documents survived.[2]

A new orientation toward relics and public documents was first evident in Alabama, which established the first state-funded archives in the South. In 1900 the newly launched Alabama Historical Commission issued a hefty report outlining the new obligations that the state should assume. It urged the establishment of a new agency charged with "the custody of state official archives" and the operation of "a state library, museum and art gallery, with particular reference to the history and antiquities of Alabama." In addition, the agency should assume responsibility for "marking historic sites." The new department's holdings would be bolstered by the addition of those of the Alabama Historical Society, which would cease collecting materials and instead devote its resources to stimulating interest in "historical discussion." In February 1901, the state legislature gave unanimous approval to a bill creating the Department of Archives and History.[3]

The success of the drive for a state archive in Alabama inspired campaigns in neighboring states, especially Mississippi. Anxious to secure prompt state support, Franklin L. Riley, a professor at the University of Mississippi, drafted a bill modeled after the legislation establishing the Alabama Historical Commission and submitted it to the state legislature in January 1899. The bill

View of the collections of the Alabama Department of Archives and History, the South's leading public archive, ca. 1915. (Alabama Department of Archives and History, Montgomery)

passed without opposition (in no small part because the only expense the commission imposed on the state was a modest subsidy for publications of the Mississippi Historical Society). Five months later, the commissioners issued a comprehensive report warning Mississippians that they risked losing irreplaceable documents to fire, decay, and collectors. If nothing were done by the state, citizens would "be forced to the inconvenience, as well as the humiliation, of going elsewhere to learn the doings of their ancestors." To prevent this ignominy, the commissioners urged that the Magnolia State follow Alabama's example and establish a state department of archives and history. In February 1902, Riley wrote and adeptly shepherded through the state legislature a carbon copy of the bill that had established the Alabama archives.[4]

In North Carolina, the creation of a state-funded historical commission was, in the words of one participant, the result of "evolution," not "sudden conversion." The first attempt to clothe public history with the dignity of the state was legislation in 1903 establishing a five-member North Carolina Historical Commission. "Realizing the reluctance with which the average legislator votes for the creation of new departments and offices," the drafters of the legislation intentionally set the new commission's appropriation at the trivial sum of five hundred dollars. But the state's obligations were in fact considerably greater because the legislation declared that all historical documents collected by the commission could be published, without restriction, at state expense. Once in operation, the commission fell under the sway of commissioner Robert Digges Wimberly Connor, a well-connected historian and activist. He soon concluded that the ongoing publication of important historical records could not proceed until materials were first collected and properly arranged. By 1906, sensing that conditions appeared to be "about right for a movement towards the proper preservation and care of historical sources,"

Connor lobbied the state legislature to fund a department of archives and a facility to house it. Connor's proposal was adopted in 1907, and the state historical commission became in fact, if not in name, the state's archives. Within two years, Connor returned to the legislature and coaxed legislation substantially expanding the scope of the existing commission. By carefully earning the benevolence of state legislators in subsequent years, he gradually secured generous funding for the commission. From a staff of one whose office was in a vacant corner of the state senate chamber, the commission grew by 1921 to consist of a staff of eight who worked in eleven rooms in a modern fireproof building and managed an enviable annual appropriation.[5]

The unprecedented extension of government support on behalf of the conservation and promotion of state heritage did not occur uniformly across the South. Even when state support was forthcoming, it was sometimes neither generous nor secure. The Tennessee legislature in 1905 refused to create a department of archives but approved funding for a secretary of the "department of Archives and History." The legislature continued to fund the position for ten years until a newly elected governor requested the resignation of the archivist, who had presided over a nonexistent department that legislators eventually abolished. In Texas the state archives fell victim to abrupt changes in leadership and mission whenever political winds shifted. And the tribulations of the Arkansas History Commission illustrated the challenges to ambitious public history plans in parts of the South. In 1905, the legislature passed a bill creating a state historical commission. A year later the commission recommended the establishment of a state archives and history department similar to those already functioning in Alabama and Mississippi. More than two years passed before the state legislature acted on the recommendations. But when it did, it failed to approve any funding for the now permanent commission. A prominent University of Arkansas historian, John Hugh Reynolds, agreed to serve as the unpaid secretary of the commission until the next legislature could appropriate funding. But two years later, tight state finances still precluded any appropriation for a full-time secretary and archivist. Intent on establishing the archives in fact as well as in name, the commission decided to elect a permanent secretary and employ him with the understanding that he must trust "to the good faith of the next legislature to reimburse him." Remarkably, the commission found a qualified applicant, Dallas T. Herndon, willing to accept the position on such precarious terms. Herndon subsequently discovered during his forty-two years as a chronically underpaid state archivist that the stinginess of Arkansas's tightfisted legislators was not momentary.[6]

That this expansion of the state into historical matters was sometimes halting and inconsistent is hardly surprising; everywhere, but especially in the South, efforts to extend government capacities generally in the early twentieth century were awkward and incomplete. The image of the overworked Dallas Herndon in his cramped office was more likely to inspire pity than awe. Nevertheless, Herndon and his fellow public historians left an enduring legacy that has shaped the public understanding of southern history throughout the twentieth century. With each additional appropriation of funds for public history, southern state legislatures acknowledged that the preservation and interpretation of the past, which previously had been a preserve of private citizens, were now matters of public policy. The privileged location of archives and museums in the civic landscapes of the region was one measure of this new state responsibility and the importance attached to it.[7]

The timing of the founding of southern public history agencies was not happenstance. The connection between public archives and the establishment of state power and administration was unmistakable. Rulers in early modern Europe had established archives to solidify and memorialize first monarchical and then state power. They looked to the documentary record to establish procedure and precedence for state practices. The ongoing destruction of public documents, advocates of historical repositories warned, made modern, efficient governance virtually impossible. Beyond interfering with the timely conduct of state business, shoddy or nonexistent record-keeping engendered mismanagement and corruption. As the scope of public business expanded and the number of state employees increased, there was a self-evident need for systematic and accessible institutional records that registered past decisions and policies. Reflecting the contemporary faith in and enthusiasm for administrative expertise and bureaucratic organizations, proponents of archives insisted that the effective provision of public services necessitated the collecting of objective information. Once established, state historical agencies quickly demonstrated their usefulness to officials. Archivists provided much-used fact-checking services for legislators, and in some instances even cooperated in the crafting of legislation. They also produced widely distributed compendiums of data on their states intended to boost their prestige by chronicling historical milestones and investment opportunities. Modern archives, in short, became a prerequisite for the modern state.[8]

A properly nurtured sense of history that promoted allegiance to state and nation also complemented the Progressive-era drive for social order in the South. The campaign for public history, seldom pitched as a crude mechanism for social control, was instead presented in elevated terms as fostering an organic solidarity among residents who shared a distinctive and proud history. Historical education, broadly conceived, offered an instrument of communal transformation that would overcome worrisome cleavages in the South. Unstated but often implied was the notion that white southerners, having endured extraordinary hardships during the Civil War and Reconstruction as well as chronic political turmoil since then, lacked a unifying civic culture. History, moreover, could be used to affirm that white leaders and institutions had in the past pursued elevated goals that could not be reduced to crass politics. By implication, the vote buying, violence, ballot stuffing, and other tawdry practices that had tainted politics in the late nineteenth-century South were historical anomalies. History would show that the South had fostered democratic institutions and nurtured enlightened statesmen, and by extension, would continue to do so.

The promotion of historical awareness appealed to those white southerners who believed that "modern" and "progressive" state governance, which was essential to the South's recovery and prosperity, required an educated and unified citizenry. The North Carolina Historical Commission warned in 1904 that "it is not safe to trust the future to the control of a people who are ignorant of their past; . . . no people who are indifferent to their past need hope to make their future great." Advocates of public funding couched their proposals in the contemporary language of state activism. As R. D. W. Connor of North Carolina well understood, "The average legislator will require something more than mere ancestor worship, sentiment, or antiquarian interest before he will be convinced of the propriety and wisdom of spending the public money for such work." In order for public institutions to embody modern ideals of civic responsibility, the thinking went, southerners needed an understanding of the past that had shaped their institutions and made progress possible. In Arkansas, Dallas T. Herndon similarly explained that to understand "the aspirations of [a state's] people one must analyze the successive stages by which the community grew into an organic body-politic."[9]

State historical agencies, proponents contended, would occupy a central role in the formation of a modern civic culture.
Franklin L. Riley of Mississippi predicted that such "agencies"
would bring together "two of the influences—academic and political—which are the most powerful and progressive in any com-
monwealth." Advocates in Alabama insisted that a public archive
and museum would "increase our sense of local importance and
State pride" and become a place "to which the patriotic heart of
all Alabamians could turn with pride and delight." Other boosters spoke of the "broad and rational basis for patriotism" that
public history engendered. Herndon, for one, anticipated that
knowledge of history "will surely bear fruit in a higher order of
citizenship, in a finer appreciation of social responsibility, in a
more rational settlement of the confounding complexities of modern society."[10]

Enthusiasts were confident that state-funded historical repositories could employ the romance of the past to transform abstract notions of citizenship into deeply felt bonds of sentiment.
Thus romance and sentimentality, at least as much as "science,"
informed the founding conception of the region's public archives
and museums. Portrait galleries of great figures in history, artifacts recovered from hallowed shrines, relics of heroes and martyrs—these were the presumed holdings and exhibits of the
proposed state agencies. Merely to be in the presence of such objects would apparently allow observers to span the chasm of time
and to experience the past. As John Spencer Bassett of Trinity
College (now Duke University) explained, relics were "speaking
witnesses" that told "a story of past life." Activists emphasized the
didactic potential of their project by dwelling on the unequaled
power of preserved relics to inspire a sense of connection with the
past and to grip the popular imagination. This understanding of
the power of objects helps to explain the curiosities that graced

The systematically organized collections of the Department of History at Louisiana State Museum, New Orleans, ca. 1912, traced an elitist record of the past. (*Third Biennial Report of the Board of Curators of the Louisiana State Museum* [1912])

many exhibits. The Arkansas State Historical Museum, for example, displayed a branch purportedly from an apple tree at the site of the Confederate surrender at Appomattox, Virginia. Also on view was a prayer book molded out of clay gathered from the site of the Civil War battle of the "Crater" at Petersburg, Virginia. That objects such as a gnarled branch and a lump of soil could fire the historical imagination of all who observed them was axiomatic to historical enthusiasts at the turn of the century. Archives and museums would become theaters where generations of southerners would experience, through all of their senses, their region's past.[11]

That the archival impulse could advance the interests of the state was clear to advocates. That the state should take a lead in it was equally obvious. Although comparatively bare, state coffers in turn-of-the-century South were the only viable funding source for public history. In many northern cities, wealthy philanthropists established privately funded museums and collections that became cultural landmarks, such as the Newberry Library in Chicago, the Boston Atheneum, and the J. P. Morgan Library in New York. In the South, private philanthropy and popular appeals were sufficient to fund monuments, but not enough to sustain archives and museums. As William P. Trent, a historian at the University of the South, pointedly observed during the 1890s, "It would not be hard to name more than one Northern [historical] society that has done more for historical science than all the Southern societies have done since their inception." Most southern historical societies, as Trent suggested, existed in name only— some as vehicles for the enthusiasms of a few zealots and others as genteel social clubs that met sporadically without any discernable mission. The Historical Society of Arkansas, one of several short-lived societies that surfaced in Little Rock after the Civil War, was typical. It left no enduring legacy other than a small pamphlet "fixing the pronunciation of the name 'Arkansas.'" The modest dues collected from these societies' tiny memberships were seldom sufficient to meet even the trivial expenses of the activities the societies undertook. Few contemporaries had cause to disagree with Trent's observation that none of the southern historical societies "has ever approximated a full measure of usefulness."[12]

The new state agencies in the South, in contrast, engaged in ongoing and systematic historical work that touched southerners who had never entered the parlors or meeting halls of the region's genteel historical societies. More important, the newly established archives and museums could give the imprimatur of the state to some interpretations of the southern past and withhold it from others. In this fashion, white historians employed by the state gave a patina of professionalism and "science" to a narrative of southern history already familiar to and embraced by many white southerners.

Reflecting the diffuse influence of Darwinian evolutionism, history itself was understood as the result of a chain of discernable causes and effects, not as random variations, recurring cycles, or surface appearances. Historical events, in short, could be explained by prior events in historical time. As a consequence of cumulative change, the past was decisively different from but causally linked to the present. Powerful traces of earlier popular beliefs about heroic individualism persisted, figuring prominently in the galleries of heroes and collections of relics displayed by many public history sites. But the idea of continually unfolding, organic development directed attention to the historical role of political and economic institutions. As Alcée Fortier of Tulane University explained, "the history of institutions and social evolution" formed the core of "the history of civilization." Professional historians thus promoted careful attention to the evolution of institutions, without entirely abandoning the mawkish biographies and heroic epics that had previously passed for history.[13]

This conspicuous emphasis on the evolution of institutions and societies meshed easily with the prevailing civilizationist ideology of the era, which held that economic and political practices were benchmarks of civilization. In the "Halls of History" and in museums that complemented these new southern archives, historical relics traced heroic narratives of white civilization. More than mere happenstance explains the Native American artifacts that graced the collections of many public history repositories. Even seemingly "objective" displays of Indian arrowheads, weaving, and tools implicitly plotted the location of Indians on the universal scale of social development, demonstrating unambiguously both the perceived barbarism that had preceded European settlement and the tragic backwardness that had doomed Indian culture to extinction. Simultaneously, ethnographic displays presented contemporary Indian cultures in a temporal limbo that existed outside of any traditional historical understanding. The logical conclusion of displays that classified and naturalized such categories as primitive and civilized, backward and modern, was that Western civilization marked the highest achievement of social evolution.[14]

In ways obvious and subtle, public history in the South explained white racial privilege as the inevitable and proper consequence of history. Without exception, professional historians in the South espoused the contemporary cult of Anglo-Saxonism, and many were as diligent in tracing their esteemed Anglo-Saxon ancestry as any members of the hereditary societies. Presumptions of racial exclusivism were rife in the pronouncements of public history advocates. When Dr. William R. Garrett of Nashville's Peabody Normal College told the members of the Alabama Historical Society that "we belong to the great Anglo-Saxon race, the race of statesmen and of heroes," his listeners apparently were untroubled by his presumptions. When Dunbar Rowland announced to the alumni association of the University of Mississippi that "the Anglo-Saxon has never bowed his head to the yoke of an inferior race and he never will" and insisted that the "demands of civilization must be obeyed," he appealed to the same civilizationist ideology that suffused the writings and speeches of the leaders of patriotic and hereditary societies in the South.[15]

The contributions of the South's new professional historians to bolstering white privilege went beyond pronouncements about black inferiority and Anglo-Saxon superiority. If most white scholars agreed that moral outrage had no place in any impartial history of slavery, the Civil War, or the traumas of sectionalism, they nevertheless littered their austere monographs on legislation, legal cases, and political contests with the conventional language and assumptions of white supremacy. The southern racial order and its historical origins became prominent subjects of historical analysis, and the resulting work supported the prevailing white opinion that slavery was a patriarchal and benevolent institution, Reconstruction a benighted experiment, and the adoption of Jim Crow an enlightened policy for racial peace and order. The publications of the Mississippi Historical Society, for example, became the venue for a systematic defense of the tactics adopted by the Reconstruction-era whites who had "redeemed" the state by terrorizing blacks. Employing the techniques of "scientific" history, authors cataloged the alleged tribulations suffered by white Mississippians during Reconstruction. Apparently scholarly objectivity did not prevent one historian from concluding that the violent overthrow of Reconstruction was "one of the greatest triumphs of Southern honor and manhood" and "a lesson of Anglo-Saxon superiority." Another historian admonished contemporaries that it "should not be forgotten that what we have today we owe" to the heroes of redemption.[16]

White historians in the South made sure that the region's impressionable children encountered the latest "scientific" scholarship in their classrooms. Prof. Franklin L. Riley was typical; he promoted the latest methods of history teaching in Mississippi schools by organizing conferences for history teachers under the auspices of the Mississippi Historical Society. He and other historians compensated for their lack of direct influence over curricula by preparing the teaching materials that were widely adopted, even mandated, in many states. Among the state historians who wrote books that generations of southern children struggled to master were Connor in North Carolina, Rowland in Mississippi, and Herndon in Arkansas, as well as professors like Riley of Mississippi. Connor carried the mission of education a step further by arranging for the publication of *North Carolina Leaflets,* a series of brief pamphlets intended for use in North Carolina schools. The state history texts that Riley and others wrote methodically taught that slavery had benefited blacks by exposing them to European civilization, but that black people were woefully unfit to participate in public life as intelligent, rational, productive citizens. These texts, often complete with footnotes and lists of "authorities," placed before children simplified versions of, as Riley put it, "all of the most important [scholarly] contributions made in recent years." In this fashion professional historians lined their pockets with cash (always an important consideration for underpaid academics and archivists), bolstered their claims of public service, and helped ensure that the region's white schools taught a version of history that celebrated the rule of white elites.[17]

At its most fundamental level, the project of public history in the early twentieth century South was the archiving of white civilization. Evidently, no thought was given to preserving, displaying, or analyzing the history of the region's African American citizenry. State-funded public history in the South, like the contemporary Progressive reform movements in the region, was "for whites only." That the documents of politicians and public records made up the preponderance of the archived collections was predictable and appropriate, given the charters of most public historical repositories. Likewise, the collections of museums understandably bulged with genteel material culture. But a profound blindness toward African American institutions and history characterized virtually every facet of the public history movement in the South. When the North Carolina and Arkansas history commissions made their first forays into marking and preserving historic "shrines," as they were charged to do by their charters, they inevitably focused on sites hallowed by whites. To the extent that the history of African Americans was preserved, it was through official documents and slaveholders' records. Black newspapers, institutional records, and private correspondence went uncollected. This void in the collections of the South impeded opportunities to understand the southern racial order from any perspective other than that of its architects. Moreover, it twisted and constrained all subsequent historical research on African Americans in the region, effectively erasing black historical agency. That recognition of almost any kind was denied African Americans while public space and resources were provided to white hereditary societies, whose membership was often tiny, speaks volumes about the biases of the state historical agencies.[18]

While the promotion of public history helped to shore up the legitimacy of white southern elites after decades of political and economic upheaval, it also established the influence of an emerging cadre of white professional historians. Like other contemporary professional men, historians and archivists set out to establish communities of specialists with shared standards of competence. Having been trained in university that the study of history required new forms of expertise and critical thinking, the South's public historians pursued "objective" historical truth by embracing professional training, organizing communities of historians, and redefining the audience for historical scholarship. Of the innovations that these professional historians encountered at Johns Hopkins, Columbia, and other leading graduate schools of the era, none were more important than seminar instruction and archival research. Previously, neither was presumed to be the best means to instill knowledge or discern historical truth. During the last two decades of the century, however, the seminar and archival research became the putative criteria for certification in the profession. Seminars, perceived to be akin to scientific laboratories, rested on the deceptively simple idea of exposing students to masses of original manuscripts, documents, and other remnants of the past. An early graduate of Johns Hopkins explained, "History cannot depend upon the memory of men; it cannot depend upon folklore nor upon traditions that come to us from word of mouth. History rests upon the documents." Historical records and artifacts were like specimens that required only the application of standardized techniques to reveal historical truths. To the trailblazers of the new history, the gathering, organization, and interpretation of documents and other evidence represented the crystallization of a scientific method for history.[19]

Intent on applying their skills and asserting their presumptive authority over southern history, white professional historians inevitably challenged those who had previously assumed guardianship over historical matters. A nascent rivalry emerged over who, among white elites, would take the lead in interpreting the southern past and would garner the power and prestige that flowed from this role. This contest posed no immediate challenge to the orthodoxies of white history. But when professional historians created state-funded historical agencies and embraced a professional ethic, they laid the foundations for both historical venues and a self-conscious professional community that decades later would interpret the South's past in ways that were unthinkable at the turn of the twentieth century.

The initial challenge facing white professional historians in the South was marshaling sufficient influence to achieve their ambitions. As late as 1895 perhaps only a half-dozen full-time historians held positions at southern universities. Although their numbers grew significantly during the first two decades of the twentieth century, professional historians could not establish their cultural authority without allies sympathetic to at least some of their goals. Consequently, professional historians across the region set about garnering support for the mission of modern history.

Prof. George P. Garrison of the University of Texas took the lead in his state by organizing a "distinguished group of men and women" into the Texas State Historical Association. Even those who "ardently enjoyed" the study of the past, like Bride Neill Taylor, one of the founding members of the new association, had to be tutored to value history's odds and ends. She recalled the profound influence of Garrison's proposal in 1897 that the new association collect all manner of historic records and artifacts. "History was to us," she explained, "an art to be dearly loved and ardently enjoyed. That it was also a science, calling for the cold, exact methods of scientific investigation, was a fact just beginning to percolate down from the specialists to the rest of us." In Alabama and Mississippi, Thomas M. Owen and Franklin L. Riley adopted similar methods to expand their influence and garner an audience for their historical scholarship. Eager to establish a community of like-minded devotees of history and to provide venues for the exchange of rigorous historical scholarship, Owen and Riley revived their state's historical societies, launched state historical publications, and initiated annual meetings. The culmination of these efforts would be the establishment of state historical agencies and archives.[20]

The campaigns of Garrison, Owen, Riley, and others found receptive audiences among white veterans' and women's patriotic and voluntary groups. These groups had little difficulty grasping the value of historical repositories or of state support for public history programs. They had already participated in private-public partnerships, such as those needed for funding monuments and homes for Confederate veterans and widows. For the United Confederate Veterans and the Sons of Confederate Veterans, campaigning for historical repositories was an extension of their campaign to preserve the "true history" of the South's failed experiment in nationhood. While the federal government scrupulously preserved Union records, it had made no comparable commitment to conserve those of the Confederacy. Aside from their practical benefits to veterans, who would be able to trace more easily their war records (and secure state pensions), public archives would be reliquaries of the Lost Cause. As such, they would be "a glorious tribute to our fathers who fought so heroically and gallantly."[21]

The long-standing role of women's organizations as cultural custodians made these groups natural and dogged advocates of historical repositories and state-funded programs of public history. Many of the goals of women's voluntary associations meshed with the early ambitions of professional historians. Like the Confederate veterans, the Colonial Dames, DAR, and UDC looked on archives as long-needed shrines of public memory. They also anticipated using archives for genealogical research, which in addition to being a turn-of-the-century fad, was essential to substantiate membership applications to hereditary societies. And women's voluntary associations already advocated a lengthening list of expanded government responsibilities. It may be recalled that the Texas State Federation of Women's Clubs, as part of its promotion of public libraries, had successfully lobbied the state legislature to create the Texas Library and Historical Commission.[22]

The initial alliance between professional historians and groups that subsequently became their rivals was eased by class bonds. Thomas M. Owen was typical of the men who succeeded as public historians in the South. Born in 1866 in northern Alabama, he graduated from the state university in 1887 with a degree in law. An ambitious man, he married Marie Bankhead, the daughter of one of Alabama's most prominent politicians, and threw himself into local Democratic Party politics. When he turned his energies toward becoming the state's first official historian and archivist, he exploited all of his ties to the state's elites. Alexander S. Salley,

Thomas Owen, champion of public history and director of the Alabama Department of Archives and History, in his office in Montgomery, ca. 1915. (Alabama Department of Archives and History, Montgomery)

South Carolina's long-time state historian, also had a background that smoothed the way for new alliances. Salley, a lawyer with an enthusiasm for history, was also the son of a prominent Orangeburg politician, a graduate of the Citadel, and a former clerk for a state congressman; in addition, he had served on the editorial staff of one of the state's most influential newspapers, the *Charleston News and Courier.* This background enabled him to move effortlessly within South Carolina's seemingly byzantine social hierarchy. R. D. W. Connor of North Carolina boasted descent from a distinguished family, too. Because, as one acquaintance later observed, he had "excellent connections (at any rate a wise and influential father), [and] is very much liked, knows the professorial business . . . and has also facility in public speaking," he excelled at mustering support for historical work and for his career in North Carolina.[23]

Shared regional loyalties also united professional historians and their amateur allies. Most of the new professional historians had completed their training outside the former Confederacy and aspired to cast off the provincial history they believed had been promoted during the early nineteenth century. Above all, they sought to avoid what a mentor to many of the region's historians called the "pettiness and sterility" of patriotic and local history. John B. Henneman of Hampden-Sidney College cautioned that it would not do for southern historians "to regard ourselves as cut off from the rest of the universe in thought—as having a peculiar world all to ourselves and a history of our own." Even so, professional historians retained a strong allegiance to their native region. Like their amateur counterparts in the South, they resented the perceived provincialism and sanctimoniousness of the New Englanders who dominated the historical profession. Voicing a familiar complaint of southern historians, Ulrich B. Phillips grumbled in 1903 that "the history of the United States has been written by Boston and largely written wrong." Whether by acquiring records that confirmed the crucial role of southerners in the struggle for independence, by stressing the national service of the region's antebellum statesmen in school texts, or by celebrating the heroism of white southerners during the Spanish-American War, historians implicitly challenged the privileged place that New England held in national narratives. Just as southern members of the DAR were quick to bristle when they perceived a regional slight by their northern Daughters, so too southern historians were tireless defenders of their region.[24]

Despite sharing with their amateur allies many beliefs—as

well as bonds of class (and often of family)—professional historians nevertheless considered themselves to be misunderstood and embattled devotees of historical truth surrounded by history buffs who were, at best, sentimental accumulators of inconsequential facts and purveyors of romantic myths. If the new professionals, with the help of antiquarians and self-professed lovers of history, had created a rudimentary infrastructure for the scholarly study of the past by the second decade of the twentieth century, they had yet to secure popular deference to their expertise. Over time, amateurs, even more than tightfisted legislators, posed the greatest challenge to the influence and vision of professional historians.

The most substantial difference that divided amateur and professional historians was the professionals' quest for objectivity. Patriotic and hereditary society members as well as professionals insisted on their commitment to compiling "true history," but they differed in their tolerance of unconventional readings of the past. Few of the new professionals challenged conventional attitudes about the most contentious events in the southern past, but they periodically aroused controversy by assigning texts that included passages perceived to be hostile to the South. Indeed, some historians who failed to hew closely enough to southern verities suffered fierce censure. In 1892, William P. Trent outraged many southerners with his depictions of the shortcomings of the Old South in his biography of the South Carolina novelist William Gilmore Simms. The subsequent uproar permanently scarred Trent's reputation and contributed to his move north later in the decade. In 1904, a brief but intense controversy erupted after John Spencer Bassett of Trinity College elevated the black leader Booker T. Washington to the pantheon of great modern southerners alongside Robert E. Lee. And as mentioned earlier, in 1911, Enoch M. Banks, a young history professor at the University of Florida, earned the enmity of the UDC and the UCV when he questioned the legitimacy of secession. The lesson of these controversies was unmistakable: scholars risked swift and severe censure if they followed their research in new and controversial directions.[25]

However much these public controversies over historical interpretation revealed about tolerance for free speech in the New South, they showed far more about the struggle over who would exercise cultural authority over southern heritage. Most professional historians courted controversy not by proposing unorthodox interpretations of hallowed themes but rather by insisting that they alone were qualified to interpret southern history. The disagreements between the scholarly and the amateur historical communities often were as much about qualifications as about interpretation. Professionals tirelessly distinguished themselves from antiquarians, whose mission, they insisted, was different from and sometimes incompatible with their own. By distinguishing between "old" and "new" styles of history, the professional historians adopted a time-honored tactic of those in emerging and insecure professions. They discredited competitors by branding them as charlatans whose historical skills, if they had ever been adequate, were hopelessly out-of-date. The depth of most amateurs' understanding of history was dismissed as "the pale skim of dilettantism." Unlike history buffs, trained historians knew what good history was and it was neither "ancestor worship" nor the "worship of the past." Their training in modern research, they asserted, had equipped them with a rigorous, even iconoclastic spirit that enabled them to examine under the cold light of science timeworn myths about the past.[26]

In the drive to establish their unique qualifications as interpreters of southern heritage, professional historians predictably cast their claims to authority in gendered terms. To do so was in keeping with the contemporary evolution of scholarly disciplines.

Male historians routinely used gendered language that implicitly denied that women were capable of systematic historical study and understanding. Describing their mission with the language of rationality and progress, professional historians insisted that scientific history was neither "ornamental" nor "romantic." They stressed the need to restrain intuition, emotion, and imagination in the study of history. Only the mind of "the self-mastered man" that had been "trained to a true recognition of facts," John Spenser Bassett counseled, should be trusted "properly to form [his] own impulses or effectively to make them into social results." Richard Henneman agreed, claiming, "The *historic* sense has grown in proportion as the *personal* feeling has become blunted." He went further and argued that when imagination was given free rein over the past it "affords the basis of future romance and fiction." To women (and any men so inclined) Henneman conceded the realm of historical fiction; meanwhile he claimed the more profound labor of historical interpretation as the prerogative of those with "a more strenuously logical cast of mind"— namely, men.[27]

Professional historians often were explicit about their belief that the study of the past was "manly" work. For instance, in an 1897 list of college history instructors in the South, intended to demonstrate the unacceptably small number of qualified full-time historians, Stephen B. Weeks emphasized that the total might appear to be large, but "in a number of cases the professors are women." In the attached list, Weeks identified those historians who were women. His readers presumably understood his intent to separate the serious, male scholars from the implicitly unqualified female poseurs.[28]

Even more than the tiny number of women professional historians, women's voluntary historical organizations and hereditary societies were targets of male professional condescension.

Historical truth, as understood by such organizations, too often rested on "the fond memory of maiden aunts and worse founded traditions." William P. Trent was willing to tolerate the various patriotic and hereditary societies even though he dismissed them as "absurd." He was more generous in his attitude toward the work of "the ladies" of the Association for the Preservation of Virginia Antiquities, but he regretted that "their sympathies are rather with the sentimental than with the practical and scientific side of historic work."[29]

R. D. W. Connor, who dealt frequently with women's historical organizations during his tenure on the North Carolina Historical Commission, was much less charitable. In 1908, a spirited controversy arose when C. Alphonso Smith of North Carolina State University and the presidents of the University of Virginia and Columbia University selected the best essay in a contest organized by the UDC. In the eyes of those loyal to the Confederate tradition, the winning essay, which was written by a northern student, slandered Robert E. Lee, the South, and the memory of the war. Connor saw the ensuing controversy as symptomatic of the challenge that women posed to serious historians of the South. "Women," he concluded, "do not make good historians. They care nothing for facts unless they conform to their preconceived prejudices."[30]

Connor's contempt for women's historical activities was tempered by pragmatic concerns, as a 1912 dustup demonstrated. Controversy erupted when the North Carolina Colonial Dames launched a campaign to memorialize the so-called Mecklenburg Declaration of Independence in the state capitol. North Carolinians had claimed since at least the early nineteenth century that patriots in Mecklenburg County were the first to declare independence from Great Britain, in May 1775. But outside of the state the claim was received with incredulity. Debate over the alleged declaration began anew during the 1890s and continued for more than a decade. The commemorative plaque proposed by the Colonial Dames, a gesture that would extend new legitimacy to the disputed event, aroused yet more controversy. In the first salvo of what was to become a bitter campaign, the Colonial Dames won support for their proposed commemoration from the state's historical society, in large part by pointing to their record of commemorative work and employing their impeccable social credentials.

Charles Van Noppen, publisher of the *Biographical History of North Carolina* and a tenacious opponent of what he called "The Myth" of the declaration, led the opposition by circulating a pamphlet provocatively entitled "The Supineness of the North Carolina Historical Association and the Ignorance of the North Carolina Society of the Colonial Dames." As the invective worsened, many North Carolinians looked to Connor to resolve the controversy. But Connor, as the head of a recently established state agency whose future was not assured, was unwilling to be publicly drawn into the acrimony.[31]

The controversy prompted another bout of complaints against meddlesome women. Connor concluded that to refuse permission to the Colonial Dames to commemorate "on the wall of the capitol an event which the state herself commemorates on her flag and her great seal would have made a pretty spectacle, indeed, of itself!" Further, he regretted that the dispute was waged contentiously. He advised the detractors of "The Myth" to wage the debate as "a purely intellectual contest" with arguments made "in cool, measured language, backed by non-answerable facts and arguments." As historians rested their claims to authority more and more exclusively on the special competence that scholarly life conferred, both the substance and the manner of their participation in controversies became more critical in enforcing their

claims. Anything that impugned objectivity endangered the rationale that scholars offered for their special mission. Thus, Connor's
stated commitment to scientific, objective history led him to shy
away from shrill, partisan debates or to assert stridently the prerogatives of historical specialists.[32]

Connor's careful maneuvering in "this over-rated and overly
debated event" is revealing. His own justifications for his reserve
are a reminder that, at least during the first two decades of the
twentieth century, professional historians recognized that their
claims of intellectual authority had yet to be universally acknowledged. He was careful not to risk the commission's public support
or standing within the legislature because he recognized that in
1912 the influence and the prestige of professional historians was
not yet sufficient to challenge the Colonial Dames without the
likelihood of unpleasant consequences. "It would have been poor
policy on our part to have made martyrs out of the colonial
Dames in this case," he concluded. Even more important, Connor
came to see the work of women's organizations as so trivial that
they could be tolerated, even ignored.[33]

In the end, Connor was willing to stand by while the Colonial
Dames and other women's organizations dotted the landscape
with memorials and filled the shelves with their hagiographic
books. For Connor and his professional peers, women and non-
specialists had a place in the business of "renovating" the southern
past as long as they remained adjuncts who deferred to trained
specialists. They were welcome to contribute as fund-raisers, sec-
retaries, and social organizers. But women history enthusiasts
who displayed unwelcome ambition to participate in the serious
business of crafting history were politely reprimanded.

Bride Neill Taylor discovered as much during the early days
of the Texas State Historical Association. Taylor served on the
publications committee of the society's *Southwestern Historical*

Quarterly, but she exercised virtually no influence over the contents of the journal. Indeed, she was unaware of them until she received each printed issue. Apparently uncomfortable with her status as a mere figurehead, she offered her resignation to George P. Garrison, the journal's editor. His response revealed volumes about the roles that professionals assigned to women. He discouraged her from resigning because someone might be placed on the committee who would demand to have a voice in the publication and probably know nothing about Texas history. Garrison's implicit fear was that a man, whose opinions could not be ignored without risk, might be appointed. Thus, at the end of a decade during which many white middle-class and elite women had found in history an instrument for self-definition and empowerment, Garrison and the other new professional historians looked to women for no more than "a comforting sort of help."[34]

Over the next decade, the divide separating professional and amateur historical activities widened greatly. By 1930, white women could no longer convincingly claim sole or even primary cultural custodianship of the remembered past. The withering of the tradition of women's historical activism enabled professional scholars to extend their influence without the controversies of earlier years. Even as academic historians turned inward and addressed themselves to their scholarly peers, and even as their debates attracted less and less attention from the general public, the infrastructure that they had helped to create at the turn of the century enabled them to continue to assert influence over public memory.

After World War I, southern historians quietly consolidated the cultural authority they had struggled for more than a decade to achieve. Seemingly modest steps such as the founding of state historical journals were one measure of the process. In North Carolina, Connor encouraged the launching of a state historical journal to replace the *North Carolina Booklet* published by the Daughters of the Revolution. Connor had observed the *Booklet* since its founding in 1900, when it was the state's only historical journal. He had published articles in it and had relied upon its editor, Evelyn E. Moffitt, to wield her considerable influence on behalf of his favorite causes. Yet he admitted only disdain for the journal, then in its final days. He advised the editor of the new *North Carolina Historical Review* not to let "professional North Carolinians and professional southerners ruin the quarterly with 'patriotic' articles—as they did the N.C. Booklet. Make it a real scholarly historical publication. Avoid old hackneyed subjects—Mecklenburg Declaration." The code words of Connor's telegraphic style—"patriotic," "hackneyed," "real scholarly"—smugly dismissed decades of women's historical activities and made clear that the field of "real" North Carolina history was a vast uncharted and unoccupied landscape waiting to be explored by male professionals.[35]

The advent of a community of professional historians in the South represented more than an increase in the number of whites who were invested in promoting historical consciousness. The new professionals, whose occupations and professional ambitions were bound up in propagating awareness of southern history, claimed an authority and credibility that flowed from their "scientific" method and interpretative rigor. Ensconced in university faculties and in state agencies, professional historians methodically expanded their influence during the early twentieth century. Just like white women a generation earlier, professional historians looked to custodianship of the past as a means to carve out a prominent public role and a source of cultural authority for themselves. As important as the competition was between white antiquarians and professionals, it generated no significant openings for unorthodox readings of the southern past. Instead, for all of the jousting between professionals and clubwomen, their efforts were, in the end, complementary.

That the public history movement would flourish in the South, a region long associated with hidebound localism and antipathy to state power, demonstrates that the traditions of voluntary commemoration were no longer sufficient to advance the interests of white southern elites. The aims of these white elites were expansive in the sense that they wanted the propagation of a particular understanding of the past to be the ongoing business of the state. And after the tumult of the late nineteenth century, new and more systematic methods of promoting a shared white historical consciousness were deemed necessary.

Southern state governments, now securely in the hands of white elites, provided the resources essential to further introduce this version of the South's past into the region's public education, life, and spaces. State historical agencies would continue to grow, fitfully, alongside state governments during the twentieth century. Their influence would expand as historic preservation and public education assumed an ever larger place in public policy. The region's archives and museums (as well as, later, university collections) became monuments to a historical consciousness that William P. Trent and others had previously found wanting. Some agencies became extraordinary resources that were the envy of scholars and antiquarians in other regions.

Yet even the best-funded and best-managed repositories perpetuated ignorance about the very history that they were charged with preserving. Not until the latter third of the twentieth century would the work of archivists and public historians in the South facilitate more inclusive interpretations of the region's history. For at least the first half of the twentieth century, the archival impulse was an extension of the systematic colonization of public spaces by white elites. This development prompted no overt protest from southern blacks, who had no effective means to challenge it. But they could not fail to see these innovations as yet another illustration of white southerners' systematic exclusion of blacks from civic life. The larger message of the public history movement in the South was unmistakable: while the black past had no relevance for public life, white history was fundamental to it.

∾ 4

Black Remembrance in the Age of Jim Crow

Standing before an assembly of students and parents at the George P. Phenix School in Hampton, Virginia, in 1936, a young boy, Bill Parker, recited the verses of his "Poem of Great, Great Grandfather":

> When my great-, great-grandfather was a slave
>   They'd whip him to death if he didn't behave
> They made him carry cotton by the ton,
>   And even shipped his little son
> They didn't teach him to read or write
>   Or even let him get out of their sight.
> Now do you think it was right
> To whip poor great-, great-grandfather with all their might?

His third-grade classmates sang songs they had written about Africa and performed their own play about a Chinese woman visiting the United States to study race relations. Susie Thornton recounted the inspiring story of her grandfather, a former slave who had risen to prominence as a Baptist minister. Other students reported on their interview with Joana Shands, the oldest ex-slave in the community.

This school performance originated in the third-graders' spontaneous request to Tamah Richardson, their teacher, to "study ourselves." Inspired by a *Journal of Negro History* article on the urgent need for "Negro history" in school curricula, Richardson devised a year-long plan of study that traced African Americans from ancient Africa to the present day. Her students performed African songs and played African games, sharpened their math skills by calculating how long ago the first slaves had arrived at Jamestown, depicted "slavery scenes" for art, and studied current race relations. With their concluding public recital, the third-graders fulfilled their teacher's ambition of telling "the story of the accomplishments of men and women of [our] race who have risen above handicaps, difficulties, discrimination, prejudice and even active opposition."[1]

The program presented by the Phenix elementary students illustrates the central importance of elementary and secondary schools to black historical memory in the twentieth-century South. By the outbreak of World War II, public schools had emerged as one of the principal venues for the promotion of African American historical consciousness. As Richardson's year-long lesson plan suggests, schools, more than perhaps any other institution, had the capacity to nurture historical awareness systematically and continuously. Earlier forms of black ceremonial citizenship, such as Emancipation Day rituals, had asserted black rights to participate within the traditional spheres of public discourse and decision-making. Blacks continued to stage rousing public commemorations during the first half of the twentieth century,

but with segregation and disfranchisement sharply circumscrib-
ing their access to public space, southern blacks created in their
schools a quasi-public sphere in which they could collectively
voice and pursue common goals.

Whites, of course, never intended that schools should promote black historical awareness. Southern white legislators
chronically underfunded black schools and stymied the work of
black teachers and administrators through all manner of ploys.
Many white southerners would have been shocked to learn that
Jim Crow schools scattered throughout the South had become
centers of black public life and vehicles for spreading history
that contradicted white historical wisdom. Confident in white
administrators' control, most whites dismissed black schools as
an expensive but harmless concession to misplaced black ambitions. Had the champions of white supremacy recognized this
use of schools to nurture a black countermemory and oppositional
culture, they undoubtedly would have agreed with Senator James
Vardaman of Mississippi that "education is ruining our Negroes."[2]

Whereas white historians could harness the state to their
historical and cultural ambitions, blacks could not realistically
harbor similar ambitions. Segregation, disfranchisement, and the
consolidation of white power over the resources of the state virtually ostracized blacks from most of the institutions that whites exploited to tell their history. But, in one of the most profound ironies of the Jim Crow era, blacks used state and private resources
to turn schools into essential sites of collective memory that performed a role comparable to that of museums, archives, and other
memory theaters in the white community. The movement to incorporate "Negro history" into school curricula, then, was the an-
alogue to the much more conspicuous public-history campaign by
white professional historians. Like their white counterparts, black
professional historians supplied the scholarship and much of the

energy that sustained the movement. And like white professional historians, black scholars sought allies and audiences among school-teachers, who in turn reached the masses who would never attend college. But whereas the first generations of white professional historians supplied ideological ballast to white supremacy, black historians and teachers rebutted historical fallacies about black Americans and argued for historical truths that would hasten racial equality. Black teachers and scholars yoked their professional ambitions to the pursuit of social justice—and their battleground was the Jim Crow schools of the South.

Even before Appomattox, black educators had begun the arduous task of establishing an equitable school system in the South. By the turn of the century they had dramatically reduced black illiteracy, but were unable to come close to securing adequate facilities or resources for black education. In 1890, there were roughly three thousand black high-school students in the entire South; fewer than half of 1 percent of the eligible black children attended secondary school. A decade later, only one-third of black children between the ages of five and fourteen attended school. Fewer than 3 percent of eligible blacks enrolled in high school in 1910 and most major southern cities, including Charlotte, Columbia, Atlanta, Jacksonville, Mobile, Jackson, and New Orleans, still had no black public high schools.[3]

Black school facilities at the turn of the twentieth century were disgraceful. Chronically inequitable funding challenged blacks to derive any benefit from public education. Mississippi, for example, invested eight times more in white facilities than in black schools in 1914. Black schools inevitably were decrepit and inadequate. Most black teachers still taught unmanageably large classes in one-room schools like the "windowless log cabin" with yawning gaps in the walls and "rough plank benches without backs" that W. E. B. Du Bois had encountered as a young teacher in Tennessee during the 1880s. Growing up in Durham, North Carolina, Pauli Murray confronted manifestations of discrimination each day when she walked past a white school on her way to school. Whereas white children attended a "beautiful red and white brick building on a wide paved street," played in a modern playground, and looked out their windows at manicured lawns and colorful flowerbeds, Murray and her classmates crowded into a "dilapidated, rickety, two-story wooden building" with bad plumbing, peeling paint, noxious odors from the nearby tobacco warehouses, and a playground of "cracked clay."[4]

In many black schools during the late nineteenth century, requirements for teacher training were minimal: only rudimentary literacy and a primary school education. With fewer than four hundred black college and professional school graduates in the region in 1900, school administrators could not afford to be choosy when hiring black teachers. Low salaries exacerbated this chronic teacher shortage, so black schools resorted to staffing their classes with teachers who often had little more education than their pupils. Black educators keenly recognized the need for higher standards for teacher preparation, but they found more enemies than allies among white southerners. As Pauli Murray put it, "The crusade against starving the colored schools was a feeble whimper." White newspapers routinely dismissed black education as a fraud and waste, and, even worse, a breeding ground for dangerous black ambitions. White politicians, ranging from Senator Ben Tillman of South Carolina to Governor James Vardaman of Mississippi, scored political points by railing against the foolishness of funding black schools and toyed with proposals to abolish black public education entirely. Vardaman went so far as to close his state's only normal school for blacks in 1904 (none took its place until 1940).[5]

Gradually and unevenly, conditions in black schools improved. By World War II, two-thirds of black school-aged children attended school and more than a fifth of eligible black children enrolled in high school. During the 1930s black high schools even appeared in some rural communities, raising the total of students attending black four-year high schools to nearly 190,000. Facilities for black students also improved significantly. Had Pauli Murray attended elementary school in Durham during the 1930s, her school would have been a two-and-a-half-story brick building designed by the noted architect George Watts Carr Sr.; she would have experienced firsthand the improvements made possible through the assistance of northern philanthropic foundations, voluntary contributions from the black community, and federal funding during the New Deal. If such facilities often were too cramped for their enrollments and failed to match the luxury of white schools, they nevertheless were prominent modern structures that became a focus of community pride. Advances in teacher training simultaneously had spread across the South as the number of blacks completing high school and attending college grew during the 1920s. By the 1930s, then, even some rural schools, such as Caswell County Training School in North Carolina, boasted black teachers with credentials equal or superior to those of their white counterparts.[6]

Along with these welcome improvements, black teachers enjoyed rising prestige in their communities. They were role models for blacks who aspired to something more than menial occupations. Since Reconstruction, teachers had emphasized the transformative potential of education. Now, as the campaign for industrial education for blacks waned during the 1920s, many black educators recast their institutions by adopting modern, comprehensive curricula. These changes not only broadened students' ambitions, but also enriched the intellectual life of black schools. Earlier generations of black teachers may have been stern

A growing number of students at black high schools, like this class of 1939 at Booker T. Washington High School in Suffolk, Virginia, were exposed to "Negro History" in the classroom and at school celebrations. (Hamblin Studio Photograph Collection, Suffolk Public Library)

taskmasters admired for their commitment to their charges, but now black teachers often were esteemed for their erudition, sophistication, and sense of mission.[7]

These far-reaching changes in black education in the first half of the twentieth century by no means reflected a sea change in white southern attitudes. Overt white hostility to black education waned, but it was not replaced by generosity. Instead, public funding for black education remained cruelly inequitable. As late as 1940, Mississippi spent only thirteen cents on black schools for every dollar it spent on white schools. Perhaps the best that can be said for most white southerners is that they neglected black edu-

cation to such an extent that blacks enjoyed surprising and welcome autonomy in their schools. "The good thing about segregated schools," explained Leroy Campbell, a black principal in
Statesville, North Carolina, was that "you could do almost anything because you had no interference." Angela Davis, recalling
the public schools of Birmingham that she attended and where
her mother taught, observed, "Insofar as the day-to-day activities
were concerned, it was Black people who ran the school." Given
the continuing importance of private initiatives, especially voluntary contributions from the black community and northern philanthropies, much of the funding for black education was beyond
the control of white officials. A study of Tennessee schools conceded that "in reality, very little supervision is given to Negro
teachers." With white superintendents too burdened to supervise
properly white teachers, they were unlikely to devote time to
black schools.[8]

The challenge that black educators faced after the 1920s,
then, was the same one that their predecessors had confronted a
half-century earlier—how to nurture black abilities and black
memory despite chronic shortages of virtually every essential resource. Black teachers had long used anything handy to enrich
their lessons, but often the comprehensive curricula they envisioned could not be teased out of discarded white textbooks and
ad hoc lesson plans. Addressing the shortcomings of the school
curriculum became a focus of black teachers' associations and
black educators. The proliferation of summer teachers' institutes
was one method of redress. Another was the campaign to incorporate Negro history into the curriculum of the South's schools.

When Tamah Richardson sought inspiration for her classroom activities, she turned to the *Journal of Negro History.* First published

in 1916, the journal was part of a long but fitful drive to remedy chronic ignorance about black history. Concerned blacks felt this need with increasing urgency as more and more black schoolchildren were exposed to the corrosive version of history offered by most textbooks. In 1891, Edward A. Johnson, a North Carolina teacher, summarized the challenge that he and his peers faced. "If you teach some of the text books that we use in N.C.," he complained, "the pupils will learn from them that they belong to the most inferior race on earth and also fail to learn one single great thing done by a negro." Almost a half-century later, a survey of fourteen textbooks used in southern schools promoted a similarly deplorable lack of historical perspective. Seven of the most widely used books left students "in utter ignorance that there is a racial situation in the South," four barely touched on the subject, and three were certain to confirm and deepen racist prejudices.[9]

Although many blacks during the late nineteenth century acknowledged the need for a vigorous rebuttal to white accounts of black history, early efforts were limited in their reach. In 1883, George Washington Williams, the celebrated black author and historian, proposed "a national Negro Historical Society," but his call went unfilled. Instead, black history remained the periodic enthusiasm of black literary and social clubs. The founding of the American Negro Historical Society of Philadelphia (1897), the American Negro Academy in Washington, D.C. (1897), and the Negro Society for Historical Research in New York City (1911) demonstrated the emergence of more exacting historical aspirations. Exhibiting a robust archival impulse, the Philadelphia and New York societies systematically collected rare books, newspapers, and pamphlets relevant to the history of African Americans and the African diaspora. They also displayed a penchant for black triumphalism. The preamble of the Negro Society for Historical Research pledged that the group would "show that the

Negro race has a history which antedates that of the proud Anglo-Saxon race" by gathering "all the historical data possible . . .
to support claims as to the antiquity of Negro history and civilization."[10]

Elitism curtailed the influence of this early awakening of
Negro history. The new societies, inspired by nineteenth-century
lyceum and literary clubs, promoted a refined culture that seldom
reached beyond an exclusive audience. The pretenses of the
American Negro Academy were evident in its membership,
which was confined to "graduates or Professors in Colleges; Literary characters, authors, artists and distinguished writers." Alexander Crummell, one of its founders, bluntly charged its members
with the responsibility to elevate "the opinions and habits of the
crude masses." The goals of the earliest black historical societies
revealed the continuing grip of the civilizationist ideology on
black elites. By intent, their societies were both progenitors and
exemplars of black civilization. They were transitional institutions that broadened the resources that informed black memory
without otherwise significantly redirecting the interpretation of
black historical experience. For example, at the same time that
Arthur Schomburg of the Negro Society for Historical Research
mocked the "petty braggadocio" of the "rash and rabid amateur
who has glibly tried to prove half the world's geniuses to have
been Negroes," he proposed to offer "a credible record of group
achievement," of "group justification." Thus, timeworn assumptions about inherent racial characteristics and preordained historical destinies informed the conclusions of these groups.[11]

The National Association of Colored Women (NACW),
founded in 1896, displayed a broader, more inclusive ambition
for its promotion of black history. Beyond advocating the study
of African American history and literature as part of their local
activities, members of the NACW sought to counter the influence

that the UDC had over school texts and curriculum. In 1920, Margaret Washington and other leaders of the NACW founded the International Council of Women of the Darker Races (ICWDR) with the aim of introducing African American literature and history to school curricula throughout the country. The task was essential, Washington explained, because "our children are taught nothing except the literature of the Caucasian race." Her appeal struck a nerve with many ICWDR and NACW members, who in turn pledged to urge school administrators to redress the shortcomings of texts and curricula.[12]

Beginning in 1916, the NACW also launched a drive to restore Frederick Douglass's home, Cedar Hill, in a suburb of Washington, D.C. Mary B. Talbert, president of the NACW, envisioned the campaign as an extension of the organization's commitment to education and black history. The site, she explained, was "a hallowed spot where our boys and girls may gather . . . and receive hope and inspiration and encouragement to go forth like Douglass and fight to win." Encumbered by a mortgage, the house had left Douglass's second wife Helen too strapped to turn it into the museum and historical center that she had envisioned. After the Frederick Douglass Memorial and Historical Association failed to redeem the mortgage, the NACW took over the campaign. Two years of fund-raising garnered enough money to pay off the mortgage and restore the cottage—an accomplishment celebrated in club lore as "the redemption." By 1933, Nettie L. Napier of the site's board of trustees was rejoicing that "the Douglass home has now assumed the condition of its past glory" and could serve as a mecca for schoolchildren. Beyond an impressive testament to the resourcefulness of black club women, the restoration of Cedar Hill was a measure of the expanding ambitions of African Americans to institutionalize their historical memory.[13]

Obvious limits, however, constrained the activities of black voluntary associations. Like their white counterparts, they could urge the compilation of "true" history and champion the preservation of historical artifacts and structures. But black organizations did not have the resources or focus to undertake sustained historical activities. When Nannie Burroughs of the NACW and ICWDR suggested that club members write books appropriate for black schoolchildren, she offered at best a sincere but stopgap measure to address the chronic need for texts, curriculum reform, and scholarship. Black history was a major concern of the NACW, but so too were a long list of other commitments. Likewise, the ICWDR during its infancy soon gave itself over to the plight of Haiti during its occupation by U.S. troops. As these examples suggest, black clubs and voluntary associations would be important early advocates of and allies in the "Negro history" movement, but not its driving force.[14]

Professional historians, who were conspicuously absent from the late nineteenth-century push to expand black historical consciousness, assumed that crucial role. Until the second decade of the twentieth century, there was no systematic study of the black past within higher education. This paucity reflected the conditions at and expectations for black colleges in the South. The poverty of most black colleges severely limited their course offerings to those rudimentary subjects that their students were prepared to study and their faculties were qualified to teach. In 1900, for example, fewer than two-thirds of the black "colleges" in the South had any undergraduates; the overwhelming majority taught precollegiate pupils. Simultaneously, the preference of white philanthropists and legislators for industrial education precluded broad curricula at most black colleges.[15]

Conditions at many black colleges improved markedly after 1910. Curriculum reforms shifted resources and emphasis to new

collegiate programs, including in the social sciences. Also introduced were courses in "Negro history." In 1911 Fisk University
initiated a class devoted to the topic; a year later Morehouse College followed, as did Howard University in 1914. Within a few
years, most of the leading four-year institutions in the South offered "Negro history" in their curricula. These new courses had
far-flung effects, including the creation of a small but growing demand for textbooks. Not coincidentally, Benjamin Brawley's *Short
History of the American Negro* appeared the same year that the author himself initiated a course in "Negro history" at Morehouse.
His class, along with George Edmund Hayes's course at Fisk and
Kelly Miller's at Howard, awakened the interest of students, including several future professional historians. Once aroused, student enthusiasm led to the founding of history clubs from
Hampton, Virginia, to Saint Philip's Junior College in San Antonio. On many campuses the clubs drew enthusiastic audiences for
activities relating to black history, including pageants, plays, and
forums. For those students who were in revolt against the lingering paternalism and stifling curriculum that had long characterized many black colleges, club activities informed the "New Negro" movement that spread across campuses during the 1920s.
"Proud of their ancestry and achievements which true history is
revealing," these "Negroes of today," according to black colum-
nist Willie M. King, rejected the "servile, cowardly Negro of yes-
terday" that they believed black colleges had cultivated.[16]

Powerful external forces accelerated the changes on black
campuses. Improved college finances and burgeoning enrollments
during the 1920s created opportunities for trained black historians. Whereas fewer than four thousand students attended private
and public black colleges in the South in 1900, nearly 27,000 students did so by 1935. A corresponding increase in the number of
black historians and social scientists occurred. From a handful of

Student interest in history made the History Study Club at Tennessee State College in Nashville, ca. 1940, the most popular extracurricular organization on campus. (Merl R. Eppse Collection, Tennessee State Library and Archives, Nashville)

specialists in 1910, the number of African American social scientists at southern schools rose to more than 350 by the late 1930s.[17]

These young scholars, including the founding generation of professional black historians, brought with them the credo of academic scholarship that they had encountered while training in the leading graduate programs of the era. Carter G. Woodson, a noted historian, received the second doctorate that Harvard awarded to an African American. Most of the other black historians had been born in the Upper South and had trained at elite black liberal-arts colleges before moving on to white universities. Charles Wesley and Luther P. Jackson, for example, were among the first class at Fisk required to take black history. For W. Sherman Savage and Lorenzo Greene, it was history classes at Howard that awakened their interest. These pioneers of black history then honed their skills at the same institutions—Harvard, University of Chicago, Columbia—that trained the leading white scholars of the day. Although their interest in "Negro history" may have placed them on the extreme margins of the academic community, they were intimately familiar with the scholarly standards, methods, and aspirations that prevailed in mainstream academe.[18]

With a vigor equal to that of their white peers, these black scholars embraced the methods and mission of "scientific" history. They intentionally linked their claim of cultural leadership to the authority of science. In a 1922 address, Paul W. L. Jones of the Kentucky Normal and Industrial Institute boasted, "The historian of today is scientifically bringing to light the evidences as to the worth of the Negro and his contributions to the uplift of the World." Like their white counterparts, Jones and his peers compared archival research, which constituted the essential foundation of sound historical scholarship, to the laboratory experiments of scientists. All interpretative claims, they agreed, had to be substantiated with ample evidence gathered by means of systematic research. In 1921, Carter Woodson insisted that "interesting, comprehensive, and valuable" history must be built on the "scientific treatment" of letters, diaries, travel accounts, and other "unconscious evidence" in contemporary sources. Only then could an "non-partisan and unbiased history of the Negro" be written.[19]

The emphasis that Woodson and his fellow scholars placed on "scientific" methodology signaled an important break with previous black historical production. The new focus on the accumulation and interpretation of archival evidence marked the evolution of black historical activity away from what author Sutton Griggs had called "the age of the voice." Traditionally, black commemorative orators and authors had concentrated on the refined use of tropes of black progress and civilization. Their orations seldom deviated from familiar historical examples or conclusions. The "new" black history, in contrast, was self-consciously scholarly and its practitioners had no patience for "the spell-binding orator who comes along to entertain the public." Black historians instead adopted a dispassionate academic tone that reflected their conviction that an accumulation of historical "facts" would sweep aside historical falsehoods.[20]

The "Harvard dryasdust" style of exposition that Woodson and his circle adopted was not happenstance. For black historians their "objective" tone was an essential component of their credibility. They espoused the pursuit of objectivity more avidly than did their white counterparts, whom they chided for succumbing to racial bias. Speaking in Houston in 1935, Joseph A. Bailey of Arkansas State College outlined the challenge of teaching an "objective" history of African Americans. Despite pressures from both within and without the black community to teach "propagandistic" versions of the past, he beseeched "the teacher of Negro History" to "take as his aim the dissemination of the truth." In the same year, Charles Wesley offered perhaps the fullest explanation of this "New History." Above all, it was not "narrow, tribal, or nationalistic." "The search for truth" rather than "the encouragement of patriotism" was the paramount goal of practitioners of the new history.[21]

Black professional historians shrugged off notions of inherited racial traits and fixed destinies and instead emphasized cultural relativism and the imprecision of racial characteristics. Speaking in Durham, North Carolina, in 1925, Carter Woodson "undertook to show that civilization is the heritage of the ages, that it cannot be appropriated to any particular race or nation as its own contribution." The millennial interpretation of history that had been so conspicuous in earlier black historical memory was absent from the new scholarship. Joseph. J. Rhoads of Bishop

College in Marshall, Texas, regretted that "it is not unusual to hear members of the Negro race refer to its superior virtues." Blacks might claim that their progress in America was due "to the fact that 'we are who we are' by racial blood." But "the truth," according to Rhoads, "is that the 'Negro race' is nothing more or less than a convenient abstraction." "Race is a social fact," he emphasized, not a biological given. Human deeds and their underlying historical causes, not metaphysics, were the proper subjects of history. A 1934 survey of black faculty members measured the erosion of the older paradigm: 85 percent of respondents rejected the proposition that "Negroes have distinct racial characteristics which would lead them to develop a unique civilization of their own."[22]

Black historians recognized the urgent need to establish the legitimacy of their entire academic enterprise if their scholarship was to dislodge inherited assumptions about black identity and history held by both blacks and whites. But, in addition to crushing teaching loads, black scholars faced limited opportunities to conduct research and even fewer avenues for publication. The white academic community, moreover, dismissed black history as a minor sidebar in the larger human saga. Black historians, then, had to create a parallel scholarly community to support and disseminate their work.

Carter Woodson almost single-handedly cobbled together the scholarly infrastructure that enabled this first generation of black historians to overcome these obstacles. Despite only a brief and troubled career in higher education, Woodson influenced American historical scholarship to an extent matched by few other historians during the twentieth century. After teaching history in Washington, D.C., high schools for a decade, Woodson became dean of liberal arts at Howard University in 1919. A tumultuous stint there was followed by two years at West Virginia State College. Tiring of teaching and college life, he then returned to Washington, D.C., where he pursued historical activities on the fringes of academia for the remainder of his life. Unable to realize his ambitious plans to anchor the study of the long-neglected history of blacks within a university setting, Woodson instead nurtured an extensive network of scholars and historical enthusiasts affiliated with the Association for the Study of Negro Life and History (ASNLH).

Woodson intended the association to perform the same functions undertaken by the leading white professional societies. Founded in 1915, the ASNLH pledged to organize conferences, collect and publish material on black history, sponsor a journal, and conduct research. A year later, the association established the *Journal of Negro History,* with Woodson assuming the post of editor-director. By 1921, Woodson's burgeoning empire included Associated Publishers, Inc., which developed an extensive catalog of books on black history and culture.

Woodson initially envisioned the association as a research institute. His plans may have reflected the preference of white philanthropies for research, as opposed to activism. For the first two decades of the association's existence, the modest financial support from black donors and subscribers to *Journal of Negro History* was insufficient to cover the association's expenses, compelling Woodson to underwrite routine costs from his own modest salary. With funding considerations probably uppermost in his mind, Woodson ingratiated himself with Booker T. Washington's circle, thereby gaining an entrée with leading white philanthropies. By raising more than $100,000 from foundations during the 1920s, Woodson ensured the short-term solvency of the organization and made possible the research and publications that burnished its reputation.[23]

Grants enabled Woodson to cultivate a circle of professionally trained black historians. Indeed, he mentored eight of the first fourteen black men who received doctorates in history before World War II, and directly subsidized the education of Lorenzo Greene, Rayford Logan, and other promising young black historians. With grants he hired Greene, Alrutheus A. Taylor, James Hugo Johnston, and Charles Wesley to conduct research on colonial race relations, Reconstruction, black workers, and black churches. In this manner, Woodson gathered around himself and affiliated with the ASNLH most of the professionally trained black historians active in the 1920s and 1930s. And because he controlled virtually the only outlets for scholarship on black history—the *Journal of Negro History* and Associated Publishers— his patronage remained crucial to these black scholars long after they had secured permanent positions.[24]

Woodson simultaneously pledged ASNLH resources to ease access to archival materials—to the extent possible. As long as most white scholars and archivists ignored materials relating to black history, few sizeable black history collections existed. Equally galling, black scholars had to endure humiliating conditions and segregated facilities when they used historical resources. Luther P. Jackson was the rare black scholar who claimed that white archivists, librarians, and court clerks showed unstinting courtesy to black researchers. Other blacks complained bitterly about the indignities they endured while conducting research in the South. Hugh H. Smythe regretted that "not only are facilities denied to us, cooperation is unthinkable." The small towns of the South, he continued, were virtually "walled cities" to black scholars who risked physical harm when they conducted research there. Even Jackson conceded that few black students were willing to test white courtesy and expose themselves to insult in order to undertake research.[25] To remedy this problem, Woodson made a concerted effort to bolster the collections of the Library of Congress by donating thousands of original documents and copies of records collected during research trips in the United States and Europe. He also made important historical records accessible by publishing them in the *Journal of Negro History*.[26]

Woodson's most significant undertaking, arguably, was his popularization of black history by bridging the gap between scholars and the general public. Financial exigencies to a considerable degree prompted the public outreach by the ASNLH. After 1933, when the Depression induced philanthropic retrenchment and Woodson's history of quarrels with foundations caught up with him, the ASNLH had to find new funding sources. Woodson responded by appealing to the black community and shifted the ASNLH's emphasis from "a scholarly organization with a very limited influence on the people at large" to an organization that "reached the general public."[27]

The reorientation of the ASNLH's activities also reflected Woodson's deep commitment to combating pervasive ignorance about black history. He had founded the ASNLH in part because he was convinced that the popularity of D. W. Griffith's film *Birth of a Nation* was a shocking measure of public credulity for racist fantasies. Woodson and his fellow historians were keen to demonstrate that their scholarship was not an indefensible and pedantic luxury far removed from the daily struggles of blacks. As comparatively privileged members of an oppressed community, black academics felt duty-bound to direct themselves toward some immediately useful end. For all of their dispassionate and "scientific" mien, the first generation of black historians looked to the crusade to promote black history as a means to fuse scholarship with public outreach and political activism. Perhaps none of the founding generation of black academic historians personified this impulse more than Luther P. Jackson.

The son of former slaves who had clawed their way into the

black middle class in Lexington, Kentucky, Jackson settled on teaching as a profession while an undergraduate at Fisk. His first teaching assignment at Voorhees Industrial School in Denmark, South Carolina, introduced him to the world of small, independent black schools that remained committed to industrial education and dependent on northern philanthropists. Although Jackson's ambitions soon led to graduate school, his experiences at Voorhees were formative. They inspired him to study black history and gave him a lifelong interest in the predicament of black teachers. In 1922, while completing his graduate education, he moved to Virginia State College. There President John M. Gandy was reestablishing the school's college programs, which white legislators had abolished at the turn of the century. Gandy also restored Virginia State's reputation as one of the leading schools for black teachers in the South. Each year, graduating students fanned out from the college's Petersburg campus to staff schools throughout the South, while hundreds of experienced teachers returned to attend annual summer teachers' institutes.[28]

Jackson's scholarly aspirations and activism complemented Gandy's larger ambitions for Virginia State. Jackson embraced "scholarly excellence," as measured by the standards of academic historians, yet never believed that his sole audience was fellow scholars. Long before the emergence of public history as an academic subdiscipline, Jackson worked out a personal vision of publicly directed scholarship. Professors, he insisted, "must investigate because much of the advancement of the South and of the Negro depends on what the research professor finds." "Without the aid of research," he warned, "the people grope in darkness." At the same time, he acknowledged, "we [professors] need to get out of the classroom far more than we do." In his own activism, Jackson pledged to "expand our efforts beyond a small group of intellectuals to the smallest business man in the street." "I shall be both the scholar and a worker among the people," he pledged to Carter Woodson.[29]

Jackson's classes, whether aimed toward undergraduates or teachers, erased the line between activism and scholarship. Jackson constantly searched for justifications for "sending out students to make actual contacts" with the black community. His students conducted interviews with former slaves and elderly blacks and compiled surveys of attitudes about voting and electoral politics. Rather than treat African American history as a tangent, he made "the Negro and his problems" central to all of his American history lectures. In his government classes, he "constantly hammer[ed]" the importance of civic involvement by encouraging his students to write letters to members of Congress and to sign petitions advocating antilynching legislation and similar causes.[30]

Jackson combined his pedagogical activism with a shrewd sense of the practical. Because he was a popular professor and longtime director of Virginia State's teachers' institutes, he was able to influence a generation of Virginia teachers. Beyond teaching Negro history to future educators enrolled at Virginia State or attending summer institutes, he mobilized the Virginia Teachers' Association to promote curriculum reform, especially the teaching of Negro history. He attempted to instill in history teachers a sense of "esprit de corps" as specialists in their discipline. In 1934, he summoned them to support an ambitious grassroots fund-raising campaign for the ASNLH. Lacking established connections with churches and lodges, he instead appealed to black teachers because Virginia State was "well harnessed up with the school forces of Virginia." He shunned raising large sums from a few contributors, preferring to raise money from as many teachers and students as possible. A decade later, he boasted that more than three thousand teachers and hundreds of schoolchildren had contributed to the ASNLH. To those who complained that fund-raising for the ASNLH was peripheral to the immediate needs of the black community, Jackson responded, "The Negro fails to fight hard enough for jobs, for his civil rights, and for the ballot because he does not know his praiseworthy background." It was the ASNLH that would "supply this gap in the life of the race."[31]

Once established, the close link between the ASNLH, Jackson, and Virginia's black teachers enabled him to disseminate "scientific" history where it was likely to have an immediate effect. Sensitive to the need to offer teachers "a token of some kind in recognition for their generosity," Jackson used a portion of their contributions to subsidize publication of *Virginia Negro Soldiers and Seamen in the Revolutionary War* and *Negro Office-Holders in Virginia, 1865–1895*. These publications in turn were distributed free to virtually every black teacher in the state. The volumes, Jackson explained, were more than "a big advertising scheme for the Association"; they were lessons in the continuing relevance of black history to contemporary concerns. The record of the service of blacks in the American Revolution, Jackson stressed in 1943, was an inspiration for the "deeds of heroism of our boys in Sicily and the Mediterranean." Such information, when passed on by the teachers to the children of Virginia, would contribute to "building the race pride in our youth."[32]

Jackson simultaneously looked to the historical record to mobilize teachers in the campaign for voting rights for blacks. This commitment grew out of his conviction that black self-determination was impossible without political participation. Rather than a partisan for either political party, Jackson championed participatory democracy. His ambition was to regain the vote for blacks in general, not to marshal voters. Based on his exhaustive state-wide surveys of voting registration records, he concluded that blacks in Virginia during the 1930s and 1940s had their best opportunity to date to regain the political influence that had been wrested from them at the turn of the century. The biggest obstacle to black voting, he claimed, was the failure of blacks to pay the poll tax and to register. Jackson set out to inspire higher rates of registration and voting among blacks by recruiting teachers to lead a campaign for black voter education, thereby turning "mere teacher[s]" into "civic leaders." As early as 1941, Jackson bragged that the relationship between the Virginia Voters' League, in which he was a leading figure, and the Virginia Teachers' Association was so close that they were "virtually one and the same thing." He taught courses and administered summer institutes that instructed educators about political parties, voting, and local politics. Teachers themselves swapped ideas about classroom activities that would encourage students to challenge white political power.[33]

Jackson continued to harness his skills as a scholar to his activist goals. His 1947 publication *Negro Office Holders in Virginia* reminded apathetic blacks that there "was a time when colored people were in politics with a vengeance; not only as voters, but officeholders as well." Jackson's revisionist study repudiated the persisting interpretation, favored by both white southerners and historians, that black officeholders had been incompetent and often criminal. In Jackson's study, black politicians of post–Civil War Virginia emerged as qualified, conscientious, and effective public servants. Moreover, the benefits of black political mobilization were clear. In a 1943 newspaper column that foreshadowed the argument of his book, Jackson stressed that "the masses gained something for themselves because a political party was organized to do something for them and because they supported this party at the polls on election day." He noted acidly that blacks then "far outstripped many of the educated class today" because they "worshiped public affairs." The contemporary relevance of this research was obvious to Jackson. Every time he sold a few more copies of his books, he hoped that he stimulated "our people to vote now as they did in the days of old."[34]

Uniting all of Jackson's diverse activities was his conviction that a black population aware of its past would have the fortitude and vision necessary to plan and sustain protest. He drew inspiration for contemporary activism from the Reconstruction-era protests by Virginia blacks. Rather than historical curiosities, these obscure events were "of interest to us today as a protest and an ideal to which Virginia, the nation, and the world must strive." These protests at the dawn of black freedom had posed pressing questions that remained unanswered, including: "Will the Virginia whites and all American whites at last see . . . that there can be no permanent peace if the doctrine of the supremacy of one race over another race continues in their thinking"? In order for blacks to gain morale and for whites to gain respect for them, "each must turn to a greater study of the past of the Negro."[35]

Jackson's extraordinary career ended abruptly in 1950 with his death at the age of fifty-eight. The hectic pace of his life undoubtedly wore him down. But Jackson's public life was characterized not by conflicting or unmet obligations, but rather by a remarkable symmetry. He, like many of his scholarly peers, had an almost unbounded belief that social justice and democracy flowed from an understanding of the past. Although exceptional in his stamina and the breadth of his activism, Jackson was not unique among his peers. Most of the early black historians became enmeshed in public activism. In the process, they made sure that Negro history reached beyond the college campuses that had provided the springboards for their own civic involvement. One of their earliest and most conspicuous accomplishments, and one that Luther Jackson was deeply invested in, was the incorporation of Negro history into the rhythms and rituals of the South's black public schools.

      ◡◢

With the aim of reaching black teachers and students in even the most benighted parts of the South, Carter Woodson and the

ASNLH built on the long-established tradition of black commemorative celebrations when they launched their most successful and influential public program—Negro History Week. Beginning in 1926, Woodson scheduled the celebration each February in recognition of the anniversaries of the birthdays of Frederick Douglass and Abraham Lincoln, two holidays already celebrated by blacks. Yet Negro History Week went beyond existing traditions. Unlike earlier failed efforts to organize a national Emancipation Day, the new celebration formalized national recognition of black history. So successful was the event that it came to be celebrated virtually coast to coast and in many communities replaced Emancipation Day as the preeminent celebration of black history.[36]

From its inception, the ASNLH had been a clearinghouse for innovative curriculum ideas. Beginning with the first annual meeting of the organization in 1916, when sociologist Kelly Miller delivered a paper on "The Place of Negro History in Our Schools," association conferences unfailingly included panels devoted to pedagogy. Subsequent meetings included panels of teachers as well as keynote sessions with high school principals. In 1936, the entire annual ASNLH meeting was devoted to the status of black history in schools. Panelists, joined by contributors to the *Journal of Negro History,* exhorted teachers to incorporate black history into all levels and aspects of education, regardless of the subject. Even the sites of ASNLH meetings underscored the organization's commitment to reaching black teachers and students. The 1933 annual meeting, for example, was held in Booker T. Washington High School in Atlanta. During other meetings, delegations of association members visited with teachers and students at local schools.[37]

To fill the need for school materials relating to African Americans, Carter Woodson and his Associated Publishers began releasing suitable texts. By the late 1930s, the press's catalog included titles appropriate for all levels of students. Woodson intended his own *African Myths Together with Proverbs* to introduce third-grade students to the cultural heritage of Africans. For advanced high school and college students, Woodson's *The Negro in Our History* provided an antidote to conventional histories that offered only a litany of white triumphs. Eventually Woodson produced different versions of the book tailored for primary, secondary, and college students. In 1939 the ASNLH introduced the *Negro History Bulletin,* which provided educators with teaching resources appropriate to all ages. The *Bulletin,* Woodson explained, represented "a new educational periodical" intended to promote the study of black history among children "by simplifying what is too difficult for the young reader in books now available."[38] The *Bulletin* and the other association's titles enjoyed healthy sales; for decades *The Negro in Our History* was one of the most widely used black history texts.

The aim of the publications, conference sessions, and other activities was fundamental curriculum reform. ASNLH members envisioned a future when qualified educators who had studied black history in college would teach required courses on black history using texts that incorporated the latest scholarship. In the near term, their goal was the mobilization of black teachers and their professional organizations on behalf of curriculum reform. In Virginia, at the 1927 annual meeting of the Virginia Teachers' Association, members endorsed an unsuccessful petition to the state board of education to add black history to high school curricula. The association's bulletin published plans of study for innovative history courses that drew upon ASNLH proposals. In Alabama, H. Councill Trenholm, an officer of the ASNLH and president of both the Alabama State Teachers Association (ASTA) and Alabama State College, committed the ASTA to a two-year "Negro History Project." In addition to distributing

Students studying black history at John W. Hoffman Junior High School, New Orleans, ca. 1935. (Special Collections, Fisk University Library)

packets of information on black history to teachers, the campaign published recommendations for texts and lesson plans for black history courses. In South Carolina and Louisiana, the influence of the ASNLH inspired members of the states' black teachers' associations to review textbooks for offensive and inaccurate portrayals of African Americans. Elsewhere disciples of Woodson petitioned state and local boards of education to approve courses and adopt appropriate texts on black history.[39]

The Negro history campaign boasted notable early successes. In 1935 nearly a third of black high schools in the South—including those in Dallas, New Orleans, Birmingham, Columbia, and Atlanta—offered black history courses, and an increasing number even made these courses compulsory for graduation. By the end of the decade, Delaware, Oklahoma, and South Carolina had joined North Carolina in adopting ASNLH texts for their black schools. And in several other states officials approved black history texts but left it to the discretion of school districts to adopt them.[40]

These accomplishments, however, could not obscure enduring obstacles to region-wide curriculum reform. Black teachers needed exceptional stamina and resourcefulness to convince white school boards to add black history to the curriculum. Alice L. Turner and her fellow high-school teachers in Roanoke, Virginia, waited ten years before white authorities granted their petition for a course in black history. In Lynchburg, Virginia, more than four years of protest against inferior facilities and textbooks filled with "the usual claptrap about shiftless Negroes" and "Nordic supremacy" were required to secure the appointment of the city's first black principal and other improvements. Scarce resources and limited funds undercut curriculum initiatives even where there were black high schools. Impoverished black families could hardly be asked to buy expensive books by Associated Publishers for elective black history courses. In theory, the adoption of legislation providing free texts to all public school students in several southern states during the 1930s might have eased the burden of purchasing black history texts. But in Florida, Mississippi, and many other southern states, the "free" texts that black students received were battered, hand-me-down, outdated rejects from white schools. Because few white schools were likely to adopt the texts that Woodson and the ASNLH had endorsed, especially as long as the UDC was monitoring textbooks for heresies against the Lost Cause, blacks were most likely to inherit from white students precisely those texts that black educators most reviled.[41]

Recognizing that these conditions impeded comprehensive curriculum reform in many areas, Woodson envisioned Negro

History Week as an expedient yet vital means of injecting black history into school life. The surprisingly swift adoption of Negro History Week by many black schools across the South, and especially in the Upper South, was testimony to Woodson's skill at mobilizing his allies at many of the region's leading black schools and colleges.[42] Yet even where his direct influence was weak, communities embraced the celebration and by the late 1930s at least some communities in every southern state observed Negro History Week. The success of Negro History Week clearly owed as much to black teachers' receptiveness to the commemoration as it did to Woodson's adept promotion of it.

Woodson's stamp on Negro History Week was pervasive. The annual event differed in its comparative uniformity from the idiosyncratic local traditions that had characterized previous black commemorations. To script the event, Woodson relied on his influence with black newspapers and educators. Each year he mailed thousands of bundles of free planning materials and programs for Negro History Week, complete with suggested topics for classroom exercises and public ceremonies. In 1929, for instance, Woodson urged that each school day during Negro History Week be devoted to the study of black contributions in a specific facet of life: Monday was Literary Day; Tuesday, Government Day; Wednesday, Arts and Science Day; Thursday, Business Day; and Friday, Education Day. Teachers in schools from Maryland to Texas, as well as outside the South, scrupulously followed Woodson's program. N. V. Boyd of La Crosse, Virginia, reported that her community followed the plan in the ASNLH pamphlets "almost to the letter." E. L. Wiley, black county superintendent in Gladstone, Virginia, was similarly deferential to Woodson's program. She explained how she "received the instruction from Dr. Woodson" and then held "a teachers' meeting and ask[ed] all teachers to observe it."[43]

Active participation by students in Negro History Week, rather than passive observation of the event, was of paramount importance to Woodson and the ASNLH. In keeping with prevailing theories of pedagogy that promoted learning through group activities as opposed to rote lessons, Woodson encouraged educators to incorporate pageants, plays, and performances into their Negro History Week programs. At the same time, Woodson was keen to introduce black students to the historically informed protest dramas that black playwrights had begun to write during the 1920s. As early as 1926 a pageant entitled "The Gateway," which traced African Americans from their African origins through the travails of slavery, had entertained an ASNLH conference held at Virginia State. Thirteen years later, at another ASNLH meeting, the faculty and students of Dillard University offered "a striking demonstration of how the Negro in American life may be truly dramatized" during a session entitled "Negro History as Source Material for Drama." The ASNLH soon turned from promoting pageants and historical dramas to publishing them. In 1930 Associated Publishers issued *Plays and Pageants from the Life of the Negro* and five years later *Negro History in Thirteen Plays*. Together the two collections provided dramas that presented "the Negro . . . as a maker of civilization in Africa, a contributor to progress in Europe, and a factor in the development of Greater America."[44]

The conviction that pageants and staged dramas were an effective means of racial mobilization was not new. Elaborate and often immense historical pageants had enjoyed broad popularity during the first two decades of the twentieth century. In conjunction with the fiftieth anniversary of the Emancipation Proclamation, W. E. B. Du Bois had written and staged his "Star of Ethiopia" pageant. Like other pageant enthusiasts, Du Bois intended to create an impressive spectacle that would teach important lessons about history while encouraging a sense of communal identification and patriotism. Woodson's genius was to understand the value of such pageants while at the same time recognizing the need for simple dramas that were suited to public schools.[45]

Pageants, plays, and performances quickly became an essential component of Negro History Week.[46] Some were products of local inspiration. In 1927, the Negro History Week Committee in Norfolk, Virginia, presented "From Slavery to Freedom: From Freedom to Fame," a pageant that gathered material "from history written and unwritten." Students at Alabama State, Elizabeth State in North Carolina, Douglass Junior School in San Antonio, Tennessee State in Nashville, and other institutions staged pageants and plays that traced "The Progress of the Race," celebrated "Beacon Lights of History," depicted "Reconstruction days," and recorded "The Rise of Brown America." Many more schools, however, drew from collections published by the ASNLH for their dramatic programs.[47]

These performances, as well as other Negro History Week celebrations, acknowledged the historical and cultural complexity of both ancient and contemporary African societies to a far greater degree than had previous black historical celebrations. Conspicuous during the 1930s was interest in Ethiopia, which was then fighting desperately to fend off an Italian invasion and maintain its independence. "Ethiopia's Achievements" were the subject of a pageant staged at the Bell Street Elementary School in Atlanta in 1934. A year later, students at Morgan College in Baltimore performed Willis Richardson's "Menelik's Court," which portrayed an earlier Abyssinian king's victory over "Italian treachery." The historical verisimilitude that was evident in these and other staged representations of African history had no precedent in previous black commemorative celebrations. The grandeur of ancient Egypt and black Africa had often been invoked, but only in the most general way. By contrast, Negro History

Lucy Harth Smith, a leader in the Association for the Study of Negro Life and History (ASNLH), with a "Negro History" king and queen and their court in a Lexington, Kentucky, elementary school, ca. 1935. (Merl R. Eppse Collection, Tennessee State Library and Archives, Nashville)

Week pageants and plays dramatized the new scholarly under-standing of African civilizations, including the conclusions that Woodson had reached in *The African Background Outlined; or, Handbook for the Study of the Negro,* which extolled Africa's great-ness but eschewed a simple portrait of the continent's history or its peoples.[48]

Slavery likewise figured prominently in dramatic representa-tions and class activities during Negro History Week. As in Bill Parker's 1936 poem about his enslaved grandfather, the perspec-tive of the slave now took center stage. Unlike earlier commemo-rative depictions of slavery, which had often employed allegorical representations that softened its horrors, Negro History Week performances displayed a new forthrightness. One especially pop-ular one-act play in the Associated Publishers collection, for ex-ample, called *William and Ellen Craft,* depicted a slave's heroic es-cape, including the threats of rape and other violence if captured.

Other plays even recast slave uprisings. Included in the collections published by Associated Publishers was *Nat Turner,* a one-act play that depicted the slave rebel as a religiously inspired leader who set out "to strike de blow dat will make de whole worl' tremble at our might." In the play, Turner is portrayed as a naive but well-intentioned and charismatic figure. If his methods are extreme, it is because he faces extreme circumstances. When accused of being a murderous beast, he counters, "Ef Ah's a beast, who made me one? Ef dey buy and sell me, whip me lak dawgs, and feed me dere leavin's, how can Ah be nothin else but a beast? How can dey blame me ef Ah turns on dem and rend dem?" The play reproaches the perfidy of some of Turner's followers as much as it castigates him for his uprising's bloody conclusion.[49]

Other widely performed pageants in the Associated Publishers collection, including "Out of the Dark" by Dorothy C. Guinn, explicitly evoked the brutality of slavery by including vignettes depicting the slave trade. Among the props required for Guinn's play was a bullwhip; the costumes of the slaves were described as tattered "burlap sacks slipped over their heads." Many plays staged during Negro History Week dwelled on the psychological damage wrought by slavery. John Matheus's melodramatic play *Ti Yette* depicts the growing racial consciousness of a quadroon whose sister is secretly in love with a white planter. Set in New Orleans in 1855, the drama contrasts the brother's growing racial militancy with his sister's willful denial of her racial identity. The sister, personifying the familiar figure of the tormented mulatto, announces that she loathes her race. Her brother rages in response, "It is not the African lineage that stains! It is this avaricious, lustful Caucasian heritage that is our curse. Their civilization has damned us." The play ends in tragedy when the brother murders his sister rather than let her "pass" as white in order to marry her white suitor.[50]

Whatever creative limitations the plays, pageants, and dramatic readings may have evidenced, they were powerfully didactic performances that conveyed a consistent historical narrative to blacks of all ages. Whether in a play about Crispus Attucks or one describing Sojourner Truth, blacks were depicted as steadfast in their pursuit of and devotion to freedom. As the character Harriet Tubman said in the play of the same name, "Thar's two things Ah got a right to, an' they is death an' liberty." The harsh depiction of slavery in the productions contrasted sharply with the prevailing portrait of slavery in both white academic scholarship and American popular culture. Historian Ulrich B. Phillips and others dwelled on the purported paternalism of planters, while popular films and plays caricatured slaves as carefree buffoons. The plays staged during Negro History Week, in contrast, recalled slavery as an unjustified and unmitigated crime. It was not coincidental that the plots of several plays evolved around mock trials at which judgment is passed on whites for wrongs they inflicted on Africans and African Americans. And just as benign depictions of slavery were countered in the plays, so too were portrayals of Reconstruction as a descent into corruption and tyranny. The tragedy of Reconstruction, as portrayed in the pageants and plays, was that it ended before black equality had been secured. In many ways, the various dramatic productions continued a black historical narrative that stretched back through previous commemorative celebrations. But now the narrative was told with a specificity of place, date, and fact that had seldom been a defining trait of earlier black celebrations. Even while the black playwrights who edited the collections for the ASNLH admitted that they were more concerned to "create the atmosphere of a time past" than "to reproduce definitive history," they nevertheless stressed that each play had been subjected to the scrutiny of Woodson to verify names, dates, and historical accuracy.[51]

In keeping with the explicit pedagogical goals of Negro History Week, educators and their students assumed the most prominent roles in the celebrations, using the ceremonies as the occasion to spread "scientific" history throughout the breadth of the black community. Woodson, for example, tolerated no nostalgia for the oratorical flights of black ministers or hyperbolic celebrations. During Negro History Week, he stressed, "there should be no indulgence in undue eulogy of the Negro." Although many ministers threw their support behind Negro History Week and opened the week's ceremonies with a prayer, their roles were secondary to those of educators.[52]

By dint of their numbers in the teaching profession, black women were at once the audience and local foot soldiers for the black history campaign. In Tennessee in 1936, for instance, 75 percent of the teachers in black public schools were women. These numbers alone ensured that women teachers figured prominently in any Negro History Week activities held in schools. Moreover, black women often held positions of influence that made their support crucial to the success of the celebrations. In many rural communities, effective supervision of black schools fell to black leaders hired by the Anna T. Jeanes Foundation. Although appointed by white county supervisors to serve on the regular teaching staffs of black schools, the so-called Jeanes supervisors enjoyed both unusual prestige and independence. Charged with the task of improving rural public schools and often motivated by an acute sense of duty, Jeanes supervisors were both inclined and well situated to promote Negro History Week as another opportunity to advertise black accomplishments: they already had experience organizing "Field Days," commencements, and other school exhibitions.[53]

The prominence of women in the Negro History Week movement also testified to the comparative openness of the ASNLH to

women. Despite the absence of women from the founding generation of professional black historians, women played an important role in the ASNLH. Woodson had no patience for amateur
historians, regardless of sex, but he had considerable respect for
women educators and scholars. He, for example, sponsored research by Zora Neale Hurston, published her work, and favor-
ably reviewed her writings. During the 1930s, the *Journal of
Negro History* was almost unique among scholarly journals in
publishing articles about black women's history and articles written by black women. The journal, by one measure, published
more scholarship on women's history than all of the major white
journals combined. As early as 1923, Mary McLeod Bethune,
founder of the Bethune-Cookman Institute and a leading black
clubwoman, delivered the keynote address at the annual ASNLH
meeting. Woodson also entrusted to Bethune, along with several
other women ASNLH members, supervision of the mailing of
educational materials to ASNLH branches. Later Bethune joined
the organization's executive board and eventually served as president of the association. Nannie H. Burroughs, Charlotte Hawkins
Brown, and Lucy Harth Smith were among the prominent women who subsequently addressed ASNLH meetings. At the local
level, women such as Smith and Gertrude Green often were the
driving forces behind the observance of Negro History Week in
their communities. And as the ASNLH came to depend more
and more on the contributions of members and fund-raising drives
among teachers, women became crucial financial sponsors.[54]

The setting for Negro History Week encouraged expanded
roles for black girls in the celebrations. Neither national nor local
planners left a record of any explicit intent to expand the representations of black women in their celebrations, but they nevertheless did so. Whereas Harriet Tubman and Sojourner Truth
were seldom mentioned in nineteenth-century Emancipation Day

orations, they now were the center of attention in popular plays that were performed during Negro History Week. "The Light of the Women," Frances Gunner's contribution to the Associated Publishers' collection of pageants, went even further and included a cast composed entirely of schoolgirls in the roles of "the Slave Mother," Tubman, Truth, Phillis Wheatley, and other black heroines. In these performances as well as other Negro History Week activities, black women became historical actors whose contributions merited acknowledgment and celebration.[55]

This inclusiveness, which almost certainly contributed to the appeal of Negro History Week, reflected the character of the central sites of the celebrations—black public schools. For many teachers and administrators, the nurturing of the highest potential of each black student was an essential contribution to racial uplift. Each student's achievement was a collective success for the teacher, school, and community. In such an environment, many students inevitably acquired a strong sense of collective identity and responsibility that offset competing fissures of class, religious affiliation, and neighborhood within student bodies. Negro History Week provided a forum in which teachers and students made manifest a collective racial pride that was anchored in education.[56]

These lofty aims for Negro History Week, however, had to be reconciled with the reality of segregation. Unlike previous black commemorative ceremonies, Negro History Week was conducted within segregated institutions and spaces. Only rarely were there Negro History Week parades or other public activities staged in public spaces routinely claimed by whites. Indeed, some blacks were loathe to tolerate any white participation in Negro History Week ceremonies. Alice Turner, a teacher in Roanoke, Virginia, recalled that the 1933 ceremonies had included a number of speeches by white politicians, ministers, and businessmen.

But, she reported, "a wave of indignation swept over the community at having white speakers on a Negro History program."[57]

The controversy in Roanoke underscored the reality that the principal audience for Negro History Week was blacks themselves. Believing that Negro History Week would promote improved race relations, Woodson and the ASNLH appealed to whites to join more fully in the annual celebration. White liberals in the South agreed, viewing awareness of black history as one facet of "racial adjustment." In 1937, the Conference on Education and Race Relations, for instance, explicitly endorsed Negro History Week. In a few locales, currents of racial liberalism occasionally led to biracial observance of the event. In several Virginia schools, black teachers were invited to discuss themes in black history and literature with students at white schools. In Fredericksburg, the local white newspaper "gladly accepted the opportunity" to publish articles on Negro History Week written by local high school teachers. Elsewhere, members of white school boards and white school clubs attended celebrations.[58]

Yet white ignorance about rather than sympathy for Negro History Week was far more common. This situation was not without its benefits: black teachers might complain that white supervisors ignored Negro History Week, but at least they were little inclined to discourage it. For James W. Mask, a black principal in Richmond County, North Carolina, the state's tepid support for Negro history was of no import: "We always had Negro history as part of the curriculum [because] I went a little bit beyond what was provided" by Raleigh. That Negro History Week was not officially sanctioned in many locales hardly prevented committed teachers from conducting informal or unapproved observances. Thus, whereas the black commemorative celebrations of the nineteenth century had been testimonials to blacks' insistence on claiming a place in the nation's ceremonial civic culture, Negro

History Week demonstrated the capacity of southern blacks to exploit opportunities for autonomy within segregation.[59]

If the testimonials of teachers in the South during the 1930s are an accurate measure, Negro History Week was a success wherever it took root. Reflecting on the value of the celebration, India Hamilton, a Virginia teacher, welcomed the opportunity "to impress the young people with the idea that the Negro has made a contribution to something other than *Crime*." Anna W. Green, another Virginia teacher, was jubilant that children were "extremely fond" of the event and that adults were "elated" and "surprised" by it. Green's appraisal meshed with the recollections of Angela Davis, for whom Negro History Week was "one of the most important events each year." "The weekend before Negro History Week each year, I was always hard at work—creating my poster, calling on the assistance of my parents, clipping pictures, writing captions and descriptions." Year after year, Davis recalled, these simple activities instilled in generations of black students "a strong positive identification with our people and our history."[60]

✺

In 1935, on the occasion of the twentieth anniversary of the founding of the ASNLH, Mary McLeod Bethune recalled the organization's accomplishments and staked out its future goals. The crusade by the ASNLH to overcome ignorance about black history, she explained, was part of the much larger struggle to harness "science in the service of humanity." She noted with satisfaction that "social knowledge and information . . . shrouded in tradition" was giving way to "information that is objective and precise." She cautioned her audience that they should not be complacent, for "knowledge or information in and of itself is not power, is not progress." The times required men and women who could "play the role of mediator," standing "between the masses whose knowledge is indefinite and the research worker whose knowledge is authoritative."[61]

The goals that Bethune set for the organization almost certainly were the same as those that her audience would have identified. The pursuit of and dissemination of historical "truth" was the rallying cry of the black history movement. But segregation withheld from black educators all but the most rudimentary resources and marginalized them within the nation's scholarly communities. Segregation dictated the trajectories of their careers; where they taught, how they conducted research, and how their scholarship was received were all determined by the region's and the nation's system of apartheid.

Black educators, because of the challenges they faced and their belief in the transformative power of historical consciousness, became insurgent scholars. Unwilling to accept their marginalization, they attacked the interpretations of the founding generation of white historians. Unlike most white southern scholars, who embraced the scholarly and popular consensus about slavery as a benign institution, the Civil War as an avoidable tragedy, and Reconstruction as an ignoble and misguided mistake, black educators highlighted the record of black perseverance in the face of white oppression and the fundamental perversity of white supremacy. And at the same time that U. B. Phillips identified "white supremacy" as the central theme in southern history, black educators associated with the ASNLH were stressing the social fiction of racial distinctions. By writing against the grain of prevailing white wisdom, black scholars gave their scholarship an overtly political import. (Of course, the scholarship of white southern historians was hardly politically neutral. But white scholars whose work did not challenge the essentials of the narrative of southern history were not compelled to acknowledge its political dimensions.) Motivated by a powerful commitment to activism, black historians extended their influence far beyond the confines of middle-class lyceums and college classrooms. If few of them matched Luther Jackson's tireless activism, many others nevertheless compiled impressive records.

Given the prodigious ambitions that black historians and teachers entertained for their crusade on behalf of "true" history, it is hardly surprising that they overreached. When they charged black schools and teachers with the duty to redeem black historical identity, they imposed an unreasonable burden on themselves. In much of the South, there were too few teachers to lead and too few first-rate schools to host the crusade. Various studies conducted in the 1930s and 1940s demonstrated just how few black students had access to curricula that incorporated any black history. In the one- and two-teacher schools of the South—which accounted for 80 percent of all black schools in 1940—deplorable conditions and limited resources thwarted systematic curriculum reform. Where high schools for blacks existed, Woodson and the ASNLH were likely to have made inroads. But in much of the rural South, where as late as World War II the majority of southern blacks still lived, the message of the ASNLH was seldom heard. Woodson conceded in 1939, "In the backward parts of the country where history is written according to order there is no hope for immediate change." There and elsewhere, advocates of black history complained about the lethargy, apathy, or hostility of principals, white administrators, and even some parents. N. A. Sykes of Halifax, Virginia, for example, regretted that "the children are more interested than their elders." Undaunted by these conditions, proponents of Negro history proposed to "take hold of the mind of the humblest teacher, and fire that mind with a missionary zeal to indoctrinate her pupils." But such expectations were foolhardy in a region where surveys of schools routinely described "poorly paid and poorly prepared teachers going through the humdrum of daily recitations."[62]

The Negro history campaign was necessarily an expedient,

even temporary, response to both segregation and the ideology that condoned it. Woodson and his allies understood the limits of crusading for black history in segregated public schools. They hoped that the curriculum in white schools in time would come to reflect the historical truths promoted by ASNLH and others. But although the crusade for Negro history had made considerable headway by 1950, no significant advances had been made in revising history curriculum at white schools. This failure was hardly surprising and merely confirmed how little influence blacks had over education policy in the South. John Gandy, president of Virginia State, acknowledged, "Whatever influence we shall exert must enter through indirect channels." Blacks could exploit the transformative possibilities, however circumscribed, of segregated public schools as long as they existed. But left unresolved was the future of Negro history if integration finally came to the schools of the South. Integration held out the promise of access to better facilities, but perhaps at the cost of the curriculum and traditions that Negro history activists had nurtured over decades.[63]

Perhaps the most significant shortcoming of the Negro history movement was the continuing emphasis on "hero worship in history." Black historians should hardly be scolded for having used history to rebut racist representations of alleged black inferiority and depravity. But the exaggerated attention to compiling a record of black heroism and respectability unnecessarily limited the scope and creativity of black history. Angela Davis recalled that she was made familiar with black history, but with a particular slant. "Through the years," she observed, "I learned something about every Black person respectable enough to be allotted a place in the history books—or, as far as contemporary people were concerned, who made their way into *Who's Who in Negro America* or *Ebony*." Horace Mann Bond, a gifted historian of education and distinguished college administrator, offered a similar if fuller critique of the ASNLH and the Negro history campaign. The activities of the ASNLH, he observed in 1935, "may, in all fairness, be said to represent a Negro nationalism which is a reaction against the 'white' nationalism of the American people and against the sectionalism of the South." Especially troubling to Bond was that "Negro History" was "counter-propaganda." "Southern nationalism has been irrational; Negro nationalism is no less so, and can be defended only on the ground that it intends itself to be an antidote to the prevailing lack of reason." Bond was not suggesting that the black history campaign was the moral equivalent of white nationalism, but rather that the crusade, aside from its call for racial pluralism, was hampered by its ideological conformity. He chided Carter Woodson and his ilk for teaching black children that "the future road to racial greatness lies in constructing a society stratified by economic class, in which the great men will be manufacturers, merchants, industrialists, business men and bankers." Woodson's "Negro nationalism," Bond grumbled, was restricted to "building a racial entity within the framework of the existing, capitalistic system." The counternarrative created by black historians, Bond implied, may have incorporated blacks into the nation's history, but otherwise the familiar triumphant national narrative remained intact.[64]

Subsequent critics, especially during the 1960s, would level similar charges against Woodson and the founding generation of black historians. There was a lot of truth in these complaints. Yet the criticism was sometimes exaggerated and unfair. After all, in many communities of the South, African Americans incorporated black history into school life and by doing so created a new venue for a shared historical memory. Thus, elementary students in Mamie Fields's classes in South Carolina sang "America the Beautiful" and recited the Pledge of Allegiance but did not perform "Dixie," because, as she pointedly explained, "My school was in the United States, after all, and not the Confederacy."[65] Meanwhile, Tamah Richardson's third-graders at in Hampton, Virginia, gained a measure of historical understanding of their ancestors' enslavement. And students in San Antonio, Texas, and Campbell County, Virginia, who had inherited racist textbooks cast off from white schools, participated in plays that depicted ancient Africa's wonders; put on pageants that celebrated the lives of Nat Turner, Frederick Douglass, and Booker T. Washington; and learned the poetry of Paul Lawrence Dunbar, James Weldon Johnson, and Langston Hughes. Students and their parents even heard public addresses and read weekly newspaper columns that linked black history to contemporary crusades for the equalization of teachers' salaries, voting rights, and integration.

Blacks may not have been able to lay claim to public spaces in the manner or to the degree that southern whites did, but within their segregated sphere they shared a black history that was a counterweight to at least the most insidious aspects of the white presentation of the past. When Angela Davis opened her recycled textbook in her elementary school, she read of the "War of Southern Independence." Yet her teachers found ways to make sure that "Black identity was thrust upon us." For one journalist, Carl T. Rowen, it was his high-school history teacher, "Miss Bessie"— Mrs. Bessie Taylor Gwynn—who brought to life Booker T. Washington and W. E. B. Du Bois and instilled a healthy dose of race pride. She also explained to Rowan the enduring riches of an education that empowered rather than crippled: "What you put in your head, boy, can never be pulled out by the Ku Klux Klan, the Congress, or anybody."[66]

ᢒᢒ 5

Exhibiting Southernness in
a New Century

"UNDOUBTEDLY, TODAY QUAINTNESS is an industry in Charleston," observed North Carolina newspaperman Jonathan Daniels in 1938. Charleston's tourism industry furnished more than mere quaintness; it seemed to offer a glimpse into the southern character. Writing in the *Saturday Evening Post,* Herbert Sass, one of the city's most commercially successful writers, insisted on Charleston's larger significance as an icon of true "southernness." "Charleston has become for thousands the visible affirmation of the most glamorous of all folk legends of America—the legend of the plantation civilization of the Old South. A single morning spent wandering through its older streets, a single afternoon at one of the great plantations which were an essential part of it, prove that there was at least one region—actually there were several—where the Old South really was in many ways the handsome Old South of the legend."[1] Plantation fiction, plays, and minstrel shows had long depicted a romantic and nostalgic South.

The publication of Margaret Mitchell's *Gone with the Wind,* and its subsequent release as a film, only intensified these associations. Charleston helped to anchor this mythic South in a real place.

The years between World War I and World War II marked a watershed in the self-conscious commercialization of the southern past. The struggle to cultivate and perpetuate historical memory in the South was incorporated into the commerce of tourism. Encouraging tourism became a pressing concern of public officials across the South, but more often businessmen took the lead in creating historical attractions, which public officials then promoted. As southern tourism evolved, then, it increasingly became a commercially oriented celebration of the South's architecture, landscape, and history. By the 1930s the transformation of the southern past into a commodity, a process that would continue during the twentieth century, was well advanced in Charleston.

The tourist South became a stage on which southerners presented the South both as they wanted to see it and as they imagined tourists wanted to experience it. Memory theaters, ranging from museums to historic recreations, provided settings in which southerners performed their "southernness" before eager audiences. Such sites gave a measure of permanency to the remembered past that fleeting rituals, such as Confederate Memorial Day, pageants, and other historical commemorations, could never attain. Americans gravitated to these historical settings, which offered a vivid intensification of experience and a magical suspension of time. There tourists experienced an enchanting, innocent, exotic, and seemingly timeless past while simultaneously escaping the perceived tedium, emptiness, and artificiality of modern life.

The "quaintness" industry that caught Jonathan Daniels's eye had enduring consequences for whites and blacks alike. Historical tourism was a project conceived of by whites for white consumers. With segregation precluding black patronage at most tourist facilities, African Americans were incorporated into southern tourism not as full equals but as domesticated "others" represented for public consumption. Tourists could enjoy the picturesque spectacle created by servile African Americans without needing to understand them. Indeed, an exaggerated concern for African Americans might have interfered with the tourist experience. To acknowledge the black past, at least as understood by blacks, would have raised knotty questions about the legacies of slavery as well as current race relations, thereby subverting the carefully nurtured images of gentility, romance, and nostalgia that sustained southern tourism. As the southern past became one of the region's leading generators of wealth, it shaped and perpetuated pernicious representations of blacks in places that became icons of regional identity.

That the South would lure tourists would have surprised most antebellum Americans. During the early nineteenth century, much of the region was associated with deadly diseases, hazardous miasmas, and paralyzing heat. The primeval and malarial southern landscape was profoundly disturbing to nineteenth-century sensibilities. It was too swampy and forested to satisfy genteel tastes for landscapes embellished by the hand of humans. The Victorian aesthetic imagination apparently sank when confronted with torpid rivers, monotonous pinelands, and unsightly fields of crops. In northern eyes, moreover, the southern landscape became inseparable from both physical and moral decay.

Although these associations persisted into the twentieth century, they began to recede in the decades following the Civil War. This shift was well advanced when journalist Edward King, in a popular account of his southern travels, observed that in the South "mere existence is pleasure." In addition, medical experts began to dismiss superstitions about the South's unhealthy environment. Now southern air, water, and scenery—even at sea level—became therapeutic. During the late nineteenth century each year brought a larger harvest of health seekers to southern locales. Hotel operators and town boosters competed to demonstrate by means of scientific tests that the mineral water purges and caressing breezes of their locales offered unsurpassed therapies for most ailments. While a succession of communities rose and fell in fashionable favor, positive perceptions of the southern landscape and climate endured.[2]

As sectional reconciliation accelerated after the 1870s, animosities born in the war and Reconstruction mellowed, thereby enabling nonsoutherners to turn their attention from lingering political and social problems to the pursuit of the sublime, romantic, and serene. The popularity of the culture of reconciliation revised the expectations of tourists well before they ever reached the South. They had seen the South's landscape in engravings (and later photographs) and read about them in guidebooks and poetry. Local color writers who exalted the region's landscapes and folkways, dramatists who staged popular sentimental plays about sectional reconciliation, and throngs of New South boosters who extolled the South's progress all added to the romance of the region.[3]

But before hordes of tourists could enjoy the attractions of the South, a tourist infrastructure had to be created almost from scratch. Outside of a few locations popular with the southern planter elite—the Virginia springs, for example—no southern tourist industry had existed before the Civil War. Few locales had offered services for tourists that were distinct from those required by ordinary travelers. Antebellum vacationers had little alternative but to stay at inns and travel on stagecoaches with commercial drummers and the traveling riffraff. Because there were so few facilities or workers devoted to the whims and needs of tourists in the antebellum South, travelers were usually grateful for whatever haphazard fare and improvised accommodations they could secure.

Beginning in the 1870s, a different touring experience developed. First along the east coast of Florida and gradually in a few other locales, tourists enjoyed new possibilities, including exotic scenery, elaborate accommodations, and crowds of fellow travelers. Tourism throughout the South owed its existence to advances in transportation. With each new mile of track in the region's rapidly expanding network of railroads, previously isolated corners of the South became potential tourist attractions, at least in the minds of local boosters. Moreover, railroads made travel in the South not only quicker and easier, but also affordable. Innovations in the businesses that catered to tourists followed improvements in transportation. Railroad companies frequently assumed the leadership in building tourist resorts, as in Florida, where northern tycoon Henry Flagler launched a tourist boom at Saint Augustine in 1885 and later at Palm Beach. Here, for the first time, a tourist industry sprang up to accommodate the needs of the new style of traveler, who required fashionable hotels and marketed attractions, ranging from carriage tours to "curiosity shops" and "museumanageries," which displayed eclectic arrays of natural and historical curiosities.[4]

Despite the appearance of tourists and tourist facilities in some parts of the South, the tourist experience lacked the defining elements that became conspicuous after the turn of the century. Then the appeal of the South had little to do with any specific historical or cultural associations; rather, the southern landscape seemingly held interest only when it achieved the northern and transatlantic standards of beauty that obsessed tourists. A destination was worthy of tourists' attention if it inspired Mediterranean or Alpine similes. The setting of the French Broad River in Asheville won praise because, according to one visitor, it possessed "a majesty almost like that of the Rhine." The seaside setting of Charleston, South Carolina, prompted grandiloquent comparisons to Venice.[5]

Saint Augustine in particular hinted at the possibilities for historical tourism in the region. There the quaint Spanish architecture of the oldest buildings and the romantic history associated with them offered tourists what one writer labeled as "individuality" and "unlikeness," qualities otherwise found only in Europe or New England. On the town's narrow streets, which evoked "the far-off twilight of three centuries ago," visitors could "enjoy the consciousness" that their surroundings had "a longer stretch of authentic history" than any other in the United States. With an eye toward both exploiting and intensifying these associations, Henry Flagler and other tourist promoters adopted a Spanish Moorish architectural style for the palatial hotels they constructed in Saint Augustine and elsewhere in Florida. The resulting townscape could, as if by magic, effect "a complete and sudden change of time and place."[6]

Elsewhere, visitors searched without satisfaction for stately manors, tidy pastures, plowed fields, picturesque village skylines, or other cues that would transport them. Instead too much of the South offered untamed swamps, dreary pine barrens, decrepit plantations, and ramshackle cabins. Too often the vistas were unexceptional, the country flat, and the towns rough in appearance. "Nowhere," one traveler complained, "does one find the finished beauty of our New England villages." Many tourists dismissed large portions of the South as "a tedious region of sand and pine and swamp and cypress," "an uninviting terra incognita," or, just plain "wearisome."[7]

Tourists in the region, moreover, entered a historical landscape that remained unmapped and unimagined. Whatever historical associations and traditions were attached to a community remained the private preserve of locals and inaccessible to tourists. Unless favored by local connections, only extroverted visitors who were willing to secure impromptu guides or tease historical lore out of locals could learn much about the past as they traveled through the South. Henry Field was one such pioneering tourist. Upon arriving in Knoxville, Field was unsure of how to explore the city. Faced with the "extremity" of lacking any introductions, he sought out a fellow Presbyterian minister, who, after looking him over, provided Field with a buggy tour of the historical sites.[8] But if some tourists gained insights into southern history by employing their ingenuity and tact, others recoiled from intimate contact with locals. After relying on local hospitality in north Florida, George M. Barbour reported in 1882 that the "old class of men and women" retained "antebellum ideas of business, crops, social ranks, education, slave labor, and their bitter memories of the war." He had no inclination to linger among people "brooding upon memories."[9]

The rigors of travel in the South threatened to drain the region of whatever romance it might hold. Travelers seldom experienced the refinement that characterized tourism in the American West. Instead they endured long trips through monotonous scenery, interspersed with townscapes scarred by tangled telegraph lines, cluttered loading platforms, and unsightly factories. In addition, once tourists reached their southern destinations, they often found their accommodations short on romance. In popular destinations such as Hot Springs, Arkansas, or Saint Augustine, plush hotels did a thriving business. But elsewhere, accommodations were distinctly rustic. Eager to glimpse the ways of the cotton South, Clifton Johnson visited a small town in South Carolina that had two hotels. With regret, he reported that "I was told that no matter which one I went to I would wish that I had gone to the other." The hotel he selected "was battered, dingy, and disreputable" and his fellow hotel guests included a morphine addict, a drunkard, and several shady-looking gamblers.

However vaunted in legend, private hospitality was equally risky in the South. George Barbour warned tourists that "such villainous, disgusting cooking" as was found in Florida was "surely unequaled." Likewise, Dr. William Jarvie, an early automobile enthusiast, encountered in Statesboro, Georgia, "such food, so badly prepared and so disgustingly presented, it has never been our misfortune to meet." These experiences quickly erased preconceptions about southern charm and refinement.[10]

Despite glaring shortcomings of landscape and facilities, the South during the last decades of the nineteenth century nevertheless attracted ever-increasing numbers of tourists. The allure of travel in the region could be expressed in one word: climate. Whatever the region's failings, "the sky is blue, and bends over the earth with a warm and loving embrace, and the soft and balmy air seems to have dropped down from heaven itself, as if it were the very atmosphere that angels breathe."[11] The tourists who migrated south each winter during the late nineteenth century did so to enjoy a respite from harsh winter climates. A similar warming in attitudes toward the region's historical landscape would await both new modes of travel and new conceptions of touring.

Even more than railroads, the automobile transformed American tourism, and with it perceptions of the South. If the railroads introduced the possibilities of selling southern travel, the automobile eventually carried far more tourists southward. At first the automobile was a rich tourist's amusement rather than a viable means of transportation in a region notorious for bad roads. As late as 1910 fewer than 7 percent of the South's public roadways were classified as improved, and a decade later, long stretches of highway in the region remained little more than wishful dreams. One veteran traveler in 1912 warned, "It takes bravery to make the trip [from New York] to Florida and unparalleled heroism to risk a jaunt to Corpus Christi or El Paso." The recommended equipment for a trip in the South—a block and tackle, three hundred feet of sturdy rope, tire chains, extra tires, a spade, and "mud hooks"—testified to the conditions drivers could expect.[12]

In fits and starts after the turn of the century, communities across the South improved the quagmires and rock-strewn trails that passed for roads in the region. An alliance of railroad entrepreneurs, farmers, and public officials joined together to form "Good Roads Associations"—which won the enthusiastic backing of business leaders and real estate developers, who predicted that good roads might bring a lucrative flood of vacationing motorists. Tourism promised to draw new money southward without requiring the intensive development and investment associated with industrialization. Writing in 1918, George W. Sutton Jr. alerted readers of *Southern Good Roads* that "the northern motorist is a generous spender." Tourist dollars, he predicted, would be showered on localities favored by good roads but would be scarce where the "short-sightedness" of the inhabitants had forced tourists to go "bouncing over wretched highways."[13]

As automobile touring evolved into a middle-class fad, entrepreneurs and good-roads advocates across the South promoted the construction of interstate highways. Real estate interests in Florida and Midwestern businessmen attempted to launch the tourist bonanza by founding the Dixie Highway Association, which advocated a road linking the Midwest with Florida. Despite acrimonious rivalries among communities eager to become way stations along the road, the four-thousand-mile Dixie Highway eventually connected northernmost Michigan to Miami, and included a branch that stretched across the mountains of North Carolina to the low country of South Carolina and Georgia. The publicity surrounding the Dixie Highway prompted other highway proposals, which garnered support from governors Sidney J. Catts in Florida, Harry Byrd in Virginia, Locke Craig in North Carolina, and other elected officials in the region. Eventually motorists could choose from twelve widely publicized interstates, including the Dixie, Andrew Jackson, Robert E. Lee, James H. Bankhead, and Jefferson Davis highways, which linked the South with the rest of the nation. By 1933 over sixteen thousand miles of paved roads crisscrossed the South. Although the region's highways still lagged far behind those in the rest of the nation, they opened the South to tourists on an unprecedented scale. As early as 1925, an estimated half-million automobiles bore sun-seekers southward annually.[14]

The opportunities offered by improved roads were perhaps greatest for towns and cities that had been ill-served by railroads. Charleston, and the surrounding low country of South Carolina, for example, had suffered through decades of economic decline precipitated, to a great degree, by a shift in trade routes brought about by railroad consolidation. Unlike rival cities that lay astride important north-south rail lines, Charleston was isolated on an end-of-the-line rail spur. As a result, Charleston shipped fewer and fewer goods from the hinterland and each census registered its rapid descent to the margins of the American economy. While rival cities grew, Charleston's population remained stagnant and its wealthiest capitalists invested elsewhere.[15]

Charleston's elites fixed on tourism to halt the city's precipitous economic decline. Florida's heady and seemingly limitless growth persuaded many Charlestonians that if the streams of tourists migrating back and forth to Florida, "with their money fairly burning holes in their pockets," could be diverted to Charleston, the city would reap an economic windfall. But before the South Carolina low country could replicate Florida's tourist boom, concerned Charlestonians recognized that it had to be made accessible to vacationers. With no prospect of improved rail service, Charlestonians looked to good roads to bring tourists. The Charleston Chamber of Commerce and the city's newspapers joined forces to promote both good roads and tourism. If "[we] leave the roads as they are now," the *News and Courier* warned in 1921, "we shall be cut off from a movement which might well mean as much to us as the profits from the cotton crop in a normal year."[16]

The focus of the good-roads campaign in the low country was a coastal highway linking Jacksonville, Florida, and Wilmington, North Carolina, by way of Charleston. By providing the shortest route between northeastern cities and Florida, the road seemed destined to become the South's principal tourist thoroughfare. Meeting in 1921, southeastern road boosters organized the Coastal Highway Association, selected the highway's route, and lobbied energetically for state road funds. By 1925 the Savannah River had been bridged and most of the coastal highway had been improved. With the completion of the final link in the route in 1929—the impressive three-mile-long bridge over the Cooper River at Charleston—the principal obstacles to automobile travel along the southeastern coast had been overcome.

Good roads alone, Charlestonians understood, were insufficient to attract tourists: tourist facilities were also desperately needed. Repeated appeals for a modern tourist hotel went unheeded until 1924, when the opening of the twelve-story, three-hundred-room Francis Marion Hotel marked "the beginning of a new epoch in the city's development." Several months later, the Fort Sumter Hotel opened with rooms for nearly four hundred guests, leading some to predict that Charleston would become "a tourist center second to none." At the urging of the chamber of commerce, entrepreneurs soon added a "tourist camp" (the antecedent to the modern campground), a golf course, and a yacht basin to the city's amenities. By the end of the 1920s, in less than a decade, Charleston had acquired most of the prerequisites for a burgeoning tourist industry.[17]

Cultivation of tourism in Charleston during the 1920s and 1930s entailed commodifying the lore of the place in addition to constructing a tourist infrastructure. Promoters of tourism in Charleston had available to them a variety of marketing themes. They might have emphasized, as did their Florida competitors, the clean air and balmy climate of the low country. Or they might have dwelled on the region's recreational offerings, such as golf, hunting, and boating. Instead promoters staked the future of tourism in Charleston on nostalgia. By cultivating and celebrating the city's distinctiveness, Charlestonians turned the city into a tourist theater. Indeed, Charlestonians increasingly came to see their city—to visualize its physical and human geography—from the perspective of tourists.

Charleston's great fortune was to adopt tourism precisely when the automobile was first making possible new ways to explore the region's natural and built landscapes. The automobile, enthusiasts claimed, "brought back the romance of travel." By allowing sightseers to "ramble in intimate leisure along little roads," the automobile became, in the words of one travel writer, a "good modern servant of the moods of modern man." Summarizing the allure of "motor touring," two young women tourists in Florida explained, "We make our own schedules, stay as long or as short in a place, and after we have seen and enjoyed the things of interest we journey on where fancy may dictate." As early as 1903, R. G. Betts proclaimed that "the motor-car provides the means and is enabling Americans to really discover their own country . . . as they never have discovered, and never could discover it before."[18] The automobile made possible intimate contact with the "authentic" character of locales, thereby producing an intensity of experience impossible by any other modern mode of travel. The automobilist, who "penetrates everywhere and reaches the remotest limits of the back country," discovered unviolated areas of the country "whose face has not been cut up and slashed by man" and which "make him forget the busy marts of trade and the strident calls of daily life."[19]

So intoxicating was the sensation of auto touring that many tourists seemed to shift focus from the destination to the pursuit of picturesque and interesting sights during the journey itself. Travel writers and automobile enthusiasts quickly grasped the implications of this change and promoted automobile touring as the means to a more intimate and intense appreciation of local history and regional distinctiveness. Now historic sites and places brimming with local color became favored travel destinations. "There is," an automobile enthusiast announced, "a new and genuine interest in places, especially those of historic interest, which is rapidly dotting many important routes with tablets and other markers conveying information which a few years ago was beyond the reach of tourists going through on schedule."[20]

The need to revise tourist perceptions of Charleston and other areas of the South was obvious. Tourists like Seymour Cunningham, an early cross-country automobilist who dismissed Charleston as offering "few attractions to motorists," could hardly be faulted for failing to recognize unmarked and undeveloped spots along southern byways. By "marking and caring for the landmarks of the old South," southerners could remedy this shortcoming. Writing in *Southern Good Roads,* Katherine Clemmons Gould complained that the South did not advertise "its chief attractions." "Places of intense historic and scenic interest literally dot the South," she insisted, "and yet it is a most difficult thing for the motorist to find the majority of them." The skills and courage of a pathfinder, for instance, were needed to navigate the meandering, sometimes impassable, roads that led to the site of the Jamestown settlement in Virginia. Only a thousand tourists accomplished the feat in 1919.[21]

If "historical associations" were going to become part of the southern tourist landscape, they first had to be identified for passersby. Members of white women's organizations were among the first southerners to recognize the opportunity for historical "education" that the enthusiasm for good roads and automobiles offered. By serving as open-air classrooms, roads could promote a "love for the country." When William Ullman observed that "automobile tours can be arranged to follow the roads of history, visiting the places of historic as well as scenic interest," he was paraphrasing ideas that had circulated among women's groups for nearly a decade. In 1909, for example, Alma Rittenberry of the Alabama Daughters of the War of 1812 proposed the construction of a highway from Chicago to Mobile as a monument to Andrew Jackson. Rittenberry became a tireless spokesperson for a coalition of the Alabama Colonial Dames, DAR, UDC, and Daughters of the War of 1812 endorsing the construction of a highway that would follow historic roads and trails "as nearly as was possible." She sought out commercial groups to back her campaign, and in 1915 the Jackson Highway Association was formed. Her vision for the highway was fulfilled when the highway followed, as Rittenberry emphasized, a "historic route" along which patriotic and hereditary organizations had placed markers, boulders, and monuments commemorating "military triumph and civic achievement."[22]

Across the South, women's groups named highways and

marked historic spots along their shoulders. Following in Alma Rittenberry's footsteps, they waged successful campaigns for the creation of the Natchez Trace from Tennessee to Natchez, Mississippi, and the Colonial Parkway linking Jamestown and Yorktown, Virginia. These enterprises meshed with longstanding campaigns by women's organizations to beautify public spaces; they also gave a measure of permanence to hallowed historical associations. The Garden Club of Virginia, for example, improved roadsides by planting native trees and shrubs, campaigning for the conservation of wild flowers and the restriction of outdoor advertising, and encouraging "individuals, organizations, and whole counties to a revaluing of whatever historical or artistic treasures they possessed." For women historical enthusiasts, memorial highways offered an opportunity to reach new audiences while aligning their campaigns with the era's symbol of progress—the automobile.[23]

State officials, too, recognized the possibility of improving the tourist experience by marking historic attractions. Following his election as governor of Virginia in 1925, Harry Byrd promised to improve the state's notoriously bad roads. As part of that pledge, a new Conservation and Economic Development Commission headed by Byrd's campaign manager fused economic development, tourism, and historic preservation by authorizing state historian Hamilton J. Eckenrode to select and mark worthy sites for historical highway markers. By 1934 more than a thousand markers taught native Virginians and tourists about what was historically significant and, by implication, what was not. To travel the roads of Virginia was literally to enter a system of signs through which the state promoted a certain narrative of history—a narrative that dwelled on the state's vaunted contributions to the nation's development.[24]

Other southern states copied Virginia's much-envied highway

marker program. In many states, early programs relied on the largesse of both private groups and state officials. In South Carolina, Coleman C. Martin, secretary of the Charleston Chamber of Commerce along with members of the "Marker Committee" of the Coastal Highway Association, proposed erecting "attractive and readable historic markers" along the highways of the low country in 1932. Thirty-five markers, modeled after Virginia signs, provided "valuable aids to the visitor desirous of gaining an authentic account of the many interesting and important happenings of American history staged in this area." Research for the text and location of the markers was performed by Marie L. Webber, secretary of the South Carolina Historical Society in Charleston, Henry Dwight of Pinopolis, an authority on the history of coastal South Carolina, and A. S. Salley, the South Carolina state historian. In this instance, as in many others, tourism and economic development were united with the state's existing commitment, through the state's historical commission, to historic commemoration.[25]

The process of revisualizing the landscape and of culling sites that warranted the attention of tourists recast the region's maps as well. An early visionary who recognized the need to place history on the map was South Carolina Commissioner of Agriculture E. J. Watson. Watson published a large map of the highway system of the state, along with "the names of all historic points and the dates on which fame was earned for them in red ink." By the 1930s, a profusion of maps, markers, and tourist brochures beckoned visitors "to breathe the air of the past and vision the romance of early America while enjoying the most modern of comforts, the paved highway." With a veneer of encyclopedic objectivity, the maps and markers oriented the traveler in a historic landscape of battle sites, historic ruins, literary shrines, and noteworthy old buildings, authenticating those places and remnants of the past that should interest visitors. The simple assertion of historic importance was significant. White southerners had for at least a generation complained that their region's and their ancestors' contributions to the nation were either ignored or deprecated. To elevate places and shrines to attractions worthy of tourists' attention was to revalue southern history.[26]

Charleston's tourism boosters recognized that their success depended on advertising the low country's historical attractions. Jealous of the success of "the Florida spirit," local newspapers urged the city's business community to launch a publicity campaign for the city. The local chamber of commerce eagerly responded by adopting almost every device in the rapidly expanding arsenal of modern advertising. Arthur V. Snell, a former manager of the chamber, explained, "Selling the city . . . is not a particle different than selling any other business." The chamber of commerce made up slogans and encouraged local businessmen to use them on their letterhead and advertising material. It promoted the adoption of "America's Most Historic City" as the city's official slogan. At the cost of tens of thousands of dollars, the chamber launched a "Selling Charleston Campaign," which placed advertisements in national journals during the winter tourist season. In 1924, the chamber, along with the city government, local Rotary and Kiwanis clubs, a local bank, and the city's new tourist hotels, funded a spring tour of Florida's tourist destinations. Mayor Thomas P. Stoney urged on the campaign, announcing, "We have to sell Charleston to the outside world." In the same year, the chamber established a permanent tourist bureau, raised more than seven thousand dollars to pay for publicity, and printed tens of thousands of guidebooks and tourist brochures. Eventually, the chamber coaxed the city council to levy a tax on all property in the city "for the purpose of creating a fund to be used for advertising the City of Charleston."[27]

Charleston's businessmen and tourist boosters, despite their reputation for having an aristocratic aversion to the bustle of the business world, were quick to exploit any means available to attract the national spotlight. In diverse ways the marketing innovations of the twentieth century were harnessed to promote Charleston's charms. In 1931 Alexander M. Bishop, who had served on the editorial staff of the *News and Courier* and had directed the chamber of commerce's publicity campaign for the city, opened his own advertising agency and began publishing slick magazines targeted at tourists. Films and radio shows also spread Charleston's fame. Beginning in 1916, the chamber tried to lure film directors to the city by distributing photograph albums of suitable local film sites. In 1917 alone, at least four companies shot some footage in the city and in subsequent years Charleston's gardens and buildings usually graced several new films a year. Several movies, including *An Old City Speaks* (1932), were specifically intended to whet tourists' appetite with scenes of the city's quaint streets, beguiling architecture, and colorful inhabitants.[28]

The effectiveness of Charleston's publicity campaigns could be measured in the growing number of tourists who visited the city each winter. From a trickle of tourists in 1916, when newspapers lamented that sometimes no more than two passengers disembarked from ships that docked in Charleston, the number of visitors swelled dramatically during the next decade until armies of tourists taxed the city's facilities. During "high season" between February and May, tourist dollars accounted for more than $5 million in local payrolls alone. By the 1930s, a travel writer reported, "We are told here that 270,000 visitors come to Charleston in a single year, and naturally most of them in the spring." A visit to Charleston was "now the thing to do."[29]

In little more than a decade, a somewhat sophisticated tourist industry had developed to meet the needs of visitors. Rather than aimlessly wander the streets of Charleston, sightseers could arm themselves with the free maps and tourist materials the chamber of commerce and every hotel provided. Hotels and bookstores sold "a wealth of guides, souvenirs, and books, ranging from small pocket pamphlets to folios with magnificent photographs." And guide services and tour companies offered package tours of the city's landmarks and gardens. The essential infrastructure for a flourishing tourist industry was in place and Charleston had, in the words of one resident, "committed itself body and soul to the exploitation of tourists."[30]

In hindsight it may appear inevitable that history would become Charleston's principal attraction. White tourist boosters understandably sought to exploit the city's extensive colonial and ante-bellum-era architecture. But they still had to decide what aspects of the city's history to emphasize or ignore. White Charlestonians elected to dwell on historical qualities they believed had distinguished the city throughout its history. These attributes, including dilapidated mansions and unpaved streets, old buildings and quaint fashions, were now interpreted as something other than marks of poverty and isolation. They came to represent the serenity and dignity of the "old days." Charlestonians chose to pass over the low country's conspicuous role in fomenting the Civil War and instead dwelled on the city's colonial elegance, old-fashioned hospitality, quaint mannerisms, nostalgic atmosphere, and purported racial harmony. Over time, white Charlestonians renovated and restored the built environment of the city and adapted their habits so as to present an unusually pervasive and alluring historical experience that attracted hundreds of thousands of tourists each year.

The historical narrative presented by Charlestonians retold

the romance of the Old South, a familiar story well before Charleston became a tourist destination. If the broad outlines of that story were not distinctive, the specifics were. By all accounts, the beginning of the Charleston story was marked by the seventeenth-century arrival of English-speaking settlers. Archetypal Charlestonians were the rice and cotton planters who settled the surrounding low country and sought culture and companionship in Charleston. The city developed into one of North America's centers for the arts, learning, and commerce before the Revolution, to which low-country patriots made heroic and decisive contributions. The early nineteenth century marked the zenith of Charleston's influence and culture. The city's elite purportedly nurtured a genteel culture that held tawdry commercialism at bay while embracing refinement and respect for tradition. The Civil War, which was brought on by lamentable abolitionist extremism, destroyed this ideal society. The city's subsequent wartime and postwar tribulations, including a devastating earthquake in 1886, figured into the account mainly as testimony to Charlestonians' abiding resilience. This narrative accentuated the historical distinctiveness of the low country, placing particular emphasis on the eighteenth and early nineteenth centuries, when the region's vanished "civilization" had reached its apogee.

If one were to believe Charlestonians of the time, even the institution of slavery that undergirded the lost civilization of their ancestors was unique. The region's planters, they insisted, had displayed uncommon solicitude to the needs of the African slaves brought to the city's shores by northern traders. Denmark Vesey, the purported leader of a failed slave revolt, merited no mention in this saga. Recalling this mythic plantation era as described by her father, Alice Ravenel Huger Smith regretted the passing of the idyllic relations that had prevailed between master and slave and had nourished "the happy family life so characteristic of

Southern establishments." She took comfort that the institution of slavery had secured "the dominance of the man of civilization, of morals, and education, over the absolute savage." Herbert Sass agreed that slavery had made possible the genuine and elevated culture of Charleston's golden age, when low-country values and institutions had created a near utopia whose beneficent influence had radiated out over the entire region. Only with the firing on Fort Sumter did this old and charmed order give way to ugly, crude, modern civilization. Apparently the destruction of the plantation order was a greater tragedy than the enslavement of African Americans.[31]

White Charlestonians pointed to the splendor of their city's heritage of decorative arts and architecture as evidence of the refined civilization of the Old South. During the booming antiques market of the 1920s, the city gained a national reputation as a repository of decorative arts and architecture on par with New England and Philadelphia. When in the early 1920s the Metropolitan Museum created a much discussed series of period rooms of antiques displayed in mock situ, but failed to include any South Carolina furniture, white Charlestonians were offended. Their wounds were not assuaged when the Minneapolis Institute of Art created two Charleston period rooms, furnished in "an authentic manner," complete with woodwork and mantels removed from a colonial-era Charleston home. Concern that these artifacts and many other things "atmospheric of Charleston" were being sold away from the city prompted some Charlestonians to urge the organization of "Charleston rooms" in Charleston. The Charleston Museum responded by creating its own period room that displayed heirlooms loaned from the collections of Charleston's old families. The rooms apparently served their purpose by demonstrating the heretofore unappreciated opulence of low-country tastes and the sophistication of regional craftsmen. Six years later, an exhibition of Charleston antiques held in the rectory of Saint Philip's Church attracted national attention to "old Charleston craftsmanship." Perhaps the zenith of Charleston's influence on furniture and interior design occurred in March 1939, when *House and Garden* devoted an entire issue to the "historical grandeur" of Charleston, which was presented as an inspiration for all manner of interior and architectural design.[32]

The aesthetics of the city's colonial and antebellum decorative arts were interpreted as having a clear social meaning. In them white Charlestonians and many visitors saw the graciousness and dignity of an aristocratic order whose sensibility lingered in the Carolina low country but elsewhere had been lost to debased, modern tastes. As a visiting antiques enthusiast explained, "Antiques show the present generation the graceful manner of living during the Eighteenth century," an age when "the men who made these things took pride and joy in their craft" and when "there was no such hurry as we experience today." Charleston's shabby but romantic gentility only added to the appeal of the decorative artifacts on display there. "Charleston, itself a veritable antique, with all the wistful charm that somehow clings to all old things, is the antique lover's dream come true."[33]

Charleston's decades as an economic backwater proved to be, as North Carolina editor Jonathan Daniels observed, "a wonderful preservative of the past. . . . [I]t will keep old things as they are because it cannot afford to change them in accordance with styles or preferences." But by the 1920s a growing number of white Charlestonians concluded that poverty alone was unlikely to conserve the city's built heritage. An organized preservation movement, which was equal parts elite romantic nostalgia for the Old South, aesthetic reevaluation of the city's architecture, and profiteering, transformed the look of the city so that it embodied a timeless elegance that was manifestly old but no longer decaying.

In particular, growing alarm about the effects of modernity and the fate of old buildings led to the founding of the Society for the Preservation of Old Dwellings (SPOD) in 1920. Susan Pringle Frost, the driving force behind the SPOD, staked out the organization's mission: "The magnificent residences which are being, and in many instances have already been, destroyed, represent a certain stability and nobility of character and taste, which a modern commercial age can ill afford to dispense with. . . . We cannot destroy these stately residences . . . without correspondingly cheapening the taste of the next generation."[34]

Initially, the campaign by the SPOD was in keeping with voluntary preservation efforts elsewhere in the country that were staffed predominantly by white women and were sustained by a largely nostalgic impulse to safeguard individual buildings from destruction. Ernest H. Pringle and his wife devoted their limited means to preserving the Manigault House, one of the city's most notable colonial-era mansions. He explained the deep filial connections bound up in the Charleston landscape. "Since boyhood, I have been used to hearing the women of my family talk of Preservation—of furniture, landmarks, tradition. As a little boy, my mother used to talk to my father, and the rest of us, of the value of works of art, of furniture then being sold from the homes of so many of our neighbors. . . . So when I married my wife it was a sweet and familiar thing to find her loving old Charleston furniture and old Charleston houses." For the Pringles, Frost, and other society members, the preservation of the domestic settings where low-country refinement had been acted out was at least as important as veneration of great men and deeds.[35]

During the late 1920s, the preservation movement in Charleston entered a second stage when the city government and a "Board of Architectural Review for Historic Charleston" acquired power over preservation policy. Yet again female voluntarism gave way to government-backed and male-led historical activism when the society was reincorporated as the Preservation Society of Charleston and men assumed the leadership in 1927. Dilettante preservationists still were the foot soldiers, but now prominent local architects and professional museum directors directed the campaign. Bolstered by the backing of the American Institute of Architects (AIA) and the city's mayor, the preservationists secured tax exemptions for restored homes from the South Carolina legislature, as well as funding for their preservation and urban planning goals from federal agencies. On October 13, 1931, they won ratification by the city council of the nation's first government-supported planning and zoning ordinance.[36]

Aesthetic concerns assumed new importance in the preservation movement during the 1930s, as was evident in the AIA's campaign to preserve Charleston's colonial architecture from decay and destruction. In 1932 Robert D. Kohn of the AIA made a national appeal for the conservation of Charleston's "priceless eighteenth century landmarks": "We are not pleading for the sake of Charleston, but because the whole country would be the loser if these buildings were destroyed." Charleston's architectural significance, according to Albert Simons, was the number of standing colonial buildings. Although a few other cities had equally old buildings and many of Charleston's buildings were "not the finest architectural examples," Simons boasted that "they form an excellent exhibition" unmatched in any other American city.[37]

The city's architectural heritage, as well as the culture that produced it, also won praise from the low-country artists who participated in the so-called Charleston Renaissance, an effervescence of low-country arts and letters during the 1920s and 1930s. Charleston's emergence as an art colony coincided precisely with the city's tourist boom. In 1924, only seven artists advertised their services in Charleston's "city directory"; seven years later, thirty-one maintained studios in the city. Their ranks included both native Charlestonians, like Alice Ravenel Huger Smith and Elizabeth O'Neill Verner, as well as migrants like Michigan-born etcher Alfred Hutty. Despite their diverse origins and life histories, their work distilled a romantic, eternal essence of Charleston, emphasizing what they believed to be the elemental, traditional character of their subject. Both Hutty and Verner used etchings to give the city and region a genteel and nostalgic atmosphere. Verner expunged from her scenes any signs of modernity; she portrayed, for example, black peddlers pushing rustic carts in cityscapes bereft of streetcars, telephone poles, electrical wires, or automobiles. Her premodern scenes were not happenstance. She explained in 1939, "It is one of my deepest regrets that I did not begin etching until 1923, for by that time so much which to my generation represented Charleston had disappeared. I would prefer to have etched the Charleston of my childhood." Alice Ravenel Huger Smith similarly adopted the technique of vivid washes of luminous watercolors to convey the region's colorful human and lush natural landscapes.[38]

Charleston's white artists shared the conviction that Charleston's old architecture and traditions could both attract and educate tourists. Because the city's distinctive architecture and ambience were so important to their own work, the artists joined with the preservationists in their campaign to preserve "that essential atmosphere which makes these buildings valuable and purposeful." Elizabeth O'Neill Verner, whose art was especially favored by tourists, admitted that "Charleston's climate is not the best in the world, that its golf courses are not the best, and its fishing not more remarkable than many other places," but the tourist "is happy no matter how gray the day may be if he has plenty to see." Charleston's tourist trade hinged on the city's ability to look quaint—and its economic survival depended on the tourist trade. As the Historic Charleston Foundation, a spin-off of the preservation movement, later would insist, "Proper preservation is good business."[39]

The efforts to preserve the city's appearance turned a significant portion of it into a memory theater. With the creation of the historic district in 1931, and its gradual expansion in subsequent decades, more and more of the city was recast or "restored" so as to capture and intensify the distinctive ambience valued by preservationists, artists, and tourists. Restored Charleston made tangible the mythic colonial and antebellum South, allowing visitors to experience firsthand remnants of what was purportedly one of the nation's most elegant and refined societies. As a brochure for a Charleston hotel explained, "The grandeur of other days lingers still in the wide streets with their chaste architectural relics." So evocative was the city's landscape that few tourists who were informed of its storied past were immune to the appeal of the civilization that had built it.[40]

Visitors to the city understandably concluded that the destruction of the civilization that had created this "Venice of North America" was a tragedy, not just for its residents but also for the nation. Only the tenacity of Charlestonians and their loyalty to traditions of the Old South had made it possible for modern Americans to glimpse and experience a vanished "way of life." Contemporary lifestyles in Charleston, no less than the cityscape, became a measure of the city's distinctiveness and the superiority of its traditions. At a time when many "old stock" Americans were anxious about the diminution of the nation's Anglo-Saxon character, Charleston offered a reassuring glimpse of a traditional and stable social order. "Her exclusive families," a tourist brochure announced, "are keeping alive in America some of the best heritages of our ancestors." Travel writer T. C. Smith agreed, observing that "Charleston is the last stand of the traditional and original in place and people against the leveling, common-place aspect which is the most marked characteristic of the twentieth century."[41]

Charlestonians appeared to live for hospitality. Travel accounts dwelled on the city's leisurely, Mediterranean pace of life. In Charleston, an envious visitor observed, "business is not the mainspring of a man's thought and the tyrant of the hours of his day." The city and its elite seemed to exist in a cocoon of tradition, outside the flow of the hurly-burly modern age. White Charlestonians apparently had almost no business to pursue and instead lingered over elaborate afternoon dinners. The social protocols of the past, which elsewhere had been corrupted by "the vulgarity of materialism," endured in Charleston. The city's charm and fascination lay in its "ancient traditions and customs," its very "strangeness."[42]

No travel account was complete without some serendipitous encounter with a member of one of Charleston's old families, who welcomed the tourist into the dream world of the city's private gardens and homes. Within the walls of Charleston's imposing colonial mansions and landmarks, city residents themselves became performers for tourists. Charleston's "family histories," proclaimed G. M. Allen, "are full of romance more dramatic than any of fiction's pages, and of incidents or real life filled with poetry." White Charlestonians (at least those who interested tourists) became representatives of a cultured elite that had vanished elsewhere in the nation. Various homes, such as the Manigault and Brewton-Pringle houses, were opened to tourists in order to raise money for historic preservation. "Pilgrimages" of paying tourists visited old plantation homes in the surrounding countryside. And some owners of restored homes adapted to the tourist market by renting rooms to visitors during the spring "season." A stay at Susan Frost's Brewton-Pringle House or any of Charleston's grand homes was like a trip to a living history museum where white Charlestonians, with their apparently quaint and eccentric ways, had not "lost the art of living."[43]

Just as the material culture of colonial and antebellum Charleston demonstrated the gentility of the Old South, the apparently serene race relations in the contemporary low country vouched for the benign character of white rule during and after slavery. Low-country African Americans and their folkways figured prominently in the human pageant presented to tourists, but only in narrowly circumscribed ways. Artist Elizabeth O'Neill Verner was not unique in insisting that blacks were "an integral part of the beauty of Charleston." But white tourist boosters were preoccupied with providing charming and benign glimpses of a childlike race that flourished under the indulgent protection of descendants of the white planter aristocracy. With its purported stable, harmonious, and time-honored racial order that properly fixed whites and blacks in their appropriate roles, Charleston stood in marked contrast to northern cities, where southern migrants had acquired the troubling ambitions and manners of the "New Negro."[44]

Low-country blacks warranted attention in proportion to their perceived simplicity and exoticism. Charleston's black street merchants who peddled seafood and vegetables from picturesque carts became emblems of the city's distinctive old-world charm. Gullah language, slave spirituals, and curious African traditions also loomed large in whites' renderings of low-country blacks. In DuBose Heyward's wildly popular and critically acclaimed novel *Porgy,* blacks were rendered as authentic primitives who seemed to exist outside of the flow of history. Repeatedly Heyward contrasted the "barbarism" of black Charleston to the gentility of white Charleston. He recounted the street antics of a black fraternal society and the capture of the "reticent, old Anglo-Saxon town" by a people who were "exotic as the Congo and still able to abandon themselves utterly to the wild joy of fantastic play." Heyward's attention to the violence, sexuality, and hedonism of the colorful characters who populate Catfish Row in *Porgy* was of a piece with the interest displayed by other Charleston literati and artists in the Negro as a "primitive" who had "resisted American standardization and had retained a native delight in color and song." The etchings of Hutty and Verner depict African Americans as almost primeval. That they often are faceless and seemingly inseparable from the landscape itself was intentional. As Verner explained in 1929, "The negro is Nature's child; one paints him as readily and fittingly into the landscape as a tree or marsh."[45]

Whites even mediated the contact that tourists had with black artistry. One of the few traditional black art forms that tourists embraced was sea grass basketry. A laborious and highly skilled craft, basketry was in decline in the low country during the early twentieth century. Before then the Penn Normal, Industrial, and Agricultural School, located near Beaufort, had kept the tradition alive by including basket weaving in its program of vocational education. By the 1920s few blacks had acquired the skills or found basket weaving lucrative. But, anticipating the appeal of the baskets to tourists, Clarence W. Legerton, a white bookstore owner in Charleston, began marketing sea island baskets to tourists through mail order. Basket weavers adapted their designs to Legerton's mail order business and to the tastes of buyers, who preferred more decorative shapes and designs than traditional "work" baskets. Legerton soon was annually selling perhaps as many as five thousand baskets with a mark-up of nearly 100 percent. By virtue of the scale of his business, he dominated the trade in baskets until the early 1930s, when basket makers began to build rustic stands along the Coastal Highway to market their art directly to tourists. In this manner, black artisans regained a measure of control over the marketing of their craft and a sufficient share of its profits to ensure its perpetuation until the present day.[46]

Yet even as black artisans carved out a place for themselves in the basket trade, the marketing of basket making by regional tourist boosters affirmed the prevailing image of low-country blacks. Beginning with Legerton, the craft tradition was depicted as another example of the region's timelessness. Both Legerton and the Charleston Chamber of Commerce publicized basketry as "An Art as Old as Africa" that had been "handed down through the generations." An exotic artifact of slavery, basketry was the antithesis of machine-age production. A 1938 chamber of commerce brochure boasted that the baskets demonstrated "Hand Work Superior to Any Other Woven Work in America." More troubling, Legerton invoked stereotypes of the "proverbially lazy . . . genuinely southern darky" in his advertising, while the chamber of commerce traced the refinement of contemporary low-country basketry to whites, who had supposedly persuaded basket makers to turn a "utilitarian" skill into a "decorative" craft.[47]

Black Charlestonians who flaunted whites' preconceptions risked scorn. Irksome to tourists were the "swarms of little knaves of spades who practice the double profession of shining shoes and selling papers, with dancing and singing as a side line." Even more vexing were the habits of the blacks who occupied crowded and derelict housing in the historic district. The real-life counterparts to the characters who populated Catfish Row in *Porgy* were too colorful and rustic to appeal to preservationists or tourists. Not coincidentally, when preservationists restored "historic integrity" to the city's neighborhoods, they also hastened the isolation of several black enclaves. For centuries, blacks and whites had lived in close proximity in Charleston. Not even the advent of legalized segregation at the beginning of the twentieth century had resulted in racial enclaves. But preservationists and city officials capitalized on federal largesse during the early years of Franklin Roosevelt's New Deal administration and secured funding from the Public Works Administration to move black residents away from the "Old and Historic District" and into African American public-housing projects. The process of racial relocation continued in 1939 when a historic black neighborhood in the northern downtown area was leveled and replaced by an all-white housing project. Thus, the "restoration" of historic Charleston effectively purged black residents from the tip of the Charleston peninsula for the first time in the city's history.[48]

Even the city's colorful African American flower women were not above reproach. Before the advent of tourism in Charleston, itinerant flower women, with baskets balanced on their heads, had wandered the streets peddling their goods with "melodious calls." The arrival of tourists prompted the women to gather together in large groups at prominent street corners. The exotic folkways of the flower women earned mention in most travel accounts. "Tourists," the *Charleston News and Courier* reported, "almost always are impressed by the colorful sight of the blooms and the picturesque poses of the pipe-smoking women." But some tourists complained that they were not sufficiently picturesque. One observer who was appalled by their "ratty winter coats" and "torn dirty sweaters" implored the chamber of commerce "to make them less like black buzzards and more like the market women of the West Indies. Make them wear gay bandanas, bright calicoes for their dresses, and if they must have a pipe let it be a corncob."[49]

Neither tourist boosters nor tourists displayed much interest in the city's black middle class. Historic black neighborhoods and institutions seldom warranted extended mention in tourist literature. Whereas tourists to the city could not easily avoid the "pic-

Black flower vendors contributed to Charleston's exotic
and picturesque allure for tourists, ca. 1938. (National
Geographic Society)

turesque" artwork of Alice Ravenel Huger Smith and Elizabeth
O'Neill Verner, they were unlikely to see visual art created by
Charleston's African Americans. Painter Edwin Harleston, who
was a prominent businessman and a founder of the local branch
of the NAACP, depicted the street life of Charleston without the
nostalgia and exoticism that characterized the "Charleston Renaissance." Harleston won acclaim nationally before his death in
1931, but he enjoyed virtually no recognition as an artist in his na-

tive city. That his work remained unappreciated in Charleston was no accident. A proposal to exhibit Harleston's work at the Charleston Museum, broached by the museum's northern-born director, was thwarted by community opposition.[50]

Black institutions that contradicted the image of blacks as un-educated, subservient, and tradition-bound were not readily ac-knowledged by whites. The Jenkins Orphanage, founded in 1891 by Rev. Daniel J. Jenkins, was a thriving private institution with a national reputation for its educational programs, especially its superb bands. Although DuBose Heyward's *Porgy* depicted the musicianship of these bands as an especially colorful facet of the city's black culture, the orphanage nevertheless galled some white Charlestonians. Irked by the comportment of modern city blacks in general, which was off-putting to tourists, Mark A. Abney wrote the editor of the *Charleston Evening Post* in 1933 urging the expulsion of the orphanage from the city. Perhaps then its oc-cupants would "learn to till the soil and be the useful citizens that they are intended to be." Evidently, too many blacks revealed more polish and airs than whites thought appropriate. One travel writer regretted that "those younger negroes who drive the clumsy two-wheeled carts in town and out over rough-paved streets have learned no good manners. And when the burly negresses who amble up the sidewalks, balancing huge trays of crabs or fresh fruits or baked stuffs, smile at you, theirs is the smile of insolence."[51]

Indeed, to the regret of some tourists and white Charlestonians, too few blacks retained the deferential manners of old. "The older negroes," one traveler glowed, "will touch their hats, if not re-move them, when you glance at them. They will step into the gut-ter when you pass them upon the narrow sidewalks of the narrow streets." He lamented, "They are rapidly disappearing from the streets of the old city." A tourist magazine reported that Becky, an elderly black plantation hand, had offered her previous employer the highest possible compliment: "It was jest like slavery time." With her "bright kerchief around her head, her skirt tied at intervals around her body to keep it from trailing the ground," Becky was "among the last of the colorful pictures distinctive of the Carolina coastal country." These remnants of the Old South seemed to grow more precious to whites as ever fewer blacks were willing to play the part.[52]

Because white tourists had few occasions to interact with so-called plantation blacks, whites in Charleston staged events that allowed them to observe suitably rustic blacks. "Authentic" black singers were displayed during spring tourist season beginning in the early 1930s. "Southern Echoes," a choir of old "plantation ne-groes," performed concerts of unadorned, traditional gospel and work songs in ratty plantation garb. Another black performance, "Heavenbound," also attained the status of "one of those items on the [tourist's] must list."[53]

For many tourists, their exposure to African American life came not through contact with blacks but through the most ec-centric cultural preservation movement in the South Carolina low country, the Society for the Preservation of Spirituals (SPS). Founded in 1922 by white descendants of planters, the society pledged to preserve black spirituals, educate "the rising genera-tion in their character and rendition," and "to relieve the distress of the old time negro and his people." As the children of former slave plantation owners, SPS members boasted that they under-stood "the negro character probably as well as any white man ever does." They pointedly confined their campaign to the preserva-tion and performance of spirituals sung during slavery and the quarter-century after emancipation. These spirituals alone pos-sessed the "pure African wildness and beauty of tone, only touched by the religion of the Anglo-Saxon" cherished by the

SPS. Society members viewed black artistic expression as something that African Americans had produced naturally. Or rather, it was something that African Americans who had not been corrupted by mass culture or unfortunate ambitions produced. They sang when they worked, their prayers were dances, and their everyday language was poetry. But because too few "authentic" blacks existed, concerned whites had to appropriate their culture in order to preserve it.[54]

Had society members recorded blacks singing spirituals or published versions of low-country spirituals, they would have been inconspicuous partners of other contemporary white folklorists who were keenly interested in black music and culture. But society members went further and actually performed black spirituals. Dressed in hoop skirts and in tuxedos with antebellum-era bow ties, they sang spirituals in the low-country black dialect of Gullah. In addition to singing and "shouting," society performances included commentary by the performers about the meaning of the spirituals and the splendors of the antebellum society that had produced them. Either refusing to recognize or incapable of hearing the slaves' anguish or longing for freedom in spirituals, the society instead bowdlerized them so they became uncomplicated testaments to black religious devotion. Their versions of black spirituals were intended to demonstrate that slavery had nurtured beauty and faith; the brutality of the institution was pointedly absent. The irony of descendants of white slaveholders appropriating and performing black spirituals to glorify slavery, and the social order it made possible, drew no comment from either society members or their audiences. To the contrary. Many in their audiences apparently agreed with a listener at a 1927 SPS concert that "the negroes themselves could not do so well."[55]

Both the mission and the performances of the SPS were assertions of cultural and social authority. In these endeavors, descendants of slave owners were insisting that only some whites possessed sufficient familiarity with and understanding of black culture to be able to perform spirituals in an authentic manner. In no obvious way did they intend to assume the appearance or persona of the stereotypical blacks of minstrelsy; the SPS had little to do with the role-playing and release that whites found in both performing and watching blackface minstrelsy. Their performances never left any doubt that they were whites, blue-blooded whites at that, who possessed an inherited grasp of black folkways. The rhetoric of noblesse oblige suffused their activities. The charitable work of the society, which was an extension of its profoundly nostalgic mission of cultural preservation, targeted elderly blacks, especially former slaves, who possessed a character and manner peculiar to the "old time negro." The SPS doled out donations of food, clothing, medicine, and other necessities as though it were restoring the benevolent traditions of antebellum plantation life. The paternalism of the SPS members even extended to educating contemporary African Americans about the value of spirituals and proper techniques to perform them.

Just what blacks made of the activities of the Society for the Preservation of Spirituals, or the other touristic representations of blacks, is difficult to know. Although their hospitality, colorful traditions, and "quaint" mannerisms were all part of Charleston's distinctive charm, blacks left little evidence of their own thoughts about their role in the tourist economy. Some apparently adapted well to the influx of new visitors. Pushcart peddlers reportedly became "self-conscious for the tourist trade and have dolled up their carts with gay colors and odd legends." Newsboys and shoeshine boys honed the requisite skills needed to lighten the pockets of tourists. But tourists were warned that the flower women were sullen and that they often demanded recompense when they were photographed. Further, other blacks also chafed at the expectations of the white tourists. As noted earlier, the "insolence" displayed by some "contemporary" blacks demonstrated their refusal to accept the new roles they had been assigned.[56]

The drive to turn Charleston into a tourist destination and memory theater culminated with the Azalea Festival. The annual event was perhaps the most characteristic institution of the new era in southern tourism. Nothing better symbolized the marketing of the idea of the South, and its shift away from the climate or scenic curiosities that had attracted tourists in earlier times, than the annual festivals that arose in Charleston, Natchez, and elsewhere.[57] The Azalea Festival was a judicious mixture of boosterism and local color in a contrived tourist event intended as "a wonderful opportunity to advertise Charleston." Launched in March 1934 by Mayor Burnett Rhett Maybank, it mobilized all of the city's cultural producers and resources. Initially the festival was something of a street frolic, but by 1936 festival planners had added events that exploited local historical lore and myth and gave the occasion a highbrow tenor. Various costumed historical pageants were staged during the festival, including an antebellum lancing tournament and the reenactment of the hanging of a pirate on the city's famed Battery. The Preservation Society offered house and plantation tours to raise money for its campaigns. Exhibitions at the city's Gibbes Museum of Art and at art shows placed the work of white artists before the city's visitors. Festival organizers also made a point of incorporating their circumscribed vision of black life into the festival. A troupe of black singers, including former slaves, performed spirituals in "Plantation Echoes." "Picturesque" street vendors competed in a contest of "negro street criers." The Charleston Museum sponsored a popular demonstration of rice husking by black field hands

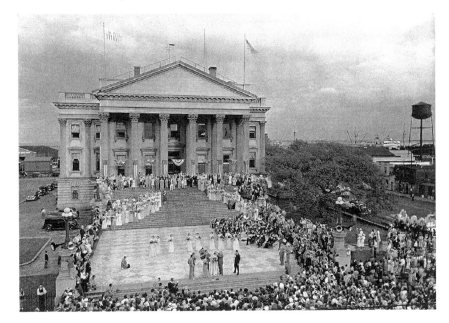

The climax of the tourist spectacle in Charleston was the Azalea Festival. Here U.S. vice president John Nance Garner presents the 1938 festival queen on the steps of the Customs Building. (National Geographic Society)

singing traditional work songs. Taken together, the musical performances, exhibitions, artwork, and tours composed the most grandiose example of white Charlestonians' efforts to fashion themselves in the image of their own myth.[58]

Few of the elements of historical tourism displayed during the Azalea Festival were complete innovations. What was new and important was the magnitude of the campaign. Nothing on the scale of the historical tourism industry in Charleston had been attempted previously in the South. And no comparable commitment of public resources to historical tourism had been made elsewhere in the region. Ambitious entrepreneurs across the South drew inspiration from Charleston when they tried to market the attractions of their communities. Most southern cities were too young or too busy with the present to go as far as Charleston did in shaping itself after the past. Nor could they recapture the authentic flavor of history as easily as Charleston, New Orleans, or Saint Augustine, which only had to dust off the past to put it on display. Thus, in some locales, such as Gatlinburg, Tennessee, tourist boosters resorted to building patently commercial southern charades during the 1930s and 1940s.[59]

The success of Charleston and the South's gamble on tourism became evident after World War II. During the 1960s the industry grew annually by more than 5 percent. Tourists accounted for almost a fifth of retail business in the city by the end of the decade. By 1970 more than one million tourists a year visited Charleston and spent more than $25 million. As the tourism industry grew region-wide, the city became more financially dependent on it. In 1961 alone, more than 50 million tourists visited Virginia, Florida, and the Carolinas and spent $2.5 billion. Tourism, by then, was the second or third largest employer and generator of wealth in the South.[60]

The advent of tourism on such a scale literally transformed public space in Charleston and many other southern locales. The tourist market, with its proliferation of shrines to white heroes and accomplishments, complemented and extended the white hegemony over public space. In Charleston, the adaptation of the city to tourism went hand in hand with zoning laws and de facto racial segregation. The cityscape was both reconfigured and restored to suit the tastes of local white elites and tourists. Henceforth, the preservation of Charleston's historic cityscape would be an enduring theme in civic affairs. The simultaneous mapping of history on the city's landscape, ranging from historical plaques to sophisticated guidebooks filled with recommended itineraries, sage advice, and précis of the prescribed emotions that tourists should anticipate at various attractions, became a model for other southern communities eager to exploit their heritages.

Charleston's tourism boom during the first half of the twentieth century mirrored the evolution of heritage tourism elsewhere. White Charlestonians, like elites across the region, were eager to create a useable past. But they had in mind uses quite distinct from those of earlier historical activists. As early as the 1930s, the tourist brochures, advertisements, and souvenirs that invoked the low country and southern past, in a real sense, commodified it. The Azalea Festival presaged the future; it retained some of the solemn ritual that had been conspicuous in previous historical representations, but it also incorporated robust doses of local boosterism and spectacle intended to promote and entertain at least as much as to edify. This mix of nostalgia, revelry, and boosterism was an essential element of the emerging tourist industry in the South in general. Since the 1920s the promotion of low-country culture and consumerism have been inextricably linked. By reducing the region's history to a romantic essence, and by remembering only those events that complemented that romantic character, Charleston's marketeers rendered the low country an ideal tourist destination.

Charlestonians adeptly responded to and exploited the modern craving for authenticity. The emphasis on historical authenticity could be traced back to the late nineteenth century, when genealogists, antiquarians, and newly trained professional historians had all insisted on the inherent superiority of the verifiably authentic. But after the turn of the century, interest in the authentic took on both a new intensity and a different quality. The pursuit of the authentic became bound up with the contemporary preoccupation to escape the banality of modernity. This impulse manifested itself in all manner of leisure activities that offered "temporary escapes to a realm of intense experience." Growing numbers of Americans found that by touring "quaint and picturesque" old towns and by collecting remnants of the past, they could transcend the tedium of everyday life. For them, the presence of aged objects offered intense gratification by awakening the imagination with memories of earlier, more heroic ages. So too were the senses excited by the beauty of hand craftsmanship and colonial aesthetics. Tourists, whether engaged in fleeing the perceived meaninglessness of modern life or, more often, merely seeking a brief respite from it, fused the pursuit of the authentic with the idea of history as a commodity. Charleston's wealth of old buildings, historic landscapes, antique furnishings, and exotic folkways made the city alluring to tourists in search of the picturesque. Charleston's decades as an economic and cultural backwater, ironically, facilitated the modern commercialization of place by making the city, according to writer Owen Wister, "the most appealing, the most lovely, the most wistful town in America. Its visible sadness and distinction seem almost to speak audibly."[61]

The allure of Charleston and the low country reflected a rejection of mass culture. Because the region was especially distant from the main currents of popular culture, resources for unique and authentic culture were plentiful there. Always implicit, and frequently explicit, in paeans to the evident superiority of the city's aesthetic was an unapologetic elitism. By embracing regional distinctiveness, Charleston's boosters proclaimed their independence from the aesthetic offenses of popular culture. Mass culture merited suspicion precisely because it was "mass," common, ubiquitous.

The city's white elite retained a vital interest in the image of the city; indeed, the rise of tourism intensified their interest. They were eager to emphasize qualities that most appealed to tourists. Charleston's economic and political decline after the Civil War had left these privileged whites sensitive to their diminished influence within the state and the nation. Tourism offered new sources of wealth and prestige. By nurturing images of a genteel and benevolent white heritage and invoking a vision of the Old

South, tourism offered a way for white Charlestonians to confirm the significance of their heritage, vaunt their fidelity to tradition, and venerate their bloodlines. White Charlestonians did not market their city so as to justify their previous power, to extend their influence, or to defend their racial privilege. But the advent of tourism in Charleston accomplished all of these ends by providing elite Charlestonians with a lucrative field in which to present their version of the past and thereby to renew their cultural power.

Despite the hostility to mass culture and modern tastes that permeated the promotion of Charleston, the city's historical tourism was, in fact, a form of mass leisure. All of the technological and marketing innovations of the age were enlisted to create and advertise Charleston's image. In this manner, the image of Charleston as an icon of a vanished southern civilization reached audiences and transfixed visitors who had never witnessed a Confederate veterans' reunion or visited a southern museum. An astute travel writer pointed out that a visit to Charleston exerted a grip on the visitor's imagination that nothing else could approximate. "The world has read of the glamorous life of the old southern plantation til it is more than weary of the subject," she observed. Yet one had only to visit the low country "to feel that he, himself, has just made fresh discovery of the subtle, inexpressible charm that cannot be captured in cold printers' ink, but must be breathed, a charm bred of the wistful leisure that still exists . . . where one's hosts entertain with the wit and grace of his cavalier ancestors."[62] Few words could have been more gratifying to the white Charlestonians who contributed to turning Charleston into one of the South's preeminent tourist destinations.

Whether black Charlestonians were equally gratified by the success of heritage tourism in the low country is difficult to discern. The representations of blacks in low-country tourist literature and attractions discouraged any appreciation of the complexity of either black culture or ambitions. Although contemporaneous with the Harlem Renaissance, the Charleston "Renaissance" provided no stage for the proud, independent, ambitious "New Negro." By encouraging the fantasy that the Old South persisted, even if only tenuously, in the South Carolina low country, historical tourism contributed powerfully to the perpetuation of crippling images of black abilities and sensibilities. Blacks with specialized trades that appealed to tourists, such as flower women and basket weavers, profited from new customers. But otherwise tourism offered African Americans the same menial jobs they had long performed in the South. And while white tourists splurged on etchings that objectified low-country blacks, they ignored more humane renderings by African Americans. Black spirituals performed by white aristocrats left white audiences elated, but performances of contemporary black music were appealing only to the degree that they confirmed stereotypes of black exoticism.

Although it is hardly surprising that white tourists and southerners opted for a romantic past that actively ignored ongoing racial oppression, their preference had enduring consequences for the public culture of the South. Perhaps the most extraordinary aspect of Charleston's transformation into a memory theater of the Old South is that it seemed so natural, so appropriate, and so inevitable that it aroused little dissent. But Charleston's evolution, along with that of Natchez, Williamsburg, New Orleans, and other southern communities favored by tourists, was the culmination of the steady advance of white southerners' control over prominent public spaces. Beginning during the late nineteenth century with cemetery monuments to Confederate dead, and continuing as courthouse squares were claimed for white memorials and as state-funded archives and museums were situated beside state capitols, whites dominated the historic landscape. The next step was the transformation of neighborhoods and even cities into shrines of white memory. Henceforth, white cultural and political ambitions—to create public spaces that at once demonstrated and justified their power—were advanced by powerful market forces. The local taxi driver who aspired to provide guide services, the dry-goods merchant who craved a piece of the antique trade, and the black flower peddler keen to sell bouquets to tourists all had an incentive to foster the South's "romantic" ambiance. As long as Old South gentility alone was what the South offered and what tourists wanted, the region's tourist landscape would continue to extend and perpetuate white history and power.[63]

∽ 6

Black Memorials and the Bulldozer Revolution

At 8:30 in the morning, July 18, 1963, a work crew began demolishing the "Old Boys' Club" in the Hayti neighborhood of Durham, North Carolina. An observer versed in architecture might have noted that the wood frame clubhouse, with its triple-A roof line and turned porch pylons graced with decorative spandrels, exemplified architectural styles favored by local black elites during the late nineteenth century. Although now dilapidated, the rambling structure had been home to a succession of prominent inhabitants. Its first owner was John Wright, a barber and leading businessman. Later Rev. A. Kirkland, a noted minister, and Dr. James Edward Shepard, the founder and longtime president of North Carolina College, lived there. Eventually the building housed the Harriet Tubman branch of the YWCA before becoming the quarters for the John Avery Boys' Club. One witness to the building's demolition mused, "A lot of people goin' miss that old place; they carried on a whole lot of things in there."

Within days, workmen had reduced the building to piles of old bricks, splintered boards, and crumpled tin, "all with a few tears covering them."[1] Urban renewal had erased the first of many landmarks in Hayti. Within a decade, the bulldozer revolution that had claimed the clubhouse would pull down hundreds of homes, businesses, and churches in Durham.

The razing of Hayti was part of a nationwide clearing of black neighborhoods. Between 1957 and 1968, federally funded renewal projects destroyed more than 300,000 housing units as highway builders and downtown redevelopers joined in a national frenzy of urban clearance, in the name of eliminating "blighted areas." Part of Jackson Ward, a neighborhood in Richmond that had been the home of celebrated black leaders John Mitchell and Maggie Walker, was cleared for an interstate, and another black neighborhood was leveled to accommodate a city jail and an industrial park. In Chattanooga, urban renewal dislocated the black neighborhood of West Side, eventually quarantining its remnants between multilane highways and the Tennessee River. In Nashville, an interstate plowed directly through the center of the city's historic black business district. In Miami, highway planners gutted the neighborhood of Overtown to make space for parking lots and an interstate cloverleaf.[2]

These and other mid-twentieth-century "civic improvements" may appear far removed from issues of collective memory. But places provided the "raw material" for the collective memory of blacks no less than for whites. Southerners' sense of place and identity was bound up in their memories of and historical associations with distinct locations in their past. Physical settings became sites of memory that elicited enduring and intense recollections of emotion and experience. When the demolition crew began splintering the boards of the Boys' Club in Hayti, they set about erasing a black neighborhood, along with its landmarks of black his-

The John Avery Boys' Club, photographed here ca. 1940, was one of the first buildings destroyed during the urban renewal of Hayti. (Durham Public Library)

tory, leaving in its place a landscape unlikely to sustain a viable civic culture. The leveling of Hayti and other black neighborhoods accentuated the differences between the landscapes inherited by southern African Americans and those handed down to whites.

By necessity blacks anchored their memory in spaces that served multiple purposes. The campuses of historically black colleges were the rare sites in the South that blacks could encumber with overt commemorative significance. Otherwise, it was on the street corners and front porches in black neighborhoods that blacks nurtured their sense of community and were in the presence of their shared history. Black "memoryscapes" came to include churches, schools, businesses, private residences, and natural landscapes. As Ralph Ellison observed, "a whole unrecorded history" was spoken in the gin mills, barber shops, juke joints, churches, and beauty parlors of black neighborhoods.[3]

Southern whites demonstrated an equally strong appreciation of the interrelationship of shared place and collective memory. For three-quarters of a century they erected monuments, restored buildings, located highway markers, and opened museums so as to create public spaces that assuaged their anxieties and reaffirmed their aspirations. Burgeoning historic preservation campaigns garnered support from whites precisely because they saw them as a way to strengthen the bonds of community in their cherished but vulnerable neighborhoods.

But blacks in the South, unlike whites, could not control how market forces and government policy reshaped their communities. Instead they watched with mounting alarm as whites simultaneously launched ambitious preservation campaigns in white neighborhoods and unleashed the urban renewal juggernaut in black neighborhoods. Just when the civil rights movement seemed poised to secure for blacks full and equal access to the public spaces of the South, white power, manifest in urban renewal, threatened to radically degrade the traditionally black spaces that had sustained black community life.

Moreover, urban renewal demonstrated white resolve to extend white control over urban spaces that whites previously had ceded to black control. Blinded by both hubris and racism, whites ignored the wholeness of black community life in targeted areas and instead saw only degraded environments that impeded their ambitions for their cities. Whites took for granted that they had both the right and the wisdom to dictate how all public space, whether traditionally used by whites or others, should be arranged and used. It was this persisting inequality of power that would exile blacks in Hayti and countless other communities from familiar landscapes and treasured sites of memory.

Local circumstances, of course, dictated when and where the wrecking ball of urban renewal swung. But the examples of Durham and Savannah are illustrative. Few black communities in the South were more renowned for their wealth, power, and culture than Durham's, and few had more that was worth preserving than Hayti. As Durham's principal black business and residential area, the neighborhood boasted landmarks associated with business, education, and community organizations. In addition, the black communities in Durham and Savannah stood a better chance of directing urban renewal to their benefit than perhaps any others in the South. Politically mobilized and influential even before the passage of civil rights legislation during the 1960s, Hayti's and Savannah's black residents were by no means powerless. Thus, the stories of Durham and Savannah demonstrate the tragic consequences of urban "renewal" in even what were arguably the most promising of circumstances.

The history of Hayti stretches back to the founding of Durham. Chartered as a small railroad town in 1869, Durham grew to be a noted center of the tobacco industry. From its ragtag origins, the city expanded steadily and by 1910 the "Chicago of the South" boasted nearly twenty thousand residents. By then, blacks who had escaped the hardships of rural life by finding employment in Durham's booming tobacco factories made up about a third of the city's residents. Hayti was the largest of the city's several black neighborhoods. First mentioned in an 1877 deed as a "settlement of colored people," it was located "on the other side of the tracks" in the shadows of tobacco factories southeast of downtown. Just what Hayti's founders intended by its name is unclear, but Haiti's hard-earned independence as a black republic undoubtedly inspired many recently emancipated freed people across the South, including those who had staked their futures in Durham. By century's end, the neighborhood boasted imposing landmarks, such as Saint Joseph's AME and White Rock Baptist churches. Although Hayti remained outside the town limits (and beyond the reach of municipal taxes) throughout the late nineteenth century, it warranted inclusion on Durham maps. Eventually, in 1920, city boundaries incorporated the entire neighborhood.[4]

Well before that year, Hayti had earned Durham a reputation as a "Mecca of Black Capitalism." Booker T. Washington, W. E. B. Du Bois, and other visitors hailed Hayti as an example of black accomplishment. Writing in 1912, Du Bois marveled that the city possessed "a group of five thousand or more colored people, whose social and economic development is perhaps more striking than that of any similar group in the nation." He noted that "quite a number of the colored people have built themselves pretty and well equipped homes . . . and that they are rebuilding their churches on a scale almost luxurious." A decade later, sociologist E. Franklin Frazier agreed, describing black Durham as "a city of fine homes, exquisite churches, and middle class respectability." The *Richmond Planet,* at once envious and proud of its southern neighbor, urged readers, "Go to Durham and see the industrious Negro at his best." Tax rolls confirmed these impressions. At the turn of the twentieth century, blacks owned most of the businesses, land, and homes in southeastern Durham. Although these homes typically were modest, one-story frame buildings, many were attractive, comfortable homes renowned for their tasteful adornments of decorative plants, woven honeysuckle vines, paint, and glasswork.[5]

Hayti's vaunted affluence and gentility rested on the entrepreneurial prowess of its black elite. The most celebrated and important black business in Durham was North Carolina Mutual, then (and now) one of the largest black-owned financial institu-

Another symbol of Hayti's storied history was the John Merrick House, built by one of Durham's leading black businessmen, ca. 1910. (Durham Public Library)

tions in the United States. In 1898 John Merrick, a successful barber, enlisted several local black investors and founded the company. He and his partners then reinvested their profits in various enterprises in Hayti and elsewhere in Durham, nurturing businesses that offered an alternative to factory work. James Edward Shepard, another important figure in the black community, catered to the aspirations of Hayti's black middle class by opening his National Religious Training School in 1910. For the next thirteen years, he struggled to keep the school afloat until the state assumed responsibility and renamed it North Carolina College for Negroes. Charged with providing a liberal arts education to the state's African American undergraduates, the school was both a symbol of black Durham's ambitions and an important source of employment.[6]

Other cities may have had comparably affluent black communities, but few had black residents as politically mobilized as Hayti's. Durham's black elite initially relied on their relations with the city's white leaders to influence civic affairs. But by the 1920s those relations, often rooted in slavery or family ties, had withered and younger blacks were chafing at their comparative powerlessness. First through the Colored Voters League, founded in 1922, and then through the Durham Committee on Negro Affairs (DCNA), launched in 1935, they organized one of the most effective black political organizations in the Jim Crow South. Because Durham was home to North Carolina Mutual and other black-owned businesses, as well as black-run North Carolina College, many blacks were shielded from economic reprisals and other tactics that whites employed elsewhere to suppress black activism. In addition, Durham blacks marshaled sufficient resources and organizational fortitude to overcome traditional obstacles to registration and voting. With the DCNA energizing the community, nearly 70 percent of Durham's eligible blacks—more than three thousand—had registered by the late 1930s. The DCNA even began fielding black candidates for city and county offices, successfully electing a black city councilor in 1953.[7]

By World War II, Hayti had a national reputation as a bustling neighborhood with active black commerce, political activism, higher education, and entertainment. Separated from Durham's downtown by unsightly coal yards and railroad tracks, Hayti's residents met most of their needs along the main thoroughfares of their neighborhood. There black florists, pharmacists, auto mechanics, barbers, dry cleaners, grocers, tailors, restaurateurs, hoteliers, morticians, and other businesses catered to them. One Hayti resident remembered, "We never had to go into downtown Durham . . . because we had everything we needed right there in Hayti."[8]

The neighborhood's notorious nightlife, located in a district evocatively named "Mexico," lured customers from as far away as Virginia. The atmosphere surrounding the saloons, billiard rooms, restaurants, cinemas, and vaudeville houses of Hayti resembled that of larger and better-known districts like Decatur Street in Atlanta and Beale Street in Memphis. Reginald Mitchiner, a Durham native, recalled locals and transients streaming into "Mexico" on weekends because "they ain't living if they don't come to Hayti." While upscale homegrown and national talent performed at Hayti's two black-owned theaters and stayed at the Biltmore Hotel (purportedly the finest black hotel between Richmond and Atlanta), harder-edged Piedmont blues musicians played in bars and barbershops. The area became so popular that Pettigrew Street came to be the favored destination for thousands of off-duty servicemen from nearby military camps during World War II. "The place was jumping," Mitchiner remembered. "It turned into a Vegas strip almost."9

Yet Hayti also displayed the unmistakable scars of racial segregation and discrimination. Although blacks in Durham bragged that they owned more homes per capita than anywhere else in the United States, a 1916 survey disclosed that four out of five of the city's blacks lived in unsanitary, substandard, overcrowded rental housing. A quarter-century after the first housing survey, conditions had not improved. Eighty percent of Durham's African Americans still occupied substandard housing. Despite the availability of generous federal loans to finance slum clearance and public housing during the New Deal, Durham's urban blight remained unaddressed. In 1939 white landlords discouraged a local committee from applying for any federal funds, prompting a local newspaper to fume that city council members and county commissioners, who were "heavily invested in 'shanty property,'" opposed slum clearance because it "might seriously destroy or curtail their earnings." Hayti's business elite and voluntary organizations, consequently, had to cajole white officials for each improvement, however modest, in city services.[10]

Not until local white elites awakened to Durham's apparent decline following World War II did Hayti become the focus of white concern. City leaders concluded that Durham's fortune was waning: industrial employment had fallen, wages were sagging, and the downtown was suffering from haphazard streets and deteriorating buildings. Although these problems had festered for years, their cumulative effects had been obscured by boomtown conditions during the war. By the mid-1950s Durham clearly had fallen from its perch as one of North Carolina's leading cities. Officials wrung their hands over the "exodus" of taxpaying businesses from the downtown and acknowledged an urgent need to "keep up property values" there. With Nashville's redevelopment plans promising an 800 percent increase in property taxes from renewed neighborhoods, Durham's white leaders concluded that only a comparable campaign could reverse their city's decline.[11]

Fundamental to the vision of a renewed Durham was overdue adaptation to the automobile. The inadequacy of the city's roadways could no longer be ignored after federal highway planners placed an interstate highway immediately north of the city's boundaries. The need for a freeway to bisect Durham and reduce traffic congestion became urgent. With the federal highway program offering local governments up to 90 percent of construction costs for inner-city beltways, Durham could now afford to modernize its antiquated roadways. Downtown business and shopping interests, who worried about the threat posed by suburban shopping centers, were especially keen to tap federal funds to make their district easily accessible to motorists.[12]

The revitalization of the city's economy was the main consideration for the advocates of freeway construction and urban renewal. Any other outcomes, such as slum clearance and social reconstruction, were welcome, but secondary, benefits. Even so, the startling juxtaposition of Hayti's "blight, obsolescence, dilapidation, and deterioration" bordering on the downtown's office buildings and department stores distressed advocates of downtown revitalization. When the city launched the Durham Redevelopment Commission in 1958, Hayti emerged as a focus of its concern. Before funding sources had even been identified, the commission's director enlisted the University of North Carolina's Department of City and Regional Planning to recommend a renewal strategy. The resulting study proposed that two hundred blighted acres of Hayti "be made an attractively clean and modern residential section." The main objective, however, remained improving the city's tax base and making room for the planned expressway.[13]

The vision that planners and city leaders had for Durham belied their reputation for conservatism. When completed, the redesigned streets, new construction, and downtown improvements would, for the first time, weave together the city's neighborhoods, including Hayti. By locating the planned freeway along the southern edge of the downtown and the railroad right-of-way that formed the northern boundary of Hayti, they sought to break down the isolation they believed had led to neighborhood blight. New commercial development would replace the grim industrial landscape that separated Hayti from the city center, and improved streets would facilitate the flow of traffic between the neighborhood and the downtown.[14]

The ambitious urban renewal campaign gathered momentum when Durham's leaders seized the opportunity to exploit federal funds. While highway funds would cover the costs of slum clearance to make way for the expressway, urban renewal funds could be used to redevelop the cleared area. The longstand-

ing opposition of Durham landlords to urban renewal melted after revisions in federal policies allowed land cleared with federal
funds to be developed privately. Conveniently, the city's investment in the downtown would count toward its financial contributions to the larger renewal project. The city, in short, could get
downtown redevelopment and an expressway, with slum clearance thrown in, as well as generous opportunities for private
profit, for only a modest outlay of local funds.[15]

Wherever urban renewal found a place on the civic agenda,
similar ambitions and rationales were evident. Whether in Houston or Durham, city planners were concerned with abstract principles of urban efficiency; elected officials focused on taxes and infrastructure. Accordingly, the conventional measures of the health
of urban neighborhoods were their assessed property values and
quality of infrastructure. Obsolete and decrepit buildings, stagnant property values, and conditions that menaced public health
and morality—these were the telltale signs of blighted neighborhoods.[16]

Because only extreme, intractable blight could warrant wholesale destruction on the scale of "slum clearance," Durham planners, officials, and newspaper editorialists seemed compelled to
depict Hayti as a "slum" that jeopardized the entire city's progress. Employing graphic language usually associated with conta-
gious diseases, they warned of Hayti's potential to contaminate
Durham. Editorials in the white newspapers predicted that
Hayti's "devaluing effect" would "spread" to adjoining areas unless immediate steps were taken. Urban renewal became an extension, albeit on a dramatic scale, of much older public health
campaigns to cleanse American cities of filthy streets, homes,
and lots, which purportedly bore witness to their occupants' lack
of self-discipline, self-respect, and good character. According to
planners, Hayti harbored a tangle of pathologies: it was a

"blighted eyesore," an "economic and esthetic drag" on the city, and a detriment to "public health, safety, morals, and welfare." As evidence of the "unsanitary and unsafe conditions" that prevailed there, officials emphasized that although only 11 percent of the city's population lived in the neighborhood, 20 percent of tuberculosis cases, 23 percent of infant mortality, 15 percent of major crimes, 20 percent of juvenile delinquency, 41 percent of venereal disease, and 20 percent of illegitimate births could be traced to it. These data actually demonstrated the comparative well-being of Hayti; the crime rate was lower and public-health indicators better than might have been expected for a segregated community in the urban South. Indeed, Hayti's problem was overcrowded and inferior housing, not a pervasive, crippling ghetto culture. Yet the language of urban renewal, reflecting both longstanding racist assumptions about dysfunctional black communities and the pragmatic politics of mobilizing support for a major public commitment, inevitably became characterized by inflated, vivid imagery, all of which hastened the razing of Hayti.[17]

Given these dire descriptions of Hayti, advocates of urban renewal never entertained any notions of neighborhood conservation or historic preservation in the district. The eventual disfigurement of Hayti during the 1960s was possible precisely because there was no competing vision of historic preservation. In this regard, Durham's white officials were typical of their peers across the nation. The evolution of historic preservation in the United States after World War II demonstrated the continuing power of expansive property rights. Lacking robust national historic preservation bodies or strict regulations over privately owned historic structures and spaces, U.S. preservationists relied on ad hoc methods. Variations in the relative power and competing aims of developers, preservationists, and local officials gave historic preservation in the United States a special randomness and complexity.

Here and there, preservation campaigns challenged private property rights or secured the adoption of new authority to regulate the use of privately owned historic buildings; neighborhood zoning ordinances, for example, protected the architecture of "old" Charleston, the French Quarter of New Orleans, and Savannah's historic downtown. But despite such precedents, no one in Durham during the late 1950s and early 1960s suggested that Hayti's streetscapes merited preservation. The vernacular architectural forms that were commonplace in Hayti—narrow one- and two-story shotgun homes with simple gable roofs and modest front porches—were inconceivable candidates for preservation, at least as historic preservation was then commonly understood. Neither were the impressive mansions and historic commercial buildings that lined the major thoroughfares of the neighborhood.[18]

By any measure, the scale of plans for Hayti was ambitious, especially for a city that had never undertaken any previous redevelopment project. Within the first seventy-acre redevelopment zone, 459 of 463 buildings were declared "structurally substandard" and slated for clearance. More than six hundred families and one hundred businesses were to be relocated. Despite the magnitude of the undertaking, editorialists and planners anticipated no unwelcome consequences. "In the long run," the *Durham Herald* explained, "there can be no losses in a program that restores the social and economic values of a deteriorating neighborhood." These predictions seemed borne out during the initial phases of relocating Hayti's residents. White newspapers published glowing accounts of black families who were moved to superior housing; one paper quoted an elderly woman who claimed to have suffered stomach pains when urban renewal was first mentioned but who now pronounced it a "godsend."[19]

Despite the scale of the project, Hayti's redevelopment aroused little initial opposition from neighborhood residents. True, experience had taught southern blacks to view both federal and local housing policies with suspicion. Subsidized housing programs, which invariably discriminated against black tenants and home-owners, had perpetuated and even intensified residential segregation throughout the nation. But because urban renewal in Hayti did not revolve around the issue of residential integration, blacks in the neighborhood were more trusting of white intentions. The presumption of planners and residents alike was that the "renewed" Hayti would remain African American. Whites in Durham never expressed any intention of relocating the city's black neighborhoods or of using urban renewal as a pretext to open Durham's traditionally white neighborhoods to blacks. If nothing in these ambitious plans threatened to erode residential segregation, neither did they envision the destruction of Hayti.[20]

Opposition was also muted because urban renewal funds held out the promise of addressing some of Hayti's longstanding problems. Gullied, unpaved streets would give way to modern, well-lit thoroughfares; dilapidated structures, which accounted for "some of the nation's most squalid housing," would be replaced by modern, upgraded homes. Landowners in the area stood to gain whether they sold out to the urban renewal commission or held onto their property until the neighborhood reblossomed. Hayti's commercial district would also be improved, thereby enhancing the ability of black businesses to compete with the city's proliferating shopping centers.[21]

The participation of blacks on crucial city committees also assuaged concerns about renewal in Hayti. Although most Hayti residents had little opportunity to participate in the planning process, John S. Stewart, president of the Mutual Savings and Loan Association, served on the city council throughout urban renewal. Simultaneously, John Wheeler, president of Mechanics and Farmers Bank and former chair of the DCNA, served on the five-member Redevelopment Commission. With Stewart and Wheeler representing the interests of Hayti and with apparently straightforward goals for redevelopment, few blacks anticipated the neighborhood's future.[22]

Had residents of the neighborhood wanted to stymie the project, they had an early opportunity to do so in 1962. In order to raise the local funds required to receive the crucial federal subsidy, the mayor and city council proposed an $8.2 million bond issue, one of the largest in the city's history. An ensuing referendum on the bond issue sharply divided the white community, with die-hard segregationsts opposing urban renewal as a waste of money and an example of dangerous governmental activism, and white professionals and liberals endorsing it as essential to Durham's modernization. When the referendum votes were tallied, it became clear that blacks in Hayti had provided the crucial votes that passed the bond issue. The *Carolina Times,* the city's black weekly, grumbled that the referendum vote demonstrated that a significant proportion of Durham whites "will not respond favorably to any movement that means the betterment of the Negro's lot." At the same time, the referendum exposed the political muscle of Durham's black community and its overwhelming support for improving Hayti.[23]

Some victims of Hayti's clearance later complained that urban renewal had been forced on them. A quarter-century after the destruction of the neighborhood began, one former resident seethed, "When they [whites] voted to put the highway through Hayti . . . blacks in Durham were helpless." Others complained that Durham's black elite had failed to defend their community's interests and had "sold the black masses down the drain" when they supported urban renewal. According to neighborhood lore, well-heeled black property owners had been eager to sell their holdings to the redevelopment agency and, after doing so, took no interest in subsequent redevelopment. Elite black families, including the Merricks, Stewarts, Spauldings, and Wheelers, had been prominent landlords in the neighborhood and did sell land to the Redevelopment Commission. In addition, North Carolina Mutual, Mechanics and Farmers Bank, and Mutual Savings and Loan heavily invested in property in Hayti. Urban renewal offered an opportunity for these families and firms to unload, at a profit, property that otherwise held only modest promise. But Durham's segregation-era black elites were neither so callous norso prescient that they could have anticipated the outcome in Hayti. Their error was to assume that the traditional forms of politics that had developed during the Jim Crow era would secure Hayti the benefits of urban renewal.[24]

Political traditions honored by both white and black elites in Durham precluded blacks from controlling the pace and extent of urban renewal in Hayti during the 1960s. Instead, during the crucial period of urban renewal, the mayor and white members of the city council systematically pursued a politics of cautious, controlled change. Durham's redevelopment, like renewal programs throughout the country, was an attempt to reconcile market forces, private initiative, and the use of public funds to arrest the decline of a troubled urban district. In simple terms, the role of public authorities and federal agencies was to facilitate private interests. In Durham, advocates of redevelopment included the twelve voting members of the city council, six of whom were directly involved in real estate. The city council members, predictably, were virtual lobbyists for urban renewal. But their advocacy never included any vision of social reform. Instead, with their commercial and political fates tied to Durham's downtown, the city's elected leaders saw renewal as an acceptable compromise that did not threaten private interests with any unwelcome social agenda. Unlike public housing, which was seen as a challenge to the private market, urban renewal was supported by developers who saw profit opportunities through public-private partnerships. Given this orientation, it was predictable that comprehensive "social rehabilitation" as part of the nation's "war on poverty" was never incorporated into Durham's urban renewal campaign. In this regard, Durham was typical of cities throughout North Carolina and the nation. From its inception, urban reconstruction in Durham was narrowly conceived by white leaders eager to keep power within the hands of a small number of private and public interests.[25]

The tenor of public life in the South contributed to the caution of Durham's elected white officials. Keenly aware of the strength of segregationists within the white community, Mayor R. Wensell "Wense" Grabarek scrupulously avoided open discussion of the explosive issues that confronted the city. He owed his election to black voters, to whom he was more responsive than had been his predecessors. But the mayor, an accountant by profession, displayed more caution than vision. Intent on maintaining firm control of his city and ensuring that all public debates took place within traditional forums (where he could control or at least moderate them), the mayor and his allies accepted that gradual change was inevitable, but they recoiled from confrontation with or concessions to grassroots activism.[26]

This traditional approach to debate over public policy encouraged black elites, a "benevolent oligarchy," to speak for the black community before white councils. Durham's black elites had long boasted that an extraordinary "harmony between the races" characterized the "spirit of Durham." Yet only a small number of elite blacks could vouch for this harmonious spirit. In the eyes of many, Durham's established black leaders exerted undue influence over the "indigenous leadership of the poor." The DCNA in particular came under periodic criticism from Louis E.

Austin, feisty editor of the *Carolina Times,* and others for "becoming too high-brow, too soft and too compromising" and for its tendency "to repulse rather than attract wider community participation." White leaders made no such complaint; they were accustomed to dealing with the DCNA and the black Business Chain, groups that worked within the "golden mean of permissible black power." These groups enjoyed the privilege and prestige associated with their role as intermediaries between the white elite and Hayti. From the outset, the DCNA and the Business Chain championed the benefits of renewal and tirelessly promoted it in Hayti. Thus, the city's tradition of orderly procedures and circumscribed biracial politics actually impeded Hayti's residents from influencing the day-to-day unfolding of urban renewal. By the time grassroots activism had matured in the city, bulldozers had already ploughed through much of Hayti.[27]

Over time, optimism about urban renewal in Hayti gave way to impatience, then skepticism and disappointment, and eventually anger. The slow progress of the renewal plan was the first indication that the project would not unfold as predicted. Ben Perry, director of the redevelopment commission, acknowledged in late 1962, "We expect that there will be chaos for a while." Federal agencies failed to release funds for the project until April 1963, five years after the first discussion of the project and two years after the launching of the redevelopment commission. By the spring of 1964, redevelopment officials acknowledged that land acquisition in Hayti had "slowed to a walk" because many residents refused to sell their property at the offered prices. Forecasts that it would take two years to relocate families and to raze Hayti proved ludicrously optimistic. About 160 families were moved in the first year, but several hundred more remained in limbo, waiting for new housing. Even while families remained in condemned buildings, demolition crews used bulldozers to knock down structures in Hayti at a rate of five a day. Other buildings were set afire and used to train city firemen, giving the neighborhood the appearance of a war zone. While officials fretted about the glacial speed of the project, residents of Hayti, who had to endure their dislocation without any clear timetable, understandably grew anxious.[28]

Redevelopment authorities tried to stay ahead of the demolition crews by relocating residents. At least in its initial phases, the relocation office, run by Mrs. Charlie Swift, eased some of the hardships of the displaced. In theory, residents were to be moved into a transitional area until they could return to their former community. Swift, trained as a social and public health worker, created a web of church groups, local voluntary organizations, and public agencies to address the effects of urban renewal. This solicitude for the social consequences of the enterprise garnered national recognition, but as the renewal project advanced, the needs of Hayti's relocated families overwhelmed the relocation office. Whatever empathy the relocation specialists displayed was offset by the growing impatience of the redevelopment commission. Irked by the reluctance of some Hayti residents to move, the director of the renewal project grumbled, "They've got to move to make way for the expressway. When people are offered decent, safe, sanitary housing . . . they're just going to have to take it."[29]

Urban renewal compounded the housing woes in Hayti. In theory, the private market and public housing would absorb displaced residents. But realistically, the private market offered no solutions because established residential racial boundaries held firm throughout the 1960s, confining blacks to the same neighborhoods they had occupied since the beginning of the century. Urban renewal increased congestion in already overpopulated southeast Durham by forcing families into neighborhoods that were already under stress. To add insult to injury, relocated families endured higher rents while low-income residents dependent on public assistance remained trapped in the gutted renewal zone. Conditions there rapidly worsened as landlords withheld maintenance on buildings that would eventually be bought by the redevelopment commission. As the president of the Durham Board of Realtors explained in 1966, "We've been told not to make repairs . . . since 1958." Relations between redevelopment authorities and residents deteriorated steadily, and by 1966 forced evictions were necessary to empty the last homes in the urban renewal zone. Moreover, Hayti residents bitterly resented the fact that only blacks were subject to forced relocations.[30]

The speed of "slum clearance" and the absence of new residential construction fueled mounting criticism of urban renewal. William O'Neal, an early and persistent opponent, fumed, "As of now, urban renewal seems to mean Negro removal and Negro re-location, with the crowding of the low income Negroes into buildings similar to the cleared area." Must the dislocated, he asked, "become lost beings in other areas of Durham . . . more slum-like or blighted than the area from which they moved?" Louis Austin of the *Carolina Times* reached a similar conclusion, labeling urban renewal a "farce." The speed with which some of the "best dwellings" in Hayti had been torn down contrasted sharply with the lethargy in replacing them with the promised housing and shopping district. Some of the demolished buildings were not only "far better than many Negroes had ever lived in" but also were superior to the nonexistent housing provided by urban renewal.[31]

Contrary to common sense, the destruction of residential structures in Hayti began before Durham public housing had space for any of the dislocated families. Public housing was already crammed to capacity, with a waiting list of more than two thousand. The clearing of Hayti and the construction of the freeway exacerbated the crisis by displacing another 1,600 families. Even had all of the public housing under construction during the decade been completed in a timely fashion, more than a thousand families still would have lacked low-cost housing. Displaced Hayti residents, moreover, had no cause to be sanguine about the compassion of the Durham Housing Authority. Families concluded that the redevelopment commission was "kicking them out of their homes" while the city's director of public housing was "keeping them out of public housing." Blacks who lived in public housing complained bitterly about their treatment at the hands of the housing authority, especially its director, Carvie Oldham. Oldham treated black residents with open disrespect and even connived with the local Ku Klux Klan to intimidate tenants. In 1964, the National Urban League censured the authority for its discriminatory practices, and branded it one of the worst in the nation. The housing office and the commission that oversaw it blithely ignored black opinion when locating badly needed and long-delayed public housing projects. By 1968, housing authority policies had so eroded any lingering trust and optimism in Hayti that violent confrontations erupted between public housing protesters and police.[32]

Renewal and the ensuing dislocation proved equally jarring to Hayti's businessmen. Initially, Durham planners displayed uncommon concern for Hayti's businesses. In other North Carolina cities, officials made no systematic effort to address the needs of dislocated businesses. But in Hayti, after surveying affected businesses, redevelopment planners designed a thirteen-acre shopping district to house some dislocated establishments. An earlier study, however, anticipated with disconcerting accuracy the effects of urban renewal on neighborhood businesses. Relocated firms bore unanticipated and uncompensated costs during relocation and, most important, often had difficulty regaining their old

By the late 1960s, when these marchers protested against public housing and urban renewal, Hayti had been reduced to a landscape of highways and barren lots. (Durham Public Library)

clientele. Most of the displaced businesses were small, shoestring retail stores and service enterprises, run by the proprietor and a handful of employees. Often elderly and lacking any other means of support, Hayti's small-business owners were unlikely to qualify for commercial loans. In addition, because most were renters, they stood to gain nothing from compensation offered to property owners whose assets were taken by renewal. Indeed, even before urban renewal inflated rents throughout southeast Durham, many businesses there had struggled to meet them. Urban renewal administrators downplayed these repercussions because they assumed that many dislocated businesses were doomed to eventual failure anyway. Unusual was the planner who admitted openly that "many of the businesses probably will not survive [urban renewal]." Whether by design or not, redevelopment threatened to level Hayti's small businesses along with its slums.[33]

Subsequent decisions exacerbated the plight of Hayti's businesses. Renewal plans called for many of Hayti's businesses to be relocated to the new shopping district. But even before the demolition of Hayti began, the city planning commission approved the construction of a large shopping center just south of the renewal area. The Business Chain, representing more than 130 businesses slated for relocation, immediately cried foul, pointing to the threat that the new shopping center would pose to them. Abraham Greenberg, a leading realtor, notorious slumlord, and the investor behind the shopping center, confirmed the fears of Hayti's business owners when he observed that the redevelopment of Hayti was years off and "the people of the community want a shopping center now." After a market survey concluded that the neighborhood could not support both the proposed shopping center and a rehabilitated Hayti shopping district, Greenberg agreed to shrink his project. Grudgingly, the Business Chain withdrew its objections. When the shopping center opened a year later,

Hayti's residents turned out in droves. The success of Greenberg's shopping center, however, contrasted starkly with the failure of the proposed Hayti shopping district, which never advanced beyond architects' sketches. This key component of redevelopment received no federal funding and instead was left to private investors, who were reluctant to invest in a large enterprise whose clients would be high-risk businesses displaced by urban renewal. With the resale of land in the Hayti renewal zone held up until the summer of 1967, commercial redevelopment was also precluded until more than two years after many of the neighborhood businesses has been forced to move. When a "shopping district" finally was constructed, it was a temporary sheet metal structure, popularly known as "Tin City." The pitiful structure was at once an eyesore and an enduring reminder of the unfulfilled promise of urban renewal.[34]

For former residents the whirlwind of urban renewal took a form they had never anticipated. As it unfolded, many scrambled to salvage mementos from the wrecking ball. If many homes in Hayti appeared to be "shacks and huts," they nonetheless held "strong sentimental value" for their occupants. One family saved a carved front door that had been passed down for generations; others purchased from the redevelopment commission the shrubbery and flowers that had adorned their former homes. Such gestures, however, preserved only a small portion of Hayti's heritage.[35]

Razed to make way for the freeway and urban renewal were numerous irreplaceable landmarks. Wrecking crews leveled the Primitive Baptist Church, founded in 1906, along with several other small storefront churches. Even the historic White Rock Baptist Church was demolished. Home to one of the largest and oldest congregations in the city, the ivy-covered neo-Gothic brick church was a particular source of community pride. It displayed the craft of noted black architect W. Sidney Pittman, who designed its expansion and remodeling in 1910, and of the black contractors who completed the work. Not only was White Rock one of the most impressive turn-of-the-century buildings erected by Durham's black elite, it had been the pulpit for many of the city's most respected ministers. For more than thirty years, Miles Mark Fisher had presided over the church. With a doctorate from the University of Chicago and family ties to Chicago's black elite, Fisher garnered a national reputation as an advocate of church activism and racial uplift. Among his congregation were the "town moguls," including many of the founders and presidents of North Carolina Mutual. During the 1950s and early 1960s, White Rock, along with nearby Saint Joseph's AME Church, was a favored meeting place for civil rights activists. It was White Rock, in February 1960, that had hosted Martin Luther King Jr. when he praised the Greensboro and Durham sit-ins and embraced the technique of nonviolent direct action. A year later, the church hosted a planning meeting for a National Association for the Advancement of Colored People (NAACP) campaign to desegregate Durham's movie houses. Despite this storied history, White Rock Baptist announced in August 1966, two months before its hundredth anniversary, its pending relocation on account of the advancing expressway. After the church organ and several stained glass windows were saved, the building was leveled in the fall of 1967.[36]

Nor were landmarks of black business history spared. A casualty of renewal was an attractive three-story brick building that served as the headquarters of the Royal Knights of King David. Launched in 1883, a half-century later the fraternal society boasted a membership of nearly thirty thousand in one hundred chapters. Out of the Royal Knights had emerged black Durham's most important business enterprise, North Carolina Mutual. Also

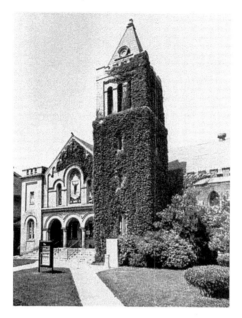

Built in the 1890s, White Rock Baptist Church (ca. 1950) was one of the most important centers of community life until it was demolished in 1967. (Durham Public Library)

demolished were the anchors of Hayti's renowned entertainment district on Pettigrew Street. Another significant building lost was the Regal Theater, which had hosted most of the big performers who had come to Hayti, including Bessie Smith, Ella Fitzgerald, Cab Calloway, Count Basie, Duke Ellington, Ethel Waters, and Fats Waller. (The Biltmore Hotel, located next door to the Regal, had accommodated traveling black artists and dignitaries. It would not be toppled until 1978, a very late victim of neglect brought about by urban renewal.) The Lincoln Café, Wonderland Theater, and other popular night spots disappeared as well. Along with these centers of genteel nightlife, the spaces that had sustained the city's famed Piedmont bluesmen were swept clean. Gone was the factory for the blind where Sonny Terry, a famed harmonica player, had worked making mattresses and chairs. So too the sidewalks and alleys, such as the evocatively named "Death Alley," where Blind Boy Fuller, Sonny Terry, Bull City Red, and Richard and Willie Trice had earned pocket change by performing for tobacco workers and night owls.[37]

Wrecking crews also demolished the homes that had sustained Hayti's reputation for bourgeois elegance. Among the monuments to black gentility that had so impressed Booker T. Washington and W. E. B. Du Bois was John Merrick's imposing three-story Queen Anne–style home, built around 1910 and graced with a wraparound porch and a polygonal tower. Also razed were large Queen Anne and colonial revival homes associated with Charles C. Spaulding, president of North Carolina Mutual; Joseph N. Mills, a leading doctor and early neighborhood political activist; Dr. Aaron McDuffie Moore, a cofounder of North Carolina Mutual and a public health advocate; Janie Marie Spaulding, one of Durham's earliest women realtors; and other elite residents. Aside from the prominence of the inhabitants, the homes were monuments to the skills of the black contractors and craftsmen who built them. Also erased were the rustic shotgun homes that predominated in Hayti. Although they were commonplace across the region, some had been home to notable residents, such as Blind Boy Fuller and other musicians who were pioneers of Carolina blues. Indeed, the razing of mansions and huts, juke joints and theaters, underscored the indiscriminate character of Hayti's clearance.

By 1968, a decade of planning, razing, and construction had wrought devastation to Hayti. The letter writer to the *Durham Herald* in 1963 who had worried that urban renewal would produce "just another segregated Ghetto" had assumed optimistically that the neighborhood would survive. But had he known the findings of a 1963 survey of North Carolina redevelopment commissioners, he might have predicted more accurately the future of Hayti. The study concluded that authorities responsible for urban renewal displayed no "local interest in or concern for the appearance of the sections of the cities to be rebuilt." The postrenewal appearance of Hayti bore out the survey. Although urban renewal in Hayti had been intended to end the isolation of southeastern Durham from the downtown, it had the opposite effect. Residents of the city's other neighborhoods had even less incentive than before to stray south of the downtown. Where once hundreds of homes and businesses had stood, an expressway and weed-infested lots remained. Rather than hosting the rowdy nightlife of "Mexico" and the bustling commerce of Fayetteville Avenue, Hayti's "improved" streets were now barren.[38]

During the 1950s, Savannah, Georgia, was beset by the same urban problems that challenged Durham and other American cities. Especially chronic was the neglect of the downtown housing stock by absentee owners after whites moved to the suburbs to escape growing concentrations of blacks in deteriorating inner-city neighborhoods. The threat of integration of downtown schools following the *Brown v. Board of Education* decision exacerbated "white flight," and disinvestment in the downtown worsened as white business owners followed their customers to the city's outskirts. Savannah's distinctive urban heritage posed additional challenges. The downtown's colonial layout, distinguished by narrow tree-lined streets that form an elaborate grid of squares, defied easy adaptation to automobiles. An exceptionally high number of notable eighteenth and early nineteenth-century buildings in the downtown were ill-suited to modern commercial use. Plans to redress the city's ills had to take into account this unique character.[39]

That Savannah would become one of the nation's showplaces of historic preservation was perhaps predictable. But more surprising was that the accelerating historic preservation movement went hand in hand with wholesale urban renewal. At the same time that white preservationists were launching the largest preservation campaign in the United States, they ignored the razing of black neighborhoods. Indeed, the destruction of historically black neighborhoods complemented the restoration of downtown Savannah.

The immediate catalyst for Savannah's preservation movement in 1955 was the threatened destruction of the stately Isaiah Davenport House, an English Regency–style home built in 1821. Outraged by plans to replace the house with a downtown parking lot, seven white women who had long been active in women's clubs and civic organizations established the Historic Savannah Foundation (HSF). They and other Savannah residents had become alarmed by the piecemeal destruction of one-third of the city's historic structures between 1930 and 1950. The threat to the Davenport house focused these inchoate concerns about the integrity of the city's architectural landscape. By exploiting their social connections and mobilizing the local garden club, Colonial Dames, Junior League, and others, the founders of HSF saved the endangered building. But the women also recognized that the threat to the city's architectural heritage was not adequately addressed by such desperate last-minute campaigns. So they set up a fund for ongoing preservation work, initiated a comprehensive architectural survey of the downtown, and began to educate business leaders, civic groups, and elected officials about the value of the city's buildings and ambience. The foundation found a receptive audience, especially among the city's white realtors and businessmen, who looked to rehabilitation to reinvigorate the downtown property market and expand the tourist trade.[40]

Although Savannah's white preservationists faced little opposition from white elites, they needed to explain why preservation was preferable to urban renewal at a time when generous federal funds were readily available for more drastic forms of urban renovation. Preservationists shrewdly invoked civic pride and economic revitalization by insisting that preservation made better economic sense than demolition. John J. Rauers, an early president of the HSF and a prominent realtor, explained, "Any thinking businessman must realize that something that can never be rebuilt must not be destroyed without grave consideration." Rather than turn the city's faded but unique downtown into a sterile landscape of business high-rises and parking decks, preservationists proposed exploiting the city's picturesque architecture and atmosphere through tourism. These features, they contended, provided a viable economic base without threatening the city's heritage. Albert Stoddard of the HSF cautioned in 1960, "We cannot expect to fully develop tourist-trade potential if we persist in destroying the very sites and atmosphere the tourist wishes to see. This is no mere day-dreaming, but a cold hard fact." Stoddard and other preservationists shifted the discussion from short-term economic value, which often justified demolition and new construction, to long-term returns that resulted from preserving the city's cultural resources. These arguments won over the editors of the city's two newspapers, both run by whites who endorsed a "progressive spirit of preservation" as part of a coordinated plan to revitalize the downtown. At the same time, the preservationist movement coaxed the chamber of commerce and city officials to stress tourism in future economic and civic planning.[41]

Within less than a decade, the HSF and its allies had succeeded in incorporating historic preservation into the city's ongoing policy. When the city published its first master plan in 1957, the influence of preservationists was obvious. The plan committed the city to preserving founder James Oglethorpe's 1733 city plan by encouraging "the conservation of the original pedestrian-oriented atmosphere" and prohibiting any future construction that "would destroy the historically significant pattern, scale, and atmosphere" of the downtown.[42]

Savannah's energetic and innovative white preservationists, however, displayed no concern for the threat that urban renewal posed to the city's black neighborhoods. At the very same time that the HSF began to promote preservation, the city sought federal funds to clear and redevelop a large area west of the historic downtown, bounded by West Broad Street, the main black business thoroughfare. In October 1955, the West Broad urban renewal project received federal approval. Touted as the "largest urban renewal area" in the southeast, 80 percent of the existing structures in the area were slated for demolition. Three years later, federal and city officials finalized the project, and by the end of the decade bulldozers and wrecking crews had begun the transformation of West Broad and neighboring Currytown and Frogtown.[43]

Savannah officials justified urban renewal in historically black neighborhoods with familiar arguments. White newspapers and city authorities insisted on the immediate need for slum clearance in order to connect Savannah's downtown with the planned terminus of interstate I-16. Tourists, the argument went, could not be expected to travel through black "slums" to reach the historic downtown. In addition, advocates of urban renewal described West Broad and the other targeted black neighborhoods as breeding grounds for disease, fire, and crime. And because of the public costs associated with these neighborhoods' deteriorating infrastructure, the region was draining precious city resources needed to address the ills of the downtown. The *Savannah Evening Press* summed up the view of the city's white elites by labeling the black neighborhoods a "black shadow" across the city.[44]

To the extent that urban renewal preoccupied white preservationists, they worried that it might increase pressure on the downtown housing market. As long as black renters moved into the deteriorating housing on the borders of the downtown, the restoration and revival of the city's center would lag. The wholesale clearance of black neighborhoods risked magnifying this problem if displaced black families searched for housing in a real estate market that offered them few options outside of downtown. To address this threat, city officials adapted the urban renewal policy to complement their nascent preservation campaign. First, elected officials aggressively sought federal funding for low-cost public housing as part of the city's redevelopment plan. By design, urban renewal channeled blacks displaced by slum clearance and historic preservation into public housing and neighborhoods outside of the historic downtown. Second, city authorities simultaneously used the federal requirement of a comprehensive zoning ordinance (as a prerequisite for federal funding) as the pretext to create historic district zoning for the downtown. Once armed with restrictive zoning, city officials and preservationists began the incremental process of gentrifying the downtown.[45]

The indiscriminate demolition on the west side of Savannah contrasted sharply with the advancing restoration movement just blocks to the east. Much of the housing in Frogtown and Currytown were hovels that lacked modern plumbing, and many of the commercial buildings along West Broad Street needed substantial improvements. Half of the structures in the city's black neighborhoods were unsound, and 20 percent were "dilapidated." But buildings of obvious historic significance, including the city's

train station, Saint Phillip Monumental Church, and Saint Paul
CME Church, also were razed. So too was the heart of the city's
black entertainment district, which longtime residents fondly recalled as "a hot street" and "the most exciting place that I have
ever known." Also gutted was the business district. Before the advent of urban renewal, blacks owned more than two hundred
businesses, earning Savannah a reputation as one of the South's
centers of black capitalism. Urban renewal, as in Durham, dispersed black businesses into new neighborhoods where they often failed to retain their former customers or to win new ones.
"They tore out the businesses," complained Floyd Adams Jr., son
of the founder of the city's weekly black newspaper. "Urban renewal," agreed Leroy Beavers Jr., "came through here and cleared
us out."[46]

In stark contrast to the west side, black neighborhoods in the
historic district became restoration rather than demolition projects. In Troup Ward, located on the eastern edge of the historic
downtown, white preservationists rehabilitated a line of high-
stoop row houses. Adeptly exploiting generous federal renewal
loans, the HSF worked closely with city officials to save the buildings. Restoration of the neighborhood, however, inevitably led to
the displacement of black residents who could not afford the increased rents in the renovated buildings. The consequences of the
restoration for blacks were made manifest when a wall was constructed to separate the newly renovated Troup Ward from black
neighborhoods to the east. But the success of the Troup Ward restoration encouraged preservationists and city officials to launch a
far more ambitious urban rehabilitation project that doubled the
historic district and extended it southward into neighborhoods
occupied largely by blacks.[47]

When white preservationists spoke of reclaiming the city,
they displayed little regard for the residents whom they dislo-

cated. Although Savannah's mayor conceded that preservation "did displace the poor," other preservationists denied that displacement was even a problem. An early activist in the HSF claimed that the restoration of the historic district "didn't displace anybody, because everybody had already left." Apparently, the "everybody" he had in mind were middle-class whites. To the extent that the city's blacks were acknowledged, it was often to disparage them for contributing to the city's blight. As an HSF supporter observed, "People, not conditions, make slums." An HSF memorandum seemed to suggest that the only possibility for downtown Savannah was to be occupied either by "slum dwellers" or by middle-class homeowners committed to "restored and renovated—improved—neighborhoods." During the first two decades of the city's preservation movement, only isolated voices advocated enabling blacks to return to restored neighborhoods. More characteristic of conventional attitudes was the opinion of a white Savannah resident who scoffed at blacks living in restored neighborhoods: "I mean, these people live in squalor. (I'm sorry but what can I do?) And they deserve better, but a restored Victorian townhouse? They won't keep it up. They'll wreck these homes. It just won't do." Real estate interests offered a different critique, arguing that subsidized and improved low-income housing sapped the initiative of tenants. With such attitudes commonplace among Savannah's white civic leaders, the displacement of working-class blacks from Savannah's historic downtown was assured.[48]

Savannah's black communities bore the brunt of urban renewal and historic preservation despite their uncommon political influence. Like their counterparts in Durham, Savannah blacks were not powerless victims of white plans to revitalize the city. Instead, they anticipated urban renewal as part of their much larger campaign to redress their long-standing grievances. Beginning in the 1940s, the local NAACP branch, under the leadership of Rev. Ralph Mark Gilbert, launched a highly successful voter registration campaign. Throughout the 1950s and early 1960s, at least half of Savannah's eligible black voters were registered. White politicians could not afford to ignore this black electorate, and as early as the late 1940s black policemen patrolled black neighborhoods, a black committee advised the mayor, and tangible improvements were made to public facilities in black communities. Black voters even played a decisive role in the 1960 city elections, ensuring the election of moderate Malcolm Maclean to replace Mayor Lee Mingledorff, who had presided over the initial stages of urban renewal and was openly hostile to black civil rights agitation. Savannah, to a far greater degree than Durham, nurtured a highly organized and effective local civil rights campaign, led by W. W. Law, a postal worker and charismatic activist who succeeded Gilbert as president of the Savannah branch of the NAACP. At the same time that bulldozers were leveling large swaths of black neighborhoods, black Savannah residents sustained a successful eighteen-month boycott against segregated downtown businesses. By 1963, the Savannah movement had brought about the nearly complete desegregation of the city's public facilities, eight months before the passage of national desegregation legislation.[49]

The speed and breadth of change that Savannah underwent during the late 1950s and early 1960s may help to explain why blacks underestimated the threat posed by urban renewal. As in Durham, Savannah blacks had reasons to be optimistic; after all, they had helped elect the mayor who presided over the completion of urban renewal. Only in the late 1960s did black opposition to the intertwined programs of urban renewal and preservation begin to impinge on the vision of Savannah's white authorities and preservationists. W. W. Law complained that the historic downtown was receiving all of the city's attention while conditions in black neighborhoods remained deplorable. He denounced urban renewal and historic preservation for exclusively benefiting whites. "Negroes in this city," he pointed out, "have been pulled from one end of the city to the other" by urban renewal and gentrification. Hosea Williams, formerly Law's aide and now with the Southern Christian Leadership Conference, agreed, blasting Savannah's urban plans that "subjugated humane values" by placing "too much emphasis" on "parks and old buildings." Adamant that city policies had to change, W. W. Law and other black activists began to marshal blacks' new political power to challenge city policies and plans that threatened or ignored black cultural resources. But by then, many of the city's irreplaceable black institutions and historic sites had already been lost.[50]

Although white monuments dominated the southern landscape during the era of Jim Crow, blacks had transformed the streets, buildings, and spaces of their communities into important sites of memory. Because whites largely ignored these spaces, and failed to recognize their importance for blacks, African Americans enjoyed a small measure of control over them. But events during the 1950s and 1960s exposed the limits of that control. Urban redevelopment transformed black neighborhoods despite the burgeoning power of black communities. And the urgency of the civil rights movement's assault on white supremacy and the institutions that supported it redressed only some of the glaring inequities in the South's civic spaces. Many developments of the period arguably worsened the disparities between traditionally white and black civic spaces, especially at a time when urban renewal was shrinking the inventory of sites of black memory. If civil rights legislation promised blacks new access to public spaces, myriad forces, ranging from insensitive government planning and crass economic motives to deep structural changes in American life, were creating new obstacles to more inclusive civic spaces.

Only with hindsight does the course of urban renewal in Durham and Savannah appear inevitable. What contemporaries could not anticipate was how rapidly the urban spaces of the South would be transformed. Even before the tumult of the 1950s and 1960s, World War II had altered the urban South. As whites and blacks moved off farms, as industries located in the region, and as the number of southern military bases increased rapidly, southern cities came under tremendous pressure. Scurrying to regain control, postwar leaders launched ambitious plans to order their municipalities. They hustled after federal funds for highway construction, urban renewal, public housing, and public works. They revised tax codes and introduced urban planning and zoning on an unprecedented scale. The broad social and economic forces that were overwhelming urban infrastructures everywhere in America were especially acute in black neighborhoods. By 1950 African Americans were the most urbanized of all Americans, and they experienced in large numbers the hardships of inadequate housing, spotty public services, insufficient public transit, overcrowded streets, and haphazard zoning. Black neighborhoods that earned opprobrium as "slums" were singled out as breeding grounds for crime and public health threats. That such neighborhoods might have been invested with black civic pride was inconceivable to white city officials, who viewed them only as apt targets for government intervention.

Even without the heavy hand of government, black neighborhoods would have been altered, perhaps drastically, by long-term social and economic forces at work in postwar America. Inner-city black business districts were almost certainly destined to wither along with their white counterparts. But the long-term effects and implications of urban decline and urban renewal differed in important ways. The urban renewal that swept through Durham and Savannah cannot be easily described as a form of "creative" or beneficial destruction. The demolition wrought in the name of urban renewal all too often obliterated black neighborhoods and with them physical reminders of black experience. Urban decline, in contrast, left open the possibility of eventual rehabilitation, of future use of derelict or untidy areas. Advocates of renewal admittedly proposed to preserve rather than destroy targeted communities; they anticipated that thriving, renewed communities would foster new civic spaces. But too often their experiments in community renewal fell prey to hostile "market" forces, political infighting, budget constraints, faulty planning, and overt hostility to black concerns. Whatever the precise causes, the legacy of urban renewal was a drastic reduction of cultural resources that might have made possible a biracial landscape of memory in the urban South.[51]

As the events in Savannah and Durham suggest, the institutions that blacks had fashioned during the Jim Crow era were ill-equipped to stave off or control these dramatic changes. The traditional black leaders who spoke for most southern black communities were not "bought off" so much as they were unlikely to question the assumptions that undergirded urban revitalization plans in postwar America. The black business elite in Hayti, on West Broad, and elsewhere no more approved of public controls on property rights than did their white counterparts. They were deeply invested, literally and figuratively, in traditional American property rights and the marketplace. Serious consideration of alternative, more egalitarian visions of urban revitalization were possible only if discussion revolved around social justice rather than preventing white middle-class flight or propping up land values. Only after the experience of urban renewal and the antipoverty movements of the 1960s did a new cadre of black leaders denounce the inequities that they traced to unfettered American capitalism. Consequently, during the crucial planning stages for urban renewal in Durham, Savannah, and other southern cities, black elites endorsed the policy of publicly funded "slum" clearance and private reconstruction.

That many blacks, especially community leaders, initially aligned themselves with urban renewal reflected the reality of U.S. urban politics after World War II. The proponents of urban renewal in the white community were typically white moderates who saw urban revitalization, including of black neighborhoods, as crucial to the region's modernization. White urban planners and officials who reimagined southern cities during the 1950s and 1960s sounded distinctly different from the champions of white supremacy. They promised revitalized public spaces without stressing that white racial privilege would be bolstered as well. Meanwhile white liberals endorsed urban renewal as an overdue redress of discriminatory public policies. Opposition to urban renewal, in contrast, came from segregationists who denounced any plans that squandered public resources on blacks. To black leaders who had patiently campaigned for improved facilities and services for their communities, the choice was clear. In the 1950s or early 1960s it was inconceivable that blacks would embrace the retrograde critique of urban renewal that segregationists offered. The choice they had was simple: support urban renewal and hope for the best, or oppose it and hand the segregationists a victory. If black leaders were naive to endorse urban renewal, that only became clear in retrospect.

Even if blacks had attacked the rationale for and methods of urban renewal during its crucial early years, they lacked the power necessary to shape policy. They were barely represented on the formal planning bodies and lacked the informal, "back door" connections that white business interests routinely exploited to in-fluence policymaking. Leroy Beavers Jr. of Savannah insisted, too, that "the black man didn't know enough" to be suspicious of ur-ban renewal. Public life in the Jim Crow era, after all, guaranteed that "the black man [didn't] know what the white man is doing . . . or what is going to happen." And because the complex plan-ning process was dispersed among local and federal agencies, blacks could seldom exert whatever local influence they had where it might have been most effective. It was not coincidental that urban renewal swept through the South in the years prior to grassroots black political mobilization. "The black community," Floyd Adams Jr. of Savannah concluded, "didn't have the re-sources" to defend itself. In Durham, blacks did provide crucial support for the bond referendum that partially funded urban re-newal. To that degree, they had a hand in the devastation of their own community. But in Savannah, white city authorities ignored the black community; they also proceeded with urban renewal even after white voters rejected a bond referendum to fund the project. Simply put, only concentrated power at the highest levels of local government, which no blacks anywhere in the South pos-sessed, could have slowed or halted urban renewal.[52]

The events in Durham and Savannah made it clear who in the South was able to protect the landmarks that met their con-ception of cultural importance, aesthetic merit, and historical sig-nificance. It is telling that white planners and officials could not imagine a strategy to shore up southern cities that did not include the destruction of black cultural resources. The buildings and me-morials that could have educated subsequent generations about strategies of collective survival and individual accomplishment during the Jim Crow era ceased to exist after the "urban revital-ization" campaigns of the 1950s and 1960s. Today, an act of un-common imagination is required to accept that something historically significant might have happened where Hayti once stood. As one historian points out, "It is difficult to value what cannot be seen." Former residents continue to keep alive the memory of Hayti, but it is a chimera detached from any physical reality. Thinking of the black churches, historic commercial structures, and black homes that were razed, Floyd Adams Jr. asked, "Where were [the preservationists] when we were talking about saving all of these buildings? . . . you didn't save the original black churches and some of the architectural treasures that we had then. So where were you?"[53]

The destruction of the public spaces that had sustained black community life and the dislocation of entire black neighborhoods ruptured traditions of black sociability. Black neighborhoods after urban renewal became notorious for dense concentrations of public housing and underclass poverty, coming closer to fulfilling white stereotypes than they ever had before. Postrenewal landscapes discouraged older, more expansive forms of neighborliness and impoverished black public life. Before black neighborhoods fell to the bulldozer, wealthy blacks admittedly had withdrawn into the private spaces of their commodious and elegant homes. But these luxurious homes were scattered throughout black neighborhoods rather than in distinct enclaves, and the black elite had used neighborhood amenities alongside their neighbors. Less affluent residents often displayed a broad public neighborliness, socializing from porches and stoops where they escaped from the heat and clutter of their small, unair-conditioned homes. Black business thoroughfares, too, lined with theaters, fraternal halls, stores, professional offices, restaurants, bars, hair salons, and churches, provided these black residents with a place to promenade in their "Sunday best" and to be seen by their friends and neighbors. On the sidewalks of Hayti and West Broad Street in Savannah, residents had nurtured "a feeling for the public identity of people, a web of public respect and trust." The destruction of these spaces did not deprive blacks of all forums for public debate, culture, or sociability. But the greater class differentiation, institutional fragmentation, and spatial isolation that followed urban renewal raised additional obstacles to black participation in public life and claims on public spaces. Residents displaced into public housing found that its design—austere hallways and desolate grounds—discouraged spontaneous socializing, and few were likely to wander the depressing landscapes of gutted black business districts.[54]

For many residents of Currytown in Savannah, Hayti in Durham, Auburn Avenue in Atlanta, Fulton in Richmond, Market Street in Greensboro, Overtown in Miami, Beale Street in Memphis, Treme in New Orleans, and so on, urban renewal and highway construction left a trail of desolation, like a latter-day Sherman dividing the recent past into "before" and "after" urban renewal. Ruminating over his personal experiences in Savannah and Atlanta, William Fonvielle, whose family owned one of the nation's oldest black pharmacies, asked himself, "All over the South it was happening, and I'm going, why the hell they've got to have the highways going through our community? It's bad enough building the projects, and then you've got to have the highway." "They took it all," he concludes. For some embittered blacks, urban renewal has become a convenient explanation for problems that have plagued their communities since the 1960s. Simultaneously, the lingering scars of urban renewal have contributed to disappointment and resentment about the costs of integration borne by blacks. We may wonder whether time will assuage Leroy Beavers Jr.'s or William Fonvielle's sense of loss or overcome their skepticism about the possibility of any equitable urban polity in the contemporary South. Forty years after urban renewal cut through his Savannah neighborhood, Beavers still boils with outrage; in his words, "It was murder . . . a type of genocide of a social life."[55]

Contested History in the Sunbelt South

On a sweltering July day in 1999, a group of fifty blacks and whites gathered beside a highway in Walton County, Georgia, to unveil a roadside historical marker. Although hundreds of state markers had been dedicated during the previous half-century, this new marker was the first to acknowledge any of the more than four hundred African Americans lynched in Georgia. The ceremony, which occurred on the fifty-third anniversary of the beating and shooting of two black couples by a small mob of whites, was remarkable in many ways. It was the result of an ongoing local campaign for racial reconciliation that included a memorial service for the lynching victims, the marking of their graves for the first time since their furtive burial in 1946, and the establishment of a college scholarship fund for public school graduates in the victims' honor. The group responsible for the marker was motivated by the conviction that acknowledgment of the region's tortured past was not only long overdue, but also essential for improved race relations and civic harmony. A local newspaper agreed, editorializing that "the best way to ease a wound is to treat it, not . . . hope it goes away. It is time to heal the wounds."[1]

Other southerners turned to commemoration in the hopes of fostering racial reconciliation during the closing decade of the twentieth century. But unpredictable fissures sometimes complicated these efforts. In 2000, an extended controversy in rural Caroline County, Virginia, just north of Richmond, erupted after the county board of supervisors refused to approve a proposed black history monument that would have been erected in the county's courthouse square. Several supervisors objected to the monument's commemoration of Gabriel's Rebellion, a failed slave revolt in 1800 that ended with the execution of dozens of alleged conspirators, including its purported leader, Gabriel Prosser. The supervisors subsequently rejected a proposal to commemorate Mildred and Richard Loving, a local interracial couple whose 1957 conviction for violating Virginia's ban on interracial marriage was overturned ten years later by the U.S. Supreme Court in a landmark decision. Proponents of the monument then turned to the NAACP, claiming that their equal-protection guarantees as citizens had been violated by the county board, which imposed standards on the black history monument that had not been applied to previous monuments, including the Confederate memorial that towered over the courthouse square.

Despite superficial appearances, the flap was not a familiar contest between African Americans insistent on drawing attention to the South's troubled past, and whites equally intent on using their inherited power to avoid doing so. Certainly, Cleo Coleman, an outspoken advocate of the Prosser monument, saw herself as a crusader for truth in the face of willful ignorance. "Until we accept Gabriel, we accept the myth that slaves were content with their condition, had no interest in freedom and were not entitled to it."² Stan Beason, the chairman of the tourism committee that originally proposed the monument, agreed. "All we want to do is balance out how history is told. With all the tributes to the Confederacy around here, many of us thought that there should be something more, something to celebrate what blacks had done in this county." Opponents of the monument also stood on principle, insisting that the monument glorified violence and inflamed racial tensions. Calvin Taylor, one of the county supervisors, explained, "We should have no part as a county in glorifying someone who wanted to kill whites and kidnap the governor." But if the lines of argument were predictable, the race of the combatants was not. Beason, one of the monument's most ardent champions, was a white Alabamian who had moved to the county after achieving prominence in the national antiabortion movement. Taylor, one of the leading opponents of the monument, was an African American who represented a majority white district on the board of supervisors. One of his fellow supervisors who voted for the monument was a white man who was elected in a majority black district. After a circuit court judge eventually dismissed the NAACP suit, the fractured community struggled to come up with a "multicultural" monument on which they could agree.³

Yet even while these efforts hint at new alliances and new conversations about the region's past, timeworn controversies still have the capacity to reopen wounds. Bitter arguments, rife with emotional language and one-dimensional caricatures, have grabbed headlines. The stakes are clear to large numbers of southerners, white and black, who agree about perhaps only one thing: the continuing relevance of history for the contemporary South. Recurring controversies surrounding Confederate History Month in Virginia are illustrative. Governor George Allen's proclamation honoring the Confederacy in 1997 prompted Linda

Byrd-Harden, the state director of the NAACP, to denounce it as "deceptive, fascist, and racist" and to demand the governor's immediate resignation. Three years later, when Allen's successor, James Gilmore, proclaimed Confederate History Month, Gerald O. Glenn, pastor of a black church in suburban Richmond, wondered why government officials declared special commemorations "to glorify those who battled to keep us in shackles and slave shanties." Robert "Red" Barbour, president of the Roanoke chapter of the Sons of Confederate Veterans, fired back, "Do I not have a right to my heritage and history? I do not deny [the NAACP] their black history." Governor Gilmore's subsequent effort to appease African Americans by using his 1998 Confederate History Month proclamation to condemn slavery in turn offended Confederate enthusiasts. R. Wayne Byrd Sr. of Danville, state president of the Heritage Preservation Association, fumed, "I feel insulted that this man [Gilmore] would cater to a racist hate group like the NAACP." He and other defenders of "southern" heritage warned that Gilmore would suffer for his "shameful attempt" to "pander" to black groups.[4]

The solemn unveiling of a highway marker in rural Georgia, the confusing ruckus in a rural Virginia county, and the barrage of invective surrounding Confederate History Month exemplify contemporary contests over the southern past. Controversy, of course, is not new. From the first celebrations of Emancipation Day to the present, white and black southerners have labored to advance and enshrine their preferred interpretations of the region's history. Contemporary disputes are continuations of this long-established struggle over the control and meaning of the South's past. Yet significant changes, especially in the relative power of the participants, are evident in present-day contests. Defenders of white southern historical narratives are now challenged by southerners whose competing claims are accorded greater respect than at any time in the region's past. Historical insurgents have political influence and financial resources that command the attention of public officials. As a result, the recalled past that prevails in the South's schools, museums, and civic spaces is under broader revision than at any time since the Civil War. What once were exclusive and enduring preserves of white memory now increasingly acknowledge a past they had, for so long, both ignored and suppressed.

෴

Desegregation necessarily raised questions about the symbolic content of previously segregated spaces in the South. Addressing the preponderance of white memory in the region's public spaces was never a major focus of civil rights activists, who predictably concentrated on more immediate concerns. They acknowledged, assailed, and regretted the southern past. But they directed their energies against the conspicuous mechanisms of white supremacy—above all, segregated education, voting restrictions, public segregation, and economic discrimination. They assumed that once they had uprooted the institutional foundations of white power, its cultural detritus, in time, would be swept aside as well.

White intransigence impeded but could not altogether forestall the revolution in southern institutions that activists struggled to bring about. The *Brown v. Board of Education* decision was a milestone in the long struggle for educational equity, but whites across the South found ways to delay meaningful desegregation until the late 1960s and early 1970s. Through ruses ranging from legal challenges to "freedom of choice" plans, white officials stymied all but the most intrepid black students from transferring to white schools. Only after the administration of President Lyndon B. Johnson threw the full weight of the federal government behind integration and the Supreme Court mandated it in 1968 did southern white resistance crumble and school desegregation take place.

The end of legal exclusion, whether in public schools or facilities, entailed much more than merely legalizing the physical proximity of blacks and whites in public areas. As part of a fundamental reformation of American society, civil rights activists imagined a nation of inclusive public spaces accessible to all citizens. The Supreme Court acknowledged as much when it banned segregated public schools in 1954. Physical proximity was a precondition for racial equality and, more broadly, meaningful interaction across race lines. Shared civic spaces, the court posited, were essential to shared culture.

When school desegregation finally occurred, it transformed the cultural resources that southerners, both white and black, had fashioned over the previous century. In a region where texts and curricula had long been subject to the scrutiny of the UDC and their ilk, it was a small revolution when white students began to encounter classroom materials and lessons that promoted racial tolerance and equality. Integrated schools also exposed white students to black teachers and students whose talents contradicted racist stereotypes. Black students likewise found themselves in unfamiliar environments where they had access to the superior resources and expanded curricula that had previously distinguished white schools. The unforeseen consequences of merging thousands of schools, tens of thousands of educators, and millions of students were inevitably jarring. Some hardships, however, were the result of conscious design. Once integration became inevitable, white educators and politicians were intent on controlling the process and ensuring that blacks bore the heaviest costs. And, without question, they did.

Schooled by Jim Crow to expect the worst, black educators during the late 1950s and early 1960s anticipated that once inte-

gration began they might face intimidation, dismissal, and demotion at the hands of white administrators. Leroy Campbell, principal of a black high school in Statesville, North Carolina, quickly
discerned a pattern: "The trend was that almost all schools that
were segregated took from the black schools and added to the
white schools. . . . We knew we were going to pay a price." But
even he did not envision the cumulative cost of integration for
African American educators and schools. Because federal over-
sight of integration failed to guarantee employment for black
teachers in merged schools, the ranks of black teachers and administrators in the South were drastically thinned during the late
1960s. Between 1963 and 1971 the number of black principals in
Arkansas shrank from 134 to 14, in North Carolina from 277 to 8.
Between 1968 and 1970, 68 black principals were eliminated and
68 white principals were added in Louisiana. A 1970 study estimated that integration had resulted in the termination of more
than 31,000 black teachers and principals.[5]

Despite the scale of the phenomenon, white officials claimed
ignorance of the drastically shrinking ranks of black educators.
The Tennessee and Texas departments of education kept no official statistics on the racial composition of educators and there-
fore did not measure the effects of integration on their faculties.
In Florida, state and local administrators brushed aside complaints about widespread dismissals without conducting any in-
vestigations. Deploring the convenient absence of data on the
problem, a North Carolina observer remarked, "You can see the
tracks, but you can't find the body."[6]

Black teachers who weathered the purges that followed integration often faced organized discrimination, especially de facto
demotion. Under the pretext of maintaining professional standards, school boards pledged to assess the qualifications of black
teachers by the same standards as their new white colleagues.

School boards and teachers eager to defend white seniority and power, however, discounted black teachers' training and experience. Black principals were routinely demoted, or given figurehead status. With gallows humor, black educators joked about black principals who were "promoted" to "assistant to the superintendent in charge of light bulbs and erasers." Dorothy Redus Robinson, a Texas teacher, recalled black principals who "drove buses while wearing the title assistant superintendent or executive assistant." At times, black teachers found themselves ensnared in bureaucratic subterfuges seemingly drawn from the pages of Franz Kafka. School boards demoted experienced black teachers who specialized in advanced subjects to teaching introductory subjects. A black teacher whose competence was English, for instance, might be assigned to teach math in an integrated school and then would be dismissed for incompetence in her new subject. And even when qualified black teachers were not fired or driven to retirement, they often were transferred to majority white schools, leaving less competent white teachers to fill their former assignments.[7]

As the costs of integration became clear, black educators looked to their teachers' associations for redress. But these remnants of segregation, which were in the process of being merged with white teachers' associations, were frail defenders of black teachers. In 1964, in the interest of social justice and maximizing the influence of teachers, the National Education Association voted to abolish segregated teachers' associations. The merging of white and black associations entailed more than distributing positions of authority and creating biracial memberships. During Jim Crow, white and black associations had developed sharply divergent cultures that defied easy amalgamation. As if to avoid controversy, white associations scrupulously focused on narrow professional issues, such as working conditions and salaries. Black associations, in contrast, pursued far broader agendas, and sometimes were at the forefront of voting rights campaigns and civil rights agitation in general. The Virginia Teachers' Association, for instance, virtually became a voting rights organization during the 1940s, as did the Louisiana Education Association (LEA). In the words of the LEA's president, Alphone Jackson Jr., it "functioned with equal vigor in the area of civil and human rights," conducting voter education and registration campaigns while also fighting for school desegregation and equal pay for black teachers. In addition, black teachers' groups promoted curricula attuned to their communities. Their support for Negro History Week and their close relationship with the Association for the Study of Negro Life and History (ASNLH) were only two expressions of this commitment.[8]

Black educators were wary of surrendering the reform traditions of their organizations. But the merger of black and white teachers' organizations and the shrinking ranks of black teachers deprived activist educators of much of their former influence. In some instances, they negotiated recognition of their long-standing reform commitments into the merger with their white counterparts. The black Alabama State Teachers Association, for example, insisted that the previously all-white Alabama Education Association agree to support Negro History Week and to fund the ASNLH. But such legalisms could not compensate for blacks' becoming a minority in both the membership and leadership of the merged associations. Henceforth, to the extent that teachers' associations acknowledged activist traditions, it was largely with nostalgia.[9]

The trauma of integration was compounded by the closing of black schools. As repositories of community lore and pride, black schools were civic spaces whose importance far exceeded their function of teaching children. But with integration, the costly duplication of infrastructure necessitated by segregated school systems became untenable. Because whites were unwilling to integrate into majority black schools, black students typically were transferred to "unitary," majority white schools. The "surplus" schools in black neighborhoods were then closed or converted to administrative facilities. In either case, they no longer served black communities, and their traditions, lore, and spirit expired. In addition, when black students were integrated into previously white schools, they confronted unfamiliar schoolteachers and traditions. School names offered one measure of the distance that black students were asked to travel. They found themselves transferred from schools named after Booker T. Washington, Frederick Douglass, and other black heroes to buildings adorned with rebel mascots and named after such illustrious Confederates as Nathan Bedford Forrest, P. G. T. Beauregard, and Robert E. Lee. A black student who entered a previously all-white high school in Americus, Georgia, in the early 1970s observed, "It wasn't really our school. Like we had lost our own school, you know, and all we had was the whites' school."[10]

Protests by black students and parents during the early 1970s slowed but could not halt school consolidation. In scattered counties across the South, organized campaigns against school closings and teacher firings demonstrated the depth of black ambivalence toward desegregation. In a few instances, black boycotts and protests succeeded in keeping black schools open and in preserving the jobs of black faculty, school names, and traditions, including classes in African American history. But these campaigns seldom enjoyed support from national civil rights organizations, which hesitated to slow desegregation and struggled to consolidate gains in the face of the hostility of President Richard M. Nixon's administration. Here and there, federal court decisions commanded school boards to distribute the burdens of school desegregation equitably. But adroit school administrators found ways to evade court rulings and black school closings continued.[11]

The cumulative toll of the dismissal and demotion of black teachers, the closing down of black teachers' associations, and the shutting up of black schools remains inestimable. Blacks had not anticipated the extent to which desegregation would mean the loss of black role models in the classroom and the denial of cherished school traditions when black schools were closed, merged, or renamed. These losses were tangible to students who made the transition from segregated to integrated schools. Brenda Tapia, for example, remembered her teachers at the black Ada Jenkins High School in Davidson County, North Carolina, with special fondness and respect. "One of the differences that I saw in being educated in a segregated school as opposed to an integrated school is that black teachers taught you not only the academics but they taught us about life. . . . You were constantly being given your history in informal ways." Desegregation uprooted in particular the tradition of black history in public schools that had been nurtured by Carter Woodson, Luther P. Jackson, and countless other activists since the 1920s. Each time a black history teacher retired rather than accept a demeaning reassignment, and each time a black school closed, traditions and public spaces that had sustained Negro History Week were lost.[12]

With desegregation thrusting most black students into formerly all-white schools, black parents and students were forced to consider a new school curriculum and atmosphere. Controversies flared, sparking protests, boycotts, and even violence at schools across the region. A few examples from 1972 suggest the depth of black frustration and the response of authorities to it. In Portsmouth, Virginia, where black students were already anxious over a proposal to turn a historically black high school into a vocational school, the cancellation of a Black History Week assembly sparked a massive demonstration. After police used dogs and physical force to disperse protesters, the school superintendent suspended more than eight hundred students. When black students in Fort Mill, South Carolina, protested the absence of Black History Week ceremonies at a newly integrated high school, police responded with mace and arrests. In James Island, South Carolina, dissatisfaction with a cursory black history program in the local high school became so explosive that the school had to be closed for several days. And in Wilson, North Carolina, a march by white students flying Confederate flags provoked a counter-march by black students; school administrators suspended hundreds of students before tensions eased.[13]

A particular point of friction was the continued use of objectionable textbooks and lesson plans in the South's public schools. The invidious racism of the textbooks commonly used in southern schools was now being presented to black students without the comparative protection provided by black teachers and schools—and black parents and white allies fought back by demanding root-and-branch textbook revision. Concerned parents drew inspiration from the ASNLH, which cautioned, "With the beginning of public school integration . . . some people may presume that emphasis upon Negro history should be unnecessary. Nothing could be further from the truth!" Joining in the chorus were the major civil rights organizations: the NAACP resolved in 1961 that school texts should acknowledge the contribution of blacks to American culture, and two years later the Urban League assailed the exclusively "white" perspective of most textbooks. In 1965 the Congress of Racial Equality agreed, denouncing "the stereotypes and distortions" that littered textbooks.[14]

Revision of texts and curricula, nevertheless, was slow to come about. Throughout the 1960s publishers continued to sell to southern schools "segregation" editions—which typically included few pictures of blacks and avoided sensitive topics in southern history—while supplying so-called integrated books elsewhere. Despite federal subsidies for school districts that adopted "multiracial" textbooks, white administrators displayed a mixture of lethargy and outright hostility to calls for new texts. Charles F. Carroll, North Carolina's superintendent of public education, demonstrated both when questioned during a 1966 congressional hearing on the "treatment of minorities" in school texts. Defending the "freedom of choice" of local school boards over texts and even integration, Carroll remarked, "If they want to integrate, fine. If they don't, fine."[15]

In Virginia, desegregation did not redress the explicitly segregationist and Cold War–inspired history taught to fourth-, seventh-, and eleventh-graders. The state-approved textbooks for these classes had been developed after a 1949 state legislative commission proclaimed that "a thorough training in America and Virginia history and government is needed today to combat the trends toward statism." A year earlier, the Southern States Industrial Council had warned Virginians not to underestimate "how much Civil Rights propaganda has infiltrated the schools." Menaced by the perceived danger of "socialistic" policies emanating from Washington, D.C., the legislature created a state commission to oversee the writing and publication of suitable texts. The authors of the volumes, however, failed to achieve the proper "tone" demanded by legislators, prompting the commission and the state's attorney general to undertake extensive and heavy-handed editing. The vetted texts reached Virginia's classrooms in 1957 and for the following decade and a half, students waded through them, learning that Virginia's Indians had been "sly and cruel," that "slavery made it possible for Negroes to come to America and make contacts with civilized life," and that Negro "servants" during the Civil War "had risked their lives to protect the white people they loved." The texts purposefully ignored the disfranchisement of blacks after 1902 because "there were enough hard feelings already" but reassured students that the poll tax was responsible for improving education in the state.[16]

With mounting urgency during the late 1960s, blacks, joined by growing numbers of whites, criticized the textbooks as "out-and-out propaganda" that "glorified the Cavalier past" and were "slanted toward a conservative political outlook at the expense of learning." Organized opposition to the texts was a direct outgrowth of black political empowerment. As one critic of the texts pointed out, "There were few public attacks [on] history textbooks so long as the ideals they represented remained dominant." But the destruction of segregation had changed everything; "What used to be good politics has become bad politics." With the Virginia Council of Social Studies castigating the texts as "ridiculous" and "reprehensible," the Virginia State Board of Education finally voted unanimously to discontinue their use after 1972. The board's decision won applause for ending, as one newspaper put it, an "embarrassing and degrading attempt by the state to package thought." Admittedly, the new texts that replaced the Jim Crow–era books were often lackluster and still shied away from some contentious aspects of the region's history. They nevertheless represented an important step toward a more inclusive history and ensured that white and black southerners, for the first time in the twentieth century, shared texts that endorsed racial equality, not white privilege.[17]

Another notable transformation in curricula was the introduction of Black History Week ceremonies into the calendars of all schools. Carter Woodson's long-delayed hope that white students would be exposed to African American history finally came to pass during the 1970s. Even Governor George Wallace, the one-time advocate of "segregation forever," endorsed Black History Week in Alabama in 1973 and by 1980, public schools in every southern state participated in the celebration of Black History Month (the successor to Woodson's Negro History Week). However unfavorably these integrated celebrations may have compared to the ceremonies previously staged by all-black schools, they perpetuated the tradition and familiarized white students with a record of black historical accomplishments.[18]

The promise of integrated education remained unrealized two decades after *Brown v. Board of Education,* but public schools in the South had nevertheless been transformed. When the wrenching process of school consolidation ended, black and white students met each other on a daily basis in the classroom and on the athletic field, while their parents participated in integrated school associations. Whereas the South's system of education had previously perpetuated unequal resources for white and black schools, now administrators were obligated to ameliorate inequalities. Opinion polls measured changed attitudes about integrated education among whites; in the early 1960s a large majority of white southerners opposed integrated schools, but by 1970 only 16 percent did. Even the tense controversies over curricula had the salutary effect of hastening negotiation between whites and blacks over the content of their children's education. Blacks may have borne the heaviest costs of school integration, but at least at the end of the 1970s there was cause to hope that the region's schools might become a crucible for racial reconciliation.

൭൭

The end of legal segregation left unresolved the future of all historically black spaces. During the era of Jim Crow, blacks had looked to their communities, their "home sphere," to provide a sense of security and affiliation that American society otherwise denied to them. The urban renewal programs of the 1950s and

1960s, however, demonstrated that blacks were unable to protect their spaces from unrivaled white political and economic power. Instead, urban renewal devastated public spaces and cultural resources that blacks had built over generations. But during the 1970s and 1980s, blacks marshaled their new political power and creatively recast urban renewal and historic preservation, thereby enabling some embattled black neighborhoods to survive.

The contrasting fates of two churches in Durham, North Carolina, attest to this evolution in strategies to preserve black heritage. When the congregation of Saint Joseph's AME Church moved into a new church building in 1975, the towering brick structure they left behind was spared the destruction that had claimed much of the surrounding Hayti neighborhood during urban renewal. The church, designed by Philadelphia architect Samuel Linton Leary—who integrated Romanesque and Gothic Revival styles to give it a monumental presence—had been, along with White Rock Baptist, one of Durham's most impressive buildings. It was also a testament to the local black craftsmen who had built it in 1896. Unlike White Rock, which had been razed in 1967, Saint Joseph's attracted the attention of local preservationists, who secured its listing on the National Register of Historic Places. A foundation eventually acquired the building and has used it as a performance space and museum that recalls Hayti's history. A mere eight years separated the leveling of White Rock and the preservation of Saint Joseph's.[19]

Only after Hayti had been cleared did urban planners begin to combine historic preservation with community revitalization. When the executive director of Durham's Redevelopment Commission conceded in the spring of 1967 that "a community can and will withstand just so much total clearance" and that "rehabilitation-conservation projects are the salvation of urban renewal," he spoke for many urban specialists. The National

Historic Preservation Act of 1966 and other federal legislation encouraged new conceptions of urban renewal by increasing federal subsidies for the preservation of historic properties and by expanding legal protections for historically significant properties. Whereas earlier historic preservation campaigns targeted once opulent but now faded white neighborhoods, restoration projects during the 1970s began to address areas noted for their "vernacular" architecture. One example of successful public intervention to stem a neighborhood's decline was the restoration of Inman Park, a deteriorating area in Atlanta. A consortium of private lenders joined with city authorities and a neighborhood association to renovate the community. Within a decade, virtually all of its structures had undergone rehabilitation, earning Inman Park a place on the National Register of Historic Places and the title of Atlanta's first and most successful historic district.[20]

Successful renovation of Inman Park, however, highlighted the obstacles to preservation of black neighborhoods like Hayti. After urban renewal had gutted many inner-city communities, sharp cutbacks in federal funds for urban redevelopment meant that most rehabilitation henceforth had to be privately sponsored. At the same time, the focus of urban renewal shifted away from the most blighted neighborhoods and toward marginal districts with salvageable structures that might attract middle-class residents. Local authorities, who usually only had "seed money" for renovation projects, now funneled community development funds to neighborhoods where real estate interests and lenders took the lead in rehabilitation. Federal tax incentives introduced during the 1970s encouraged these campaigns by offering generous tax deductions and credits. Although these incentives spurred the most extensive urban redevelopment campaign in American history, they typically followed the path of Inman Park's preservation campaign, becoming an instrument of "gentrification" that displaced working-class, elderly, and black residents. By intent, the shift to private reinvestment in older urban communities led to increased rents, taxes, and property values, outcomes that middle-class professionals, city officials, and commercial interests welcomed but displaced residents resented.[21]

In the face of this threat, black activists began to adapt the techniques of and rationales for historic preservation to serve the interests of their communities and their heritage. Historic preservation no longer is synonymous with a profoundly conservative and exclusively elite, white understanding of cultural value and place. In recent years, black preservationists have campaigned for the conservation of abandoned commercial buildings in Jacksonville, Florida; the home of an early twentieth-century black physician in Little Rock, Arkansas; and a Jim Crow–era black school in rural Georgia. Public officials now promote the role of the state in the preservation of black heritage, even identifying historic sites that they subsequently pledge to preserve.[22]

Perhaps nowhere in the South have the effects of black heritage preservation been more marked than in Savannah. By the late 1960s, blacks there had become bitterly resentful of the hardship and loss inflicted on them by the city's urban renewal and historic preservation projects. When the city announced plans in 1975 for yet another urban renewal and public housing project in the Wheaton Street area, a black downtown neighborhood, black frustration mounted. While the Georgia Historic Preservation Office assessed the historic significance of the structures threatened with demolition, black activists, including W. W. Law, president of the local branch of the NAACP, led the mobilization of black residents. The city and the Historic Savannah Foundation (HSF) insisted that nothing in the project area warranted saving, but the National Register of Historic Places concluded that six buildings merited preservation. City officials demurred, but infuriated Law with their cavalier attitude. Given the previous pattern of urban renewal, Law contended that he was "by no means surprised" that the city and HSF had failed to acknowledge the historic worth of the threatened buildings. Law and the NAACP supported public housing, but they opposed "anyone going into a Negro area and recklessly wiping out everything standing as if black people have nothing of value."[23]

The organized opposition to the Wheaton Street project alerted city officials that they could no longer ignore the concerns of African American residents. Even so, city authorities complained that preservation of the threatened buildings was a waste of resources and jeopardized a major urban renewal project. Law and his supporters in the black community remained adamant. After resigning from the presidency of the local NAACP branch, a position he had held for more than two decades, Law founded in 1977 the Yamacraw branch of the Association for the Study of Afro-American Life and History (ASALH; the renamed organization that Carter Woodson had founded). Law hoped the organization would teach residents and tourists about the history of the city's African Americans while simultaneously protecting black historic sites. Law's indefatigable lobbying of state and local politicians failed to preserve all of the endangered buildings, but he succeeded in raising enough funds to protect one of them. The relocated and restored building, subsequently known as the King-Tisdell Cottage, was formally dedicated in 1981. A superb example of black craftsmanship, the Queen Anne–style cottage, built in 1896, became the headquarters for the local branch of the ASALH and one of the city's first museums devoted to black history.[24]

By the early 1980s, Law and his allies were engaged in comprehensive neighborhood preservation. The particular focus of their efforts was a residential enclave on the eastern edge of the historic downtown. Anchored by the Beach Institute, which had been built by the American Missionary Association in 1867 as a school for freed people, the neighborhood had languished throughout the preceding decades of urban revitalization. Initially a racially mixed working-class neighborhood, the area became predominantly African American during the twentieth century. The district was home to black professionals and tradesmen, as well as a remarkable array of architectural styles, from late eighteenth-century Federal-style cottages to Carpenter Italianate row houses and multistoried Second Empire homes. By the 1980s encroaching gentrification was threatening the neighborhood. Because fewer than one in five of the neighborhood's residents owned their homes, they could not easily defend the integrity of the community. Neighborhood activists, led by Law and the pastor of a neighborhood black church, pressured city officials to prevent the displacement of longtime residents. Rallying behind the Beach Institute Historic Neighborhood Association, which Law founded in 1980, residents requested city funds to purchase buildings as they came on the market and then adopted restrictive covenants to protect existing residents. Law made clear the larger significance of the campaign: "This may be the last opportunity that blacks will have to own anything in the downtown area." In an act that Law described as "one of the finest hours" in the city's history, the city council approved a major loan to the neighborhood organization. In subsequent years the association worked to hold down rents while subsidizing owners who rehabilitated their homes. It made available unprecedented financial resources and know-how to Savannah blacks intent on preserving their neighborhood, enabling them to participate in public subsidy programs and court private foundations. For the first time, a black neighborhood in the city had access to the funds necessary to preserve its architectural and cultural resources.[25]

Law's crusade to preserve Savannah's black history was an extension of his lifelong civil rights activism. Indeed, it was fitting that the ASALH would be a vehicle for his activism. Law's conviction that historical awareness was essential to black community development was consonant with the beliefs that had inspired Carter Woodson to found the ASNLH eight years before Law's birth. Law's gift was his shrewd appreciation of the possibilities of fusing blacks' emerging political power with historic preservation to transform policies that had previously victimized black neighborhoods. If Savannah's future was going to rest on the commercialization of the past, Law insisted that blacks had as large a stake in that past as did whites. Not only should black history be incorporated into the historical record that Savannah presented, but blacks should also profit from it alongside whites.

Law and other black activists in Savannah and elsewhere have transformed the South's historic landscape on a scale that would have been previously unimaginable. They have demanded recognition of their cultural heritage by identifying historic resources worthy of preservation and interpretation that had been ignored by most white preservationists and officials. Taking advantage of state and local policies to gain new leverage in property markets, activists revised notions about preservation. Law and his allies demonstrated that the concerns of the civil rights movement—access to and inclusion in American public life—remained a pressing issue more than a decade after the passage of civil rights legislation. They promoted civil rights, articulated an alternative version of history, and launched neighborhood development programs as a means to achieve a measure of economic equality. One measure of their influence on urban planning in the city was the Savannah Neighborhood Action Conference, held in 1983. Joining the well-established white preservation organizations were Law and other black preservationists. Participants voiced sentiments that would have been inconceivable only a decade earlier. One conference attendee, for instance, insisted that "the concept of neighborhoods integrated socially, economically, culturally, and racially, is of incredible importance for the further development of cities." The evolution of historic preservation in Savannah raised the possibility that even if historic preservation may not be a force for social justice, it need not be a threat to it.[26]

Since the 1960s a broad and momentous shift in interpretation has transformed many southern museums, finally loosening the grip of whites on these important repositories of historical memory. Whereas southern museums during the era of Jim Crow actively discouraged black patronage while advancing the ideology of white supremacy, they recently have made significant strides toward becoming the most inclusive historical spaces in the region.

When Virginia celebrated the 350th anniversary of the settlement of Jamestown in the summer of 1957, such a transformation was inconceivable. Ceremonies provided "a tribute to the fortitude, determination, and character" of the state's founders and their descendants, as well as a pretext for attracting tourists to the Jamestown site. Organizers rose above the narrowest ethnocentrism when they staged a ceremony to commemorate eight Spanish Jesuits who led a nearby failed mission that antedated the founding of Jamestown. Yet the Indians whose land was invaded and the enslaved Africans who were brought to the colony in 1619 went virtually unacknowledged. State officials, who were embroiled in a campaign of "massive resistance" against the integration of public schools, went out of their way to exclude African Americans from the ceremonies. When Governor Thomas B. Stanley's staff mistakenly included six blacks among six hundred dignitaries invited to attend the opening ceremonies, their invitations were quickly withdrawn because the event was a "social occasion" where "race mixing" would be inappropriate. And although the legislature had appropriated $750 in 1942 for a memorial to the "African Negroes" purchased at Jamestown in 1619, no official recognition took place. As one black observer complained, "The only evidence of race at the current Jamestown Festival are very prominent signs indicating segregated rest rooms." Unable to enforce segregation on the portion of the Jamestown site administered by the National Park Service, Virginia authorities located the festival's reception center on state land, where Jim Crow arrangements prevailed. State officials were noticeably absent when a small ceremony, independently organized by a group of blacks, commemorated the arrival of Africans at Jamestown. These competing Jamestown ceremonies underscored whites' continuing resolve, more than three years after the Supreme Court's landmark *Brown v. Board of Education* decision, to exclude any meaningful recognition of black history from southern museums.[27]

The past that had been so purposefully ignored during the Jamestown celebration in 1957 was conspicuous in 2000 when the members of the Georgia Association of Black Elected Officials opened their annual meeting at the Ralph Mark Gilbert Civil Rights Museum in Savannah. Founded in 1970 by the then newly elected Atlanta mayor Maynard Jackson, the organization promoted black political empowerment, especially the election of blacks. The selection of the museum as the opening venue for the meeting was appropriate. The four-year-old museum was named for a man who had been the pastor of the First African Baptist Church, a charismatic president of the Savannah branch of the NAACP during the 1940s, and a founder of the influential Citizens' Democratic Club, an African American political organization in the city. Gilbert exemplified black leadership, and the mu-

Westley Wallace ("W. W.") Law (1923–2002), civil rights and community activist in Savannah, Georgia, in the Ralph Marks Gilbert Civil Rights Museum. (*Savannah Morning News*)

seum itself commemorated the movement that had made possible the careers of the black politicians who gathered there. The museum itself was the culmination of W. W. Law's three-decade-long crusade to preserve his city's rich black heritage. The legacy of the past extended to the meeting's agenda, when members affirmed the organization's long-standing opposition to the incorporation of the Confederate battle flag in the Georgia state flag.[28]

Revision of exhibits that unabashedly defended white supremacy, glorified the Confederacy, or celebrated the antebellum South was probably inevitable after desegregation began. Even so, reinterpretation at most sites came about slowly and unevenly. No major southern museums made significant efforts to present the history of African Americans with any complexity before the 1970s. Not even the U.S. bicentennial celebration, which planners hoped would promote national unity after the turmoil unleashed by the civil rights movement and Vietnam, prompted any major revisions. The exploits of southern white men who had achieved fame in politics, business, and the military remained in the spotlight.[29]

This inertia reflected practical and ideological constraints that plagued many southern museums. Although some museum staffs remained committed to traditional interpretations of the region's history and actively obstructed innovation, elsewhere reinterpretation came about slowly because it demanded more time and funds than stretched staffs could muster. The limitations of extant collections also hindered reinterpretation. Earlier museum directors and staffs had spent decades gathering artifacts of the region's white elites, leaving their successors with few materials with which to present the experience of African Americans and non-elite whites. Prevailing ideas about how to interpret artifacts also impeded creative reinterpretation. The emphasis placed on the "authentic" provenance of museum objects led curators to highlight the creators and owners of objects, but the unnamed slaves who might have made or used many artifacts preserved in museum collections went unmentioned. Curators shied away from incorporating such conjecture into exhibits because it might erode the museum's commitment to presenting a purportedly objective, "factual" account of the past.[30]

All of these factors were evident at Colonial Williamsburg. As the South's premier historic restoration since it opened as a museum in 1932, Colonial Williamsburg was a shrine to American democracy and individualism. The private foundation that operated it made ongoing, albeit modest, amendments to its presentation of colonial history during the first four decades of its operation. Gradually the focus at the site shifted from restoration to interpretation, and the staff in "simulated ancient costume" grew accordingly. During the 1950s and 1960s, Colonial Williamsburg carefully avoided challenging traditional white southern attitudes about race, on the purported grounds that "by pushing too fast too far we might only aggravate a prejudice we want to see disappear." The staff, in fact, seemed anxious to cater to prejudices. A 1967 training manual, for example, sketched the ideal "hostess" (that is, interpreter) as "a well-informed, well-bred individual, who speaks in a grammatically correct and culturally acceptable manner" and who showed "good taste in dress and behavior." As late as 1976 some staff described the prevailing ethos there as "antediluvian." Such attitudes discouraged discussion of the colonial African American experience. The staff continued to refer to slaves as "servants" and slave housing as "dependencies." Although half of colonial Williamsburg's population had been African American, visitors were far more likely to encounter black service workers than site interpreters. Displays of artifacts related to slavery were conspicuously absent, and there was little mention of the institution itself, aside from a brief prerecorded audio presentation at two locations.[31]

By the late 1970s, the silence about African American history at Williamsburg and other southern museums provoked mounting criticism. Visitor discontent with the avoidance of the topic of slavery at some heavily visited sites became evident, especially after the publication of Alex Haley's *Roots: The Saga of an American Family* in 1976, and the airing of a twelve-hour television adaptation in January 1977. Haley's work had a catalytic effect on popular attitudes toward slavery, especially among African Americans. His depiction of his slave ancestors' struggle to retain their dignity and to attain freedom removed the stigma from slavery for many African Americans, transforming their past into a saga of perseverance and quiet heroism. Informed of their slave ancestors' courage and resilience, blacks displayed unprecedented interest in genealogy. As more and more blacks traced their family lines, some also visited historic sites to learn about the slave experience. But those who did so were often dismayed by "the almost total absence of any reference to slavery" at Williamsburg and other historic sites. This silence undoubtedly discouraged larger numbers of blacks from visiting historical museums. Previously, during the era of Jim Crow, attracting black audiences had never been a concern of white site managers. After desegregation, however, museum staffs gradually acknowledged that the inclusion of black history was essential to expanding their clientele.[32]

Criticism from visitors was echoed by critiques by trained museum specialists, who often played prominent roles in initiating new interpretations. At the same time that museums provided a refuge for historians exiled from academia by a tight job market, they also hired more and more graduates trained at the burgeoning museum studies programs at Winterthur, Cooperstown, and elsewhere. Renouncing the tradition-bound aesthetics and patriotism that had characterized the vision of their predecessors, this 1970s generation of professional historians and museum specialists brought with them a commitment to social history, often succinctly described as "history from the bottom up." Whether manifested in an interest in folk art, working-class culture, vernacular architecture, or the history of African Americans and women, the historical preferences of these new specialists could not easily be reconciled with the elitist, white focus that prevailed at most southern sites. This revisionist impulse was by no means unique to the South; public historians across the nation saw themselves as insurgents working to free museums and sites from outdated interpretations. Indeed, many younger staff members in the South considered themselves members of a larger national professional community and distanced themselves from the often parochial allegiances of earlier museum staffs.[33]

These practitioners of what became known as the "new

museumology" agreed with their predecessors about the didactic potential of museums. But instead of reaffirming moral precepts and conventional wisdom about the past, museum innovators proposed that they should expose the often obscure underlying economic and social structures of society. Whereas earlier exhibits had often promoted the timelessness of the principles behind the Revolution, the Civil War, or other celebrated events, museum specialists now proposed to analyze the historically specific decisions that historical actors had made. This reorientation shifted attention to historical processes and away from eternal principles. The language of "liberty" and "freedom" associated with the Revolutionary-era patriots, for example, now became an expression of ideology, rather than of ageless truths. By encouraging visitors to reconsider conventional historical verities, the new museumologists hoped to hone visitors' faculties as social critics. As Cary Carson, a leader in the reinterpretation of Colonial Williamsburg, explained: "I want [the public] to go away disturbed. I see this museum as a device to make Americans look at aspects of both the past and the present that they might not want to see."[34]

Infused with a belief that a museum should be a provocative and "liberating force," the still largely white staffs at a few southern museums began to revise their programs during the late 1970s. New exhibits began to address previously ignored historical themes, such as slavery and class privilege. Colonial Williamsburg took the lead, shifting its focus away from the gentry and toward colonial Virginia's working-class whites and "other half"—its colonial African American population. The crude furnishings and squalor of a reconstructed mental hospital in Williamsburg, for example, informed visitors about the harsh methods used to control patients whom society had labeled deviant. A larger aim of the reconstruction was to encourage visitors to reflect on how "the same issues are alive today."[35] Interpretation now paid close attention to the inequalities that undergirded the trappings of colonial wealth admired by visitors. Previously the exploitation of slaves had warranted only passing acknowledgment. Now the staff insisted that "in Virginia the history of English settlement is inextricably joined with the history of the transformation of black Africans into Afro-Americans."[36]

Disseminating this new orientation throughout the site's extensive visitor education programs required more than a decade of experimentation and innovation. In 1979, the first black reenactors, who performed roles as slave and free black characters, joined the staff. Using artifacts amassed through archaeological research, Colonial Williamsburg began to interpret the material culture of colonial African Americans. Soon, with the 1989 completion of reconstructed slave quarters at Carter's Grove, a satellite historic home owned by Colonial Williamsburg, the plantation slave experience also was addressed. Eventually, dramatic productions, such as the 1994 mock slave auction, challenged visitors to reflect on the traumas of colonial slavery and African American responses to them.[37]

The Museum of the Confederacy in Richmond emerged as another center of revisionist interpretation during the 1970s. Founded in the late nineteenth century as a Confederate reliquary by elite white women, the museum was an unlikely site for new approaches to the history of the antebellum South and the Confederacy. Even so, in 1969 the museum's board signaled its intention to transform the site from a shrine by voting to change the Confederate Museum's name to the Museum of the Confederacy. A later executive director of the site revealed the thinking behind the museum's reorientation: "We are the museum *of* the Confederacy, not *for* the Confederacy."[38] A successful fund-raising drive enabled the museum to expand its staff and begin the laborious process of reinterpreting its collections and planning major exhibits. In 1978, the appointment as executive director of Edward D. C. "Kip" Campbell, who had earned a Ph.D. in history, accelerated the changes under way at the museum. Campbell, whose dissertation had focused on the depiction of the mythic South in American film, oversaw the completion of a major exhibit, People of the Confederacy, which redirected attention from military and political elites to the populace of the southern nation at war. Encouraged by the success of the exhibit, the staff began planning more ambitious and innovative exhibitions in the early 1980s, culminating in "Before Freedom Came," which opened in 1991, and "A Woman's War," which debuted in 1996. That one of the first comprehensive American exhibits devoted to slavery, complete with leg irons and an 1863 photograph of the whip-scarred back of a slave, was staged next door to the White House of the Confederacy, where Jefferson Davis had lived during the Civil War, surprised many observers and garnered national acclaim. The exhibit underscored not only that slavery was "a key aspect of secession, the creation of the Confederacy and the Civil War," but also that the museum was committed to a far broader and more inclusive mission than its founders could have imagined or would have condoned.

Some Richmonders deplored the museum's new direction. Louis Gorr, its executive director, conceded that "I had doors slammed in my face" when he began local fund-raising for the exhibit. Sa'ad El-Amin, a local black activist, questioned the appropriateness of staging the exhibit at a museum devoted to the Confederacy: "This is sort of like [if] the Museum of the Holocaust was located in some Nazi shrine." But the public response to the exhibit was overwhelmingly positive. It was a milestone that a major show planned and staged by the Museum of the Confederacy subsequently traveled to the National Afro-American Mu-

seum and Cultural Center in Wilberforce, Ohio. Annual attendance at the Museum of the Confederacy doubled, reaching levels
that have yet to be exceeded, and African American patronage increased dramatically.[39]

For all the efforts to create more inclusive interpretations at
long-established southern historic sites during the 1970s and 1980s,
significant obstacles to reinterpretation remained. At many sites,
existing collections included too few artifacts to create exhibits
that would provide a comprehensive overview of the black experience. Some sites, such as Williamsburg and Monticello, employed archaeological research to address this lacuna. But most
museums lacked either resources or sites appropriate for excava-
tions. In order to stage the Before Freedom Came exhibit, for example, the staff of the Museum of the Confederacy had to draw
on the collections of other museums. But only major museums
were likely to attempt such exhibitions, which ultimately did little
to redress the limitations of their permanent collections. Moreover, most of the long-established museums and historic sites in
the South were tethered to particular events or eras, particularly
the colonial, antebellum, or Civil War periods. No matter how
creatively staffs might interpret their sites and collections, they
could not ignore the historical focus that they had inherited from
the sites' founders.

The staff at the Stonewall Jackson House in Lexington, Virginia, confronted these challenges during the 1970s and 1980s.
Founded by white women as a shrine to Jackson, who had owned
the home while he was a faculty member at the Virginia Military
Institute, the site attracts a steady stream of Civil War enthusiasts.
Although the museum had few obvious incentives to revise its
orientation, the staff embraced the new museumology and shifted
from a narrow focus on the idealized Jackson to a much broader
consideration of mid-nineteenth-century white middle-class cul-

ture. Visitors now learn of Jackson's penchant for exotic water cures and dietary fads, his career as an educator, his family life, and his religious beliefs. The museum forthrightly discusses Jackson's slaves and incorporates their life experiences into the interpretation. Yet no matter how skillfully the experiences of Jackson's slaves are presented, no comprehensive treatment of their lives is possible at the site and they remain, as they were in Jackson's life, appendages of their white owner. The new approach to history ultimately could only revise, not remake, sites founded by the architects of white historical memory at the dawn of the twentieth century.[40]

Despite these persisting limitations on the presentation of black history at long-established southern museums and sites, museums devoted to African American history were slow to emerge. African American interest in museums devoted to black history was long-standing, extending back to the late nineteenth century and through the black nationalist movements of the 1960s. The organization and exhibition of major permanent collections, however, were beyond the capacity of most local activists, who lacked access to the public funds and private foundations that sustained white museums. Until the 1980s, southern museums of black history were small, obscure, and often ephemeral undertakings.

The major black history sites launched in the South during the 1980s and 1990s were a legacy of the civil rights movement as much as of the new museumology. The concern for the dispossessed and the attention devoted to the historical origins of inequality that characterized the new social history certainly made the African American past a rich new field for interpretation. Simultaneously, the civil rights movement secured for blacks political rights that enabled them to prod elected officials to subsidize museums devoted to their heritage. Not surprisingly, the movement became the focus for the museums. These museums, including the National Civil Rights Museum in Memphis (1991), the Birmingham Civil Rights Institute (1992), the National Voting Rights Museum in Selma (1992), the Ralph Mark Gilbert Civil Rights Museum in Savannah (1996), and the Albany (Georgia) Civil Rights Museum (1998), were self-conscious efforts to institutionalize the links that both social historians and movement activists saw among historical awareness, black identity, and social change in the South.

Without the consolidation of black political power in many southern cities, the proliferation of new museums devoted to black history would have been unlikely. In Memphis, the city's powerful black political leadership, which had emerged during the 1970s, provided crucial allies for the Memphis activists who bought the decrepit Lorraine Motel, the site of Martin Luther King Jr.'s assassination, at a bankruptcy auction in 1982. Their ambitious plans for a museum commemorating the civil rights movement would have stalled without the infusion of $9 million of state and local public funds. With public funding assured, activists were able to pry contributions from the city's major corporations.[41] In Birmingham, Richard Arrington, the city's first black mayor, adapted long-standing plans for a civil rights museum to shore up his political machine. In 1985 he used city funds to purchase land next to both the Sixteenth Street Baptist Church, the site of a notorious bombing by white supremacists in 1963, and the park where police and firemen, under orders from Eugene "Bull" Connor, had shocked the world with their brutality toward black protesters. Although many observers questioned his motivations for supporting the museum (especially after allegations of massive corruption in its construction), he nevertheless cobbled together the $12 million necessary to complete the facility. Elected officials used similar methods to fund renovations at the site of a proposed civil rights museum in Albany, Georgia. This reliance on public funding was a recognition that blacks lacked sufficient financial resources on their own to create and sustain these major public institutions. These claims on the public purse also reflected a belief that funding was warranted on the basis of both equity and historical significance. Public resources, after all, had been used to confer prestige on white heritage for more than a century; now blacks expected the state to do the same for their heritage.[42]

The civil rights museums that opened during the 1990s displayed an even more acutely activist orientation toward the past than did most well-established museums. Beyond using new exhibit techniques to engage the largest possible audience, the civil rights museums explicitly promoted historical awareness as an agent of social change. In the eyes of their founders, the civil rights museums are continuations of the movement for racial justice. The Martin Luther King Jr. Center for Nonviolent Social Change in Atlanta, founded by King's widow in 1968, was an archetype for this fusion of shrine, interpretative site, and laboratory of social change. The overt insistence on the continuing relevance of the history presented in these museums may be explained partially by their comparatively contemporary subject matter. Exhibits that draw connections between the events of the 1960s and present-day America hardly seemed forced. Yet the civil rights museums go further and attempt to inspire visitors to activism. A panel in the final exhibit space at the Memphis museum proclaims, "We must remember our past and learn from it . . . The struggle will continue, with determination and courage." Outreach programs offered by the museum aim to "teach people their role and their responsibility today." Lawrence Pijeaux Jr., director of the Birmingham museum, boasts that his museum's conferences, such as "Transformative Justice," demonstrate that "We are more than a museum. We're not stuck in the past."[43]

This activist orientation informs both the content and display of museums' exhibits, which recount the so-called "Montgomery to Memphis narrative," tracing the struggle for racial equality through such well-known flashpoints as Montgomery, Little Rock, Greensboro, Albany, Birmingham, Selma, and Memphis. However conventional this narrative arc, the museums shy away from attention to the leaders of these campaigns and instead present the "movement" as a mass movement. The Albany museum, for example, presents "largely a story of unsung heroes. A story of ordinary people in extraordinary times." Particular emphasis is placed on recreating the visceral experience of segregation. Tennessee Circuit Judge D'Army Bailey, one of the visionaries behind the Memphis museum, described the level of historical immediacy that he hoped the site would achieve: "I wanted not only sirens and barking dogs, but I even envisioned a whiff of tear gas." The museum's exhibit designer had the same objective: "We are trying in the exhibits to give them a You Are Them feeling." Among the exhibits at the museum is a recreation of the event that sparked the famous Montgomery bus boycott in 1955. When visitors take a seat on the bus, they automatically activate prerecorded audio commands like those that a white bus driver made to Rosa Parks when she violated the segregated seating law. "That brings it right home to you . . . That's when reality sets in," the director of the museum explained. The sit-in movement is commemorated by four mannequins seated at a lunch counter while television monitors in front of them broadcast footage of the verbal and physical violence directed against them by white segregationists. Even while the exhibits aim to give patrons a sense of the degradation and violence of Jim Crow–era racism, they also emphasize that history is an unresolved, ongoing process. By reminding visitors of how recently legal segregation prevailed, the museums present a living past that is bound up in the present, one neither exotically different nor entirely escaped.[44]

The exhibits at the Birmingham Civil Rights Institute, like those at other civil rights museums, celebrate the role of black "folk" in the campaign to secure racial equality. (Birmingham Civil Rights Institute)

This reformist orientation extends to the museums' relationship to their immediate urban surroundings. Advocates for the museums predicted that they would stimulate tourism, which in turn would resuscitate the decayed black neighborhoods in which they were located. "Tourism," Juanita Moore of the Memphis museum acknowledged, "has played a major part in folks being interested" in creating museums of black history. In Memphis, the site of the museum had been a haven for prostitutes in a dilapidated neighborhood. City officials defended public funding for the site because it "is certainly going to revitalize the area." Planners in Birmingham similarly forecast that the museum there would "bring back" its neighborhood. In Savannah, W. W. Law and his Yamacraw branch of the ASALH promoted their civil rights museum as part of a campaign to redevelop the former West Broad Street, which had festered since being gutted by ur-

ban renewal during the 1960s. These sometimes rosy predictions
may have been intended to convince skeptical taxpayers of the
worthiness of public subsidies for the museums. But also at work
was the belief that an awareness of black history was a prerequisite for any campaign to address the contemporary needs and concerns of African Americans. By reviving community pride, the
argument goes, historical awareness will promote the regenera-
tion of community institutions.[45]

Almost certainly too much has been asked of the new African
American history museums in the South. They are expected to revise misconceptions about the past, teach inspirational lessons,
attract tourists, revive troubled neighborhoods, and spur political activism. These expectations, however unrealistic, are entirely
predictable. Throughout the century after the Civil War, southern whites had looked to their monuments and museums to advance similar ends. With so few venues in which to present their
collective memory, blacks understandably have anticipated that
their new museums would do the work that the myriad memory
theaters of whites have long performed. Given these pressures,
there is a risk that contemporary African American museums will
promote a form of shallow "therapeutic activism" that mutes the
searing violence and persecution so central to their heritage. Lost
also may be the ironies, nuances, and unsettling contradictions
of the past that cannot be reconciled with a preferred saga of
unflagging activism and purpose. African American history museums, like other contemporary museums, are necessarily cautious
about offending the sensibilities of important constituencies; their
aim, after all, is to attract visitors. In this light, one wonders how
many southerners, let alone others, would have the stamina for a
candid history of blacks that did not offer some sort of uplifting
resolution. Like the Emancipation Day jeremiads of old, present-
day museums of black history hold out the promise that the tra-

vails of history have had a purpose, one that we can achieve if we learn its lessons.[46]

Although of recent origin, the transformation of historical interpretation in southern museums is both broad and substantial. In 1957 Governor Stanley and other white defenders of "southern traditions" almost certainly could not have envisioned a time when the institution of slavery would be a focus of interpretation at historic sites. And although Stanley predicted many calamities following the advent of black voting, he did not anticipate that the South would be home to museums that commemorated the struggle to secure black political and civil rights. Now, in public museums where the new museumology has taken root, creative and constructive interpretations of the region's contested history are commonplace. And with the advent of museums devoted to African American history and run by African American staffs, whites no longer have exclusive control over how museums present the region's history. Some museums, especially small, privately owned sites, have resisted the revisionist impulse. Even so, it is not only possible but also realistic to anticipate that the South's museums will house some of the most substantive and productive discussions about the history that continues to divide southerners.

Since the 1920s, the commercialization of the South's past has been one of the region's largest producers of income. Until the end of the twentieth century, however, southern tourism barely acknowledged the historical experience of blacks. The advent of "heritage" tourism in the region is a signal development in an arena of commerce and public culture that would appear especially resistant to revision. To recognize blacks' past could raise contentious questions about both the legacies of discrimination and the state of current race relations. Incorporation of black heritage risks shattering long-nurtured associations of romance and nostalgia with many of the region's tourist attractions, which in turn may dissolve the separation of the past and present that is so appealing to contemporary tastes. Yet at the same time, countervailing pressures have encouraged the expansion of "heritage" tourism throughout the region and have substantially broadened the historical past on display in the South.

Heritage tours have proliferated from Portsmouth, Virginia, to Natchez, Mississippi. Tourists in New Orleans who forgo the temptations of Bourbon Street, haunted houses, picturesque graveyards, and French Quarter mansions can take a six-hour "Africans in Louisiana" tour. Beginning at the city's Old Slave Market, which was once a center of the nation's trade in human chattel, the tour travels along the "Old River Road" that hugs the Mississippi River to Baton Rouge. Hundreds of thousands of tourists travel this route each year, visiting the grandiose antebellum plantations that line it. Many visitors may be wistful for the grandeur and elegance of the Old South. The "Africans in Louisiana" tour, however, addresses the lifestyle of slave owners only as a backdrop for the enslavement and trade in Africans. When the tour guides explain how slaves developed communities, nurtured families, and resisted their bondage, they are "trying to give the enslaved Africans some humanity." Leonard Moore, the tour's founder, adds, "We look at everything through their lens." The "hidden" history of African Americans is also the focus of Negro Heritage Trail Tour in Savannah, Georgia. Initiated by W. W. Law and his Yamacraw chapter of the ASALH and led by a "conductor" whose title evokes memories of the Underground Railroad, the tour reinterprets familiar sights in the city. Savannah's famed grid of public squares warrants comment as the legacy not of James Oglethorpe, the city's founder, but of the black slaves who constructed it along with most of the city's historic buildings. Rather than parade through the restored mansions in the historic downtown, tour patrons visit the First African Baptist Church, the local slave market, historically black neighborhoods, and African American history museums.[47]

As recently as two decades ago, the southern tourism industry catered almost exclusively to whites. During the era of Jim Crow, segregated railroad cars and rustic accommodations robbed travel of most of its romance for blacks. Automobiles offered an escape from some of these hardships, but blacks still risked insult or worse whenever they sought out restaurants or lodging in unfamiliar surroundings. At a few destinations, such as Atlantic Beach in North Carolina and American Beach in Florida, black tourists could relax without fear of white harassment. But most of the South's major historic destinations offered blacks only restricted visiting hours and limited access to public amenities. Black guests at Colonial Williamsburg, for example, could visit the restored buildings, but restaurants and hotels at this American icon were strictly for whites only.[48]

Given the humiliation that generations of black travelers had endured, tourist destinations predictably became targets for civil rights activism during the 1960s. In addition to protesting segregated waiting rooms at bus and rail stations, blacks held "wade-ins," defying ordinances that had segregated public pools and beaches from Virginia to Texas. In Saint Augustine, Florida, black activists exploited the tourist industry's economic vulnerability by discouraging northern travelers from patronizing "America's oldest segregated city." Even so, tourist operators there and elsewhere showed little inclination to offend traditional white sensibilities by integrating their facilities, and only after the passage of the Civil Rights Act of 1964 were the South's tourist facilities open, in principle, to blacks.[49]

Despite the end of legal segregation, neither white businessmen nor public officials revised their promotional campaigns with an eye toward enticing black customers. Instead, tourism promoters splurged on the most expensive advertising campaign in the region's history, invoking images of the South that were little changed from those presented in the early twentieth century. Southern states accounted for three of the top five (and five of the top ten) state advertising budgets during the 1970s. Across the region, gentility and historical romance were the proffered attractions. Richmond advertised itself as "Down Where the South Begins" and Baton Rouge as "Plantation Country." A brochure boasted, without apparent irony, that Natchez, Mississippi, was "Where the Old South Still Lives." An Alabama folder acknowledged that "The Old South is Gone" but nevertheless urged visitors to visit one of the state's "elegant, stately, ornate" antebellum homes where they would "see why our ancestors went to war to save the Old South." In Arkansas, a tourist handout proclaimed that the state's antebellum mansions were a testament to "a civilization" that had been "fast refining itself into a model of grace for all ages." Columned mansions, white belles in hoop skirts, Civil War shrines—these were the icons of southern tourism during the 1970s. That these attractions might be off-putting to blacks and some whites seemingly went unacknowledged. Indeed, tourism specialists ignored potential African American customers altogether. For example, major surveys of tourism in Georgia and in Charleston, South Carolina, written during the early 1970s made no mention of the effect of integration on the industry or the traveling habits of blacks.[50]

Pragmatic political considerations, as well as economic interests, provided the impetus for the revision of southern promotional strategies. For white politicians eager to put the tumult and recriminations of the civil rights struggle behind them, the promotion of "heritage" tourism was of a piece with their efforts to publicize the "New" Sunbelt South. They pointed to the commercialization of black history as a gesture of reconciliation and progress. Alabama, which had earned international notoriety for its tortured race relations, appropriately led the way with the publication of *Alabama's Black Heritage* in 1983. Governor George C. Wallace held up the publication as "our way of telling everybody that Alabama has changed." The self-conscious revision of perceptions of Alabama meshed with Wallace's efforts to recast himself as a racial liberal. But even Wallace's conservative Republican successors endorsed the state's new tourism campaigns, proclaiming, "We're not going to hide from our past anymore." Unable to boast any nationally known tourist destinations, Alabama's promoters instead elevated "the darker side of Alabama's past" as one of the state's most marketable assets. Notorious sites in the civil rights struggle, such as the Edmund Pettus Bridge in Selma and the Sixteenth Street Baptist Church in Birmingham, now were officially promoted as tourist destinations. Each successive edition of *Alabama's Black Heritage* added more sites to the state's attractions, until the original number, fewer than sixty, became more than three hundred. By 1999, nearly 700,000 copies of the guidebook had been distributed around the world, prompting its originator, Frances Smiley, to boast, "It has become the best image builder for Alabama ever."[51]

Tourism promoters elsewhere were slow to follow Alabama's lead. But by the 1990s they could no longer afford to ignore black tourism. Survey data, which revealed that blacks spend more money than other tourists, caught the eye of public officials eager to use tourism to revitalize depressed communities across the South's hinterland. Boosters also noted that in recent years blacks have shown a much greater appetite for travel than most Americans. The success of the first *Essence* Festival, held in 1995 in New Orleans, aroused envy across the region. The music and cultural festival attracted nearly 150,000 people, mostly African Americans, and garnered an estimated $70 million for the city. Previously, New Orleans officials had made few targeted efforts to lure black tourists. But after the festival, a state official remarked, "If anybody was skeptical before about how important that [African American] market was, [they] should have those questions answered now." From Virginia to Mississippi, officials anxious to revive an industry badly shaken by international terrorism have focused on black tourism. So manifold were the benefits of "heritage" tourism that by the end of the 1990s every southern state promoted it and specifically targeted African Americans with advertising.[52]

Beyond profits, boosters promise that black heritage tourism will hasten racial reconciliation. According to Sara Fuller, Birmingham's director of tourism, heritage tourism preserves places that inspire healing and introspection and "enhance better race relations." These attitudes suggest that by acknowledging the past it can be sequestered, and the present-day South can be distanced from its antecedents. In the words of a tour guide at a faux plantation home in Greenville, Mississippi, "It happened; this is our history. We're different now." The aim of the promoters of heritage tourism is not to ignore, repudiate, or trivialize the region's history. "This is our history," the director of the Mississippi Division of Tourism readily concedes. "We have an image problem." Heritage tourism, she predicts, has a crucial role to play in a region haunted by its past. "Some parts of it [our history] we're not so proud of, but come see it and let's understand it. And let's hold hands and move on."[53]

The competitive marketplace in southern heritage almost certainly will continue to include some private museums and tourist destinations that will present interpretations of the South's history little changed from those that prevailed decades ago. But there are reasons to be cautiously optimistic about the prospects for gradual and ongoing reinterpretation, especially at publicly funded sites. Because the prevailing ethos among museum professionals stresses the active participation of patrons in exhibit planning and interpretation, broad discussion of controversial historical issues are encouraged. While most sites understandably strive to avoid controversy, they do not avoid contentious topics altogether. Instead, public sites increasingly address controversial subjects by accommodating diverse, even competing interpretations, thereby encouraging patrons to view the past as complex, contradictory, and unresolved. To the extent that the region's repositories of history do so, they will provide the South ideal settings in which to hash out arguments over a history that continues to divide southerners.

The determined refusal of blacks to surrender their claims on the South's public spaces and life sustained a tradition of contestation that began immediately after the Civil War. For most of the century following the Civil War, the contest about the South's recalled past was waged obliquely. Blacks forthrightly challenged white versions of the past, but whites typically ignored these attacks, preferring instead to use their power to push blacks to the extreme margins of southern public life. But since the 1960s, whites have had to contend with an enfranchised and mobilized black population that cannot easily be excluded from civic life. The contest over interpretation of the southern past consequently has entered the public arena more directly than at any time since Reconstruction. Some observers have mistakenly concluded that these developments have fostered an unwelcome politicization of the South's recalled past. In fact, the contest between whites and blacks over their past has always been starkly political, but now the relative powers of the participants have changed. Blacks now wield more control over their physical surroundings and more influence in public life than at any time in the region's history.

This revision of the South's civic landscape is no mere chimera but rather the tangible consequence of blacks' enlisting public institutions to record and honor their past. As blacks extended and consolidated their political influence during the 1970s and 1980s, they challenged persisting white privilege. Beyond the practical goal of depriving whites of the power that flowed from their exclusive control of public life, black activists looked to a new and inclusive civic culture to renew democracy and ease inequities in the region. Black public life, which had long been conducted outside of established political institutions and public spaces, now acquired new visibility as blacks demanded their full incorporation into the southern polity. Public institutions did not so much grant blacks a voice as blacks themselves demanded it. The dogged fund-raisers and community organizers in Savannah who amassed money to open a local civil rights museum, the activists in Bowling Green, Virginia, who envisioned a monument to black history in the town square, and the myriad other black groups who complained that the history of the South had not been fully and fairly told were all driven by the ambition of blacks to anchor their history at the very center of southern public life.

Blacks insisted that all southerners be exposed to their history, an ambition that posed a more serious challenge to the privileged status of white history than if blacks had aspired to keep their history separate. In this crusade, blacks have had important allies among southern whites. By siding with blacks during the controversy in Bowling Green and in other situations, sympathetic whites have helped black activists call for a broadening of the representations of the past that inform the public spaces and life of the South. Whether prompted by political expediency or sincere principle, some whites now endorse the proposition that history should be presented in a manner that is acceptable to African Americans.

In the wake of this profoundly important transformation, unprecedented resources are now devoted to public recognition of a history that is distinct from, if still interwoven with, southern white history. Permanent public sites that commemorate the black past have multiplied in the past quarter of a century. Fredericksburg, Virginia, a town previously associated with colonial patriots and a bloody Civil War battle, is now the site of a major museum devoted to the history of slavery. In Charleston, where the tourist experience overwhelmingly focused on the low-country white aristocracy, a museum of African American history is now open. In Richmond, bridges now bear the names of civil rights activists and in several southern states heritage trails link black history shrines. Civic calendars across the region now include a holiday honoring Martin Luther King Jr., while in Texas Juneteenth is a state holiday. Black history may not crowd the southern landscape to the extent that white history does, but it is present and visible to a degree that was unimaginable as recently as two decades ago.

Conclusion

FROM ITS INCEPTION, the monument commemorating Arthur Ashe aroused controversy. Many whites recoiled at the suggestion that an image of a black tennis star merited inclusion on Monument Avenue, a boulevard in Richmond, Virginia, honoring such Confederate heroes as Robert E. Lee, Thomas "Stonewall" Jackson, and Jefferson Davis. Proponents of the memorial disagreed, insisting that it would promote racial reconciliation by symbolically "integrating" one of the South's most famous shrines to the Lost Cause. After months of contentious debate in the city council and local newspapers, groundbreaking ceremonies for the memorial finally took place on August 15, 1995. Members of the Richmond chapter of the Council of Conservative Citizens protested the event by hoisting Confederate flags during the ceremonies, and anonymous white supremacists circulated racist leaflets in the surrounding neighborhoods. Other Richmonders defied expectations by endorsing the monument. One advocate, who boasted that her ancestors had fought for the Confederacy, explained: "My great grandfather's past actions take nothing away from the vast accomplishments and legacy of Arthur Ashe. Neither does Ashe's memorialized presence take anything away from the honor and integrity of my ancestor's deeds or memory." Another white supporter, who attended the groundbreaking in his Sons of Confederate Veterans uniform, said it more simply: "A hero is a hero."[1]

The controversy surrounding the Ashe monument is emblematic of the continuing dialectic between black and white pasts in the present-day South. More than a century after whites in Reconstruction-era Richmond had bridled at blacks celebrating their freedom on the hallowed grounds of the state capitol, the quarrel over the Ashe monument calls into question the willingness of some present-day southerners to tolerate a truly inclusive version of the past. The Jim Crow "solid" South has given way to the desegregated "Sunbelt" South, immigrants from Latin America and Asia have flocked to the region, personal incomes are now more in line with national levels, evangelical churches associated with the South have spread across the nation, suburbanization has transformed huge swaths of the region into landscapes indistinguishable from those elsewhere; yet southerners continue to look to their heritage to define themselves and their region. Public life continues to be interrupted by both familiar and new controversies over Confederate symbols, museum exhibits, historical monuments, and the naming of public thoroughfares. These clashes over the past show no signs of abating in the early twenty-first century.

Controversies continue to flare because they touch on fundamental issues of power and identity. Some observers may be tempted to dismiss these battles over heritage as shallow "identity politics" that divert attention and resources from more substantive problems in the region. To be sure, some of the contretemps over the South's past verge on farcical. Who can take seriously the unreconstructed rebel who explained to a journalist that he embraced vegetarianism so he could renounce federally inspected beef? But the stakes in the controversies that arouse the strongest passions and the widest interest are quite real. As has been true since the Civil War, claims to material resources, political power, and moral high ground are at the center of contemporary debates over the South's history. Although the future course of these debates cannot easily be predicted, there is ample reason to conclude that struggles over historical memory will remain conspicuous in southern public life. Moreover, how southerners choose to grapple with their disputed past will have enduring consequences for the region's civic culture and public institutions.[2]

Revision of the South's public landscapes continues to spark controversy. Activists target persisting historical gaps at the region's heritage sites while calling for more inclusive commemorations and memorials. Southern institutions have yet to acknowledge the divergent memories of recent traumas that divide many whites and blacks; consequently, some of the thorniest questions about the region's past remain unaddressed. And in an era when even public institutions are increasingly dependent on corporate donors and philanthropy, the underfunding of new, revisionist cultural landmarks risks perpetuating the marginalization of much of the South's heritage.

For all the talk of using museums to promote critical analysis of the connections between the past and contemporary concerns, too few museums actually do so. Exhibits that address class privilege and racial exploitation during the colonial and antebellum eras are now commonplace, but sites that delve into the political and economic underpinnings of white power during the era of Jim Crow remain rare. Apparently it is easier for museums to acknowledge the wealth and power that white slaveholders accrued than to address the benefits that whites in recent times received from the maintenance of white supremacy. Visitors to the region's museums will learn little about how residential segregation was (and is) maintained, what methods white leaders used to co-opt black resistance, or the motivations of blacks who impeded campaigns for racial equality. Police brutality, capital punishment, and other contentious issues regarding criminal justice that mobilized activists throughout the twentieth century are seldom considered, even in the region's civil rights museums.[3]

These and other controversies of contemporary racial politics cannot be evaded entirely, however, because social and economic transformations compel southerners to grapple with them. The de facto resegregation of public education in the South, for example, is contributing to an evolving historical memory of both segregation and integration. The resegregation of public schools in Atlanta is suggestive of trends throughout the region. By 2003, seventy-six of Atlanta's ninety-one public schools had fewer than five white students. Even in suburbs with significant white populations, public schools resegregated briskly. In 1969, before court-ordered integration began, 94 percent of suburban DeKalb County's 82,000 public school students were white; in 1999, less than 12 percent of the county's 95,000 students were white. Although nearly 90 percent of the residents of Avondale Estates in the same county are white, the public high school there enrolls 95 percent minority students. In rural areas, especially in the Deep South, meaningful integration often never occurred. So pronounced has been white flight to private academies that the racial divide between public and private schools is virtually complete. In Greenville, Mississippi, in 2003, for example, one public high school had only four whites among its 576 students, while a nearby Christian academy had only three blacks among its 357 students. In ten counties in the state, more than 90 percent of white students attended private schools in 2003.[4]

One effect of resegregation is that black parents and students increasingly insist that schools should adapt to the overwhelmingly minority populations that they now serve. The renaming of public schools across the region is one striking manifestation of this impulse. In 1925, when Robert E. Lee Elementary School in the West End neighborhood of Birmingham opened, its student body was exclusively white. By 2001, it was almost exclusively black. Nell Allen, a local activist, led a drive to rename the school after Martin Luther King Jr., explaining, "He [Lee] was a great example for the community that was living in the area when the school was built . . . [but] that population is no longer here." In other instances, the tin ears of school boards virtually compelled black parents to protest school names. In Saint Bernard Parish in Louisiana, black parents long tolerated that Milladoun Elementary was named after a nearby antebellum plantation. But plans to replace the dilapidated school with a new school named after Confederate P. G. T. Beauregard outraged parents. In New Orleans a grassroots movement during the 1980s, led by the Louisiana State Committee against Apartheid, campaigned to remove the names of all slaveholders from local schools. The school board eventually adopted a policy against retaining names of "former slave owners or others who did not respect equal opportunity for all." Under the 1992 policy, the decision to rename schools is left up to school faculty and students, who must initiate and vote for the change. Within five years, faculty and students had renamed twenty-two schools, including P. G. T. Beauregard Elementary (now named after black jurist Thurgood Marshall) and Jefferson Davis Elementary (now named after the city's first black mayor, Ernest N. Morial).[5]

Although many commentators have ridiculed the renaming of schools as meaningless grandstanding and "political correctness" run amok, it reflects a renewed sense of cultural custodianship among black parents and students for their schools. Having witnessed the loss of many black school traditions during the period of school consolidation during the late 1960s and early 1970s, black teachers, students, and parents are now transforming the identities of the schools that they inherited after integration. Michael L. Lomax, president of Dillard University in New Orleans, answered the critics, highlighting the combination of power and powerlessness that lay behind efforts to give schools new identities. "It's a very direct statement that I will celebrate my own history and I will compel you to recognize my heroes and heroines," he explained. "But it is also more of a statement of frustration in exercising power over one of the few things that you can exercise power over, which is the name of a street or a building."[6]

For many blacks, however, the renaming of schools cannot erase their ambivalence about integration or about its costs. Whereas black schools were once an important symbol of black achievement and perseverance, integrated schools are now seen by some as emblems of loss. In growing numbers, alumni of segregated schools assemble annually, share memories, and restore old bonds. These gatherings implicitly disparage present-day integrated schools. Recollections of the days before integration, when black schools were staffed by long-serving and highly regarded faculty who were guardians of traditions, evoke a time irretrievably lost and express an unmistakable sense of disillusionment. When Joan Cooper, an organizer of a black high-school reunion in Brunswick, Florida, boasted that her teachers "had instilled in us the importance of our heritage and pride of color that has never left us," she implied that she and her classmates had absorbed a sense of dignity that contemporary students lack. Recalling his years at Phillis Wheatley Elementary School in Louisville, Kentucky, Jim Cleaver conceded that the facility was dingy and the textbooks tattered. Nevertheless there he had gained "the spirit that comes with being proud of who and what you are." How ironic, he mused, that today's "young people" don't "have the advantage of Phillis Wheatley Elementary School." The crumbling buildings that once housed black schools foster skepticism among some blacks about the possibilities for equitable integration and serve as reminders of how vulnerable historically black spaces are to forces that blacks cannot fully control. This nostalgia for one of the most glaring features of the Jim Crow South contrasts with the more pervasive celebration of the crusade against white supremacy in the region's civil rights museums.[7]

Even more jarring contrasts occur in southern tourism. In the region's increasingly segmented tourist industry, "heritage" tourism is a label applied equally to black sites that subvert familiar tropes of the region's past and attractions offering retrograde interpretations that have changed little in decades. Heritage tourism in Natchez, Mississippi, is a case in point. Since the 1930s, the community's two white garden clubs have hosted an annual "pilgrimage" during which hoop-skirted white women and men in string ties and white suits welcome visitors into some of the South's most opulent antebellum mansions. For the women of the garden clubs, the pilgrimage started as a way to beautify the community and celebrate the traditions that they valued. The event quickly outgrew its amateurish origins and has become an engine for the community's economy and the source of its national reputation.[8]

Since its inception, the pilgrimage has unapologetically marketed Old South "romance." "Nostalgia is a big part in the attraction," a white resident of Natchez concedes. The pilgrimage offers "a chance to get away and step into another time and place." A hostess agrees, explaining, "It's kind of like a play. We open the front door and try to act like aristocrats—because everyone expects 'Gone with the Wind.'" The highlight of the pilgrimage for

Women dressed in pilgrimage costumes, Natchez, Mississippi, ca. 1930s. (Roane Fleming Byrnes Collection, J. D. Williams Library, University of Mississippi)

many tourists is the Confederate Pageant, performed for thousands at the city auditorium four nights a week during the season. When the pageant was first performed during the 1930s, it was a local counterpart to the Azalea Festival in Charleston and other community spectacles of the era. But Natchez's pageant, despite periodic controversies, has changed little since then. Offering "romance, grandeur, chivalry," and "adventure," the pageant reenacts—or, more accurately, imagines—a sequence of vignettes, culminating with a Confederate farewell ball. Performed by white girls and women in hoopskirts and ball gowns, and boys and men in frock coats and military uniforms, the tableaux unabashedly extol the city's aristocratic heritage and traditions.[9]

Blacks in Natchez have long resented the pilgrimage. One black letter writer in the local newspaper raged against it as "a revival of the Old South" that instills "those ideas in each successive generation." Early pilgrimage organizers assigned only demeaning roles to blacks, such as allowing them to don the tattered garb of "cotton pickers and pickaninnies" and sing spirituals during the Confederate Pageant. Blacks refused such roles during the 1960s, leaving white organizers bewildered. "I don't know why they stopped," a puzzled garden club member remarked in 1989. Organizers gradually recognized that the all-white pageant perhaps should be more inclusive, and so in 1986 the president of the Natchez Garden Club proposed that a "darkies' ball" tableau, recreating the slave balls of yore, be added to the festival. The outcry that followed her suggestion baffled many local whites, suggesting how strong was the grip of the mythic image underlying the pilgrimage. Such attitudes led one black resident to conclude that "There are ante-bellum minds as well as ante-bellum structures here."[10]

Beginning in the 1990s black activists and entrepreneurs, abetted by some whites, began to contest the moonlight-and-magnolia imagery that remained the lifeblood of Natchez's tourism. In 1991, the Natchez Association for the Preservation of African-American Culture opened a black history museum. Two years later, the city hired its first director of minority affairs for tourism and began promoting its black heritage. Steps were taken to identify local black history sites, such as the unmarked childhood home of Richard Wright, the city's most famous novelist. By the late 1990s, blacks had even secured a new place in the pilgrimage festivities with "Southern Road to Freedom," a musical tribute to

The cast of "Southern Road to Freedom," ca. 2000, offer a black-oriented history during the Natchez Pilgrimage. (Historic Natchez Foundation)

the struggles of African Americans in Natchez. With the establishment of the Natchez National Historic Park, which includes both Melrose, an antebellum mansion, and the William Johnson House, the home of a wealthy antebellum free black man, the city now boasts a cluster of notable attractions where black history is sympathetically presented.[11]

Still unclear, however, is whether "heritage" tourism will substantially alter the southern past encountered by most tourists. Despite the labors of Natchez's black history activists during the 1990s, they failed to gain a significant portion of the city's tourist trade. Of the more than 350,000 tourists who visited the city in 1993, for example, fewer than five thousand made their way to the Museum of Afro-American History and Culture. With the exception of the National Historic Park, the black history sites operate on shoestring budgets and without adequate publicity. As one of the women who founded the Mostly African Market, a nonprofit gallery, jokes, "We're not a low-budget agency. We're a no budget agency." And because many of the plans for the development of black history require public funding, they are hostage to shifting local priorities. For example, an extended campaign to secure public funding to purchase the site of the city's once thriving slave market ran aground when budget exigencies persuaded the city aldermen, some of whom were black, that other needs were more urgent. Even if the city had been able to purchase the site, it lacked funds to develop it.[12]

As in the past, access to resources will dictate which groups in Natchez and elsewhere are able to enshrine their version of history. Well-heeled and well-connected organizations like the Natchez garden clubs remain far more likely than other groups to secure public recognition for their version of the past. The already considerable influence of private organizations is certain to grow at a time when public funding for historical interpretation is tight and the quasi-privatization of public works gathers speed. Recent trends in highway marker programs across the South are suggestive. Although state agencies retain editorial control over the text of markers, private groups now bear the cost of manufacturing and erecting the signs. Previously whites used state funds to clutter the landscape of the South with markers that celebrated both the significant and trivial deeds of whites. Now, when there is an acknowledged need to designate notable black history sites, adequate public funding is no longer available. To take one example, as of 1998 only thirty-seven of some eight hundred highway markers in South Carolina memorialized African American history. Similar disparities are evident in most southern states.[13]

Questions persist about whether blacks can wield sufficient influence in the "heritage" industry to redress these persisting gaps. Blacks in Natchez pocket only a tiny portion of the city's $120 million annual tourist receipts. Black low-wage workers vastly outnumber black tour operators. These conditions evoke unwelcome memories of the "Old South" among some black visitors. Describing her trip "as a descent into hell," one black tourist bristled at the city's "proud atmosphere of white superiority" and complained that she saw "not one black tour guide, only black gardeners and parking attendants." The president of the African American Travel and Tourism Association concedes that blacks barely have a toehold in the tourist industry anywhere, much less Natchez: "We own very few tourism products like black museums, side attractions, black resorts." As notable as the new black history sites in Natchez and the rest of the South are, the overwhelming bulk of the city's and the region's tourist infrastructure remains in the hands of whites, who operate it as they see fit.[14]

As a consequence of the disparity in resources controlled by whites and blacks, heritage sites in Natchez and many other southern tourist destinations still fail to provide a sophisticated, inclusive synthesis of black and white versions of the past. Instead they offer competing narratives of southern heritage that exist in apparent isolation from each other. A few sites focus almost exclusively on the black experience, while many more concentrate on the white experience. For the foreseeable future it seems likely that operators of tours in Natchez and the River Road plantations of Louisiana, to take just two examples, will divide the "market," and with it the history that they offer. The owner of Oak Alley in Louisiana, one of the most famous and frequently visited plantations in the South, has already adopted this business strategy. Tour guides there wear period dress and visitors can sip mint juleps while they stroll the mansion's manicured grounds. He is unapologetic about the site's complete silence on the subject of slavery. Visitors, he explains, "come for the hoop skirts, the grandeur, and the elegance. That's a part of the story, and maybe the better part of the story for us to tell."[15]

Southerners intent on securing the moral high ground in debates over the past have increasingly looked to political and judicial leaders to arbitrate historical interpretation. This recourse to the political realm is unquestionably divisive, because it is as likely to yield disgruntled losers as gratified winners. And it is these recent struggles that have provoked the most hand-wringing about the worrisome escalation of "culture wars" in the region. Previously, white elites exploited their wealth and power to adorn their version of the past with the prestige of official recognition. The region's public archives and museums long gave inordinate privilege to the history that appealed to white elites, thereby giving it the imprimatur of both the state and the historical profession. Now, however, historical sites and public historians are more likely to accentuate both the complexities of and divergent perspectives on the past. Their stance offers little solace to those who believe that their interpretation of history qualifies as historical "truth," and that other interpretations are illegitimate. Southerners whose views were once the privileged interpretation of the past can no longer assume that public historical sites and the historical profession will bolster their claims. White southerners who hanker for an unambiguous celebration of Confederate valor are unlikely to be satisfied by exhibitions on slavery at the Museum of the Confederacy or discussions of Stonewall Jackson's eccentricities and slaveholding at the Stonewall Jackson House. Nor can black southerners who want unambiguous acknowledgment of the brutality of slavery easily tolerate the continuing celebration of Confederate History Month and similar anniversaries. Because no other contemporary institutions can resolve these disputes to the satisfaction of concerned southerners, administrative bodies, legislatures, and courts have necessarily become the battlegrounds in clashes over the past.

The humdrum business of planning commissions and zoning boards may seem to be an unlikely venue for substantive debates over contested historical matters. But however prosaic and bureaucratic disputes over land use may be, they are also one of the most important contexts in which communities self-consciously articulate the qualities that make them enduring places with an idealized past. Zoning was and remains a favored tool to protect property values and to exclude the unwelcome, as white activists in Charleston and New Orleans demonstrated during the 1930s. Since then, the preservationist ethos has expanded far beyond its earlier urban and genteel origins and is now embraced by all manner of southerners anxious about the region's headlong development. Southerners are hardly unique in dreading the "placelessness" that drains so many U.S. landscapes of a distinctive identity. In the suburbs that consume more and more of the South, builders exploit familiar southern icons of place, especially names and symbols redolent of the Old South, to give a patina of character to antiseptic residential "plantations" and "estates." Southerners who scorn these contrivances look to public agencies to defend their communities against sprawl and unwelcome development. It is hardly a coincidence that between 1960 and 1990—the advent of the South's "bulldozer revolution"—southerners founded more historical and preservation societies than during the entire preceding century. As in the past, some of these organizations have modest ambitions, but many others have taken the lead in policing commercial and residential development.[16]

The Disney Corporation discovered the obstacle that a sense of place could present when the company proposed a history theme park in northern Virginia during the early 1990s. A diverse coalition, including environmentalists, Civil War buffs, and horse enthusiasts, browbeat county officials into reversing their earlier support for the company's grandiose project. If there was any common concern that united opponents of the attraction, it was that Disney's park threatened the distinctive historical character and pastoral landscape of northern Virginia. The dispute, as is common in such controversies, pitted advocates of "jobs" and "progress" against defenders of "heritage" and local "character." Similar lines are evident wherever local activists use zoning restrictions and planning codes to harass large retailers whose stores threaten the businesses and character of small southern towns. Because the "bulldozer revolution" can only temporarily be impeded or redirected, the struggle to control landscapes is inevitably a recurring feature of public life across the region.[17]

Whether interpreted as struggles pitting elitist mossbacks against pragmatic champions of progress or embattled locals against predatory multinationals, the pervasive recourse to zoning underscores the power that officials have to shape southern landscapes and the historical memory associated with them. In the past, business leaders in southern communities exercised their power surreptitiously and without political accountability, taking for granted their right to decide the path of development for their communities. Now land-use policies assure that decisions about "place" will at the very least receive public vetting, at which time interested parties have an opportunity to participate in defining the identity of their communities. When land-use policy is directed toward conserving the "hunt country" of northern Virginia, the atmosphere of a swank San Antonio neighborhood, the character of a South Carolina mill village threatened by deindustrialization, or the integrity of one of North Carolina's oldest communities founded by freed slaves, it often stands as the only bulwark against the standardization and commercialization of the southern landscape.

The region's most vexing historical controversies necessarily require the larger public stage of legislatures and courts. The expansion of state-guaranteed rights in the South has enabled activists to bring long-unaddressed historical concerns before public bodies. During the past half-century, a "rights revolution" in American jurisprudence has substantially broadened citizens' understandings of their entitlements and rights, especially to due process. Through creative claims for these broadened rights, litigation has become a favored tool for social change and the courts an essential forum for the settlement of public disputes, including persisting claims of historical injustice. Groups and issues that would never have received a hearing in these bodies during the first half of the twentieth century now do so routinely. In recent years, for example, African American litigants have invoked the Fourteenth Amendment equal-protection clause in suits to remove the Confederate flag from the state capitol in Alabama and from the Georgia state flag. Continued displays of Confederate symbols in public spaces, the suits claim, foster an exclusionary and racist atmosphere that precludes the full and free exercise of constitutionally protected rights by blacks. While the practical aim of these suits was to remove Confederate symbols from specific public spaces, the broader goal was to establish unequivocally that all Confederate symbols are tinged with racism and that the public spaces of the South should be cleansed of them. Other legal advocates have proposed using the Thirteenth Amendment protection against "badges of inferiority" to strip Confederate symbols from public schools and institutions. Here again the aim is to demonstrate that the state has a legal obligation to regulate public displays of Confederate symbols. Although state and federal courts have not been persuaded by these arguments, litigants are certain to continue to challenge the favored status of Confederate symbols and other reminders of white supremacy.[18]

Even more ambitious are demands for reparations for historical injustices, either in the form of compensation or formal apology. Calls for slave reparations to African Americans began with antebellum abolitionists and remained a topic of public debate during the late nineteenth century. During the 1960s, Whitney Young and other civil rights activists revived the issue when they urged the nation to launch a "Marshall Plan" for blacks. Appeals to moral justice and fair play provided the justification for these early proposals. More recently, proponents of reparations have grounded their litigation to recompense blacks for the illegal confiscation of their labor, property, and rights in contemporary understandings of civil rights. Reparation activists, however, have had little success. The "rights revolution" may have created an opening for litigation, but conservative state and federal courts in the region have flatly denied legal claims for slave reparations, and the prospects for legal remedies against private firms, such as insurance companies, remain unclear.[19]

Because of daunting obstacles to redress in the courts, some reparation advocates instead have turned to legislatures, where, because of black political empowerment, they stand a greater likelihood of securing a favorable hearing. With national contrition the goal, the slave reparations campaign is necessarily national rather than regional in scope. Indeed, reparations activists are especially keen to expose the extent to which the entire nation, and not just the slave South, was implicated in slavery and white supremacy. Consequently, the long history of white privilege in the South figures prominently in the justifications for slavery reparations, but the South itself has not been the focal point of the campaign. Drawing inspiration from various recent reparation schemes, including for Holocaust survivors whose assets were illegally confiscated and for Japanese-American victims of forced relocation during World War II, blacks in Congress have annually introduced a bill to establish a commission to study reparations for African Americans. Although the bill has never made it out of committee during the past fifteen years, it remains a focal point for a substantial grassroots campaign for reparations.[20]

Reparations campaigns for African Americans have also emerged specifically in the South. In the most important reparations victory to date, the Florida legislature in 1994 acknowledged the failure of state authorities to suppress a 1923 race riot in the hamlet of Rosewood. Incited by trumped up charges of black criminality, whites in the central Florida village marauded for days, destroying black property and murdering blacks. In light of the unconscionable failure of public officials to protect life and property, state legislators, seven decades after the violence, approved more than $2 million in compensation for the riot's survivors and their descendants. In many regards the Rosewood reparations are sui generis; they compensate the victims of a specific event; the number of claimants was small; and the injustice was inflicted on identifiable victims, as opposed to a broad, indiscriminate category of people. Favorable political circumstances also smoothed passage of the reparations bill. Democrats in the state legislature were eager both to retain the allegiance of black voters and to satisfy restive black legislators. In addition, the Democratic governor, who endorsed reparations, enjoyed broad public support, and white conservative legislators saw few benefits in opposing a comparatively inexpensive gesture of contrition. Activists elsewhere have been eager to replicate the success of the Rosewood reparations. Descendants of race riot victims in Tulsa and in Wilmington, North Carolina, have called for compensation, and recently serious proposals for reparations for the descendants of lynching victims have been broached.[21]

Compelling the nation to acknowledge the systematic and ongoing injustices endured by African Americans is at least as important to reparations activists as is remunerating blacks for the uncompensated labor and suffering of their ancestors. Consequently, activists measure the success of their campaigns for reparations by the breadth and sincerity of the debate they provoke no less than by legislative or judicial victories. Although triumphs like the Rosewood settlement undoubtedly will be rare, activists will continue to use calls for reparations as a way to prod the South and the nation to confront its heritage of white supremacy.[22]

Litigation and legislative redress have been by no means used exclusively by African American activists. White southerners who venerate the Confederacy have responded to attacks on Confederate symbols by portraying themselves as an embattled minority whose heritage has been unfairly and illegally suppressed. In 2001, when the city of Selma, Alabama, at the behest of its newly elected black mayor, moved a new monument to Confederate general Nathan Bedford Forrest from a downtown park to a cemetery, a local committee initiated a federal suit, claiming that the monument's relocation amounted to "an unequal application of the law." Spokesmen for the aggrieved "Friends of Forrest" invoked the memory of the civil rights struggle in a city notorious as a battleground during the 1960s, announcing that "we have not been treated fairly" and warning that "we cannot be moved to the back of the bus." Mobilized by the events in Selma, the Confederate Heritage Association, with the support of a Republican legislator, introduced a bill in the state legislature to prevent any monument on public property from being relocated, removed, or "desecrated." The bill eventually stalled in the legislature and a federal district judge dismissed the suit, but not before the city of Selma had spent over $100,000 in legal fees. Elsewhere the Sons of Confederate Veterans and similar groups have provided legal counsel to employees fired for displaying the Confederate flag in the workplace and to students reprimanded for wearing Confederate symbols on public school property. Insisting that Confederate symbols have no association with racism and that the Constitution protects their right to free speech, present-day defenders of the Lost Cause take advantage of some of the same rights that black activists invoke.[23]

Without implying a moral equivalency between demands for slavery reparations and the legal campaign of Confederate enthusiasts, it nevertheless is clear that both efforts are driven by the same goal: to compel the broader public to accept and endorse an interpretation of the past for which there is no consensus. And although the region's courts and legislatures are unlikely to resolve debates over the past with much subtlety, they are fitting venues for jousting over the South's past. The labor of deciding what should be revered, what should be acknowledged, and what should be forgotten must incorporate the full diversity of southerners, not just a small community of historical activists and professional historians. Contests about the South's troubled history are at last unfolding precisely where they should: in the glare of public scrutiny and before publicly accountable officials. There is no guarantee that local zoning commissions, circuit courts, or state legislatures will ensure that all interested parties have an equal hand in influencing the debates over historical matters. The voices of the disadvantaged and marginalized will not easily be heard. But even the rickety procedures of administrative bodies and the sometimes unedifying debates in legislatures are an improvement over how issues relating to the past were addressed during most of the previous 150 years. When, for example, the DAR and its allies in Atlanta decided to reclaim the Fourth of July from African Americans at the end of the nineteenth century, they could count on the city's police and city council to do their bidding without public discussion. Similarly, the Charleston white elites who decided to yoke their city's future to tourism during the 1920s gave no thought to conducting an open discussion of their vision for the city. Now, at the very least, comparable and even weightier issues are subject to public scrutiny in forums that are more democratic and inclusive than at any previous time in the region's history.

Rather than lamenting the contentiousness that disputes over the South's past introduce into public life, we should applaud the process by which inequities are acknowledged and the region's civic life energized. Nostalgia for an age when some purportedly shared memory may have united the South is quixotic. To the extent that any shared sense of the past united southerners, it did so as much through coercion as consent. Because southerners, and white southerners in particular, have had little experience with according public recognition to competing historical memories, a pluralistic public culture will emerge only through the strenuous expression and airing of public differences.

The heated discussion in 2000 over the appropriateness of the monument to commemorate slave conspirator Gabriel Prosser in Caroline County, Virginia, shows how contestation can foster a deeper appreciation of the complexities of history. In addition to teaching many residents about local resistance to slavery by both slaves and Quakers, the controversy provoked substantive debate about which forms of resistance to oppression are legitimate. There was broad support for memorializing African American heritage, but residents divided over the appropriateness of recognizing a planned revolt that only tangentially involved residents of Caroline County. At the same time, some residents opposed undue recognition for white antislavery activism because it ignored the more furtive yet arguably more heroic resistance of the enslaved. Residents failed to resolve these questions. But, as one resident observed, "Many, many people have learned a part of their history that was never discussed before, that they didn't know existed. . . . It caused a lot of people who have open minds to have dialogue."[24]

Controversy for its own sake, of course, is not salutary. The biggest threat to a constructive debate over the past is not contentiousness per se, but rather polarization that precludes public civility and erodes institutions. At a time when political operatives resort to cultural "wedge issues" to polarize public debate, they will perhaps inevitably exploit divisions rooted in historical memory. At the same time, activists will press public figures to weigh in on historical controversies. As the dispute over Virginia's Confederate History Month in the 1990s demonstrates, the southern past remains susceptible to facile politicization. In the exchanges of inflammatory and categorical rhetoric between the event's critics and supporters, both nuance and tolerance were lost. Governors George Allen and James Gilmore displayed characteristic insensitivity to Virginia's African Americans; both lacked credibility when they protested that they were attentive to the concerns of the black community. And when their aides dismissed the criticism of the proclamations as mere knee-jerk political correctness, they confirmed the suspicions of many African Americans. Republicans predictably viewed the NAACP with mistrust because it first made an issue of Confederate History Month during an election year, suggesting political opportunism. Previous announcements of the month by other governors, including Douglas Wilder, the state's first black governor, had provoked no controversy. Moreover, the cavalier charges of racism and fascism by opponents of the celebration warped all subsequent debate. When foes of Confederate History Month went so far as to suggest that any recognition of the Confederacy amounted to condoning racism, and equated the Confederacy with Nazism, they exceeded the tolerance of even some of their supporters. But the Confederate enthusiasts, for their part, forfeited credibility by insisting that slavery was a benign institution that had no role in the origins of the Civil War. Rather than focusing exclusively on the sacrifice of the soldiers who fought during the Civil War, the neo-Confederates brazenly proclaimed the self-evident superiority of the antebellum South's social and political order.

Current trends in southern politics suggest that we can anticipate further corrosive debates over the past. Even while the Republican Party has consolidated its control over much of the region, including the previously Democratic rural hinterland, it has made no inroads among southern African Americans. As a result, the South is home to two political parties that are as racially distinct as at any time since the late nineteenth century. Uncomfortable with this stark racial divide, some white conservatives have actively courted African Americans by confessing their regret for failing to support racial equality during the 1950s and 1960s. For example, Ralph Reed, a historian trained at Emory University and the Christian Coalition's executive director during the 1990s, endorsed the civil rights movement's purported goal of a color-blind society, judging the movement's goal just. Reed and similarly inclined white conservatives conclude that the obstacles to black advancement have been removed and now blacks and whites need to move on. This strategy of acknowledging old racial wounds while relegating them to the distant past failed to sway many blacks, but it did dampen partisan political rhetoric about the region's contentious history. Since 1997, however, when Reed left the Christian Coalition, no other prominent southern white conservative has demonstrated comparable dedication to revising white conservatives' perceived hostility to civil rights. Instead, Reed's vision of a multiracial conservative alliance has given way to a strategy to balkanize electorates with inflammatory partisan appeals. The priority in contemporary politics is to arouse longtime partisans rather than to attract support from independents or erstwhile opponents. As partisanship gets a sharper edge and the parties fire up their supporters, appeals to sensitive historical disputes risk becoming convenient "wedge" issues.[25]

Recent events in several Deep South states suggest that this scenario is already occurring. There are signs that the Republican Party is assuming the mantle of the defender of white southern "heritage" and the Democratic Party, the guardian of black heritage. In the 2002 gubernatorial election in Georgia, the Republican Party systematically used Democratic governor Roy Barnes's role in the adoption of a new state flag as an election issue, rallying the support of rural white males who harbored grievances against what they perceived to be metropolitan, liberal, and elitist policies. In the hands of Republican Sonny Perdue's campaign, the new state flag became a synecdoche for "political correctness," affirmative action, multiculturalism, moral laxity, and other perceived modern ills. Georgians cast their votes for varied and complex reasons that cannot be reduced to simple racism or neo-Confederate nostalgia, but Perdue's unexpected victory over a deeply entrenched Democratic governor is inexplicable unless the "flag issue" is taken into account. The announcement of Senator John Edwards's selection as the 2004 Democratic vice presidential candidate is another case in point. The choice sparked a flurry of partisan letters from Sons of Confederate Veterans to the *Raleigh News and Observer* and other newspapers. Denouncing Edwards for his repeated claim that the Confederate flag is a symbol of oppression, Confederate enthusiasts urged voters to vote for George W. Bush, who purportedly displays proper respect for the Lost Cause.[26]

What is troubling about these political contests is that they suggest that for the foreseeable future white traditionalists will flock to the Republican Party, while the Democratic Party attracts virtually all of the region's African Americans and a shrinking number of white moderates and liberals. This outcome is being actively promoted by various organizations. Numerous white "heritage" groups publish "voters' guides" that endorse almost exclusively archconservative Republican politicians—like Texas Congressman Ron Paul, an ardent defender of the "Lost Cause," and Texas governor Rich Perry, a member of the Sons of Confederate Veterans who has not distanced himself from the organization even though it has connections to white supremacists. Both the Council of Conservative Citizens and the Southern League have aligned themselves with the Republican Party as part of a much broader reactionary agenda. The Council, which is the successor to the Citizens Council that led the opposition to integration during the 1950s and 1960s, promotes a strident, ultraconservative critique of contemporary race relations and public policy. It opposes interracial marriage, immigration, affirmative action, the "welfare state," and contemporary tolerance for what it perceives as black depravity, while openly endorsing white supremacy and "southern" traditional values. The Southern League is in agreement with all of these positions, but also champions the establishment of an independent white southern nation.

It is tempting to dismiss these small organizations as hopelessly out of step with mainstream opinion. But in several southern states, especially Mississippi and South Carolina, they have nurtured close ties with leading politicians. Governor Kirk Fordice of Mississippi embraced the Council, explaining that "there are some very good people in there with very good ideas." Senator Trent Lott has spoken to its members several times, entertained its leadership in his Senate office, and twice appointed a council leader to serve on his reelection campaign. John D. Ashcroft, while a Missouri senator, interceded on behalf of a Council member who was charged with conspiring to murder a federal agent. Moreover, both the League and the Council have waded into electoral politics by throwing their support behind campaigns to punish governors David Beasley of South Carolina and Roy Barnes of Georgia for their purported apostasy to southern heritage when they advocated against official recognition of the Confederate flag. In 2002, the organization supported Haley Barbour in his campaign to unseat Mississippi governor Ronnie Musgrove, who had promoted a new state flag in a statewide referendum a year before. Like Fordice, Barbour refused to denounce the Council or repudiate its support.[27]

The battle lines over the Confederate flag and other controversial historical symbols do not yet cleave strictly along partisan lines. In South Carolina, Governor Beasley, a Republican, willingly risked offending white conservatives by calling for the removal of the Confederate flag from the state capitol. Similarly, Governor Gilmore of Virginia antagonized his political base when he used his 1998 Confederate History Month proclamation to denounce slavery. Speaking for outraged Confederate enthusiasts and as state president of the Heritage Preservation Association, R. Wayne Byrd Sr. warned that Gilmore would suffer for his "shameful attempt . . . to pander to racist hate groups like the NAACP." In Mississippi, leading Republicans and Democrats endorsed the adoption of the new flag in 2001. Members of both parties are represented among the thirty-four Mississippi state legislators who are members of the Conservative Council.[28]

If, as these developments hint, the politics of memory in the South eventually will divide sharply along partisan and racial lines, substantive and productive consideration of divisive historical issues is certain to be hindered. Debates over the South's past are contentious enough without the added fuel of partisan divisions and the inevitable suspicion of motives that such partisanship will engender. Moreover, a divisive politics of memory will curtail prospects for redressing current inequalities in public representations of the region's history. Any ambitious plan to revise the southern historical landscape is doomed if African Americans cannot elicit the support of a significant proportion of whites, and especially of whites with meaningful political influence. Otherwise, whites and blacks committed to refashioning the South's public spaces and civic institutions are likely to find themselves appealing to a waning Democratic Party, which because of its need to attract white voters will be averse to stirring up controversies over southern heritage. To date, the partisan exploitation of history to polarize the southern electorate has received surprisingly little attention. But if it continues, southerners risk reviving some of the worst elements of the region's tortured politics and squandering the promise of the past two decades.

The 150-year struggle between blacks and whites over the past teaches several important lessons. In growing numbers southerners understand that the hard edges of the past cannot be smoothed over by well-meaning talk and that confronting the region's traumatic history is more than boosterism or a pleasant learning exercise. In a pluralistic nation like the United States, competing groups and individuals need to acknowledge the history they share with people who are not like themselves. In the absence of healthy exchange, privileged groups will perpetuate exclusionary pasts, thereby privatizing the past, reinforcing inequalities, and impeding salutary change. It is folly to expect that the struggle over memory in the South can resolve the region's most profound political and social problems. Yet if southerners speak freely, respect difference, deliberate collectively, and reject categorical claims that employ stark oppositions, they may avoid the divisions that have contaminated southern public life for most of the past century and a half. With time and commitment, they may enlist the region's public spaces to foster a heterogeneous public life rather than division and alienation.

Southerners, then, face, an exceedingly difficult task. The creation of a public culture that fully and appropriately acknowledges the South's contested past will require stamina, experimentation, and tolerance. As long as white and black southerners do not succumb to nostalgia, do not idealize an exclusionary past, and do not presume the inherent virtue of their idealized historical identity, they may fashion a fully democratic civic culture, an accomplishment that generations of southerners have longed for.

Can no "true" history of the region be offered? Is there no narrative of the South's past that southerners should collectively adopt? Certain interpretations of the southern past are indefensible and cannot withstand any standard of historical credibility: slavery was not a positive good for the enslaved; white supremacy after the Civil War cannot be justified by alleged black barbarism; and the modern civil rights movement was not a front for Communist subversion and atheism. These interpretations should be challenged and rebutted whenever and wherever they surface. They cannot contribute in any meaningful way to either deeper historical understanding or richer public debate. But such simplistic interpretations are unlikely to be at the center of controversies that roil the contemporary South. Instead, the complexities and contradictions of the South's history are often the points of contestation for black and white southerners. Slavery was an inhumane institution and yet both slave masters and slaves found ways to retain their humanity. How do we discuss this central facet of the history of slavery? The oppressiveness of the Jim Crow South was unquestionably soul-numbing, and yet blacks were never reduced, in the words of Ralph Ellison, to "the sum of [their] brutalization." How can this apparent contradiction be presented? And however much the civil rights movement was a triumph for social justice, it was accompanied by incalculable losses for southern blacks. These are the nuances of the South's history that complicate any search for simple historical "truth" and inspire sharply divergent interpretations. Although some historical narratives cannot be condoned, it is equally important to acknowledge that many of the most important historical questions are messy, confusing, and ambiguous.[29]

The search for historical "truth" cannot be separated from an appraisal of the unequal power that competing groups and individuals exercise over the interpretation of the past. To trace how power operates in the making and recording of historical interpretation, as this book has done, is also to acknowledge that history cannot be separated from practices of domination. Power operates at each stage of the processes that render some historical narratives credible and others beyond the pale. This power to privilege and silence narratives does not play out as a conspiracy at specific moments. Instead it operates continuously, and has always been present in debates over the past in the South. It was manifest at the end of the nineteenth century when whites etched their version of the South's past into the region's public spaces and life, and at the end of the twentieth century when black city officials in Richmond renamed bridges after civil rights activists.

Careful consideration, then, of the long history of unequal power over the meaning of the South's past may not resolve specific controversies. But it should teach valuable lessons to blacks and whites alike. Whites may gain a better understanding of how the southern landscape that their ancestors created appears to blacks. At the same time, it may help blacks to better understand the responsibility that comes with their new power over how history is told and fixed on the South's landscape. There are lessons in this contested history for all those who wield power over the past and all those on whom that power is exercised.

Notes

ABBREVIATIONS

AC	Atlanta Constitution
AHQ	Alabama Historical Quarterly
BAH	Birmingham Age-Herald
BB	Brenham (TX) Banner
CN&C	Charleston News and Courier
CS	Columbia (SC) State
CT	(Durham) Carolina Times
CV	Confederate Veteran
DH	Durham Herald
DHS	Durham Herald-Sun
DS	Durham Sun
GHQ	Georgia Historical Quarterly
IF	Indianapolis Freeman
JNE	Journal of Negro Education
JNH	Journal of Negro History
JTU	Jacksonville Times-Union

MCA	*Memphis Commercial Appeal*
NCB	*North Carolina Booklet*
NCHR	*North Carolina Historical Review*
NJ&G	*Norfolk Journal and Guide*
NOTP	*New Orleans Times-Picayune*
NVP	*Norfolk Virginian-Pilot*
NYA	*New York Age*
NYT	*New York Times*
OES	*Ocala Evening Sun*
PMHS	*Proceedings of the Mississippi Historical Society*
RN&O	*Raleigh News and Observer*
RP	*Richmond Planet*
RTD	*Richmond Times-Dispatch*
SCHS	South Carolina Historical Society
SEP	*Savannah Evening Post*
SHC	Southern Historical Collection, University of North Carolina, Chapel Hill
SMN	*Savannah Morning News*
SOHP	Southern Oral History Project, Southern Historical Collection, University of North Carolina, Chapel Hill
ST	*Savannah Tribune*
VSU	*Virginia State University*
VTB	*Virginia Teachers Bulletin*
WP	*Washington Post*

INTRODUCTION

1. *RTD,* Feb. 15, 2000, A1; *NYT,* Nov. 12, 2003, E1. On controversies over street renaming in general, see Maoz Azaryahu, "The Power of

Commemorative Street Names," *Environment and Planning D: Society and Space* 14 (1996): 311–330; Derek H. Alderman, "A Street Fit for King: Naming Places and Commemoration in the American South," *Professional Geographer* 52 (Nov. 2000): 672–684.

2. *Congressional Record* 63d Cong., 2d sess. (Feb. 6, 1914), 3036.

3. *NYT,* Nov. 17, 1996, A9, Feb. 8, 1997, A1; *Gainesville (Florida) Sun,* Nov. 20, 1997, A3; *RN&O,* Jan. 21, 2001, A4, Nov. 30, 2002, A7.

4. James Fentress and Chris Wickham, *Social Memory* (London: Blackwell, 1992), 3.

5. Harold Pinter, quoted in David Lowenthal, *The Past Is a Foreign Country* (New York: Cambridge University Press, 1990), 193.

6. Jan E. Lewis and Peter S. Onuf, eds., *Sally Hemings and Thomas Jefferson: History, Memory, and Civic Culture* (Charlottesville: University Press of Virginia, 1999).

7. Sheryl Kroen, *Letting Tartuffe Be Our Guide: Practicing Politics in an Age of Counterrevolution, France, 1815–1830* (Berkeley: University of California Press, 2001); Tony Judt, "The Past Is Another Country: Myth and Memory in Postwar Europe," *Daedalus* 121 (1992): 83–118; Guenter Bischof and Anto Pelinka, eds., *Austrian Historical Memory and National Identity* (New Brunswick, N.J.: Transaction, 1997); and Richard Rubin, "The Colfax Riot," *Atlantic Monthly* (July/Aug. 2003): 155–158.

8. Pierre Nora explains that memory "relies on the materiality of the trace, the immediacy of the recording, the visibility of the image." Nora, "Between Memory and History: Les Lieux de Memoire," *Representations* 26 (Spring 1989): 13. See also Earl Lewis, "Connecting Memory, Self, and the Power of Place in African American Urban History," *Journal of Urban History* 21 (Mar. 1995): 347–371.

9. Henri Lefebvre, *The Production of Space,* trans. Donald Nicholson-Smith (London: Blackwell, 1991), esp. chap. 2; Jürgen Habermas, *The Structural Transformation of the Public Sphere: An Inquiry into a Category of Bourgeois Society,* trans. Thomas Burger (Cambridge, Mass.: MIT Press, 1989), esp. 43–67, 232; Craig Calhoun, ed., *Habermas and the Public Sphere* (Cambridge, Mass.: MIT Press, 1992); and Harold Mah, "Phantasies of the Public Sphere: Rethinking the Habermas of Historians," *Journal of Modern History* 72 (Mar. 2000): 153–182.

10. Hannah Arendt, *The Human Condition* (New York: Doubleday Anchor, 1959), esp. 45–73; Mark Gottdiener, *The Social Production of Urban Space,* 2d ed. (Austin: University of Texas Press, 1994), 121–132;

Kendrick Ian Grandison, "Negotiated Space: The Black College Campus as a Cultural Record of Postbellum America," *American Quarterly* 51 (Sept. 1999): 529–579; David M. Henkin, *City Reading: Written Words and Public Spaces in Antebellum New York* (New York: Columbia University Press, 1998), 10; Henri Lefebvre, "Space: Social Product and Use Value," in J. W. Freiberg, ed., *Critical Sociology: European Perspective* (New York: Irvington, 1979); Richard H. Schein, "The Place of Landscape: A Conceptual Framework for Interpreting an American Scene," *Annals of the Association of American Geographers* 87 (1997): 660–680.

11. Jacques LeGoff, *History and Memory,* trans. Steven Rendall and Elizabeth Claman (New York: Columbia University Press, 1992), 54.

12. Michel-Rolph Trouillot, *Silencing the Past: Power and the Production of History* (Boston: Beacon, 1995), esp. chap. 1.

13. Eudora Welty, *One Writer's Beginnings* (Cambridge, Mass.: Harvard University Press, 1984), 104.

14. James C. Scott, *Domination and the Arts of Resistance: Hidden Transcripts* (New Haven, Conn.: Yale University Press, 1990), 56.

15. J. H. Plumb, *The Death of the Past* (Boston: Houghton Mifflin, 1970), 14.

1. A Duty Peculiarly Fitting to Women

1. *Pensacola Daily News,* June 18, 1891.

2. Confederated Southern Memorial Association, *History of the Confederated Memorial Association of the South* (New Orleans: Graham Press, 1904), 74. The fund-raising campaign may be traced in *Pensacola Daily News,* Mar. 15, 20, 22, 29, Apr. 4, 12, 15, 16, May 13, and June 14, 16, 18, 1891. See also *Bliss' [Pensacola] Quarterly* 3 (Jan. 1897): 121–123.

3. For accounts that stress the enduring significance of the activities of organized white women for southern racial politics, see Fred. A. Bailey, "The Textbooks of the 'Lost Cause': Censorship and the Creation of Southern State Histories," *GHQ* 75 (Fall 1991): 507–533; Karen L. Cox, *Dixie's Daughters: The United Daughters of the Confederacy and the Preservation of Confederate Culture* (Gainesville: University Press of Florida, 2003), esp. chaps. 6–8; Cynthia Mills and Pamela H. Simpson, eds., *Monuments to the Lost Cause: Women, Art, and Landscapes of South-*

ern Memory (Knoxville: University of Tennessee Press, 2003); and W. Scott Poole, *Never Surrender: Confederate Memory and Conservatism in the South Carolina Upcountry* (Athens: University of Georgia Press, 2004), 197–207.

4. Thomas Nelson Page, *The Old South: Essays Social and Political* (New York: Scribner's, 1894), 253, 256, 258.

5. For the international context, see David Cannadine, "The Context, Performance and Meaning of Ritual: The British Monarchy and the 'Invention of Tradition,' c. 1820–1977," in Eric Hobsbawm and Terence Ranger, eds., *The Invention of Tradition* (New York: Cambridge University Press, 1983); Alon Confino, *The Nation as a Local Metaphor: Württemberg, Imperial Germany, and National Memory, 1871–1918* (Chapel Hill: University of North Carolina Press, 1997), esp. pt. 1; Charles Dellheim, *The Face of the Past: The Preservation of the Medieval Inheritance in Victorian England* (New York: Cambridge University Press, 1982), esp. chaps. 2 and 3; Ian McKay, *The Quest of the Folk: Antimodernism and Cultural Selection in Twentieth-Century Nova Scotia* (Kingston, Ont.: McGill Queens University Press, 1994), esp. chap. 1; Jeffrey D. Needell, "The Domestic Civilizing Mission: The Cultural Role of the State in Brazil, 1808–1930," *Luso-Brazilian Review* 36 (Summer 1999): 1–18; and Daniel J. Sherman, *Worthy Monuments: Art Museums and the Politics of Culture in Nineteenth-Century France* (Cambridge, Mass.: Harvard University Press, 1989), esp. pt. 1.

6. On the limits of the U.S. state, see Nancy Cohen, *The Reconstruction of American Liberalism, 1865–1914* (Chapel Hill: University of North Carolina Press, 2002), esp. chaps. 1 and 2; Alan Dawley, *Struggles for Justice: Social Responsibility and the Liberal State* (Cambridge, Mass.: Harvard University Press, 1991), pt. 1; and Stephen Skowronek, *Building a New American State: The Expansion of National Administrative Capacities, 1877–1920* (Cambridge, Eng.: Cambridge University Press, 1982), esp. pt. 2. On the federal government and national memory, see Michael Kammen, *Mystic Chords of Memory: The Transformation of Tradition in American Culture* (New York: Knopf, 1991), 101–282.

7. Cecelia Elizabeth O'Leary, *To Die For: The Paradox of American Patriotism* (Princeton, N.J.: Princeton University Press, 1999), chap. 9.

8. Compiled from the *Annual Report of the Florida State Comptroller* (Tallahassee, 1900–1915).

9. Wallace Evan Davies, *Patriotism on Parade: The Story of Veterans' and Hereditary Organizations in America, 1783–1900* (Cambridge, Mass.: Harvard University Press, 1955); and Gaines M. Foster, *Ghosts of the Confederacy: Defeat, the Lost Cause, and the Emergence of the New South* (New York: Oxford University Press, 1987), esp. chaps. 7 and 8.

10. Francesca Morgan, "Home and Country: Women, Nation, and the Daughters of the American Revolution, 1890–1939," Ph.D. diss., Columbia University, 1998.

11. Earl Barnes, "The Feminizing of Culture," *Atlantic Monthly* 109 (June 1912): 770; Joel Chandler Harris, "The Women of the South," *Southern Historical Society Papers* 18 (Jan.–Dec. 1890): 277–281; "Critic," Letter to the Editor, *NYT,* Mar. 2, 1902. See also Kammen, *Mystic Chords of Memory,* 266–269.

12. *CV* 1 (1893): 353; Herman Hattaway, "Clio's Southern Soldiers: The United Confederate Veterans and History," *Louisiana History* 12 (Summer 1971): 214–216. On the Sons of the Confederacy, see Foster, *Ghosts of the Confederacy,* 178–179.

13. *RTD,* June 17, 1906, 2–1; Woodson to Cameron, Sarah R. Cameron Papers, box 3, folder 26, SHC; Lance Brockman, ed., *Theatre of Fraternity: Staging the Ritual Space of the Scottish Rite of Freemasonry, 1896–1929* (Jackson: University Press of Mississippi, 1996); Mark C. Carnes, *Secret Ritual and Manhood in Victorian America* (New Haven, Conn.: Yale University Press, 1989); Mary Ann Clawson, *Constructing Brotherhood: Class, Gender and Fraternalism* (Princeton, N.J.: Princeton University Press, 1989); and Lynn Dumenil, *Freemasonry and American Culture* (Princeton, N.J.: Princeton University Press, 1984).

14. See Darlene R. Roth, *Matronage: Patterns of Women's Organizations, Atlanta, Georgia, 1890–1940* (Brooklyn: Carlson, 1994), 17–72; Anastatia Sims, *The Power of Femininity in the New South: Women's Organizations and Politics in North Carolina, 1880–1930* (Columbia: University of South Carolina Press, 1997), 128–154; and Elizabeth Hayes Turner, *Women, Culture, and Community: Religion and Reform in Galveston, 1880–1920* (New York: Oxford University Press, 1997), 158–159.

15. Margaret Wooten Collier, *Biographies of Representative Women of the South, 1861–[1938]* (College Park[?], Ga., self-published [1938]), 28–31, 50–55.

16. For accounts that emphasize "republican motherhood" as a

pretext for women's historical activism, see Joan Marie Johnson, "'This Wonderful Dream Nation!': Black and White South Carolina Women and the Creation of the New South, 1898–1930," Ph.D. diss., University of California, Los Angeles, 1997, esp. chap. 2; James M. Lindgren, *Preserving the Old Dominion: Historic Preservation and Virginia Traditionalism* (Charlottesville: University Press of Virginia, 1993), 58–74; Sims, *Power of Femininity,* 128–154; and Elizabeth R. Varon, *We Mean to Be Counted: White Women and Politics in Antebellum Virginia* (Chapel Hill: University of North Carolina Press, 1998), 170–172.

17. Mrs. George T. Fry, "Memorial Day—Its Origin," *CV* 1 (May 1893): 149; *A History of the Origins of Memorial Day as Adopted by the Ladies' Memorial Association of Columbus, Georgia* (Columbus, Ga.: Lizzie Rutherford Chapter of the Daughters of the Confederacy, 1898), 24–25; Ellen M. Litwicki, *America's Public Holidays, 1865–1920* (Washington, D.C.: Smithsonian Press, 2000), chap. 1.

18. *Ceremonies in Augusta, Georgia, Laying the Cornerstone of the Confederate Monument with an Oration by Clement A. Evans* (Augusta, Ga.: n.p., 1875), 9. On women, memorialization, and gender tensions, see Faust, *Mothers of Invention,* 234–254; Foster, *Ghosts of the Confederacy,* 36–46; and LeeAnn Whites, *The Civil War as a Crisis in Gender, Augusta, Georgia, 1860–1890* (Athens: University of Georgia Press, 1995), 160–224.

19. Patricia R. Loughridge and Edward D. C. Campbell Jr., *Women in Mourning* (Richmond: Museum of the Confederacy, 1985), 25.

20. For an alternative interpretation that stresses the continuity of women's commemorative activities in the postwar years and at the turn of the century, see Drew Gilpin Faust, *Mothers of Invention: Women of the Slaveholding South in the American Civil War* (Chapel Hill: University of North Carolina Press, 1996), 252–253. On strains along white gender lines, see Laura F. Edwards, *Gendered Strife and Confusion: The Political Culture of Reconstruction* (Urbana: University of Illinois Press, 1997), 107–144; Nancy MacLean, *Behind the Mask of Chivalry: The Making of the Second Ku Klux Klan* (New York: Oxford University Press, 1994); and LeeAnn Whites, "Rebecca Latimer Felton and the Problem of 'Protection' in the New South," in Nancy A. Hewitt and Suzanne Lebsock, eds., *Visible Women: New Essays in American Activism* (Urbana: University of Illinois Press, 1993), 41–61.

21. Gail Bederman, *Manliness and Civilization: A Cultural History of Gender and Race in the United States, 1880–1917* (Chicago: University of Chicago Press, 1995), 1–44; Anne McClintock, "'No Longer in a Future Heaven': Gender, Race, and Nationalism," in Anne McClintock, Aamir Mufti, and Ella Shohat, eds., *Dangerous Liaisons: Gender, Nation, and Postcolonial Perspectives* (Minneapolis: University of Minnesota Press, 1997); Louise M. Newman, *White Women's Rights: Historical Origins of American Feminism, 1870–1930* (New York: Oxford University Press, 1998), chaps. 1 and 2.

22. Moffitt speech delivered to the DR, [1911?]. E. E. Moffitt Papers, folder 11, SHC; Cotten speech to U. D. C. meeting, [1918?], S. S. Cotten Papers, box 2, folder 22, SHC.

23. Mary Hilliard Hinton, "North Carolina's Historical Exhibit at Jamestown Exposition," *NCB* 7 (Oct. 1907): 138–144; Ellen Douglas Baxter, "A Lesson from the Lives of the Women of the Revolution," *American Monthly Magazine* 7 (Jan. 1896): 28; "The Unveiling and Dedication of the Edenton Tea Party and Memorial Tablet," *NCB* 8 (Apr. 1909): 282; *CV* 8 (May 1900): 252.

24. Baxter, "A Lesson," 32; Mrs. Patrick Matthew, "Penelope Baker," *NCB* 8 (Apr. 1909): 277.

25. Sarah B. C. Morgan, Committee Reports, *Minutes of the Eighth Annual Convention of the Georgia Division, UDC, 1902,* 13–15. On the DAR's racialized conception of nationhood, see Shawn Michelle Smith, *American Archives: Gender, Race, and Class in Visual Culture* (Princeton, N.J.: Princeton University Press, 1999), 136–145.

26. On white women and the fictional romanticization of the southern past, see David Blight, *Race and Reunion: The Civil War in American Memory* (Cambridge, Mass.: Harvard University Press, 2001), esp. chap. 7; Jane Turner Censer, *The Reconstruction of White Southern Womanhood, 1865–1895* (Baton Rouge: Louisiana State University Press, 2003); and Sarah Gardner, *Blood and Irony* (Chapel Hill: University of North Carolina Press, 2003).

27. Mildred L. Rutherford Scrapbook no. 7, 67, Museum of the Confederacy, Richmond, Va.; Odenheimer to Janet Randolph, Feb. 11, 1923, Mar. 14, 1923, box 15, Randolph Papers, Museum of the Confederacy; Catherine Clinton, *Tara Revisited: Women, War, and the Plantation Legend* (New York: Abbeville Press, 1995), 191–204; Grace Elizabeth

Hale, *Making Whiteness: The Culture of Segregation in the South, 1890–1940* (New York: Pantheon, 1998), 85–120; Micki McElya, "Commemorating the Color Line: The National Mammy Monument Controversy of the 1920s," in Mills and Simpson, *Monuments to the Lost Cause,* 203–218; and Cheryl Thurber, "The Development of the Mammy Image and Mythology," in Virginia Bernhard et al., eds., *Southern Women: Histories and Identities* (Columbia: University of Missouri Press, 1992), 87–108.

28. Dorris, *Preservation of the Hermitage.*

29. For an excellent discussion of the DAR and its sensitivity to white southern sensibilities, see Morgan, "Home and Country."

30. *Athens Banner,* Apr. 26, 1912. See also E. Merton Coulter, "The Confederate Monument in Athens, Georgia," *GHQ* 40 (Sept. 1956): 232.

31. Lindgren, *Preserving the Old Dominion,* 91–115; see also Catherine W. Bishir, "Landmarks of Power: Building a Southern Past, 1855–1915," *Southern Cultures* 1 (1993): 5–46; Kammen, *Mystic Chords of Memory,* 194–253; Karal Ann Marling, *George Washington Slept Here: Colonial Revivals and American Culture, 1876–1986* (Cambridge, Mass.: Harvard University Press, 1988), 85–114; and Morgan, "Home and Country," 28–83, 151–218.

32. *Minutes of the Third Annual Convention of the Georgia Division, UDC, 1897,* 11–13; Isobel Bryan, "Report of the President for 1903," *Yearbook of the Association for the Preservation of Virginia Antiquities, 1901–1904* (Richmond: William Ellis Jones, 1905), 7; "Marking the Site of the Old Town of Bloomsbury," *NCB* 11 (July 1911): 51; "Proceedings of the North Carolina Society Daughters of the Revolution," *NCB* 16 (Jan. 1917): 164.

33. Elna Green, "Those Opposed: The Antisuffragists in North Carolina, 1900–1920," *NCHR* 67 (July 1990): 318, 320; Janet G. Stone-Erdman, "A Challenge to Southern Politics: The Woman Suffrage Movement in North Carolina, 1913–1920," master's thesis, North Carolina State University, 1986, 83–89; UDC delegate quoted in Lloyd C. Taylor, "Lila Meade Valentine: The FFV as Reformer," *Virginia Magazine of History and Biography* 70 (Oct. 1962): 482; *Georgia House Journal, 1914,* 287. On Rutherford, see Grace Elizabeth Hale, "Some Women Have Never Been Reconstructed: Mildred Lewis Rutherford, Lucy M. Stanton, and the Racial Politics of Southern White Womanhood, 1900–1930," in John Inscoe, ed., *Georgia in Black and White: Explorations in*

the Race Relations of a Southern State, 1865–1950 (Athens: University of Georgia Press, 1994), 173–201. On Pearson and Pinkard, see Elna C. Green, *Southern Strategies: Southern Women and the Woman Suffrage Question* (Chapel Hill: University of North Carolina Press, 1997), esp. 63–66.

34. Randolph's myriad charitable activities may be traced in her papers at the Museum of the Confederacy; Felton is quoted in Rebecca Montgomery, "Lost Cause Mythology in New South Reform: Gender, Class, and Race and the Politics of Patriotic Citizenship in Georgia, 1890–1925," in Janet L. Coryell et al., eds., *Negotiating Boundaries of Southern Womanhood; Dealing with the Powers That Be* (Columbia: University of Missouri Press, 2000), 174. See also A. Elizabeth Taylor, "The Last Phase of the Woman Suffrage Movement in Georgia," *GHQ* 43 (Mar. 1959): 11–28; and Sara Bertha Townsend, "The Admission of Women to the University of Georgia," *GHQ* 43 (June 1959): 156–169.

35. Suzanne Lebsock, "Woman Suffrage and White Supremacy: A Virginia Case Study," in Hewitt and Lebsock, *Visible Women,* 62–100; Sydney R. Bland, *Preserving Charleston's Past, Shaping Its Future: The Life and Times of Susan Pringle Frost* (Westport, Conn.: Greenwood Press, 1994), esp. 47–108; Janet G. Humphrey, *A Texas Suffragist: Diaries and Writings of Jane Y. McCallum* (Austin: Ellen C. Temple, 1988).

36. Mary Ryan, *Women in Public: Between Banners and Ballots, 1825–1880* (Baltimore: Johns Hopkins University Press, 1990): 59.

37. Foster, *Ghosts of the Confederacy,* 128–131; H. E. Gulley, "Women and the Lost Cause: Preserving a Confederate Identity in the American Deep South," *Journal of Historical Geography* 19 (1993): 125–141; Morgan, "Home and Country," 151–218; Whites, *Civil War as a Crisis in Gender,* 160–198; and Joel J. Winberry, "'Lest We Forget': The Confederate Monument and the Southern Townscape," *Southeastern Geographer* 23 (Nov. 1983): 107–121.

38. CMLS Minute Book, Feb. 4, 1896, box I-1, Museum of the Confederacy; Jay Cohn, *The Palace or the Poorhouse: The American House as a Cultural Symbol* (East Lansing: Michigan State University Press, 1979), 193–212; Charles B. Hosmer Jr., *Presence of the Past: A History of the Preservation Movement in the United States before Williamsburg* (New York: Putnam, 1965), 69–72; Barbara J. Howe, "Women in Historic Preservation: The Legacy of Ann Pamela Cunningham," *Public Histo-*

rian 12 (Winter 1990): 31–61; James M. Lindgren, "Virginia Needs Living Heroes: Historic Preservation in the Progressive Era," *Public Historian* 13 (Winter 1991): 9–24; Marling, *George Washington Slept Here,* 97; Patricia West, *Domesticating History: The Political Origins of American House Museums* (Washington, D.C.: Smithsonian Institution Press, 1999), esp. chaps. 1 and 2.

39. Elizabeth Stillinger, *The Antiquers: The Lives and Careers, the Deals, the Finds, the Collections of the Men and Women Who Were Responsible for the Changing Taste in American Antiques, 1850–1930* (New York: Knopf, 1980); West, *Domesticating History,* 42.

40. Varon, *We Mean to Be Counted,* esp. chap. 1 and epilogue.

41. Cotten to Gen. W. G. Le Duc, Jan. 30, 1897, box 1, folder 1, SHC; Cotten to Evelyn E. Moffitt, Mar. 24, 1894, emphasis in original, box 1, folder 3, Sallie Southall Cotten Papers, SHC.

42. Mrs. W. C. H. Merchant, "Report of the Historical Committees, UDC," *CV* 12 (Feb. 1904): 64. On campaigns to influence "public opinion," see "Proceedings of the North Carolina Society Daughters of the Revolution," *NCB* 16 (Jan. 1917): 165; Bailey, "The Textbooks of the 'Lost Cause,'" *Georgia Historical Quarterly* 75 (Fall 1991): 507–533; "Free Speech and the 'Lost Cause' in Texas: A Study of Social Control in the New South," *Southwestern Historical Quarterly* 97 (Jan. 1994): 453–477; "Mildred Lewis Rutherford and the Patrician Cult of the Old South," *GHQ* 78 (Fall 1994): 523–530; Cox, *Dixie's Daughters,* chap. 6; Foster, *Ghosts of the Confederacy,* 163–179; Johnson, "This Wonderful Dream Nation," chap. 2; and Sims, *Power of Femininity,* chap. 6.

43. Enoch Marvin Banks, "A Semi-Centennial View of Secession," *Independent* 70 (Feb. 9, 1911): 302–303; Fred Arthur Bailey, "Free Speech at the University of Florida: The Enoch Marvin Banks Case," *Florida Historical Quarterly* 71 (July 1992): 1–17.

44. Mrs. Maurice de C. B. Moore to Janet Randolph, box 15, UDC Collection, Randolph Papers, Museum of the Confederacy, emphasis in original; Pamela H. Simpson, "The Great Lee Chapel Controversy and the 'Little Group of Willful Women' Who Saved the Shrine of the South," in Mills and Simpson, *Monuments to the Lost Cause,* 85–99.

45. On women and the preservation crusade in Charleston, see Stephanie E. Yuhl, "Rich and Tender Remembering: White Elite Women, Historical Memory and the Creation of an Aesthetic Sense of Place

in Charleston during the 1920s and 1930s," in W. Fitzhugh Brundage, ed., *Where These Memories Grow: History, Memory, and Southern Identity* (Chapel Hill: University of North Carolina Press, 2000), 227–248; on the Stone Mountain controversy, see David B. Freeman, *Carved in Stone: The History of Stone Mountain* (Macon, Ga.: Mercer University Press), chap. 4; and Grace Elizabeth Hale, "Granite Stopped Time: Stone Mountain Memorial and the Representation of White Southern Identity," in Mills and Simpson, *Monuments to the Lost Cause,* 219–233.

46. Form completed for the United Daughters of the Confederacy History Committee, Oct. 1, 1908, Janet Randolph Papers, Museum of the Confederacy. For discussions of fund-raising efforts, see E. Merton Coulter, "The Confederate Monument in Athens, Georgia," *GHQ* 40 (Sept. 1956): 235–238; and Antionette G. van Zelm, "Virginia Women as Public Citizens: Emancipation Day Celebrations and Lost Cause Commemorations, 1863–1890," in Janet L. Coryell et al., eds., *Negotiating Boundaries of Southern Womanhood* (Columbia: University of Missouri Press, 2000), 81–83, 86. On women's fund-raising techniques, see Beverly Gordon, *Bazaars and Fair Ladies: The History of the American Fundraising Fair* (Knoxville: University of Tennessee Press, 1998), chaps. 4 and 5.

47. Clinton, *Tara Revisited,* 184–185; and Angie Parrott, "'Love Makes Memory Eternal': The United Daughters of the Confederacy in Richmond, Virginia, 1897–1920," in Edward L. Ayers and John C. Willis, eds., *The Edge of the South: Life in Nineteenth-Century Virginia* (Charlottesville: University Press of Virginia, 1991), 219–220.

48. Bederman, *Manliness and Civilization,* 232–239.

49. Ellen Carol DuBois, "Making Women's History: Activist Historians of Women's Rights, 1880–1940," *Radical History Review* 49 (Winter 1991): 66; Roth, *Matronage,* 90–98; Morgan, "Home and Country," 400–479; Patricia C. Walls, "Defending Their Liberties: Women's Organizations during the McCarthy Era," Ph.D. diss., University of Maryland, 1994, 22–55. For a contrasting conclusion about the character of women's historical activism after World War I, see Montgomery, "Lost Cause Mythology in New South Reform," 193–196.

50. On the marginalization of women historians in academia, see Julie Des Jardins, *Women and the Historical Enterprise in America: Gender, Race, and the Politics of Memory, 1880–1945* (Chapel Hill: University of North Carolina Press, 2003), esp. chap. 1. On the simultaneous transfor-

mation of women's role in social work, see Robyn Muncy, *Creating a Female Dominion in American Reform, 1890–1935* (New York: Oxford University Press, 1991), esp. chaps. 2 and 5.

51. Charles W. Ramsdell, "The Preservation of Texas History," *NCHR* 6 (Jan. 1929): 6; E. W. Winkler, "Some Historical Activities of the Texas Library and Historical Commission," *Quarterly of the Texas State Historical Association* 14 (1910–1911): 294–304; and Emily Benbury Haywood, "Presentation of Joel Lane Tablet to the City of Raleigh," *NCB* 13 (July 1913): 50.

52. For suggestive accounts of women and public space outside the South, see Sarah Deutsch, *Women and the City: Gender, Space, and Power in Boston, 1870–1940* (New York: Oxford University Press, 2000), and Mary P. Ryan, *Civic Wars: Democracy and Public Life in the American City during the Nineteenth Century* (Berkeley: University of California Press, 1997).

2. Celebrating Black Memory in the Postbellum South

1. *San Antonio Express,* June 20, 1883; *San Antonio Light,* June 20, 1883; Judith Berg Sobre, *San Antonio on Parade: Six Historic Festivals* (College Station: Texas A&M University Press, 2003), 57–59.

2. *Dallas Morning News,* June 20, 1936; William H. Wiggins Jr. and Douglas DeNatale, *Jubilation! African American Celebration in the Southeast* (Columbia, S.C.: McKissick Museum, 1993), 62; David A. Williams, *Juneteenth: The Unique Heritage* (Austin: n.p., 1992), 38.

3. James Weldon Johnson, *Along This Way: The Autobiography of James Weldom Johnson* (1933; New York: Penguin, 1990), 154.

4. Alexander Crummell, "The Need of New Ideas and New Motives for a New Era," in *Africa and America: Addresses and Discourses* (1891; Miami: Mnemosyne, 1969), 36.

5. *Raleigh Baptist Sentinel,* Jan. 9, 1908. On the anti-black popular culture of the era, see Sam Dennison, *Scandalize My Name: Black Imagery in American Popular Music* (New York: Garland, 1982); David Krasner, *Resistance, Parody, and Double Consciousness in African American Theatre, 1895–1910* (New York: St. Martin's, 1997); and Eric Lott, *Love*

and Theft: Blackface Minstrelsy and the American Working Class (New York: Oxford University Press, 1993).

6. *Richmond Whig,* July 6, 1872.

7. Elizabeth Rauh Bethel, *The Roots of African-American Identity: Memory and History in Free Antebellum Communities* (New York: St. Martin's, 1997), 188–191.

8. *Christian Recorder,* Dec. 3, 1874.

9. The idea of "ceremonial citizenship" is elaborated in Mary P. Ryan, *Civic Wars: Democracy and Public Life in the American City during the Nineteenth Century* (Berkeley: University of California Press, 1997), esp. chap. 2.

10. See Mitchell A. Kachun, *Festivals of Freedom: Memory and the Meaning of African American Emancipation Celebrations, 1808–1915* (Amherst: University of Massachusetts Press, 2003), 16–98; Gregg Kimball, "African, American, and Virginian: The Shaping of Black Memory in Antebellum Virginia, 1790–1860," in W. Fitzhugh Brundage, ed., *No Deed But Memory: History and Memory in the American South* (Chapel Hill: University of North Carolina Press, 2000), 57–78; and Shane White, "'It Was a Proud Day': African American Festivals and Parades in the North, 1741–1834," *Journal of American History* 81 (June 1994): 13–50.

11. *Harrisonburg Rockingham Register,* July 6, 1871; *AC,* July 5, 1900. For similar sentiments, see *Jackson (Miss.) Clarion and Standard,* July 6, 1866. On Fourth of July in the South, see Cecilia Elizabeth O'Leary, *To Die For: The Paradox of American Patriotism* (Princeton, N.J.: Princeton University Press, 1999), chap. 7; Robert Pettus Hay, "Freedom's Jubilee: One Hundred Years of the Fourth of July, 1776–1876," Ph.D. diss., University of Kentucky, 1967, 266–273. On Memorial Day, see David Blight, *Race and Reunion: The Civil War in American Memory, 1863–1915* (Cambridge, Mass.: Harvard University Press, 2001), chap. 9.

12. *Augusta (Ga.) Colored American,* Jan. 13, 1866; Benjamin Quarles, "Historic Afro-American Holidays," *Negro Digest* 16 (Feb. 1967): 18. The anniversary of Liberia's founding prompted scattered celebrations; see *ST,* May 20, 1893.

13. *ST,* Jan. 23, Jan. 30, and May 22, 1915. For other representative church celebrations, see *NYA,* Jan. 10, 1891; and *Washington D.C. Colored American,* Apr. 9, 1898. For descriptions of Allen Day, see *IF,* Feb. 21, 1891; and Kachun, *Festivals of Freedom,* 161–166.

14. *RP,* Apr. 14, 1900. See also *RP,* Apr. 2, 1904; *IF,* June 28, 1890; *ST,* June 30, 1894, Mar. 4, 1911. On black voluntary associations, see Elsa Barkley Brown, "Uncle Ned's Children: Negotiating Community and Freedom in Postemancipation Richmond, Virginia," Ph.D. diss., Kent State University, 1994, esp. chap. 7; Lynne B. Feldman, *A Sense of Place: Birmingham's Black Middle Class Community, 1890–1930* (Tuscaloosa: University of Alabama Press, 1999), 145–155; Joan Marie Johnson, "'This Wonderful Dream Nation!': Black and White South Carolina Women and the Creation of the New South, 1898–1930," Ph.D. diss., University of California, Los Angeles, 1997, esp. chap. 3; and Howard N. Rabinowitz, *Race Relations in the Urban South, 1865–1890* (New York: Oxford University Press, 1978), 227–228.

15. *Washington Bee,* Sept. 21, 1901; H. W. Clark to Mary Church Terrell, Aug. 1, Sept. 11, 1922, Mary Church Terrell Papers, Moorland-Spingarn Research Center, Howard University; *RP,* Apr. 14, 1906. Such rural celebrations could evolve into imposing affairs. See "Juneteenth," *Ebony* 6 (June 1951): 27; DeNatale, *Jubilation,* 31.

16. *NYA,* Jan. 19, 1889; *Indianapolis Freeman,* July 19, 1890; George Brown Tindall, *South Carolina Negroes, 1877–1900* (Columbia: University of South Carolina Press, 1970), 288–290.

17. *Nashville Banner,* Jan. 2, 1893; *CS,* Jan. 3, 1893.

18. Bobby L. Lovett, *The African-American History of Nashville, Tennessee, 1780–1930* (Fayetteville: University of Arkansas Press, 1999), 212; *JTU,* July 6, 1886; *Richmond Whig,* Jan. 2, 1867. See also *Richmond Whig,* July 6, 1868; *Richmond Dispatch,* July 5, 1867, July 5, 1883, July 6, 1886; Elsa Barkley Brown and Gregg B. Kimball, "Mapping the Terrain of Black Richmond," *Journal of Urban History* 21 (Mar. 1995): 296–346.

19. Alice Ravenel Huger Smith, "Reminiscences" [1950], in Martha R. Serverens, *Alice Ravenel Huger Smith: An Artist, a Place, and a Time* (Charleston: Carolina Art Association, 1993), 75; *Charleston Daily News,* July 9, 1866; *RP,* Mar. 31, 1906; "Juneteenth," *Ebony* 6 (June 1951): 27; *ST,* Jan. 1, 1898, Apr. 19, 1913; *AC,* Jan. 6, 1874; *SMN,* July 6, 1886; *JTU,* Jan. 2, 1890; *Fredericksburg Free Lance,* Jan. 5, 1892; *Lynchburg News,* Apr. 10, 1911; *Washington D.C. People's Advocate,* Jan. 17, 1880, Jan. 2, 1890; *RN&O,* Jan. 2, 1892, Jan. 2, 1901; *Augusta Georgia Baptist,* Jan. 7, 1909; "The Fourth of July," *Southern Opinion,* July 11, 1868.

20. Williams, *Juneteenth,* 21; *Alexandria Gazette,* Jan. 1, 1866; Laura F. Edwards, *Gendered Strife and Confusion: The Political Culture of Re-*

construction (Urbana: University of Illinois Press, 1997), 194; *AC*, July 5, 1904.

21. *AC*, May 26, 1902, May 31, 1902, July 5, 1904.

22. *SMN*, Jan. 2, 1896, Jan. 2, 1906; *NVP*, Jan. 2, 1904; *JTU*, Jan. 2, 1906; Richard Zuczek, *State of Rebellion: Reconstruction in South Carolina* (Columbia: University of South Carolina Press, 1996), 163–165. For other "riots" prompted by black commemorations, see *Norfolk True Southerner*, Apr. 19, 1866; *Jackson Pilot*, July 10, 1875; Lovett, *African-American History of Nashville*, 207; George Rable, *But There Was No Peace: The Role of Violence in the Politics of Reconstruction* (Athens: University of Georgia Press, 1984), 31–32, 145–152.

23. Patricia Smith Prather, "Juneteenth: A Celebration of Freedom," *Texas Highways* (June 1988): 4–5; Lovett, *African-American History of Nashville*, 110; *RP*, Mar. 31, 1906; Rabinowitz, *Race Relations in the Urban South*, 230.

24. *ST*, May 4, 1918.

25. *Montgomery Daily Mail*, Jan. 2, 1867; *RP*, June 2, 1906, May 27, 1915; *ST*, Feb. 13, 1909, May 31, June 7, 1913, May 30, June 6, 1914, Feb. 17, 1917, May 24, 1919. On black militias, see Donald L. Grant, *The Way It Was in the South: The Black Experience in Georgia* (New York: Birch Lane, 1993), 299–300; Rabinowitz, *Race Relations in the Urban South*, 227–230; Lawrence D. Rice, *The Negro in Texas, 1874–1900* (Baton Rouge: Louisiana State University Press, 1971), 270–271; Otis A. Singletary, *Negro Militia and Reconstruction* (New York: McGraw-Hill, 1963); and Tindall, *South Carolina Negroes*, 286–288.

26. Kirk Savage, *Standing Soldier, Kneeling Slaves: Race, War, and Monument in Nineteenth-Century America* (Princeton, N.J.: Princeton University Press, 1997), 178; George Washington Williams, *A History of the Negro Troops in the War of the Rebellion, 1861–1865* (1888; New York: Bergman, 1968), 328; *NYA*, Jan. 2, 1889.

27. *ST*, Jan. 8, 1876, Aug. 3, 1889, May 26, 1894, May 15, 1897; *JTU*, July 6, 1886; *Petersburg Index*, July 6, 1880; *Petersburg Lancet*, July 7, 1883; *Charlotte Observer*, Jan. 2, 1895.

28. *ST*, Jan. 6, 1906; *RP*, Jan. 8, 1898. For an extended discussion of the Pythians in celebrations, see *Augusta Georgia Baptist*, Jan. 7, 1909.

29. Ceremonial roles of fire companies are detailed in *CN&C*, Jan. 2, 1875; *Huntsville (Ala.) Gazette*, July 7, 1883; *CS*, Jan. 1, 1892; *Natchez*

Democrat, July 10, 1892; *Wilmington Morning Star,* Jan. 2, 1895, Jan. 2, 1896; *Greenville (N.C.) Reflector,* Jan. 6, 1896; and *NVP,* Jan. 3, 1898, Jan. 2, 1902. Union participation is described in *CN&C,* Jan. 2, 1874; *Southern Workman,* Feb. 17, 1886; *Jacksonville News Herald,* July 5, 1887; *NYA,* Apr. 28, 1888; *New Orleans Pelican,* July 9, 1888; *Huntsville (Ala.) Gazette,* July 12, 1888; *Norfolk Landmark,* Jan. 2, 1889; *Norfolk Virginian,* Jan. 2, 1890; *Jacksonville Evening Telegram,* Dec. 31, 1891; *BAH,* Jan. 2, 1899, Jan. 2, 1903; *NVP,* Jan. 2, 1910; and *ST,* Jan. 6, 1917.

    30. *RP,* Apr. 1, 1916; *ST,* Jan. 13, 1917; and *Charlotte Observer,* Jan. 2, 1915.

    31. *Roanoke Times,* Jan. 2, 1892; *IF,* Mar. 4, 1893; *CS,* Jan. 3, 1893, Jan. 2, 1894, Jan. 2, 1895, Jan. 2, 1898; *SMN,* Jan. 2, 1896; *NVP,* Jan. 2, 1902, Jan. 2, 1909; *Knoxville Sentinel,* Apr. 9, 1913; and *OES,* Jan. 2, 1925.

    32. Joseph T. Wilson, "Introduction," in *Twenty-two Years of Freedom* (Norfolk: Thomas F. Paige, 1885), 10–11. For examples of Republican celebrations, see *Richmond Dispatch,* July 5, 1867; *Montgomery Daily Mail,* Jan. 2, 1868; *Montgomery Advertiser,* July 6, 1868; and *CN&C,* June 2, 1869. Republicans continued to stage commemorative celebrations in some communities as late as the 1890s; see *BAH,* Jan. 2, 1892.

    33. *Nashville Banner,* Jan. 2, 1891; *Elizabeth City (N.C.) Carolinian,* Jan. 6, 1892, Jan. 4, 1893, Jan. 5, 1895; *ST,* Jan. 9, 1909, Feb. 3, 1912; *RP,* Jan. 23, 1897, Dec. 25, 1897, Jan. 16, 1917; *IF,* Jan. 14, 1893.

    34. *ST,* Nov. 1, 1916.

    35. *NYA,* Nov. 8, 1890; *RP,* Jan. 20, 1906; *AC,* July 2, 1894, Jan. 2, 1896, Jan. 2, 1903; *ST,* Dec. 14, 1907, Dec. 21, 1907, Dec. 28, 1907, Jan. 3, 1914, Nov. 14, 1914; Sobre, *San Antonio on Parade,* 64–68. For disputes in Jacksonville and Tampa, see *Jacksonville Evening Telegram,* Dec. 30, 1892; *JTU,* Jan. 3, 1907.

    36. *ST,* Dec. 30, 1911; *RP,* Jan. 1, 1898; *ST,* Dec. 21, 1891. See also *IF,* Feb. 22, 1896. On respectability, see Campbell, *Songs of Zion,* chap. 2; Kevin K. Gaines, *Uplifting the Race: Black Leadership, Politics, and Culture in the Twentieth Century* (Chapel Hill: University of North Carolina Press, 1996), introduction, chap. 1; Evelyn Brooks Higginbotham, *Righteous Discontent: The Women's Movement in the Black Baptist Church, 1880–1920* (Cambridge, Mass.: Harvard University Press, 1993), chap. 1; and Deborah Gray White, "The Cost of Club Work, the Price of Black Feminism," in Nancy A. Hewitt and Suzanne Lebsock, eds., *Visible*

Women: New Essays on American Activism (Urbana: University of Illinois Press, 1993), 247–269.

37. *ST,* Jan. 8, 1876, Jan. 2, 1892, Dec. 16, 1893, June 30, 1894, Jan. 9, 1897, Aug. 23, 1902, Jan. 4, 1908, Aug. 22, 1914; *Jacksonville Evening Telegram,* Jan. 2, 1892, July 5, 1906; *IF,* Jan. 18, 1890, May 30, 1891. See also *BB,* June 20, 1894.

38. On John Canoe, see Elizabeth A. Fenn, "'A Perfect Equality Seemed to Reign': Slave Society and Jonkunnu," *NCHR* 65 (Apr. 1988): 127–153; Raymond Gavins, "North Carolina Black Folklore and Song in the Age of Segregation: Toward Another Meaning of Survival," *NCHR* 66 (Oct. 1989): 416–418; and Richard Walser, "His Worship the John Kuner," *North Carolina Folklore* 19 (Nov. 1971): 160–172.

39. *NYA,* Apr. 19, 1890; *RP,* June 12, 1897.

40. *Washington Bee,* Mar. 15, 1884, Mar. 31, 1888; *Washington Post,* Apr. 17, 1897; Katchun, *Festivals of Freedom,* chap. 6.

41. *RP,* May 27, 1916. For other Fourth of July frivolities, see *AC,* July 5, 1883, July 5, 1891, July 2, 1894, July 5, 1897; *SMN,* Jan. 2, 1884, July 6, 1897, July 5, 1900; *IF,* July 9, 1892; *BB,* June 21, 1896, June 20, 1897, June 21, 1900; *OES,* July 5, 1900, July 5, 1901, July 5, 1913; *Ocala Star Banner,* July 5, 1901; *ST,* May 27, 1916.

42. Theophilus G. Stewart, "The Army as a Trained Force," in Alice Moore Dunbar, ed., *Masterpieces of Negro Eloquence: The Best Speeches by the Negro from the Days of Slavery to the Present Time* (1914; New York: Johnson Reprint, 1970), 278; Gail Bederman, *Manliness and Civilization: A Cultural History of Gender and Race in the United States, 1880–1917* (Chicago: University of Chicago Press, 1995), chap. 3; Glenda Elizabeth Gilmore, *Gender and Jim Crow: Women and the Politics of White Supremacy in North Carolina, 1896–1920* (Chapel Hill: University of North Carolina Press, 1996), esp. chaps. 1 and 2; Higginbotham, *Righteous Discontent.*

43. *JTU,* July 5, 1887; *OES,* Jan. 9, 1900; "Paying the Fiddler," undated speech, Daniel Webster Davis Papers, Virginia Historical Society, Richmond; *ST,* Feb. 17, 1906. On black women and Emancipation Day celebrations, see Antoinette G. van Zelm, "Virginia Women as Public Citizens: Emancipation Day Celebrations and Lost Cause Commemorations, 1863–1890," in Janet L. Coryell et al., eds., *Negotiating Boundaries of Southern Womanhood: Dealing with the Powers That Be* (Columbia: University of Missouri Press, 2000), 71–80.

44. *ST,* Aug. 5, 1876; *CN&C,* Jan. 2, 1889; *Atlanta Daily Intelligencer,* July 6, 1866; *IF,* July 9, 1892, Jan. 13, 1894; *JTU,* Jan. 3, 1893. See also *Twenty-two Years of Freedom,* 12, 27–28; *JTU,* Dec. 28, 1890; *IF,* Jan. 24, 1891; *BB,* June 20, 1894, June 19, 1897; *NVP,* Jan. 2, 1902, Jan. 2, 1907.

45. *OES,* Jan. 2, 1901. For discussions of black clubwomen, see Gilmore, *Gender and Jim Crow;* Johnson, "This Wonderful Dream Nation!"; and White, "The Cost of Club Work."

46. *Twenty-two Years of Freedom,* 19, 24; *RP,* Dec. 25, 1897. See also *New York Globe,* July 12, 1884; and *ST,* Jan. 6, 1900.

47. Wendell Phillips Dabney, "Rough Autobiographical Sketch of His Boyhood Years," 17–18, Wendell Phillips Dabney Papers, Cincinnati Historical Society, Cincinnati, Ohio. For examples of women in processions, see *Asheville Democrat,* Jan. 8, 1891; *IF,* Jan. 24, 1891; *ST,* Feb. 14, 1914, June 15, 1915, Jan. 16, 1917, Feb. 17, 1917, Feb. 16, 1918, Dec. 29, 1918.

48. *RP,* Jan. 11, 1919. On Lincoln Day, see *ST,* Feb. 14, 1914, Feb. 17, 1917, Feb. 16, 1918; on Memorial Day and women, see *RP,* May 24, 1918; for examples of black women's prominence in Emancipation Day celebrations, see *[Nashville] Tennessee News,* Feb. 15, 1917; *ST,* Jan. 4, 1919, Jan. 7, 1926, Jan. 6, 1927.

49. *ST,* Jan. 1, 1898, Jan. 4, 1902, Jan. 10, 1914; *AC,* Dec. 29, 1896, Jan. 2, 1897, Dec. 30, 1899; *RP,* Jan. 5, 1895, May 27, 1915; *IF,* Jan. 12, 1895, Feb. 9, 1895, Mar. 20, 1897, Jan. 15, 1898.

50. *Twenty-two Years of Freedom,* 24; *JTU,* Jan. 2, 1891; *Ocala Star Banner,* Jan. 9, 1891; *Jacksonville Evening Telegram,* Dec. 29, 1892; *OES,* Jan. 2, 1901; *ST,* Jan. 8, 1910, Dec. 27, 1913; *RP,* Jan. 6, 1917.

51. On black women and the jeremiad tradition, see David Howard-Pitney, *The Afro-American Jeremiad: Appeals for Justice in America* (Philadelphia: Temple University Press, 1990), 81–86; Higginbotham, *Righteous Discontent,* chap. 5.

52. *San Antonio Express,* June 20, 1883; *San Antonio Light,* June 20, 1883; Sobre, *San Antonio on Parade,* 57–59.

53. Laurie Maffly-Kipp, "Mapping the World, Mapping the Race: The Negro Race History, 1874–1915," *Church History* 64 (Dec. 1995): 610–626.

54. *JTU,* Jan. 2, 1901; Tunde Adeleke, *Un-African Americans: Nineteenth-Century Black Nationalists and the Civilizing Mission* (Lexington: University Press of Kentucky, 1998), esp. chap. 1; Bederman, *Manliness*

and Civilization, esp. chaps. 1 and 2; Louise Michele Newman, *White Women's Rights: The Racial Origins of Feminism in the United States* (New York: Oxford University Press, 1999), esp. chap. 1; Wilson Jeremiah Moses, *Afrotopia: The Roots of African American Popular History* (New York: Cambridge University Press, 1998), chaps. 4 and 6.

55. *ST,* Jan. 4, 1902; *RP,* Apr. 27, 1907; *OES,* Jan. 9, 1900. See also *New Orleans Louisianian,* Jan. 8, 1881. On "Ethiopianism," Freemasonry, and Egypt, see Moses, *Afrotopia,* 47–50; and Albert J. Raboteau, *A Fire in the Bones: Reflections on African-American Religious History* (Boston: Beacon, 1995), chap. 2.

56. *RP,* Apr. 27, 1907; *ST,* Jan. 4, 1902, Feb. 24, 1917; *OES,* Jan. 9, 1900; *Asheville (N.C.) Gazette,* Jan. 2, 1901.

57. *Huntsville Gazette,* Jan. 4, 1890. For examples of the acknowledgment of former slaves during ceremonies, see *IF,* Jan. 15, 1898; *ST,* Feb. 3, 1912, Jan. 6, 1917; *RP,* Jan. 6, 1917. For orations that discussed the horrors of the Middle Passage, the courage displayed by runaway slaves, and the hardships of slavery, see *Washington D.C. People's Advocate,* Jan. 7, 1882; *CN&C,* Jan. 2, 1889; *Charlotte Observer,* Jan. 2, 1909.

58. Wilson Jeremiah Moses, *The Golden Age of Black Nationalism, 1850–1925* (New York: Oxford University Press, 1978), 72; Untitled speech, Apr. 13, 1885, Charles N. Hunter Papers, Rare Book, Manuscript and Special Collections Library, Duke University; *Richmond Dispatch,* Jan. 2, 1866; *Richmond Whig,* Jan. 2, 1866, *Richmond Examiner,* Jan. 2, 1866; *ST,* Jan. 5, 1889, Feb. 13, 1909, Jan. 10, 1914; *AC,* Jan. 3, 1888, Feb. 24, 1917. See also *OES,* Jan. 9, 1900, Jan. 2, 1901; *Southwestern Christian Advocate,* Jan. 3, 1901; James Walker Hood, *Negro in the Christian Pulpit; or, The Two Characters and Two Destinies* (Raleigh: Edwards, Broughton, 1884), 119.

59. *Richmond Dispatch,* Jan. 2, 1866; *ST,* Jan. 5, 1889; *CS,* Jan. 1, 1892; *RP,* Dec. 11, 1897; *ST,* Feb. 24, 1917. See also *New Orleans Louisianian,* July 9, 1881; *Petersburg Lancet,* Jan. 13, 1883, Jan. 17, 1885; *Nashville Banner,* Jan. 2, 1891; *OES,* Jan. 2, 1901; Emancipation Day Resolutions, page 2, Jan. 2, 1899, Charles N. Hunter Papers. For a cogent discussion of black millennialism, see Timothy E. Fulop, "'The Future Golden Day of the Race': Millennialism and Black Americans in the Nadir, 1877–1901," *Harvard Theological Review* 84 (1991): 75–99.

60. *Savannah Daily Republican,* July 6, 1867; Edwards, *Gendered*

Strife, 194; *ST,* Jan. 5, 1889, Jan. 7, 1893, Mar. 14, 1896, Jan. 4, 1902. For other accounts of black heroism, see *Twenty-two Years of Freedom,* 42–43; *IF,* Jan. 13, 1894; *ST,* Jan. 9, 1904, Jan. 5, 1907, Jan. 10, 1914, *OES,* Jan. 2, 1906; *RP,* Jan. 9, 1915.

61. *Raleigh Baptist Sentinel,* Jan. 11, 1912; Emancipation Day Oration, Jan. 1, 1912, box 4, Charles N. Hunter Papers; *New Berne Daily Times,* Jan. 3, 1873; *JTU,* July 5, 1887; *ST,* Jan. 12, 1895; *OES,* Jan. 9, 1900.

62. *BB,* June 21, 1894; *ST,* Jan. 12, 1895, Jan. 9, 1904, Jan. 8, 1910, Jan. 10, 1914.

63. *Raleigh Baptist Sentinel,* Jan. 9, 1908; *SMN,* Jan. 2, 1892; *IF,* July 18, 1896; *RP,* Jan. 9, 1915. For other examples, see *Twenty-two Years of Freedom,* 44–45; *CS,* Jan. 2, 1898; *RN&O,* Jan. 2, 1900; *Star of Zion,* Jan. 29, 1914; Emancipation Day Address, Jan. 1, 1907, box 3, Charles N. Hunter Papers; Undated Emancipation Day Speech, 21–22, box 3, Charles N. Hunter Papers.

64. *JTU,* Jan. 3, 1884; *AC,* Jan. 2, 1890; *SMN,* Jan. 3, 1899; *BAH,* Jan. 3, 1899; *ST,* Jan. 4, 1902; *IF,* Jan. 14, 1893; *RN&O,* Jan. 3, 1922. See also *Twenty-two Years of Freedom,* 47; *CS,* Jan. 2, 1896; *BAH,* Jan. 3, 1899; *NVP,* Jan. 2, 1900, Jan. 2, 1907; *OES,* Jan. 9, 1900; *RN&O,* Jan. 2, 1901; Emancipation Day Oration, 6–8, [n.d.], box 12, Charles N. Hunter Papers; *Birmingham Reporter* Jan. 7, 1928.

65. *RP,* Oct. 28, 1899; *ST,* Feb. 24, 1917.

66. *ST,* May 27, 1893, Jan. 6, 1900. See, for instance, *SMN,* Jan. 2, 1900; *AC,* Jan. 2, 1904; *Raleigh Post,* Jan. 3, 1905; *Raleigh Liberator,* Jan. 7, 1905; *Raleigh Times,* Jan. 1, 1907; *ST,* Jan. 5, 1907; *RN&O,* Jan. 2, 1917. A few orators, contrary to the general pattern described here, were so pessimistic that they advocated emigration to Africa or virtual black autonomy in the United States. See *SMN,* Jan. 2, 1890, Jan. 6, 1917; *IF,* Jan. 13, 1894; and *ST,* Jan. 7, 1898.

67. For jeremiads about proper behavior and "race pride," see *AC,* Jan. 3, 1888, Jan. 2, 1897, Dec. 30, 1899; *JTU,* Jan. 2, 1902; *ST,* Jan. 9, 1904; and "Lectures of Daniel Webster Davis," undated orations, Daniel Webster Davis Papers, Virginia Historical Society. On the black jeremiad tradition, see Howard-Pitney, *Afro-American Jeremiad,* especially the introduction and chap. 2; and Wilson Jeremiah Moses, *Black Messiahs and Uncle Toms: Social and Literary Manipulations of a Religious Myth* (University Park: Pennsylvania State University Press, 1982), chap. 3.

68. Emancipation Day speech, Jan. 1, 1912, box 4, Charles N. Hunter Papers.

69. *AC,* July 4–5, 1902, July 4–5, 1903, July 4–5, 1904.

70. Moses, *Golden Age of Black Nationalism,* 255.

71. *IF,* July 18, 1896.

3. Archiving White Memory

1. *Montgomery Advertiser,* Dec. 8, 1898.

2. Theodore H. Jack, "The Preservation of Georgia History," *NCHR* 4 (July 1927): 239–240; John Hugh Reynolds, "Public Archives of Arkansas," *Annual Report of the American Historical Association, 1906* (1908), vol. 2: 28; David Y. Thomas, "Report on the Public Archives of Florida," *Annual Report of the American Historical Association, 1906* (1908), vol. 2: 151–152; R. D. W. Connor, "How Can the States Be Persuaded to Take Care of Their Historical Archives?" *Annual Report of the American Historical Association* (1922), vol. 1: 121; St. George Leakin Sioussat, "A Preliminary Report upon the Archives of Tennessee," *Annual Report of the American Historical Association* (1906), vol. 2: 206.

3. Thomas McAdory Owen, ed., *Report of the Alabama History Commission to the Governor of Alabama: December 12, 1900,* vol. 1 (Montgomery, Ala.: Brown Printing, 1901), 37; Thomas M. Owen, *The Establishment, Organization, Activities, and Aspirations of the Department of Archives and History of the State of Alabama* (Montgomery: Brown, 1904); Peter A. Brannon, "The Alabama Department of History and Archives," *AHQ* 24 (Spring 1962): 1–6; Mitchell B. Garrett, "The Preservation of Alabama History," *NCHR* 5 (Jan. 1928): 10–13; Wendell H. Stephenson, "Some Pioneer Alabama Historians: Thomas M. Owen," *Alabama Review* 2 (Jan. 1949): 51–54.

4. Riley to Thomas M. Owen, Aug. 15, 1898, Thomas M. Owen Papers, Alabama Department of Archives and History, Montgomery; "Report of the Mississippi Historical Commission," *PMHS* (1902), vol. 5: 33; "Development of Historical Work in Mississippi," *Publications of the Southern History Association* 6 (July 1902): 335–340; William H. Weathersby, "The Preservation of Mississippi History," *NCHR* 5 (Apr. 1928): 142–145.

5. R. D. W. Connor, "Lessons from North Carolina," *Annual Report of the American Historical Association, 1922* (1926), vol. 1: 121, 124; Waldo G. Leland to Thomas M. Owen, Feb. 6, 1906, Thomas M. Owen Papers. See also *The North Carolina Historical Commission: Forty Years of Public Service, 1903–1943* (Raleigh: North Carolina Historical Commission, 1942); J. G. de Roulhac Hamilton, "The Preservation of North Carolina History," *NCHR* 4 (Jan. 1927): 10–15; Frontis W. Johnston, "The North Carolina Historical Commission, 1903–1978," in Jeffrey J. Crow, ed., *Public History in North Carolina, 1903–1978* (Raleigh: North Carolina Department of Cultural Resources, 1979), 1–4.

6. A. P. Foster, "Tennessee Department of Library, Archives, and History," *Tennessee Historical Magazine* 6 (1920–1921): 271–272. See also Philip M. Hamer, "The Preservation of Tennessee History," *NCHR* 6 (Apr. 1929): 130–131; Charles L. Lewis, "Robert Thomas Quarles and the Archives of Tennessee," *Tennessee Historical Magazine* 9 (Apr. 1925): 3–8.; Charles W. Ramsdell, "The Preservation of Texas History," *NCHR* 6 (Jan. 1929): 9; "Proceedings of Later Meetings of the Arkansas Historical Commission," appendix B of the *Third Report of the Arkansas History Commission* (1911), vol. 3: 42. For a sampling of Herndon's tribulations, see Dallas T. Herndon to John Hugh Reynolds, May 15, 1915 (box 1, folder 2), Aug. 2, 1921 (box 1, folder 6), and Apr. 12, 1923 (box 1, folder 6), John Hugh Reynolds Papers, Arkansas History Commission, Little Rock.

7. On the evolution of state authority, see Stephen Skowronek, *Building a New American State: The Expansion of National Administrative Capacities, 1877–1920* (Cambridge, Eng.: Cambridge University Press, 1982), esp. chaps. 3, 6, and epilogue. For a case study of the limits of state authority in the South, see Stephen W. Wrigley, "The Triumph of Provincialism: Public Life in Georgia, 1898–1917," Ph.D. diss., Northwestern University, 1986.

8. *North Carolina Historical Commission,* 34–35, 88–89; *First Biennial Report of the Texas Library and Historical Commission* (Austin: Austin Printing, 1911), 20–21; *Second Biennial Report of the Texas Library and Historical Commission* (Austin: Von Boeckmann-Jones, 1914), 10–11. The archival impulse in Europe and elsewhere is discussed in Michel Foucault, *The Archaeology of Knowledge* (New York: Routledge, 1972), 79–131; Jacques Le Goff, *History and Memory* (New York: Columbia

368 Notes to Pages 114–118

University Press, 1992), 87–89; Thomas Richards, *The Imperial Archive: Knowledge and the Fantasy of Empire* (New York: Verso, 1993); and Carolyn Steedman, *Dust: The Archive and Cultural History* (New Brunswick, N.J.: Rutgers University Press, 2002).

9. Dallas T. Herndon, "Arkansas History Commission and Its Work," address prepared for the Forty-fourth Annual Session of the Arkansas State Teachers' Association, Dec. 27–29, 1911, 9; Connor, "Lessons from North Carolina," 125; North Carolina Historical Commission, *Report of the Historical Commission to Governor Charles B. Aycock* (Raleigh: E. M. Uzzell, 1904), 1.

10. Franklin L. Riley, "The Work of the Mississippi Historical Society," *PMHS* 10 (1910): 42; *Report of the Alabama History Commission*, vol. 1: 38; John Hugh Reynolds, "A Comprehensive Historical Policy for Arkansas," Arkansas Historical Commission, Circular no. 3 (1905), 11; see also comments of C. Alphonso Smith and William A. Dunning, quoted in "Opinions of Men of Letters on the Work of the Mississippi Historical Society," (n.p.: n.p., 1909[?]), 4, 11; Herndon, "Arkansas History Commission," 10.

11. *Trinity Archive* (Jan. 1898): 177–187; Dallas T. Herndon, *The Arkansas History Commission Catalogue* (n.p.: n.p., 1923), 7, 8.

12. William P. Trent, "Notes on Recent Work in Southern History," *Proceedings of the Virginia Historical Society* (1892): 49–50; David Y. Thomas, "The Preservation of Arkansas History," *NCHR* 5 (July 1928): 269; Allen J. Going, "Historical Societies in Alabama," *Alabama Review* 1 (Jan. 1948): 43. On the plight of the Florida Historical Society, see Watt Marchmann, "The Florida Historical Society," *Florida Historical Quarterly* 19 (July 1940): 22.

13. Alcée Fortier, "The Teaching of History in the South," *Iowa Journal of History and Economics* 3 (1905): 93; John Higham, *History: Professional Scholarship in America* (Baltimore: Johns Hopkins University Press, 1983), 94; Dorothy Ross, "Historical Consciousness in Nineteenth-Century America," *American Historical Review* 89 (1984): 923; David D. Van Tassel, "From Learned Society to Professional Organization: The American Historical Association, 1884–1900," *American Historical Review* 89 (Oct. 1984): 941. For the emerging professional social sciences, see Thomas L. Haskell, *The Emergence of Professional Social Science: The American Social Science Association and the Nineteenth-Century Crisis of Authority* (Urbana: University of Illinois Press, 1977), esp. chap. 2.

14. R. D. W. Connor, "A State Library Building and Department of Archives and Records," *North Carolina Booklet* 6 (Jan. 1907): 171; Herndon, *Arkansas History Commission Catalogue; First Biennial Report of the Board of Curators of the Louisiana State Museum* (1908): 24–46; *Second Biennial Report of the Board of Curators of the Louisiana State Museum* (1910): 12–29; *Third Biennial Report of the Board of Curators of the Louisiana State Museum* (1912): 19, 21–57; and *Fourth Biennial Report of the Board of Curators of the Louisiana State Museum* (1914): 25, 34–47, 59–85. On museums as temples to white domination, see Steven Conn, *Museums and American Intellectual Life, 1876–1926* (Chicago: University of Chicago Press, 1998), 117; Donna Haraway, *Primate Visions: Gender, Race, and Nature in the World of Science* (New York, 1989), 26–58; Curtis M. Hinsley, *Savages and Scientists: The Smithsonian Institution and the Development of American Anthropology, 1846–1910* (Washington D.C., 1981), 89–91, 97–99, 104–109, 112; Robert W. Rydell, *All the World's a Fair: Visions of Empire at American International Expositions, 1876–1916* (Chicago: University of Chicago Press, 1984), 100.

15. William R. Garrett, "The Work of the South in the Building of the United States," *Transactions of the Alabama Historical Society, 1898–1899* (1904), vol. 3: 43; Dunbar Rowland, *A Mississippi View of Race Relations in the South* (Jackson, Miss.: Harmon, 1903), 4, 16. On the racial attitudes of southern historians, see Bruce Clayton, *The Savage Ideal: Intolerance and Intellectual Leadership in the South, 1890–1914* (Baltimore: Johns Hopkins University Press, 1972); and John David Smith, *An Old Creed for the New South: Proslavery Ideology and Historiography, 1865–1918* (Athens: University of Georgia Press, 1991), chaps. 5–6. Thomas M. Owen and Dallas T. Herndon, for example, were both devotees of genealogical research.

16. Charles Hillman Brough, "The Clinton Riot," *PMHS* 6 (1902): 63; Alfred Holt Stone, "Mississippi's Constitution and Statues in Reference to Freemen, and their Alleged Relation to the Reconstruction Acts and War Amendments," *PMHS* 4 (1901): 226.

17. Franklin L. Riley, "Proceedings of the Decennial Meeting of the Mississippi Historical Society," *PMHS* 10 (1910); Riley, "Work of the Mississippi Historical Society," *PMHS* 10 (1910): 43–44; Frederick W. Moore et al., "The Teaching of History in the South," *School Review* 11 (Feb. 1903): 107; "The Study of History in Schools," *Annual Report of the American Historical Association, 1898* (1899): 427–518; Dunbar Rowland,

"The Rise and Fall of Negro Rule in Mississippi," *PMHS* 2 (1899): 189; Charles Hillman Brough, "The Clinton Riot," *PMHS* 6 (1902): 63; Alfred Holt Stone, "Mississippi's Constitution and Statues in Reference to Freemen, and Their Alleged Relation to the Reconstruction Acts and War Amendments," *PMHS* 4 (1901): 226; *North Carolina Historical Commission,* 92–93; Willard B. Gatewood Jr., "Rendering Striking Historical Service: North Carolina's Historical Publications Program, 1903–1978," in Jeffrey J. Crow, ed., *Public History in North Carolina, 1903–1978* (Raleigh: North Carolina Department of Cultural Resources, 1979), 38; Franklin L. Riley, *School History of Mississippi* (Richmond: B. F. Johnson, 1900), 5.

18. Thomas M. Owen, "State Departments of Archives and History," *Annual Report of the American Historical Association, 1904* (1905): 237–257; Brannon, "Alabama Department of History and Archives," 9–11; Garrett, "Preservation of Alabama History," 13–19; Stephenson, "Some Pioneer Alabama Historians," 53–61; North Carolina General Assembly, *Public Laws of North Carolina, 1907* (Raleigh, 1908), 1031–1032.

19. James A. Woodburn, "Promotion of Historical Study in America Following the Civil War," *Illinois State Historical Society Transactions* 29 (1922): 48. On the influence of Johns Hopkins, see Higham, *History,* 11–14; Wendell H. Stephenson, "Herbert Baxter Adams and Southern Historical Scholarship at Johns Hopkins University," *Maryland Historical Magazine* 42 (Mar. 1947): 1–20; and Bonnie G. Smith, "Gender and Practices of Scientific History: The Seminar and Archival Research in the Nineteenth Century," *American Historical Review* 100 (Oct. 1995): esp. 1154–1158. On transformations in American higher education, see Mary O. Furner, *Advocacy and Objectivity: A Crisis in the Professionalization of American Social Science, 1865–1905* (Lexington: University Press of Kentucky, 1975), esp. chaps. 7–10; and Haskell, *Emergence of Professional Social Science.*

20. Bride Neill Taylor, "The Beginnings of the Texas State Historical Association," *Southwestern Historical Quarterly* 33 (July 1929): 2; Tom B. Brewer, "A History of the Department of History of the University of Texas, 1883–1951," master's thesis, University of Texas, 1957, 211; "Proceedings of the Annual Meeting of the Alabama Historical Society, June 19, 1899," *Transactions of the Alabama Historical Society, 1898–1899*

(1904), vol. 3: 13–22; Riley, "Work of the Mississippi Historical Society," 35–39.

21. United Sons of Confederate Veterans, *Minutes of the Tenth Annual Reunion* (Louisville, 1905), 22. See also Gaines M. Foster, *Ghosts of the Confederacy: Defeat, the Lost Cause, and the Emergence of the New South* (New York: Oxford University Press, 1987), 180; Robert Reynolds Simpson, "The Origin of State Departments of Archives and History in the South," Ph.D. diss., University of Mississippi, 1971, 95–101.

22. Ramsdell, "Preservation of Texas History," 6; E. W. Winkler, "Some Historical Activities of the Texas Library and Historical Commission," *Quarterly of the Texas State Historical Association* 14 (1910–1911): 294–304. UDC lobbying is discussed in Karen L. Cox, *Dixie's Daughters: The United Daughters of the Confederacy and the Preservation of Confederate Culture* (Gainesville: University Press of Florida, 2003), 76–82; and R. B. Rosenberg, *Living Monuments: Confederate Soldiers' Homes in the New South* (Chapel Hill: University of North Carolina Press, 1993).

23. Stephenson, "Some Pioneer Alabama Historians," 45–62; David Duncan Wallace, ed., *History of South Carolina* (New York: American Historical Society, 1934), 4, 611; Yates Snowden, *History of South Carolina* (New York: Lewis, 1920), 14–15; Simpson, "Origin of Southern Departments of Archives and History," 187–188; J. Franklin Jameson to Herbert Putnam, July 26, 1927, in Elizabeth Donnan and Leo F. Stock, *An Historian's World: Selections from the Correspondence of John Franklin Jameson* (Philadelphia: American Philosophical Society, 1956), 325; Hugh T. Lefler, "Robert Digges Wimberly Connor," in Clifford L. Lord, ed., *Keepers of the Past* (Chapel Hill: University of North Carolina Press, 1965), 109–123.

24. J. Franklin Jameson to Herbert Baxter Adams, Feb. 21, 1890, in W. Stull Holt, *Historical Scholarship in the United States, 1876–1901, as Revealed in the Correspondence of Herbert B. Adams* (Baltimore: Johns Hopkins University Press, 1938), 128; John B. Henneman, "Historical Studies in the South since the Civil War," *Sewanee Review* 1 (Nov. 1892): 339; Phillips to George J. Baldwin, May 2, 1903, quoted in John David Smith, "Du Bois and Phillips—Symbolic Antagonists of the Progressive Era," *Centennial Review* 24 (Winter 1980): 94.

25. Fred Arthur Bailey, "The Textbooks of the Lost Cause: Cen-

sorship and the Creation of Southern State Histories," *GHQ* 75 (Fall 1991): 507–533; Bailey, "Free Speech at the University of Florida: The Enoch Marvin Banks Case," *Florida Historical Quarterly* 71 (July 1992): 1–17; Bailey, "Free Speech and the 'Lost Cause' in Texas: A Study of Social Control in the New South," *Southwestern Historical Quarterly* 97 (Jan. 1994): 453–477; Clayton, *Savage Ideal*, chaps. 3 and 4; Foster, *Ghosts of the Confederacy*, 182–183; John McCardell, "Trent's *Simms:* The Making of a Biography," in William J. Cooper et al., eds., *A Master's Due: Essays in Honor of David Herbert Donald* (Baton Rouge: Louisiana State University Press, 1985), 177–203.

26. John Spenser Bassett, quoted in Nannie M. Tilley, *The Trinity College Historical Society, 1892–1941* (Durham, N.C.: Duke University Press, 1941), 53; John Spencer Bassett, *Trinity Archive,* Jan. 1898.

27. John Spenser Bassett, *Trinity Archive,* Jan. 1898; Henneman, "Historical Studies in the South since the Civil War," 324–325, 333–334, emphasis in original; Smith, "Gender and the Practices of Scientific History," 1153.

28. Weeks, "Historical Studies in the South," 22.

29. Henneman, "Historical Studies in the South since the Civil War," 337; William P. Trent, "Tendencies of Higher Life in the South," *Atlantic Monthly* 79 (1897): 775; Trent, "Notes on the Outlook for Historical Studies in the South," *American Historical Association Papers,* 5 vols. (New York: American Historical Association, 1885–1891), vol. 4, 391.

30. Connor to Captain Ashe, Feb. 5, 1909, series 1, box 1, folder 68, R. D. W. Connor Papers, SHC. See also Connor to C. Alphonso Smith, Feb. 3, 1909, series 1, box 1, folder 68, R. D. W. Connor Papers. On the controversy, see Foster, *Ghosts of the Confederacy,* 186–188.

31. Charles L. Van Noppen, "The Supineness of the North Carolina Historical Association and the Ignorance of the North Carolina Society of the Colonial Dames" [Greensboro, N.C., 1912].

32. Connor to H. Addington Bruce, Jan. 20, 1910, series 1, box 2, folder 99, R. D. W. Connor Papers; Connor to S. A. Ashe, Mar. 8, 1912; Connor to Ashe, Mar. 12, 1912; Connor to Ashe, Mar. 19, 1912; and Connor to Charles Von Noppen, [Mar. 1912], all in series 1, box 2, folder 157, R. D. W. Connor Papers. For similar attitudes about the form and tone of scholarly debate among social sciences specialists, see Furner, *Advocacy and Objectivity,* esp. chaps. 12 and 13.

33. Connor to S. A. Ashe, Mar. 8, 1912; Connor to Ashe, Mar. 12, 1912; Connor to Ashe, Mar. 19, 1912; Connor to Charles Von Noppen, [Mar. 1912], all in series 1, box 2, folder 157, R. D. W. Connor Papers.

34. Taylor, "Beginnings of the Texas State Historical Association," 11–12.

35. Connor to Robert B. House, Nov. 18, 1923, quoted in Thomas C. Parramore, "Forging a Tremulous Link: The First Half Century of the *North Carolina Historical Review*," *North Carolina Historical Review* 51 (Oct. 1974): 363. For a laudatory survey of the campaign to purge southern historical scholarship of "romance," see James P. Hendrix, "From Romance to Scholarship: Southern History at the Take-Off Point," *Mississippi Quarterly* 30 (Spring 1977): 193–211.

4. Black Remembrance in the Age of Jim Crow

1. Tamah Z. Richardson and Annie L. Rivers, "Progress of the Negro: A Unit of Work for the Third Grade," *VTB* 13 (May 1936): 3–8.

2. Vardaman quoted in Ray Stannard Baker, *Following the Color Line: An Account of Negro Citizenship in the American Democracy* (New York: Doubleday, Page, 1908), 247.

3. The plight of black education is surveyed in James D. Anderson, *The Education of Blacks in the South, 1860–1935* (Chapel Hill: University of North Carolina Press, 1988); Louis R. Harlan, *Separate and Unequal: Public School Campaigns and Racism in the Southern Seaboard States, 1901–1915* (1958; New York: Atheneum, 1968); Leon F. Litwack, *Trouble in Mind: Black Southerners in the Age of Jim Crow* (New York: Knopf, 1998), chap. 2; and Robert A. Margo, *Race and Schooling in the South, 1880–1950: An Economic History* (Chicago: University of Chicago Press, 1990).

4. W. E. B. Du Bois, *The Souls of Black Folk* (1903; New York: New American Library, 1982), 99; Pauli Murray, *Proud Shoes: The Story of an American Family* (New York: Harper & Row, 1978), 269.

5. Murray, *Proud Shoes;* James L. Leloudis, *Schooling in the New South: Pedagogy, Self, and Society in North Carolina, 1880–1920* (Chapel Hill: University of North Carolina Press, 1996), 177–179; Neil R. McMillen, *Dark Journey: Black Mississippians in the Age of Jim Crow* (Urbana: University of Illinois Press, 1989), chap. 3, 90–91, 107–108.

6. Adam Fairclough, *Teaching Equality: Black Schools in the Age of Jim Crow* (Athens: University of Georgia Press, 2001), 50–51; Carol Townsend Gilkes, "The Politics of Silence: Dual-Sex Political Systems and Women's Traditions of Conflict Resolution," in Paul Johnson, ed., *African American Christianity: Essays in History* (Berkeley: University of California Press, 1994), 94; Myrtle R. Phillips, "The Negro Secondary School Teacher," *Journal of Negro Education* 9 (July 1940): 482; Sonya Y. Ramsey, "More Than the Three R's: The Educational, Economic, and Cultural Experiences of African American Female Public School Teachers in Nashville, Tennessee, 1869 to 1983," Ph.D. diss., University of North Carolina, 2000, 30, 220; Vanessa Siddle Walker, *Their Highest Potential: An African American School Community in the Segregated South* (Chapel Hill: University of North Carolina Press, 1996), esp. chap. 1.

7. Michael Fultz, "African American Teachers in the South, 1890–1940: Powerlessness and the Ironies of Expectations and Protest," *History of Education Quarterly* 35 (Winter 1995): 406–407, 408, 418.

8. Leroy Campbell interview, folder 7, series M, SOHP; Angela Davis, *Angela Davis: An Autobiography* (New York: Random House, 1974), 90; George W. Gore, *In-Service Professional Improvement of Negro Teachers in Tennessee* (New York: Teachers College, Columbia University, 1940), 58; Valinda W. Littlefield, "'I Am Only One, But I Am One': Southern African-American Women Schoolteachers, 1884–1954," Ph.D. diss., University of Illinois, Urbana, 2003, 74–75, 108; Ramsey, "More Than the Three R's," 91–92.

9. Johnson to Booker T. Washington, in Louis Harlan, ed., *Booker T. Washington Papers* (Urbana: University of Illinois Press, 1974), vol. 3: 121; R. B. Eleazer, *School Books and Racial Antagonism: A Study of Omissions and Inclusions That Make for Misunderstanding* (Atlanta: Conference on Education and Race Relations, 1937), 7; Mamie Garvin Fields with Karen Fields, *Lemon Swamp and Other Places: A Carolina Memoir* (New York: 1983), 45.

10. Constitution of the Negro Society for Historical Research, quoted in Elinor Des Verney Sinnette, *Arthur Alfonso Schomburg: Black Bibliophile and Collector* (Detroit: Wayne State University Press, 1989) 43. On early black historical activities, see Julie Des Jardins, *Women and the Historical Enterprise in America: Gender, Race, and the Politics of Memory, 1880–1945* (Chapel Hill: University of North Carolina Press, 2003), 132–133; Robert Hill, "On Collectors, Their Contributions to the Docu-

mentation of the Black Past," in Elinor Sinnette, Paul Coates, and Thomas C. Battle, eds., *Black Bibliophiles and Collectors: Preservers of Black History* (Washington, D.C.: Howard University Press, 1990), 47–55; Elizabeth McHenry, *Forgotten Readers: Recovering the Lost History of African American Literary Societies* (Durham, N.C.: Duke University Press, 2002), 156–157, 174–179; Sinnette, *Schomburg: Black Bibliophile and Collector,* esp. chaps. 2 and 3; James Spady, "The Afro-American Historical Society: The Nucleus of Black Bibliophiles, 1897–1923," *Negro History Bulletin* (June–July 1974): 255–256; Charles Wesley, "Racial Historical Societies and the American Heritage," *JNH* 37 (Jan. 1952): 25.

11. August Meier and Elliot Rudwick, *Black History and the Historical Profession, 1915–1980* (Urbana: University of Illinois Press, 1986), 7; Alfred A. Moss Jr., *The American Negro Academy: The Voice of the Talented Tenth* (Baton Rouge: Louisiana State University Press, 1981), 24; Crummell quoted in Willard B. Gatewood, *Aristocrats of Color: The Black Elite, 1880–1920* (Bloomington: Indiana University Press, 1990), 218; Arthur A. Schomburg, The Negro Digs Up His Past," in Alain Locke, ed., *The New Negro* (1925; New York: Atheneum, 1968), 236–237. Early black historical societies also marginalized black women. See Des Jardins, *Women and the Historical Enterprise in America,* 120–124.

12. Margaret Washington to Lugenia Burns Hope, Sept. 15, 1922, folder 240, Mary Church Terrell Papers, Moorland-Spingarn Research Center, Howard University; Joan Marie Johnson, "'This Wonderful Dream Nation!': Black and White South Carolina Women and the Creation of the New South, 1898–1930," Ph.D. diss., University of California, Los Angeles, 1997, 288–291; Cynthia Neverdon-Morton, *Afro-American Women of the South and the Advancement of the Race, 1895–1925* (Knoxville: University of Tennessee Press, 1989), 198–200; Jacqueline Anne Rouse, *Lugenia Burns Hope: Black Southern Reformer* (Athens: University of Georgia Press, 1989), 115.

13. The Napier quotation is in Elizabeth L. Davis, *Lifting as They Climb* (Washington, D.C.: National Association of Colored Women, 1933), 80, 82. See also Mary Talbert, "The Frederick Douglass Home," *Crisis* 14 (Feb. 1917): 174; Mary Talbert, "Concerning the Frederick Douglass Memorial," *Crisis* 14 (Aug. 1917): 167; Wesley, "Racial Historical Societies," 79–85, 89, 91; Des Jardins, *Women and the Historical Enterprise in America,* 124–125.

14. Mary A. Renda, *Taking Haiti: Military Occupation and the Cul-*

ture of U.S. Imperialism, 1915–1940 (Chapel Hill: University of North Carolina Press, 2001), 266–267.

15. Anderson, *Education of Blacks in the South,* 249.

16. *NJ&G,* Feb. 5, 1927. See also Carter G. Woodson, "Negro Life and History in Our Schools," *JNH* 4 (Jan. 1919): 277–278; Meier and Rudwick, *Black History and the Historical Profession,* 6–8. On club activities at various black colleges, see *Atlanta World,* Feb. 12, 1932; *Houston Informer,* Feb. 10, 1934; *NJ&G,* Feb. 15, 1936; *Pittsburgh Courier,* Feb. 8, 1936; *Nashville Globe,* Jan. 20, 1939; *San Antonio Register,* Feb. 14, 1941.

17. U.S. Commissioner of Education, *Report, 1899–1900* (Washington, D.C.: U.S. Government Printing Office, 1901), vol. 2, 2506–2507; David T. Blose and Ambrose Caliver, *Statistics of the Education of Negroes, 1933–1934 and 1935–1936,* U.S. Department of the Interior, *Office of Education Bulletin* 13, 1935 (Washington, D.C.: U.S. Government Printing Office, 1939), 37–40; Anderson, *Education of Blacks in the South,* chap. 7; "Directory: Teachers of the Social Sciences in Negro Colleges and Universities," undated list [1940?], Luther P. Jackson Papers, VSU.

18. Kenneth Robert Janken, *Rayford W. Logan and the Dilemma of the African American Intellectual* (Amherst: University of Massachusetts Press, 1993), chap. 3; Meier and Rudwick, *Black History and the Historical Profession,* 73–95.

19. Paul W. L. Jones, "Negro Biography," *JNH* 8 (Apr. 1923): 129; *JNH* 6 (Jan. 1921): 129.

20. Sutton E. Griggs, *Life's Demands; or, According to Law* (Memphis: National Public Welfare League, 1916), 51–52; John Hope Franklin, "On the Evolution of Scholarship in Afro-American History," in Darlene Clark Hine, ed., *The State of Afro-American History: Past, Present, and Future* (Baton Rouge: Louisiana State University Press, 1986), 14–15.

21. W. E. B. Du Bois, *Freeman,* Oct. 4, 1922; Joseph A. Bailey, "Perspective in the Teaching of Negro History," *JNH* 20 (1935): 25–26; Charles H. Wesley, "The Reconstruction of History," *JNH* 20 (Oct. 1935): 416, 421.

22. *JNH* 10 (July 1925): 581; Joseph J. Rhoads, "Teaching the Negro Child," *JNH* 19 (Jan. 1934): 17, 20; Irwin V. Shannon, "The Teaching of Negro Life and History in Relation to Some Views of Educators of Race Adjustment," *JNE* 2 (Jan. 1933): 63.

23. Jacqueline Goggin, *Carter G. Woodson: A Life in Black History* (Baton Rouge: Louisiana State University Press, 1993), 38–45, 79–84; Meier and Rudwick, *Black History and the Historical Profession,* 13, 15–19, 31–46.

24. Luther P. Jackson, "The First Twenty-five Years of the *Journal of Negro History* Digested," *JNH* 25 (Oct. 1940): 438.

25. Luther P. Jackson to Dr. [?] Hunter, June 9, 1945; Jackson to Hunter, June 8, 1947, both in Luther P. Jackson Papers.

26. "Opportunities of Negro College Professors for Research in the South," *Norfolk Journal and Guide,* May 17, 1944; Jackson to Carter G. Woodson, Sept. 18, 1947, Smythe to Luther P. Jackson, Nov. 27, 1944, Luther P. Jackson Papers; *JNH* 23 (Oct. 1938): 418–419; *JNH* 7 (Jan. 1922): 123; *JNH* 16 (Jan. 1931): 3; *JNH* 21 (Apr. 1936): 235; *NJ&G,* Feb. 8, 1930.

27. Luther P. Jackson, "The Work of the Association and the People," *JNH* 20 (Oct. 1935): 385; John Hope Franklin, "The Place of Carter G. Woodson in American Historiography," *Negro History Bulletin* 13 (May 1950): 174–176.

28. So close were Virginia State's ties with teachers that the Virginia Teachers' Association, the black teachers' professional organization, was "virtually the child of Virginia State College" during Gandy's tenure. See Luther P. Jackson to Alruethus A. Taylor, June 14, 1949, Luther P. Jackson Papers. On Jackson's career, see Michael Dennis, *Luther P. Jackson and a Life for Civil Rights* (Gainesville: University of Florida Press, 2004).

29. *NJ&G,* May 17, 1944; Jackson to Henry J. McGuinn, Nov. 10, 1941, box 6, folder 141, Luther P. Jackson Papers; *NJ&G,* May 17, 1944; Jackson to Dr. F. D. Patterson, Aug. 22, 1940, box 6, folder 137, and Jackson to Woodson, May 20, 1944, box 35, folder 990, both in Luther P. Jackson Papers.

30. Jackson to Dr. I. A. Derbigney, Oct. 26, 1941, box 6, folder 140, Luther P. Jackson Papers; Luther P. Jackson, *A History of the Virginia State Teachers Association* (Norfolk: The Guide, 1937), chap. 5.

31. Luther P. Jackson, "Secondary Education and the Teachers Association," *VTB* 7 (Mar. 1930): 10; Jackson, "The High School Division of the State Teachers Association: Its Organization, Aims, and Policies," *VTB* 8 (Apr. 1931): 8; Jackson to Carter G. Woodson, Apr. 4, 1935, Lu-

ther P. Jackson Papers; *NJ&G*, Sept. 3, 1947. See also Luther P. Jackson, "The Teachers of Virginia and the Annual Drive of the Association for the Study of Negro Life and History," *VTB* 15 (Jan. 1938): 23, 28; Jackson, "The Annual Negro History Drive in Virginia," *VTB* 16 (Apr. 1939): 13–14. As early as 1927, Jackson proposed lesson plans in black history; see his "Negro History in the Virginia High School Curriculum," *VTB* 5 (Mar. 1928): 8, 9–11.

32. *NJ&G*, Aug. 21, 1943, Feb. 3, 1944, box 7, folder 164; Jackson to Carter G. Woodson, Oct. 9, 1943, box 7, folder 164; Jackson to Carter G. Woodson, Sept. 11, 1945, box 35, folder 992; and Jackson to W. A. Jordan, Sept. 24, 1944, box 8, folder 182, all in Luther P. Jackson Papers.

33. Jackson to Dr. Charles S. Johnson, Mar. 13, 1943, box 7, folder 156; Jackson to Dr. Carter G. Woodson, Dec. 12, 1941, box 35, folder 983; C. N. Bennett to Jackson, Nov. 20, 1944, box 8, folder 184, all in Luther P. Jackson Papers. See also Luther P. Jackson, "Citizenship and Governmental Participation," *VTB* 12 (Nov. 1935): 4–5.

34. *NJ&G*, June 24, 1943, Jan. 26, 1945; Jackson to Mr. C. V. Wilson, May 6, 1946, box 10, folder 210, Luther P. Jackson Papers.

35. *NJ&G*, Feb. 9, 1944, Aug, 15, 1945. See also *NJ&G*, Oct. 30, 1946.

36. Luther P. Jackson to C. G. Wolkskill, Jan. 9, 1950, box 12, folder 252, Luther P. Jackson Papers.

37. *JNH* 2 (Jan. 1917): 448; *JNH* 15 (Jan. 1930): 5; *JNH* 18 (Jan. 1933): 3; *JNH* 19 (Jan. 1934): 13, *JNH* 20 (Jan. 1935): 1–3; *JNH* 22 (Jan. 1937). See also *JNH* 8 (Jan. 1923): 117; Jones, "Teaching of Negro History"; *JNH* 10 (July 1925): 577; *JNH* 14 (Apr. 1929): 113; *JNH* 15 (Jan. 1930): 4, 7; *JNH* 20 (Apr. 1935): 127–128; *JNH* 21 (Apr. 1936): 108; *JNH* 23 (Apr. 1938): 143; *JNH* 24 (Apr. 1939): 140.

38. *JNH* 23 (Oct. 1938): 413.

39. "Report of Finding Committee," *VTB* 5 (Jan. 1928): 2; Ethel Howerton, "A Unit of Instruction in Negro History," *VTB* 10 (Mar. 1933): 10–13; Lillian A. Carter, "The Story of Cotton," *VTB* 11 (Mar. 1934): 12–15; John F. Potts Sr., *A History of the Palmetto Education Association* (Washington D.C.: National Education Association, 1978), 173; Ernest J. Middleton, *History of the Louisiana Education Association* (Washington D.C.: National Education Association, 1984), 65.

40. "Negro History Week—The Tenth Year," *JNH* 20 (Apr. 1935): 127–128.

41. Turner to Luther P. Jackson, Aug. 28, 1942, box 5, folder 148, Luther P. Jackson Papers; Charles Scott Wright, "Creating a New Deal: The Importance of Black Self-Help Organizations in Lynchburg, Virginia, 1930–1940," master's thesis, University of North Carolina, Charlotte, 1998, 87; Gilbert L. Porter and Leedell W. Neyland, *History of the Florida State Teachers Association* (Washington D.C.: National Education Association, 1977), 54; Cleopatra D. Thompson, *The History of the Mississippi Teachers Association* (Washington D.C.: National Education Association, 1973), 17.

42. "Negro History Week—The Eighth Year," *JNH* 18 (Apr. 1933): 109; "Negro History Week—The Tenth Year," *JNH* 20 (Apr. 1935): 128; "Negro History Week—The Twelfth Year," *JNH* 22 (Apr. 1937): 145; "Negro History Week—The Fourteenth Year," *JNH* 24 (Apr. 1939): 140.

43. *Baltimore Afro-American,* Feb. 16, 1929; N. V. Boyd to Luther P. Jackson, Aug. 31, 1935, and E. L. Wiley to Luther P. Jackson, Sept. 4, 1935, Luther P. Jackson Papers. See also M. O. Townes to Jackson, Sept. 23, 1935; Anna W. Green to Jackson, Aug, 29, 1935; N. A. Sykes to Jackson, Sept. 5, 1935; and India Hamilton, Aug. 29, 1935, all in Luther P. Jackson Papers.

44. *JNH* 11 (Apr. 1926): 231–232; "Negro History Week—The Fourth Year," *JNH* 14 (Apr. 1929): 111; *JNH* 25 (Jan. 1940): 3–4; Willis Richardson and May Miller, eds., *Negro History in Thirteen Plays* (Washington D.C.: Associated Publishers, 1935), v. See also "Negro History Week—The Fourteenth Year," 140. On the emerging black protest theater, see Samuel A. Hay, *African American Theatre: An Historical and Critical Analysis* (Cambridge, Eng.: Cambridge University Press, 1994), 78–134.

45. David Glassberg, *American Historical Pageantry: The Uses of Tradition in the Early Twentieth Century* (Chapel Hill: University of North Carolina Press, 1990), 132–135; David Krasner, *A Beautiful Pageant: African American Theatre, Drama, and Performance in the Harlem Renaissance, 1910–1927* (New York: Palgrave, 2002), 81–96.

46. "Negro History Week—The Fourth Year," *JNH* 14 (Apr. 1929): 111; *JNH* 15 (Jan. 1930): 3; *JNH* 17 (Jan. 1932): 3; "Negro History Week—The Eighth Year," *JNH* 18 (Apr. 1933): 117; *JNH* 22 (Jan. 1937): 5; *JNH* 25 (Jan. 1940): 3–4; Myrtle Brodie Crawford, "The Negro Builds a Pyramid," *Social Studies* 32 (Jan. 1941): 27.

47. *NJ&G,* Feb. 12, 1927; *Birmingham Reporter,* Feb. 25, 1928; *NJ&G,*

Feb. 18, 1928; *San Antonio Register,* Feb. 9, 1940; *Houston Informer,* Feb. 24, 1934; *Atlanta Constitution,* Feb. 18, 1940; Ramsey, "More Than the Three R's," 220–221.

48. *Atlanta World,* Feb. 18, 1934; *Baltimore Afro-American,* Feb. 23, 1935; Carter G. Woodson, *The African Background Outlined; or, Handbook for the Study of the Negro* (Washington D.C.: Associated Publishers, 1936).

49. *Baltimore Afro-American,* Feb. 22, 1930; *NJ&G,* Feb. 7, 1942; Richardson and Miller, *Negro History in Thirteen Plays,* 202, 215. For a description of the performance of *Nat Turner* at Tennessee State in 1940, see *Nashville Globe,* Feb. 2, 1940.

50. *Houston Informer,* Feb. 24, 1934; Willis Richardson, *Plays and Pageants from the Life of the Negro* (Washington D.C.: Associated Publishers, 1930), 94–95, 311–312, 328. *Ti Yette* was performed during Negro History Week celebrations in Norfolk in 1933. See *NJ&G,* Feb. 18, 1933. Schools in Caroline County, Virginia, mapped the African slave trade; see "Programme for the Observance of Negro History in Caroline County Schools, Beginning Feb. 6, 1938" by Mayme H. Coleman, box 37, folder 1084, Luther P. Jackson Papers.

51. Richardson and Miller, *Negro History in Thirteen Plays,* vi, 279; Richardson, *Plays and Pageants,* vii.

52. "The Celebration of Negro History Week, 1927," *JNH* 12 (Apr. 1927): 105; N. V. Boyd to Luther P. Jackson, Aug. 31, 1935, box 37, folder 1054, Luther P. Jackson Papers.

53. Michael Fultz, "African-American Teachers in the South, 1890–1940: Growth, Feminization, and Salary Discrimination," *Teachers College Record* 96 (1995): 2–6; Gore, *In-Service Professional Improvement of Negro Teachers,* 34; Lattie H. Fennell to Luther P. Jackson, Aug. 30, 1935, box 36, folder 1018, Luther P. Jackson Papers; Littlefield, "I Am Only One, But I Am One," 100. On Jeanes teachers and women teachers in general, see Fairclough, *Teaching Equality,* 51–52; Glenda Elizabeth Gilmore, *Gender and Jim Crow: Women and the Politics of White Supremacy in North Carolina, 1896–1920* (Chapel Hill: University of North Carolina Press, 1996), 157–165; Leloudis, *Schooling the New South,* 186–191; and Littlefield, "I Am Only One, But I Am One," chaps. 1 and 2.

54. *JNH* 9 (Jan. 1924): 105; *JNH* 19 (Oct. 1934): 373; Des Jardins, *Women and the Historical Enterprise in America,* 149–158; Jacqueline

Goggin, "Countering White Racist Scholarship: Carter G. Woodson and the *Journal of Negro History,*" *JNH* 68 (Fall 1983): 365, 374.

55. Richardson, *Plays and Pageants,* 333–344.

56. Fairclough, *Teaching Equality,* 4–6; Walker, *Their Highest Potential,* esp. chap. 6.

57. Turner to Luther P. Jackson, Sept. 1, 1935, box 36, folder 1037, Luther P. Jackson Papers.

58. R. B. Eleazer, *School Books and Racial Antagonism: A Study of Omissions and Inclusions That Make for Misunderstanding* (Atlanta: Conference on Education and Race Relations, 1937), 1; Paul E. Bowes, "Celebrating Negro History Week," *VTB* 18 (Mar. 1941): 14; Alice L. Turner to Luther P. Jackson, Sept. 1, 1935, box 36, folder 1037, Luther P. Jackson Papers. See also N. V. Boyd to Jackson, Aug. 31, 1935, box 37, folder 1054, Luther P. Jackson Papers; *Bristol Herald Courier,* Feb. 7, 15, 1943.

59. L. V. Williams, "Teaching Negro Life and History in Texas High Schools," *JNH* 20 (Jan. 1935): 15; Anna W. Green to Luther P. Jackson, Aug. 29, 1935, box 37, folder 1005; E. L. Wiley to Luther P. Jackson, Sept. 4, 1935, box 37, folder 1062, both in Luther P. Jackson Papers; James W. Mask interview, folder 13, series M, SOHP.

60. Hamilton to Luther P. Jackson, Aug. 29, 1935, box 37, folder 1077, emphasis in original; Green to Luther P. Jackson, Aug. 29, 1935, box 37, folder 1076; Winston to Luther P. Jackson, Sept. 5, 1935, box 37, folder 1084, all in Luther P. Jackson Papers; Angela Davis, *Angela Davis: An Autobiography* (New York: Random House, 1974), 90.

61. Mary McLeod Bethune, "The Association for the Study of Negro Life and History: Its Contribution to Our Modern Life," *JNH* 20 (Oct. 1935): 406–409.

62. "Negro History Week—The Fourteenth Year," 139; "Negro History Week—The Tenth Year," 124; N. A. Sykes to Luther P. Jackson, Sept. 5, 1935, box 36, folder 1043, Luther P. Jackson Papers; Albert L. Turner, "Higher Education in Alabama," *Quarterly Review of Higher Education among Negroes* 5 (Oct. 1937): 154, 158; Phillips, "Negro Secondary School Teacher," 491; Fultz, "African American Teachers in the South, 1890–1940: Powerlessness and the Ironies of Expectations and Protest," 402.

63. Gandy quoted in Fultz, "African American Teachers in the

South, 1890–1940: Powerlessness and the Ironies of Expectations and Protest," 413.

64. Davis, *Angela Davis,* 91; Horace Mann Bond, "The Curriculum and the Negro Child," *Journal of Negro Education* 4 (Apr. 1935): 163–164. See also Fairclough, *Teaching Equality,* 44–45.

65. Fields, *Lemon Swamp,* 127.

66. Davis, *Angela Davis,* 90–91; Carl T. Rowan, *Breaking Barriers: A Memoir* (Boston: Little, Brown, 1991), 32–33. See also Langston Hughes, "Simple on Negro History Week," *Chicago Defender,* Feb. 13, 1960, 10.

5. Exhibiting Southernness in a New Century

1. Jonathan Daniels, *A Southerner Discovers the South* (New York: MacMillan, 1938), 328; Herbert Ravenel Sass, "Charleston," *Saturday Evening Post* (Feb. 8, 1947): 72.

2. Edward King, *The Great South* (Hartford, Conn.: American Publishing, 1875), 380. The remaking of the southern image is traced in Elliot J. Mackle Jr., "The Eden of the South: Florida's Image in American Travel Literature and Painting, 1865–1900," Ph.D. diss., Emory University, 1977; David C. Miller, *Dark Eden: The Swamp in Nineteenth-Century American Culture* (New York: Cambridge University Press, 1989), esp. 53–76; Anne Rowe, *The Enchanted Country: Northern Writers in the South, 1865–1910* (Baton Rouge: Louisiana State University Press, 1978); Rowe, *The Idea of Florida in the American Literary Imagination* (Baton Rouge: Louisiana State University Press, 1986), esp. chaps. 1 and 2; and Nina Silber, *The Romance of Reunion: Northerners and the South, 1865–1900* (Chapel Hill: University of North Carolina Press, 1993), chap. 3. On the South and disease, see Billy M. Jones, *Health-Seekers in the Southwest, 1817–1900* (Norman: University of Oklahoma Press, 1967); and Todd L. Savitt and James Harvey Young, eds., *Disease and Distinctiveness in the American South* (Knoxville: University Press of Tennessee, 1988).

3. Silber, *Romance of Reunion,* chap. 3.

4. For a concise, perceptive history of early southern tourism, see Rempert W. Patrick, "The Mobile Frontier," *Journal of Southern History* 29 (Feb. 1963): 5–9. See also Harvey K. Newman, *Southern Hospitality: Tourism and the Growth of Atlanta* (Tuscaloosa: University of Alabama Press, 1999), chaps. 1 and 2.

5. "Rambler," *Guide to Florida* (1875; Gainesville: University of Florida Press, 1964), 63, 91, 128; Henry M. Field, *Bright Skies and Dark Shadows* (1890; Freeport, N.Y.: Books for Libraries Press, 1970), 18, 37, 39, 40; John Grimball Wilkins, "Old Charleston by the Sea," *Confederate Veteran* 33 (Dec. 1925): 452; Edward Hungerford, "Charleston of the Real South," *Travel* 21 (Oct. 1913): 33; David Gray, "The Lure of the South," *Collier's* 46 (Feb. 11, 1911): 19; Julian Ralph, *Dixie; or, Southern Scenes and Sketches* (New York: Harper & Brothers, 1896), 106, 118.

6. "Rambler," *Guide to Florida,* 99; Field, *Bright Skies and Dark Shadows,* 40; George M. Barbour, *Florida for Tourists, Invalids, and Settlers* (1882; Gainesville: University of Florida Press, 1964), 99.

7. Ralph, *Dixie,* 160; Henry MacNair, "Motoring in the Land of Cotton," *Travel* (1918): 12; Field, *Bright Skies and Dark Shadows,* 36, 99.

8. Field, *Bright Skies and Dark Shadows,* 20–21.

9. Barbour, *Florida for Tourists,* 69.

10. Ibid., 57; William Jarvie, "From Richmond over Proposed Highway to Florida," *Club Journal* 2 (May 28, 1910): 182.

11. Field, *Bright Skies and Dark Shadows,* 41.

12. Percy H. Whiting, "Motoring Conditions in the South," *Country Life in America* 21 (Jan. 1, 1912): 37, 38.

13. George W. Sutton Jr., "The South and the Motorist," *Southern Good Roads* 17 (Mar. 1918): 11.

14. Forrest Crissey, "Scenery: A Cash Crop," *Saturday Evening Post* 198 (Sept. 12, 1925): 121; Howard Lawrence Preston, *Accessibility and Modernization in the South, 1885–1935* (Knoxville: University of Tennessee Press, 1991), 126.

15. Don H. Doyle, *New Men, New Cities, New South: Atlanta, Nashville, Charleston, and Mobile, 1860–1910* (Chapel Hill: University of North Carolina Press, 1990), chap. 7; Walter J. Fraser Jr., *Charleston! Charleston! The History of a Southern City* (Columbia: University of South Carolina Press, 1991), 327–328; Jamie W. Moore, "The Low Country in Economic Transition: Charleston since 1865," *South Carolina Historical Magazine* 88 (Apr. 1979): 156–171.

16. *CN&C,* Jan. 7, 1921, Apr. 3, 1919, Sept. 29, 1919, Feb. 23, 1921.

17. *CN&C,* July 6, 1921, May 6, 1924, Apr. 17, 1928.

18. "Automobiling to Old Virginia," *Travel Magazine* 12 (Apr. 1907): 264; R. G. Betts, "The Rediscovery of America by the Automo-

bile," *Outing* 42 (May 1903): 168, 169; Edna Lynn Simms, "Motor Tours in Sunnyland," *Hollywood Magazine* 1 (Mar. 1925): 7; Crissey, "Scenery," 84.

19. Frank Presbrey, "Opening up the 'Back Country,'" *Collier's* 44 (Jan. 15, 1910): 16; John R. Eustis, "The Automobile, The Ideal Vehicle of Travel," *Travel* 14 (Jan. 1909): 177; Effie Price Gladding, *Across the Continent by the Lincoln Highway* (New York: Brentano's, 1915), ix.

20. Robert Bruce, "Named and Marked Roads," *American Motorist* (Apr. 1917): 9.

21. MacNair, "Motoring in the Land of Cotton," 12, 15; Seymour Cunningham, "Motor Migrants to the Southland," *American Motorist* 3 (Mar. 1911): 155; Katherine Clemmons Gould, "The Highways of the South," *Southern Good Roads* 17 (Mar. 1918): 3, 5; James M. Lindgren, *Preserving the Old Dominion: Historic Preservation and Virginia Traditionalism* (Charlottesville: University of Virginia Press, 1993), 190.

22. William Ullman, "Springtime Is Motoring Time: A Medley of Thoughts," *American Motorist* (Apr. 1916): 10; Alma Rittenberry, "The Jackson Highway," *Southern Good Roads* 12 (Sept. 1915): 12; Rittenberry, "The Jackson Highway," *Southern Good Roads* 13 (Apr. 1916): 11–13; Rittenberry, "Every Automobile Club Should Establish Tourist Bureaus," *Southern Good Roads* 16 (Aug. 1917): 10–13.

23. Agnes Rothery, *New Roads in Old Virginia* (Boston: Houghton Mifflin, 1937), 36–37.

24. Lindgren, *Preserving the Old Dominion,* 189–190.

25. *Coastal Tourist* 2 (Nov. 1932): 20.

26. Katherine Clemmons Gould, "The Highways of the South," *Southern Good Roads* 17 (Mar. 1918): 3; "The King's Highway: A Region of Romance and History Is Now Readily Accessible to the Autoist," *Coastal Tourist* 1 (Nov. 1931): 3. On tourist maps and their influence on conceptions of place, see James Akerman, "Selling Maps, Selling Highways: Rand McNally's 'Blazed Trails' Program," *Imago Mundi* 45 (1993): 77–89; Akerman, "Blazing a Well Worn Path: Cartographic Commercialism, Highway Promotion, and Auto Tourism in the United States, 1880–1930," *Cartographica* 30 (Spring 1993): 10–20; and Susan Schulten, *The Geographical Imagination in America, 1880–1950* (Chicago: University of Chicago Press, 2001), 185.

27. *CN&C,* May 29, 1924; Thomas P. Stoney, "Mayor Stoney's Annual Review," *Year Book, City of Charleston* (1924), ix; *Annual Report,*

1913 (Charleston: Chamber of Commerce, 1913), 16; *CN&C,* Sept. 2, 1922, Mar. 15, 1924, May 5, 1924, July 17, 1924, May 22, 1925, May 22, 1925, July 8, 1926, Aug. 9, 1926, Mar. 9, 1927; *Proceedings of the City Council of Charleston, 1928,* Apr. 10, 1928, 60; repeated on Mar. 12, 1929 (p. 225); Feb. 25, 1929 (p. 420); Mar. 24, 1931 (p. 617); Apr. 14, 1931 (p. 622).

28. *Who's Who in South Carolina, 1934–1935* (Columbia: Current Historical Association, 1935); *CN&C,* Feb. 10, 1926, Oct. 29, 1928.

29. "Impressions of the Manigault House on Its Pilgrims" [1930s?], 11–278B-1, Manigault House Papers, SCHS.

30. *CN&C,* Nov. 10, 1916, Dec. 2, 1933; William Oliver Stevens, *Charleston: Historic City of Gardens* (New York: Dodd, Mead, 1939), 50, 51; Philip H. Gadsden to B. A. Hagood, Oct. 18, 1927, Waring Papers, SCHS.

31. Alice R. Huger Smith, "Doorways, Gateways, and Stairways of Quaint Old Charleston," *Art in America* 4 (Aug. 1916): 296; Herbert Ravenel Sass, *Look Back to Glory* (Indianapolis: Bobbs-Merrill, 1933). On the literary production of the Charleston Renaissance, see Stephanie E. Yuhl, *A Golden Haze of Memory: The Making of Historic Charleston* (Chapel Hill: University of North Carolina Press, 2005), chap. 3.

32. *CN&C,* Apr. 30, 1931, Jan. 20, 1933, Mar. 10, 1939, Mar. 15, 1939, Mar. 30, 1939; *House and Garden* (Mar. 1939): 24.

33. *CN&C,* Apr. 6, 1931, Mar. 11, 1939, Mar. 15, 1939. See also *CN&C,* Jan. 18, 1934. The number of antique shops in the city mushroomed from five in 1923 to more than thirty only six years later. See *New Charleston City and Suburban Directory, 1923* (Charleston: Southern Printing and Publishing, 1923), 699; *Walsh's Charleston City Directory, 1930* (Charleston: Southern Printing and Publishing, 1930), 916. On the Charleston antique trade, see also Daniels, *Southerner Discovers the South,* 327–328.

34. Daniels, *Southerner Discovers the South,* 222; Susan Pringle Frost, Apr. 12, 1920[?], 11–278B-3, Manigault House Papers. On Frost's colorful career, see Sidney R. Bland, *Preserving Charleston's Past, Shaping Its Future* (Westport, Conn.: Greenwood, 1994), chaps. 3–5.

35. Ernest H. Pringle to G. Corner Fenhagen, Apr. 16, 1932; undated and unsigned note, 11–278B-2, Manigault House Papers. On the preservation movement, see Michael K. Fenton, "Why Not Leave

Our Canvas Unmarred?' A History of the Preservation Society of Charleston, 1920–1990," master's thesis, University of South Carolina, 1990; William H. Hanckel, "The Preservation Movement in Charleston, 1920–1962," master's thesis, University of South Carolina, 1962; Charles Hosmer, *Preservation Comes of Age: From Williamsburg to the National Trust, 1926–1949* (Charlottesville: University Press of Virginia, 1981), 231–269; Christopher Silver, "Revitalizing the Urban South: Neighborhood Preservation and Planning since the 1920s," *Journal of the American Planning Association* 57 (Winter 1991): 70–73.

36. Yuhl, *Golden Haze of Memory,* 24–43. See also Stephanie E. Yuhl, "Rich and Tender Remembering: Elite White Women and an Aesthetic Sense of Place in Charleston, 1920s and 1930s," in W. Fitzhugh Brundage, ed., *Where These Memories Grow: History, Memory and Southern Identity* (Chapel Hill: University of North Carolina Press, 2000), 227–248.

37. *NYT,* Apr. 6, 1932; *CN&C,* Apr. 20, 1934.

38. *Walsh's Charleston City Directory, 1924* (Charleston: Walsh Directory, 1924), 821–822; *Walsh's Charleston City Directory, 1934* (Charleston: Southern Printing and Publishing, 1934), 889; Elizabeth O'Neill Verner, *Prints and Impressions of Charleston* (Columbia, S.C.: Bostick & Thornley, 1939), 2–3.

39. Margaret Simons Middleton to *Charleston News and Courier,* Feb. 25, 1935; *CN&C,* Dec. 30, 1937; "Statement of Purpose of the Historic Charleston Foundation: The Value for Charleston," doc. 30–14–37, 1949[?], Historic Charleston Foundation, SCHS.

40. *The Fort Sumter—Newest and Finest* (New York: Amsterdam Agency, [1925], 4–5, South Caroliniana Library, University of South Carolina; "Charm of Charleston: A City of Personality and Refinement," *AGWI Steamship News* (May 1921), 18.

41. "Charm of Charleston," 18; T. Culyer Smith, "The Ivory City," *Frank Leslie's Popular Monthly* 53 (Mar. 1902): 511; Margaret Lathrop Law, "Charleston—Queen of Colonial America," *Travel* 44 (Nov. 1929): 46.

42. *Fort Sumter—Newest and Finest;* "Charm of Charleston," 10, 18.

43. G. M. Allen, "Charleston: A Typical City of the South," *Magazine of Travel* 1 (Feb. 1895): 128; Richard N. Cote, July 12, 1989, Miles Brewton House Research Memo, 28-636, Allston-Pringle-Frost Collec-

tion, SCHS; Susan Pringle Frost to Isabel Pringle, Jan. 19, 1918, Susan Pringle Frost to "My precious Nina," Jan. 24, 1918, and Frost to "My precious Nina," May 23, 1939, all in Pringle Papers (microfilm copies from Bancroft Library, University of California, Berkeley), SCHS; "Charm of Charleston," 10.

44. Elizabeth O'Neill Verner, *Mellowed by Time: A Charleston Notebook*, 3d ed. (Charleston: Tradd Street Press, 1978), 33; Yuhl, *Golden Haze of Memory*, 57–59.

45. DuBose Heyward, *Porgy* (Charleston: Tradd Street Press, 1985), 110; Elizabeth O'Neill Verner, "Spirituals of the Low Country," *CN&C*, Apr. 29, 1929.

46. Dale Rosengarten, *Row upon Row: Sea Grass Baskets of the South Carolina Low Country* (Columbia: McKissick Museum, 1987), 25–39.

47. "Sea Grass Baskets: An Interesting Industry," *Picture and Art Trade and Gift Shop Journal* (1918), cited in Rosengarten, *Row upon Row*, 37–38; "Hand Made Basketry, the Art of South Carolina Negroes," quoted in Rosengarten, *Row upon Row*, 37–38. See also Dale Rosengarten, "Low Country Basketry: Folk Arts in the Marketplace," *Southern Folklore* 49, no. 3 (1992): 240–255.

48. Yuhl, *Golden Haze of Memory*, 49–50.

49. Stevens, *Charleston*, 73–74. The flower women were such an "institution" that a 1934 police campaign to regulate them prompted an outcry. One local fumed to the *Charleston Evening Post* that "If the Police Department don't like flowers that's their hard luck, the people do, and strangers who visit us [also] must be considered." *CN&C*, Feb. 27, 1933, Dec. 12, 1934; Wilkins to *Charleston Evening Post*, Dec. 18, 1934.

50. Maurine Akua McDaniel, "Edwin Augustus Harleston, Portrait Painter, 1882–1931," Ph.D. diss., Emory University, 1994; and Yuhl, *Golden Haze of Memory*, 58–59.

51. Mark A. Abney to *Charleston Evening Post*, Apr. 20, 1933; Hungerford, "Charleston of the Real South," 33.

52. Hungerford, "Charleston of the Real South," 33; "Plantations Reminiscent of Antebellum Days," *Resort Life* (Dec. 17, 1930): 3.

53. Stevens, *Charleston*, 319.

54. "Constitution of the Society for the Preservation of Negro Spirituals" and SPS Minutes, SPS Papers, SCHS; Gavin James Campbell,

Music and the Making of a New South (Chapel Hill: University of North Carolina Press, 2004), 75, 80; Yuhl, *Golden Haze of Memory,* 127–156.

55. Matthew Page Andrews, quoted in *CN&C,* Nov. 26, 1927.

56. Stevens, *Charleston,* 75.

57. For other discussions of tourism and southern identity, see Jack E. Davis, *Race against Time: Culture and Separation in Natchez since 1930* (Baton Rouge: Louisiana State University Press, 2001), chap. 2; Richard D. Starnes, ed., *Southern Journeys: Tourism, History and Culture in the Modern South* (Tuscaloosa: University of Alabama Press, 2003); Anthony Stanonis, "Creating the Big Easy: New Orleans, American Culture, and the Emergence of Modern Tourism, 1915–1950," Ph.D. diss., Vanderbilt University, 2003.

58. *CN&C,* Mar. 11, 1934. On Maybank's efforts to revitalize Charleston, see Marvin L. Cann, "Burnett Rhett Maybank and the New Deal in South Carolina, 1931–1941," Ph.D. diss., University of North Carolina, 1967.

59. On tourism in the early twentieth century South, see Starnes, *Southern Journeys.*

60. Lewis Copeland, *The Travel Business in Charleston, 1963* (Knoxville: University of Tennessee Bureau of Business Research, 1964), 8; Robert L. Frank, "The Economic Impact of Tourism in Charleston, South Carolina, 1970," master's thesis, University of South Carolina, 1972, 108–117; Patrick, "Mobile Frontier," 14–18; Newman, *Southern Hospitality,* chaps. 4 and 5.

61. T. Jackson Lears, "From Salvation to Self-Realization," in Richard Wightman Fox and T. J. Jackson Lears, eds., *The Culture of Consumption: Critical Essays in American History, 1880–1980* (New York: Pantheon, 1983), 11; Owen Wister, *Lady Baltimore* (New York: Macmillan, 1906), 9.

62. Law, "Charleston—Queen of Colonial America," 25. A fusion of consumerism, nostalgia, and modernity was also characteristic of the age's culture; see Jonathan Freedman, *Professions of Taste: Henry James, British Aestheticism, and Commodity Culture* (Stanford, Calif.: Stanford University Press, 1990); Jennifer Wiche, *Advertising Fictions: Literature, Advertisement and Social Reading* (New York: Columbia University Press, 1988).

63. For a rare but trenchant critique of Charleston's "myth," see Edward Twig, "Charleston: The Great Myth," *Forum* 103 (Jan. 1940): 1, 4, 7.

6. BLACK MEMORIALS AND THE BULLDOZER REVOLUTION

1. *CT,* Aug. 3, 1963, 5.

2. Ronald H. Bayor, *Race and the Shaping of Twentieth-Century Atlanta* (Chapel Hill: University of North Carolina Press, 1996), chap. 3; Scott C. Davis, *The World of Patience Gromes: Making and Unmaking a Black Community* (Lexington: University Press of Kentucky, 1988); Raymond A. Mohl, "Race and Space in the Modern City: Interstate 95 and the Black Community in Miami," in Arnold R. Hirsch and Raymond A. Mohl, eds., *Urban Policy in Twentieth-Century America* (New Brunswick, N.J.: Rutgers University Press, 1993), 100–158; Christopher MacGregor Scribner, *Renewing Birmingham: Federal Funding and the Promise of Change, 1929–1979* (Athens: University of Georgia Press, 2002), chap. 3; Christopher Silver, "Revitalizing the Urban South: Neighborhood Preservation and Planning since the 1980s," *Journal of the American Planning Association* 57 (Winter 1991): 76–78; Christopher Silver and John V. Moeser, *The Separate City: Black Communities in the Urban South, 1940–1968* (Lexington: University Press of Kentucky, 1995), chap. 4.

3. Ralph Ellison, *Invisible Man* (1947; New York: Vintage, 1995), 471.

4. Jean Bradley Anderson, *Durham County: A History of Durham County, North Carolina* (Durham: Duke University Press, 1990), chaps. 9–12; Garrett Weaver, "The Development of the Black Durham Community, 1880–1915," Ph.D. diss., University of North Carolina, Chapel Hill, 1987, 48–54, 92–94.

5. W. E. B. Du Bois, "The Upbuilding of Black Durham," *World's Work* 23 (Jan. 1912): 334, 337; E. Franklin Frazier, "Durham: Capital of the Black Middle Class," in Alain Locke, ed., *The New Negro* (1925; New York: Antheneum, 1968), 333; Jerome Dowd, "Art in Negro Homes," 90–93, Special Collections, Perkins Library, Duke University.

6. Anderson, *Durham County,* 220–224, 256–258, 351, 368; Weaver, "Development of the Black Durham Community," chaps. 5, 7; Walter B. Weare, *Black Business in the New South* (Urbana: University of Illinois Press, 1973).

7. *DHS,* Feb. 19, 1995, A1; Anderson, *Durham County,* 372–373; William R. Keech, *The Impact of Negro Voting: The Role of the Vote in the Quest for Equality* (Chicago: Rand McNally, 1968), chaps. 2 and 3; Weare, *Black Business in the New South,* 240–246.

8. *DHS,* Sept. 5, 1995, B5; *Hill's Durham City Directory, 1958* (Richmond: Hill's Directory Co., 1958), 95–97, 199–201; Rebecca Kathleen Blackmon, "When the Bulldozers Came: A Historical Analysis of Urban Renewal and Community Action in a New South City," honors thesis, University of North Carolina, Chapel Hill, 1996, 26–27; Weaver, "Development of the Black Durham Community," 384–386.

9. Reginald Mitchiner interview, Nov. 15, 1976, H-212-1, sort P, Southern Oral History Project, SHC.

10. *DHS,* May 12, 1935, I-4, III-1, 10; *DHS,* Sept. 26, 1937, I-3; *DHS,* Aug. 24, 1938; *DHS,* Mar. 10, 1940, I-6, II-4; *DH,* Aug. 26, 1938, II-10; *DH,* Aug. 27, 1938, I-4; *DH,* Jan. 27, 1940, I-1; *DH,* Mar. 17, 1940, II-4; *DH,* Mar. 18, 1940, IV-1; *CT,* Nov. 17, 1956, 2.

11. *DS,* Oct. 16, 1956; *DS,* Jan. 28, 1958, B4; *DH,* Jan. 28, 1958, A1; *DH,* Jan. 29, 1958, A4; *DH,* Mar. 2, 1958, D4; *DH,* Nov. 20, 1958, A4; *DH,* Mar. 22, 1959, A1; *Downtown Development Association, Report No. 1* (Durham: Downtown Development Association, 1959); Anderson, *Durham County,* 399–400, 406–409.

12. Robert L. Isaacson Jr., "A Revitalization Proposal for the Central Business District of Durham, North Carolina," master's thesis, Regional and Urban Planning, University of North Carolina, Chapel Hill, 1957, 2; *DH,* Mar. 24, 1959, A1; *DH,* Mar. 25, 1959, A1, A4, A9; *DH,* Mar. 26, 1959, A1.

13. *DH,* June 19, 1962, A4; *DH,* Sept. 2, 1962, D1; *DS,* July 25, 1962, A1; *CT,* Feb. 15, 1958, 1; Isaacson Jr., "Revitalization Proposal," 2.

14. Isaacson Jr., "Revitalization Proposal," 75–82.

15. *DS,* Mar. 26, 1959.

16. Charles Abrams, "Downtown Decay and Revival," *Journal of the American Institute of Planners* 27 (1961): 3–9; Morton Schussheim, "Urban Renewal and Local Economic Development," *Journal of the*

American Institute of Planners 27 (1961): 118–120; George Sternlieb, "Bulldozer Renewal Is More Needed Now than Ever—Even Though Politically Unpopular," *Journal of Housing* 25 (1968): 180–182; Robert M. Fogelson, *Downtown: Its Rise and Fall, 1880–1950* (New Haven, Conn.: Yale University Press, 2001), chap. 7; Mark I. Gelfand, *A Nation of Cities: The Federal Government and Urban America, 1933–1965* (New York: Oxford University Press, 1975), chap. 8.

17. *DH*, Nov. 20, 1958, A4; *DS*, July 27, 1962, A1. On depictions of black degeneracy, see Daryl Michael Scott, *Contempt and Pity: Social Policy and the Image of Damaged Black Psyche, 1880–1996* (Chapel Hill: University of North Carolina Press, 1997), chaps. 4 and 5.

18. Early proposals for urban renewal through historic preservation emphasized architectural aesthetics and the economic benefits of preservation. See "Historic Preservation through Urban Renewal," *Journal of Housing* 19 (1962): 296–315; Ross McKeever, "Urban Renewal Means More than Slum Clearance," *Urban Land* 21 (1962): 2, 7; Barbara Snow, "Preservation and Urban Renewal: Is Coexistence Possible?" *Antiques* 84 (1963): 442–453; William J. Murtagh, *Keeping Time: The History and Theory of Preservation in America* (New York: John Wiley & Sons, 1997), 62–77.

19. *DH*, Nov. 20, 1958, A4; May 16, 1963, C1; May 25, 1964, B1.

20. Bayor, *Race and the Shaping of Twentieth-Century Atlanta,* chap. 3; Karen Ferguson, *Black Politics in New Deal Atlanta* (Chapel Hill: University of North Carolina Press, 2002), chaps. 7 and 8; Marc V. Levine, "The Politics of Partnership: Urban Redevelopment since 1945," in Gregory D. Squires, *Unequal Partnerships: The Political Economy of Urban Redevelopment in Postwar America* (New Brunswick, N.J.: Rutgers University Press, 1989), 12–34; Raymond A. Mohl, "Making the Second Ghetto in Metropolitan Miami, 1940–1960," *Journal of Urban History* 21 (1995): 395–427; Thomas J. Sugrue, *Origins of the Urban Crisis: Race and Inequality in Postwar Detroit* (Princeton, N.J.: Princeton University Press, 1996), chap. 2.

21. James V. Cunningham, "Chapter Six: The Negro and Community Action," 26, folder 4351, North Carolina Fund Papers, SHC.

22. Anderson, *Durham County,* 373, 412, 430, 431, 432, 433, 434, 439, 486, 487.

23. *CT,* Sept. 15, 1962, 2; David H. Rice, "Urban Renewal in Dur-

ham: A Case Study of a Referendum," master's thesis, Department of Political Science, University of North Carolina, Chapel Hill, 1966.

24. Christopher L. Johnson, "Fight on Christian Soldier: The Role of Black Churches in the Freedom Struggles of Durham, North Carolina, 1955–1970," History honors thesis, University of North Carolina, Chapel Hill, 1996, 49; Blackmon, "When the Bulldozers Came," 34.

25. Raymond A. Mohl, "Shifting Patterns of American Urban Policy since 1900," in Hirsch and Mohl, *Urban Policy in Twentieth-Century America,* 14–17; Jon C. Teaford, *The Rough Road to Urban Renaissance, 1940–1985* (Baltimore, Md.: Johns Hopkins University Press, 1990), 44–81.

26. "Durham's On and Off Again Mayor," *CT,* Aug. 5, 1967; Anderson, *Durham County,* 439–441; Osha Gray Davidson, *Best of Enemies: Race and Redemption in the New South* (New York: Scribner's, 1996), 140–141, 159, 219.

27. Walter B. Weare, *Black Business in the New South: A Social History of the North Carolina Mutual Insurance Company* (Urbana: University of Illinois Press, 1973), 90, 246; *DS,* Mar. 22, 1965; *CT,* June 15, 1957; *CT,* Jan. 11, 1958, 11; Bertie Howard and Steve Redburn, "UOCI: Black Political Power in Durham," folder 4563, subseries 4.8, North Carolina Fund Papers; William Pursell, "Crisis and Conflict: The Case of Durham," folder 7416, subseries 6.10, North Carolina Fund Papers; Allan P. Sindler, "Negro Protest and Local Politics in Durham, N.C.," folder 4393, subseries 4.8, North Carolina Fund Papers; Vernaline Watson, "The Durham Rent Strike," folder 7456, North Carolina Fund Papers; Davidson, *Best of Enemies,* 88–91. The workings of the "benevolent oligarchy" are traced in Weare, *Black Business in the New South,* 211–264.

28. *CT,* Feb. 10, 1962, 6; *CT,* Apr. 20, 1963, 1; *DS,* Apr. 30, 1964, C1; *DS,* July 22, 1964, B1. For studies of dislocation in other cities, see Jon E. Burkhardt and Margaret T. Shaffer, "Social and Psychological Impacts of Transportation Improvements," *Transportation* 1 (Aug. 1972): 207–226; Chester Hartman, "The Housing of Relocated Families," *Journal of the American Institute of Planners* 30 (Nov. 1964): 266–282; Patricia A. House, "Relocation of Families Displaced by Expressway Development: Milwaukee Case Study," *Land Economics* 46 (Feb. 1970): 75–78.

29. Minutes of the Meeting of the Religious Affiliate Committee of the Redevelopment Commission, folder 5, White Rock Baptist Church Records, SHC; *DS,* May 19, 1965, C1; *DS,* May 27, 1965, C1; *DS,* Dec.

29, 1966, B1; *DS,* Jan. 4, 1967, A9, B1; *DS,* Mar. 21, 1967, A5; *DS,* Apr. 20, 1967, C1; *DH,* Nov. 16, 1963, A6; *DH,* Dec. 28, 1963, B1; *DH,* June 15, 1965, B1; "Urban Renewal in North Carolina Cities," Progress Report no. 4 (Chapel Hill: Institute of Government, University of North Carolina, 1964), 1.

30. *DS,* Apr. 30, 1964, C1; *DS,* Mar. 5, 1965, A1; *DS,* Oct. 11, 1966, A4; *DS,* Apr. 21, 1967, A9; *DS,* Apr. 26, 1967, A4, B1; *DH,* May 17, 1964, D1; *DH,* Mar. 7, 1966, B1; *DH,* Oct. 17, 1966, B1; *DH,* Dec. 17, 1966, B1; *CT,* Aug. 28, 1965, 1.

31. *DH,* Aug. 28, 1963, A4; *CT,* Sept. 25, 1965, 2. See also *CT,* Mar. 7, 1964, 1.

32. *CT,* Oct. 17, 1964, 2; *CT,* Oct. 9, 1965, 1, 2; *CT,* Jan. 15, 1966, 2; *CT,* Feb. 12, 1966, 1; *CT,* Dec. 10, 1966, 1; *CT,* June 24, 1967, 2; *CT,* July 22, 1967, 1; *CT,* Sept. 9, 1967, 1; *CT,* Sept. 20, 1967, 2; *DH,* Feb. 7, 1965, G10; *DH,* Aug. 7, 1966; *DS,* Sept. 22, 1966, B1; *DS,* Oct. 4, 1966, B1; Davidson, *Best of Enemies,* 163, 212–213.

33. Robert Nelson Anderson Jr., "Business Relocation or Dislocation? An Analysis of Commercial Renewal in North Carolina," master's thesis, University of North Carolina, Chapel Hill, 1964, 29–30, 36; *DH,* Nov. 9, 1963, A4; *DH,* June 2, 1965, B1; *DS,* June 2, 1965, A16; *DS,* Aug. 17, 1965, B1; William N. Kinnard Jr. and Zenon S. Malinowsi, *The Impact of Dislocation from Urban Renewal Areas on Small Businesses* (Storrs: n.p., University of Connecticut, 1960), quoted in Anderson, "Business Relocation or Dislocation?" 32.

34. *CT,* Apr. 15, 1961, 1; *CT,* June 17, 1961, 1, 4; *CT,* July 22, 1961, 4; *CT,* Aug. 19, 1961, 1, 4; *CT,* July 2, 1966, 1; *DH,* June 16, 1961; *DS,* May 3, 1967, A1. On Greenberg's reputation as a slumlord, see "The Greenburg Housing Controversy," folder 4585, North Carolina Fund Papers; Chris Gioia, "How They Get Out of Hell by Raising It: Race and Politics in Durham's War on Poverty," History honors thesis, University of North Carolina, Chapel Hill, 1966, 43–52; Davidson, *Best of Enemies,* 172–175; Patrick O'Connell, "Hayti," *Tobacco Road* 3 (1979): 8.

35. *DH,* Mar. 8, 1963, A4.

36. W. J. Kennedy, "First Century of White Rock Baptist Church," 2.1, file 51, White Rock Baptist Church Records, SHC; Anderson, *Durham County,* 138, 160, 224, 259, 286, 287, 351, 370, 371, 373, 405, 438.

37. Bruce Bastin, *Red River Blues: The Blues Tradition in the South-*

east (Urbana: University of Illinois Press, 1986), 265, 266; *Durham Architectural and Historic Inventory* (Durham: Historic Preservation Society of Durham, 1982), 113–119.

38. "Urban Renewal in North Carolina Cities," Progress Report no. 3 (Chapel Hill: Institute of Government, University of North Carolina, 1963), 3.

39. Anthony Wolff, "The Heart of Savannah," *American Heritage* 22 (Dec. 1970): 55–61.

40. *Savannah Morning News,* June 18, 1955, 16, June 28, 1955, 20, 24, Sept. 14, 1955, 16, Sept. 29, 1955, 12, 36; *Savannah Evening Press,* June 23, 1955, 28, June 25, 1955, 16, Aug. 16, 1955, 20, Aug. 24, 1955, 20; *NYT,* Oct. 30, 1955, 27; Robert S. Hodder Jr., "Savannah's Changing Past: A Generation of Historic Preservation Planning in a Southern City, 1955–1985," Ph.D. diss., Urban Planning, Cornell University, 1993, 52–93; Wolff, "Heart of Savannah," 61, 103.

41. *SMN,* Nov. 16, 1955, 18, May 15, 1956, 22, 24, Jan. 18, 1960, A4, B5, May 8, 1961, B10, May 25, 1961, D7, D10, Jan. 10, 1963, D8, May 17, 1963, B4, June 11, 1963, B8, Apr. 4, 1965, C1, Apr. 10, 1965, B10. See also *SMN,* Mar. 11, 1956, 6, Jan. 8, 1958, B10; *SEP,* Oct. 23, 1957, 20, Jan. 7, 1958, 6, Jan. 17, 1958, 24, Jan. 18, 1958, 6, Jan. 2, 1959, 2.

42. *Development of Zoning Standards and Procedures for the Chatham–Savannah Metropolitan Planning District, Master Plan Report Number 5* (Savannah: Chatham County–Savannah Metropolitan Planning Commission, 1957), 40; *Savannah's Golden Heritage* (Savannah: Metropolitan Planning Commission, 1958), 46; Hodder, "Savannah's Changing Past," 69–79.

43. *SEP,* Mar. 23, 1955, 24; *SMN,* May 3, 1958, B10.

44. *SEP,* Oct. 6, 1955, 32, Mar. 28, 1959, 6, Apr. 1, 1959, 32, Apr. 20, 1959, 20, Apr. 25, 1959, B12.

45. Hodder, "Savannah's Changing Past," 94–127.

46. Charles Elmore interview, SOHP; Leroy Beavers Jr. interview, SOHP: Stephen G. N. Tuck, *Beyond Atlanta: The Struggle for Racial Equality in Georgia, 1940–1980* (Athens: University of Georgia Press, 2001), 45, 129.

47. *Atlanta Journal Constitution Magazine,* June 4, 1961, 14; *SMN,* July 9, 1962, B8, Jan. 19, 1963, B10, Mar. 2, 1964, B8, July 22, 1964, A2; Hodder, Savannah's Changing Past," 134.

48. *Chicago Tribune,* Aug. 28, 1977, 10; *Atlanta Journal Constitution,* Sept. 4, 1977, B20, July 24, 1978, B1; *SMN,* Sept. 27, 1965, B8; *Atlanta Journal Magazine,* Oct. 29, 1978, F26.

49. Tuck, *Beyond Atlanta,* 49–50, 128–129.

50. *SMN,* Apr. 22, 1971, D1; *SMN,* Dec. 2, 1971, D1; *SMN,* Feb. 17, 1972, D1; *SMN,* Mar. 7, 1980, B1; *Wall Street Journal,* Nov. 13, 1970, A12.

51. For the argument that redevelopment can be a form of "creative destruction," see Max Page, *The Creative Destruction of Manhattan, 1900–1940* (Chicago: University of Chicago Press, 1999), esp. chap. 8.

52. Leroy Beavers Jr. interview, Aug. 8, 2002, and Floyd Adams Jr. interview, Aug. 16, 2002, both in "Remembering Black Main Streets," SOHP.

53. David Glassberg, *Sense of History: The Place of the Past in American Life* (Amherst: University of Massachusetts Press, 2001), 124; Floyd Adams Jr. interview.

54. Jane Jacobs, *The Death and Life of Great American Cities* (New York: Vintage, 1961), 56. On porches and sociability, see Trudier Harris, *The Power of the Porch: The Storyteller's Craft in Zora Neale Hurston, Gloria Naylor, and Randall Kenan* (Athens: University of Georgia Press, 1996), xii–xiii; Eric Sandweiss, *St. Louis: The Evolution of an American Urban Landscape* (Philadelphia: Temple University Press, 2001), 106–107.

55. William Fonvielle interview, Aug. 2, 2002, "Remembering Black Main Streets," SOHP; Leroy Beavers Jr. interview.

7. Contested History in the Sunbelt South

1. *Walton Tribune,* Aug. 6, 1997, 6–1; *Athens Banner-Herald,* July 26, 1999, A1. Groups even revisited the legacy of slavery. In 1986, Somerset Plantation in Creswell, North Carolina, a state historic site, hosted its first "homecoming" for descendants of its slave-era white and black residents. For the more than 1,500 blacks whose ancestors had worked the plantation, the homecoming was, in the words of its organizer, a "living monument" to "our toil, our lives, our lineage." *NYT,* Aug. 31, 1986, A26.

2. *RTD,* Nov. 26, 2000, C1.

3. *WP,* Dec. 4, 2000, B1; *RTD,* Dec. 4, 1997, B6; *RTD,* Nov. 17,

2000, B3; *RTD,* Nov. 26, 2000, C1; *RTD,* Nov. 29, 2000, B2; *RTD,* Dec. 4, 2000, B1; *RTD,* Nov. 29, 2002, B2; *RTD,* Mar. 10, 2003, B1; *RTD,* June 20, 2003, B1; *RTD,* June 23, 2003, B1; *RTD,* Sept. 12, 2003, B7; *WP,* Dec. 4, 2000, B1; *WP,* Nov. 30, 2002, B3.

4. *RTD,* Apr. 11, 1997, A1; *RTD,* Mar. 23, 2000, B1; *Roanoke Times and World News,* Apr. 12, 1997, A1, May 11, 2000, A1; *WP,* May 19, 1997, B3; *Washington Times,* Mar. 28, 1998, A11, Apr. 10, 1998, A1, Apr. 7, 2000, C1, May 11, 2000, A1; *Boston Globe,* Apr. 26, 1998, A8; *NVP,* Apr. 5, 2000, B5, Apr. 27, 2000, B3.

5. Leroy Campbell, folder 7, series M, SOHP; Hurley H. Doddy and G. Franklin Edwards, "Apprehensions of Negro Teachers Concerning Desegregation in South Carolina," *JNE* 24 (Winter 1955): 26–43; Jonas O. Rosenthal, Negro Teachers Attitudes toward Desegregation," *JNE* (Winter 1957): 63–71; Gregory C. Coffin, "The Black Administrator and How He's Being Pushed to Extinction," *American School Board Journal* 159 (May 1972): 33–34. See also Everett E. Abney, "The Status of Florida's Black Principals," *JNE* 43 (Winter 1974): 3–8; Johnnny Butler, "A Question of Survival," *JNE* 43 (Winter 1974): 9–24.

6. Robert W. Hooker, "Displacement of Black Teachers in the Eleven Southern States," *Afro-American Studies* 2 (Dec. 1971): 165; John Egerton, "When Desegregation Comes, the Negro Principal Go," *Southern Education Report* 3 (Dec. 1967): 10; Hooker, "Displacement of Black Teachers," 173–174.

7. Hooker, "Displacement of Black Teachers," 166; Dorothy Redus Robinson, *The Bell at Four: A Black Teacher's Chronicle of Change* (Austin: Madrona Press, 1978), 129; John W. Smith and Betty M. Smith, "For Black Educators: Integration Brings the Axe," *Urban Review* 6 (Apr. 1973): 8, 10, 11. See also Sonya Y. Ramsey, "More than the Three R's: The Educational, Economic, and Cultural Experiences of African American Female Public School Teachers in Nashville, Tennessee, 1869 to 1983," Ph.D diss., University of North Carolina, Chapel Hill, 2000, 255–284.

8. Ernest J. Middleton, *History of the Louisiana Education Association* (Washington D.C.: National Education Association, 1984), 118; Adam Fairclough, *Race and Democracy: The Civil Rights Struggle in Louisiana, 1915–1972* (Athens: University of Georgia Press, 1995), 62–63, 99–101, 454–455.

9. Jerome A. Gray, Joe L. Reed, and Norman W. Walton, *History of the Alabama State Teachers Association* (Washington D.C.: National Education Association, 1987), 224, 261.

10. Quoted in David R. Goldfield, *Black, White, and Southern: Race Relations and Southern Culture, 1940 to the Present* (Baton Rouge: Louisiana State University Press, 1990), 268.

11. David S. Cecelski, *Along Freedom Road: Hyde County, North Carolina, and the Fate of Black Schools in the South* (Chapel Hill: University of North Carolina Press, 1994), 170–173; Adam Fairclough, *To Redeem the Soul of America: The Southern Christian Leadership Council and Martin Luther King, Jr.* (Athens: University of Georgia Press, 1987), 394–396.

12. Brenda Tapia, folder 445, series K, SOHP; Nancy L. Arnez, "Implementation of Desegregation as a Discriminatory Process," *JNE* 47 (Winter 1978): 28–45; James Bolner and Arnold Vedlitz, "The Affinity of Negro Students for Segregated Schools: Obstacles to Desegregation," *JNE* 40 (Fall 1971): 313–321; Leon Hall, "The Implementor's Revenge," *Southern Exposure* 7 (Summer 1979): 122–124.

13. *Southern Patriot* 36 (Jan. 1972): 6; 36 (Feb. 1972): 3; 36 (Mar. 1972): 6, 7; 36 (Dec. 1972): 5. For an account of the turmoil of integration in one locale, see James V. Holton, "The Best Education Provided: A Social History of School Integration in Polk County, Florida, 1863–1994," Ph.D. diss., George Washington University, 2002, 142–178.

14. *Thirty-third Annual Celebration of Negro History Week* (Washington, D.C.: Association for the Study of Negro Life and History, 1958), 3; Lerone Bennett Jr., "The Negro in Textbooks: Reading, 'Riting, and Racism," *Ebony* 22 (Mar. 1967): 130–138; Jonathan Zimmerman, *Whose America? Culture Wars in the Public Schools* (Cambridge, Mass.: Harvard University Press, 2002), 112–115.

15. "House Committee Studies Treatment of Minorities in Text and Library Books," *Publishers' Weekly* 190 (Sept. 19, 1966): 40.

16. *Roanoke Times,* Feb. 18, 1948, A4; *The Teaching of Virginia and Local History and Government in the Public Schools,* Virginia Senate Document no. 4 (Richmond: Division of Purchases and Printing, 1949), 9; Frederic R. Eichelman, "A Study of the Virginia History and Government Textbook Controversy, 1948–1972," Ph.D. diss., Virginia Tech, 1975, 36; Raymond C. Dingledine Jr., Lena Barksdale, and Marion Belt

Nesbitt, *Virginia's History and Georgaphy* (New York: Scribner's, 1956), 56, 60, 268–269; *Norfolk Virginian-Pilot,* Oct. 28, 1965, 52; Frances Butler Simkins, Spotswood Hunicutt, and Sidman P. Poole, *Virginia: History, Government, Georgraphy* (New York: Scribner's, 1957), 98, 186–187, 508.

17. Marvin W. Schlegel, "What's Wrong with Virginia History Textbooks," *Virginia Journal of Education* 64 (Sept. 1970): 10; Schlegel, "What a Good Virginia History Textbook Should Be," *Virginia Journal of Education* 64 (Oct. 1970): 6–7; Eichelman, "Study of the Virginia History and Government Textbook Controversy," 98–120.

18. Zimmerman, *Whose America?,* 126.

19. Claudia P. Roberts et al., *Durham Architectural and Historic Inventory* (Durham, N.C.: Historic Preservation Society of Durham, 1982), 120; *DHS,* Oct. 27, 1996, A13, Nov. 4, 2001, C1.

20. *DH,* Feb. 2, 1967, B1; *DH,* Feb. 12, 1967, H5; Rick Bear, "From Suburb to Defended Neighborhood: The Evolution of Inman Park and Ansley Park, 1890–1894," *Atlanta Historical Journal* 26 (1982): 113–154; Christopher Silver, "Revitalizing the Urban South: Neighborhood Preservation and Planning since the 1920s," *Journal of the American Planning Association* 57 (Winter 1991): 69–84.

21. Clarence N. Stone, *Economic Growth and Neighborhood Discontent: System Bias in the Urban Renewal Program of Atlanta* (Chapel Hill: University of North Carolina Press, 1976), esp. chaps. 10 and 12.

22. For accounts of communities that successfully fended off destruction, see Paul Luebke, "Activists and Asphalt: A Successful Anti-Expressway Movement in a 'New South' City," *Human Organization* 40 (Fall 1981): 256–263; Anne E. Petty, "Historic Preservation without Relocation," *Journal of Housing* 35 (1978): 422–423; Alice Ratliff and Michael D. Calhoun, "Use of Last Resort Housing Benefits and Redevelopment Powers to Preserve a Low-Income Community Threatened with Displacement," *Clearinghouse Review* 22 (1988): 79–110; William M. Rohe and Scott Mouw, "The Politics of Relocation: The Moving of the Crest Street Community," *Journal of the American Planning Association* 57 (Winter 1991): 57–68.

23. *SMN,* Feb. 16, 1975, B1.

24. Ibid., May 14, 1976, D1; *WP,* May 20, 1979, F7; Robert S. Hodder, "Savannah's Changing Past: A Generation of Historic Preser-

vation Planning in a Southern City, 1955–1985," Ph.D. diss., Cornell University, 1993, 234–235.

25. *SMN,* Mar. 7, 1980, B1; Apr. 27, 1980, B1; Allyne T. Owens, "Can Historic Preservation Succeed in Minority Communities? A Look at the Beach Institute Historic Neighborhood in Savannah, Georgia," master's thesis, Urban Planning, University of Florida, 1986, 3–43, 99–106. On the need for black know-how, see Andrea Kirsten Mullen, "A Black Preservationist Speaks Out," *Historic Preservation* 35 (Nov.–Dec. 1983): 13.

26. *SMN,* Dec. 6, 1983, B1. For each successful campaign to preserve a historic black site, there are many more that fail. Jackson Ward, Richmond's historic black neighborhood, remains at risk despite Richmond's robust preservationist movement. See *RTD,* May 15, 2002, B4. See also *NYT,* May 26, 1991, A22; *AC,* Aug. 27, 1993, E1; *JTU,* Feb. 7, 2001, A1; *Little Rock Arkansas Democrat-Gazette,* July 15, 2001, B1; *NOTP,* Dec. 9, 2001, B1; and Christopher Silver, "Revitalizing the Urban South: Neighborhood Preservation and Planning since the 1920s," *Journal of the American Planning Association* 57 (Winter 1991): 78–80.

27. *NYT,* Nov. 10, 1957.

28. *Associated Press,* June 22, 2000; *JTU,* June 22, 2000, B1; *Associated Press,* June 24, 2000.

29. Michael Kammen, *Mystic Chords of Memory: The Transformation of Tradition in American Culture* (New York: Vintage, 1993), 572, 588–589.

30. Eric Gable, Richard Handler, and Anna Lawson, "On the Uses of Relativism: Fact, Conjecture, and White and Black Histories at Colonial Williamsburg," *American Ethnologist* 98 (1996): 791–805.

31. Quotations are from Rex M. Ellis, "Presenting the Past: Education, Interpretation and the Teaching of Black History at Colonial Williamsburg," Ph.D. diss., College of William and Mary, 1989, 83, 139, 231; Kenneth Chorley to Broadus Mitchell, Apr. 22, 1953, quoted in Anders Greenspan, *Creating Colonial Williamsburg* (Washington, D.C.: Smithsonian Institution Press, 2002), 115.

32. Kammen, *Mystic Chords of Memory,* 641–645; Greenspan, *Creating Colonial Williamsburg,* 145.

33. Richard Handler and Eric Gable, *The New History in an Old*

Museum: Creating the Past at Colonial Williamsburg (Durham, N.C.: Duke University Press, 1997), 3–27.

34. Fergus M. Bordewich, "Revising Colonial America," *Atlantic Monthly* (Dec. 1988): 31.

35. Ibid., 26.

36. Colonial Williamsburg Foundation, *Teaching History at Colonial Williamsburg* (Williamsburg, Va.: Colonial Williamsburg Foundation, 1985), 4.

37. Michael Olmert, "Colonial Williamsburg Corrects the Record," *American Visions* 1 (Sept.–Oct. 1986): 44–52; *NYT,* Feb. 11, 1988, C9, Sept. 12, 1988, A10, June 4, 1999, E29; Edward A. Chappell, "Social Responsibility and the American History Museum," *Winterthur Portfolio* 24 (Winter 1989): 259–264; Ellis, "Presenting the Past," 272–280; Greenspan, *Creating Colonial Williamsburg,* 151–157.

38. *AC,* Sept. 8, 1991, M1.

39. Tim Wheeler, "Of Human Bondage," *Virginia Magazine* (Oct. 24, 1982): 7–10; Sandra R. Gregg, "Museum of the Confederacy," *American Visions* (Oct. 1990): 43–45; *Richmond News-Leader,* July 11, 1991, A3; *Richmond Afro-American,* July 17, 1991; *AC,* Sept. 8, 1991, M1; *WP,* Aug. 11, 1991, G1; John Coski to author, Dec. 5, 2003; Edward D. C. Campbell to author, Dec. 8 and Dec. 9, 2003.

40. Jennifer L. Eichstedt and Stephen Small, *Representations of Slavery: Race and Ideology in Southern Plantation Museums* (Washington D.C.: Smithsonian Institution Press, 2002), 196–199.

41. Michael Honey, "Doing Public History at the National Civil Rights Museum: A Conversation with Juanita Moore," *Public Historian* 17 (Winter 1995): 72, 76–77.

42. Glenn T. Eskew, "Memorializing the Movement: The Struggle to Build Civil Rights Museums in the South," in Winfred B. Moore Jr., Kyle S. Sinsi, and David H. White Jr., *Warm Ashes: Issues in Southern History at the Dawn of the Twenty-first Century* (Columbia: University of South Carolina Press, 2003), 363–372.

43. *MCA,* Sept. 28, 1992, A1; *MCA,* Sept. 26, 1996, A1; *AC,* Aug. 24, 1997, R1; *Boule Journal* 66 (Summer 2002): 153. For an extended description of the Memphis museum exhibits at the opening, see *MCA,* June 30, 1991, G6.

44. Honey, "Doing Public History," 73; description of Albany

Civil Rights Movements Museum at Old Zion Church, found at http://www.museumstuff.com/rec/org_20020201_10135.html (accessed Dec. 12, 2003); Walter Shapiro, "The Glory and the Glitz," *Time* 138 (Aug. 5, 1991): 56; *MCA,* Jan. 15, 1992, A1.

45. Honey, "Doing Public History," 82; *MCA,* June 27, 1991, C1; *SMN,* May 18, 2001.

46. For a critique of "therapeutic activism" at one museum, see *NYT,* Aug. 18, 2004, B5.

47. *NOTP,* Feb. 2, 2003, Living section, 1; on black history tours, see http://africansinlouisiana.com (accessed Dec. 24, 2003); *Chattanooga Times Free Press,* June 17, 2001, D1; Eichstedt and Small, *Representations of Slavery,* 246–250.

48. Greenspan, *Creating Colonial Williamsburg,* 88–91; Grace Elizabeth Hale, *Making Whiteness: The Culture of Segregation in the South, 1890–1940* (New York: Pantheon, 1998), 130–134; Marsha Dean Phelts, *An American Beach for African Americans* (Gainesville: University Press of Florida, 1997); Russ Rymer, *American Beach: How "Progress" Robbed a Black Town—and Nation—of History, Wealth, and Power* (New York: Harper Perennial, 2000); Richard D. Starnes, "Creating a Variety Vacationland: Tourism Development in North Carolina, 1930–1990," in Richard D. Starnes, ed., *Southern Journeys: Tourism, History, and Culture in the Modern South* (Tuscaloosa: University of Alabama Press, 2003), 148–149.

49. David R. Colburn, *Racial Change and Community Crisis: St. Augustine, Florida, 1877–1980* (New York: Columbia University Press, 1985), esp. 137–154.

50. Quotations from Stephen A. Smith, "The Old South Myth as a Contemporary Southern Commodity," *Journal of Popular Culture* 16 (1982): 25–26; Polly W. Hein and Adolph Sanders, *The Georgia Travel Industry, 1960–1972* (Athens: Division of Research, College of Business Administration, University of Georgia, 1974); Robert L. Frank, "The Economic Impact of Tourism in Charleston, South Carolina, 1970," master's thesis, University of South Carolina, 1972.

51. *NOTP,* Jan. 21, 1996, B3; *Knoxville News-Sentinel,* Feb. 7, 1999, E1; "Black History in Alabama," *American Demographics* 15 (Jan. 1993): 48–49; Christy Anderson, Dorothy Walker, and Trina Binkley, "Civil Rights Resources in Alabama," *CRM: The Journal of Heritage Steward-*

ship 1 (Fall 2003): 93–96; Glenn T. Eskew, "From Civil War to Civil Rights: Selling Alabama as Heritage Tourism," *International Journal of Hospitality and Tourism Administration* 2 (2001): 201–214.

52. *NVP,* June 9, 2001, A1; Nov. 16, 2002, D1; Feb. 20, 2003, D1; *Knoxville News-Sentinel,* Feb. 9, 1999, E1; *Greensboro News and Record,* Feb. 24, 2002, I1; *NOTP,* July 16, 1995, F2; *RTD,* June 4, 2000, C5. On trails in Louisiana, Tennessee, Virginia, and Florida, see *NOTP,* July 16, 1995, F1; *MCA,* July 2, 1998, CC2; *NVP,* Feb. 20, 2003, D1; *St. Petersburg Times,* July 14, 1992, D1; *JTU,* Mar. 5, 2003, L1; *NYT,* Aug. 10, 2004, A1.

53. *NOTP,* July 16, 1995, F1; *RTD,* Apr. 27, 2003, H1.

CONCLUSION

1. *WP,* Aug. 16, 1995; Jane G. Atkinson, "Letter to the Editor," *RTD,* undated article in vertical file, Valentine Museum, Richmond, Va.; Brian Black and Bryn Varley, "Contesting the Sacred: Preservation and Meaning on Richmond's Monument Avenue," in Cynthia Mills and Pamela Simpson, eds., *Monuments to the Lost Cause: Women, Art, and Landscapes of Southern Memory* (Knoxville: University of Tennessee Press, 2003), 241–248.

31. Tony Horwitz, *Confederates in the Attic: Dispatches from the Unfinished Civil War* (New York: Pantheon, 1998), 81.

3. Owen J. Dwyer, "Interpreting the Civil Rights Movement: Place, Memory, and Conflict," *Professional Geographer* 52 (Nov. 2000): 666–667.

4. *AC,* Sept. 30, 1999, A1; *AC,* Jan. 19, 2003, A13; *AC,* June 22, 2003, E1; *St. Petersburg Times,* Sept. 29, 2002, D1; *Charleston Post and Courier,* Feb. 6, 2000, A1; Associated Press, Mar. 14, 2003; Ronald H. Bayor, *Race and the Shaping of Twentieth-Century Atlanta* (Chapel Hill: University of North Carolina Press, 1996), chap. 7.

5. *Birmingham News,* July 26, 2001; *NYT,* Nov. 16, 1997, D5. See also *AC,* Mar. 7, 1993, A1; *NOTP,* Jan. 5, 1993, B6; *NOTP,* Jan. 22, 1992, B1; *NOTP,* Feb. 1, 1993, B5; *NOTP,* Apr. 3, 1994, B7; *NOTP,* Sept. 18, 1994, B7; *NOTP,* July 1, 1995, B3; *NOTP,* Sept. 24, 1997, B1, B2; *NOTP,* Dec. 2, 1997, B3; *NYT,* Jan. 27, 1993, A16; *NYT,* Nov. 12, 1997, A1; *JTU,* Feb. 21, 1999, D3; *San Antonio Express-News,* June 18, 1999, B4; *Birmingham News,* July 26, 2001, Sept. 5, 2001; *RTD,* Oct. 1, 2003, B1; *RN&O,*

Dec. 28, 2003, D5; Jack E. Davis, *Race against Time: Culture and Separation in Natchez since 1930* (Baton Rouge: Louisiana State University Press, 2001), 255.

6. *NYT,* Nov. 16, 1997, D5.

7. *WP,* June 14, 1992, B3; *Los Angeles Sentinel,* Feb. 4, 1982, A7. See also *Charleston Gazette,* Aug. 12, 1994, C1; *Jacksonville Florida Times-Union,* July 3, 1998, B1; and Peter Frizsche, "Spectres of History: On Nostalgia, Exile, and Modernity," *American Historical Review* 106 (Dec. 2001): 1588.

8. Davis, *Race against Time,* chap. 2.

9. *Baton Rouge Sunday Advocate,* Mar. 14, 1999, Sunday magazine, 3; *MCA,* Mar. 22, 1991, C1; Davis, *Race against Time,* 64–66; Steven Hoelscher, "'Where the Old South Still Lives': Displaying Heritage in Natchez, Mississippi," in Celeste Ray, *Southern Heritage on Display: Public Ritual and Ethnic Diversity within Southern Regionalism* (Tuscaloosa: University of Alabama Press, 2003), 218–250.

10. Quoted in Davis, *Race against Time,* 266, 268, 269.

11. *Baton Rouge Sunday Advocate,* Mar. 14, 1999, Sunday magazine, 3; *MCA,* Mar. 14, 1993, E1; Davis, *Race against Time,* 268–273; Hoelscher, "Where the Old South Still Lives," 238–243.

12. Celeste Garrett and Bennie M. Currie, "Tours to Fill the Gaps of Mississippi's History," *Emerge* (June 1994): 58–59.

13. *South Carolina Highway Historical Marker Guide* (Columbia: South Carolina Department of Archives and History, 1998). For a catalog of historical errors and silences on the southern landscape, see James W. Loewen, *Lies across America: What Our Historic Sites Get Wrong* (New York: New Press, 1999). On the broader problem of a "diversity deficit" in heritage sites, see Ned Kaufman, "Historic Places and the Diversity Deficit in Heritage Conservation," *CRM: The Journal of Heritage Stewardship* 1 (Summer 2004): 68–85.

14. *AC,* Mar. 30, 1993, A13; *NOTP,* July 16, 1995, F2.

15. *NOTP,* Feb. 2, 2003, Living section, 1. See also Tara McPherson, *Reconstructing Dixie: Race, Gender, and Nostalgia in the Imagined South* (Durham, N.C.: Duke University Press, 2003), 40–44, 96–101.

16. Although there are no studies of the history of land-use controls in the South, valuable discussions of zoning can be found in Michael Kammen, *Mystic Chords of Memory: The Transformation of Tradi-*

tion in American Culture (New York: Knopf, 1991); and Lawrence M. Friedman, *American Law in the Twentieth Century* (New Haven, Conn.: Yale University Press, 2002), 399–406.

17. *NYT,* Sept. 29, 1994, Sept. 30, 1994; *Wall Street Journal,* Sept. 29, 1994; William M. S. Rasmussen and Robert S. Tilton, *Old Virginia: The Pursuit of a Pastoral Ideal* (Charlottesville: Howell Press, 2003), 227–230.

18. Kathleen Rilley, "The Long Shadow of the Confederacy in America's Schools: State-Sponsored Use of Confederate Symbols in the Wake of *Brown v. Board*," *William and Mary Bill of Rights Journal* 10 (Feb. 2002): 533–534; Alexander Tsesis, "The Problem of Confederate Symbols: A Thirteenth Amendment Approach," *Temple Law Review* 75 (Fall 2002): 539–612. On the "rights revolution" see Friedman, *American Law,* 280–348; and Samuel Walker, *The Rights Revolution: Rights and Community in Modern America* (New York: Oxford University Press, 1998), esp. 61–114.

19. Roy L. Brooks, "History of the Black Redress Movement," *Guild Practitioner* 60 (Winter 2003): 1–12; Walter B. Hill Jr., "The Ex-Slave Pension Movement: Some Historical and Genealogical Notes," *Negro History Bulletin* 59 (Oct.–Dec. 1996): 7–12; Raymond A. Winbush, ed., *Should America Pay? Slavery and the Raging Debate over Reparations* (New York: Amistad, 2003).

20. For an especially valuable discussion of the legal, institutional, political, and moral complexities of reparations, see Eric A. Posner and Adrian Vermeule, "Reparations for Slavery and Other Historical Injustices," *Columbia Law Review* 103 (Apr. 2003): 689–747.

21. Michael D' Orso, *Like Judgment Day: The Ruin and Redemption of a Town Called Rosewood* (New York: Putnam, 1996); Richard A. Ryles, "The Rosewood Massacre: Reparations for Racial Injustice," *National Bar Association Magazine* (Mar.–Apr. 1995): 15, 24; Alfred L. Brophy, *Reconstructing the Dreamland: The Tulsa Riot of 1921. Race, Reparations, and Reconciliation* (New York: Oxford University Press, 2002).

22. On reparations as a means to a "mass-based antisubordination agenda," see Robert Westley, "Many Billions Gone: Is It Time to Reconsider the Case for Black Reparations?" *Boston College Law Review* 40 (Dec. 1998): 429–476.

23. *MCA,* Oct. 9, 2000, A10; *Birmingham News,* Dec. 21, 2000, A1; Feb. 13, 2001, B4; Feb. 22, 2001, B4; Feb. 27, 2001, B6; Mar. 13, 2001, A2;

May 19, 2001, n.p.; Aug. 9, 2003, n.p.; Suzanne M. Alford, "Student Display of Confederate Symbols in Public Schools," *School Law Bulletin* 33 (Winter 2002): 1–7; James M. Dedman IV, "At Daggers Drawn: The Confederate Flag and the School Classroom—A Case Study of a Broken First Amendment Formula," *Baylor Law Review* 53 (Fall 2001): 877–927; David L. Hudson Jr., "Stars and Bars Wars: Confederate Flag-Wavers, Many of Them Students, Storm the Courts under a Banner of Free Speech," *ABA Journal* 86 (Nov. 2000): 28.

24. *RTD,* Mar. 10, 2003, B1.

25. *NYT,* June 19, 1996; Ralph Reed, *Active Faith: How Christians Are Changing the Soul of American Politics* (New York: Free Press, 1996); Ann Burlein, *Lift High the Cross: Where White Supremacy and the Christian Right Converge* (Durham, N.C.: Duke University Press, 2002); David John Marley, "Riding in the Back of the Bus: The Christian Right's Adoption of Civil Rights Movement Rhetoric," in Leigh Raiford and Renee Romano, eds., *Freedom Is a Constant Struggle: The Civil Rights Movement in United States Memory* (Athens: University of Georgia Press, forthcoming).

26. *Washington Times,* Aug. 10, 2004, A5.

27. On the "flag" controversy in South Carolina, see K. Michael Prince, *"Rally 'Round the Flag, Boys": South Carolina and the Confederate Flag* (Columbia: University of South Carolina Press, 2004).

28. *RTD,* Apr. 11, 1997, A1; *RTD,* Mar. 23, 2000, B1; *Roanoke Times and World News,* Apr. 12, 1997, A1; *Roanoke Times and World News,* May 11, 2000, A1; *WP,* May 19, 1997, B3; *Washington Times,* Mar. 28, 1998, A11; *Washington Times,* Apr. 10, 1998, A1; *Washington Times,* Apr. 7, 2000, C1; *Washington Times,* May 11, 2000, A1; *Boston Globe,* Apr. 26, 1998, A8; *NVP,* Apr. 5, 2000, B5; *NVP,* Apr. 27, 2000, B3.

29. Ralph Ellison, "A Very Stern Discipline," *Harper's* (Mar. 1967): 84.

Index

Abney, Mark A., 215
Ada Jenkins High School (Davidson, NC), 280
Adams, Floyd, Jr., 260, 267, 268
Addison, Lucy, 87
African American colleges: curriculum at, 149–150; growth of during early twentieth century, 150–151; as centers of scientific history, 152–154; faculty activism at, 157–162
African American history museums, 301–304
African American militias, 73–74
African American public celebrations: 55–104; need for in postbellum South, 59–60; variety of, 60–64; scale of, 64; use of public space, 65–70; importance of parades in, 71; organization of, 71–77; divisions during, 77–79; concern with respectability during, 79–82; gender roles during, 82–88; oratorical traditions during, 88–99; representations of Africa in, 91; depictions of slavery, 91–93; interpretation of Civil War, 93–94; record of black progress, 95–97; expressions of black politics, 97–98; as vehicle for counter-memory, 99–104

African American schools: as site of historical memory, 138–182; poor resources for, 141–143, 144-145; status of black teachers in, 143–144; ties to civil rights movement, 159–160; and Negro History Week, 162–177; limits of, 178–182; desegregation of, 274–278; loss of traditions in integrated schools, 278–282; resegregation of, 319–320; nostalgia for, 321–322

African American Travel and Tourism Association, 327

Alabama's Black Heritage, 311

Alabama Department of Archives and History, 108, 109

Alabama Historical Commission, 105, 108

Alabama Historical Society, 105, 108

Alabama State College, 164, 169

Alabama State Teachers Association, 164, 278

Albany Civil Rights Museum (GA), 302

Allen, G. M., 209

Allen, George (Gov. of Virginia), 272, 337

Allen, Richard, 62, 94

Allen University (SC), 65

American Beach (FL), 309

American Institute of Architects (AIA), 206

American Missionary Association, 289

American Negro Academy, 146, 147

American Negro Historical Society, 146

"An Old City Speaks" (film), 200

Andersonville (GA), 69

Archives: and historical memory, 105–137; nineteenth century record keeping practices, 107–108; founding of early archives, 108–112; and expansion of state authority, 112–118; promotion of ideology of civilization, 118–120; educational activities of, 120–121; and professional ambitions of male historians, 122–135

Arkansas, Historical Society of, 117

Arkansas History Commission, 111, 121

Arkansas State College, 153

Arkansas State Historical Museum, 116

Arrington, Richard, 302

Ashcroft, Sen. John D., 340

Ashe, Arthur, 316

Asheville (NC), 91, 188

Associated Publishers, 156, 163, 166, 168; *Negro History in Thirteen Plays,* 168; *Plays and Pageants from the Life of the Negro,* 168; *The African Background Outlined; or Handbook for the Study of the Negro,* 170

Association of the Army of Northern Virginia, 19

Association for the Preservation of Virginia Antiquities (APVA), 24, 37, 131

Association for the Study of Negro Life and History (ASNLH), 155, 157, 163, 278, 281, 288, 290, 305, 308

Atlanta (GA), 68, 77–78, 96, 269, 286, 319, 335

Atlantic Beach (NC), 309

Attucks, Crispus, 94, 172

Austin, Louis E., 244, 247

Avery Boys' Club, 227

Azalea Festival (Charleston, SC), 219–221, 323

Bailey, D'Army, 304

Bailey, Joseph A., 153

Bankhead, James H., 192

Bankhead, Marie, 125

Banks, Enoch M., 46, 128–129

Barbour, George M., 189, 190

Barbour, Haley (Gov. of Mississippi), 341

Barnes, Earl, 20

Barnes, Roy (Gov. of Georgia), 339, 341

Bassett, John Spencer, 115, 128

Baton Rouge (LA), 308, 310

Baxley, Jerry, 1, 3

Baxter, Ellen Douglas, 30, 31

Beach Institute (Savannah, GA), 289

Beach Institute Historic Neighborhood Association, 289
Beasley, David (Gov. of South Carolina), 341
Beason, Stan, 272
Beaufort (SC), 64
Beavers, Leroy, Jr., 260, 267, 269
Bethune, Mary McLeod, 174, 177
Bethune-Cookman Institute, 174
Betts, R. G., 194
Birmingham (AL), 302, 311, 320
Birmingham Civil Rights Institute, 302, 303
Birth of a Nation, 157
Bishop, Alexander M., 200
Bishop College, 154
Blackshear (GA), 97
Bond, Horace Mann, 180–181
Booker T. Washington High School (Atlanta, GA), 144
Booker T. Washington High School (Suffolk, VA), 144
Boyd, N. V., 167
Brawley, Benjamin, 150
Brewton (AL), 79
Brewton-Pringle House (Charleston, SC), 209
Brown, Charlotte Hawkins, 174
Brunswick (FL), 321
Brunswick (GA), 87
Bryan, Belle, 38
Burroughs, Nannie, 149, 174
Bush, George W., 339
Business Chain (Hayti, NC), 245, 250
Byrd, Harry, 192, 197
Byrd, R. Wayne, Sr., 273, 341
Byrd-Harden, Linda, 273

Campbell, Edward D. C. "Kip," 299
Campbell, Leroy, 145, 276

Capehart, Dr. L. B., 58
Carnes, J. R., 56
Carolina Times, 242, 245, 247
Caroline County (VA), 271, 336–337
Carr, George Watts, Sr., 143
Carroll, Charles, 103
Carroll, Charles F., 282
Carson, Cary, 297
Carter's Grove, 298
Caswell County (NC) Training School, 143
Catts, Sidney J., 192
Caxtons Club (Pensacola, FL), 23
Chambers, Rev. Andrew, 60
Charleston (SC), 75, 83, 188, 240, 310, 315, 329, 335; and tourism: 183–226; campaign to promote, 192–196, 199–200; reinterpreting the landscape of, 196–199; marketing history of, 201–219; and glorification of plantation era, 201–203; antiques and material culture of, 203–205; historic preservation of, 205–206; artistic representations of, 206–208; exotic representations of African Americans in, 210–215
Charleston Chamber of Commerce, 193, 198, 199, 212
Charleston (SC) Light Dragoons Monumental Association, 19
Charleston Museum, 203, 215, 219
Chase, W. Calvin, 64, 81
Chatham County (GA) Emancipation Association, 78
Chattanooga (TN), 228
Chicago, University of, 152
Chipley, Ann Elizabeth Billups, 37
Chipley, William D., 13
Christian Coalition, 338
Civil Rights Act of 1964, 309

Cleaver, Jim, 321
Coastal Highway Association, 193, 198
Coleman, Cleo, 271
Coles, Lula, 86
Colfax (LA) Riot, 5
Collective memory. *See* Historical memory
Colonial Dames, 22, 24, 41, 125, 196; and Mecklenburg "Declaration of Independence," 131–133
Colonial Parkway (VA), 197
Colonial Williamsburg, 294–298, 309
Columbia (SC), 65, 94
Columbia University, 131, 152
Columbus (GA), 25
Confederate Flag controversy, 331, 334–35, 339, 341
Confederate Heritage Association, 334
Confederate History Month, 272, 328, 337–338
Confederate Memorial Literary Society (CMLS), 39, 43, 47–48
Confederate Veteran, 21, 32
Confederate "White House," 39, 43, 47–48
Conference on Education and Race Relations, 176
Congress of Racial Equality, 281
Connor, Eugene "Bull," 302
Connor, Robert Digges Wimberly, 110–111, 114, 120, 126, 134–35; and Mecklenburg "Declaration of Independence," 131–133
Cook, Fields, 93
Cooper, Anna Julia, 83
Cooper, Joan, 321
Corpus Christi (TX), 191
Cotten, Sallie Southall, 29, 30, 44–45

Council of Conservative Citizens, 316, 340–341
Covington (VA), 63
Craig, Locke, 192
Crawford, Virgil A., 95
Crummell, Alexander, 57, 100
Cunningham, Seymour, 195

Daniels, Jonathan, 183, 184, 204
Dare, Virginia, 30, 31, 38, 44–45
Darien (GA), 77
Daughters of the American Revolution (DAR), 20, 24, 35, 36, 46, 101, 125, 127, 196, 335; post WWI conservatism of, 50
Daughters of Colonial Governors, 24
Daughters of the Founders and Patriots of America, 24
Daughters of the Pilgrims, 24
Daughters of the Republic of Texas (DRT), 14
Daughters of the Revolution (DR), 29, 42, 43
Daughters of the War of 1812, 24, 196
Davis, Angela, 145, 177, 180, 182
Davis, Daniel Webster, 83
Davis, Jefferson, 12, 192, 316; monument in Richmond (VA), 49
Declaration of Independence, 89
Descendants of the Barons of Runnemede, 24
Dillard University, 168, 321
Disney Corporation, 329
Dixie Highway Association, 191
Dixon, Thomas, 97
Dixon, Rev. W. H., 93
Douglass, Frederick, 62, 92, 94, 104, 163, 182
Douglass Junior School (San Antonio, TX), 169

DuBois, Ellen, 50

Du Bois, W. E. B., 142, 168, 182, 232, 254

Dunbar, Paul Lawrence, 182

Durham (NC): urban renewal of, 227–255; founding of Hayti, 231–232; as center of African American "progress," 232–233; political activism in, 234; slum housing in, 235–236, 238–239; efforts to revitalize, 236–238, absence of preservationist ethos in, 239–240; urban renewal project in, 240–251; destruction of historic sites in, 251–254; emergence of historic preservation movement in, 285–286

Durham Board of Realtors, 247

Durham Committee on Negro Affairs (DCNA), 234, 241, 244, 245

Durham Herald, 254

Durham Housing Authority, 248

Durham Redevelopment Commission, 237, 242, 243, 245, 285

Durham, Rev. J. J., 97

Dwight, Henry, 198

Eckenrode, Hamilton J., 197

Edenton (NC) Tea Party, 30, 31, 42–43

Edgefield County (SC), 69

Edwards, Sen. John, 339

El-Amin, Sa'ad, 299

Elizabeth State College (NC), 169

Ellison, Ralph, 229, 343

El Paso (TX), 191

Emancipation Day: origins of, 62; organization of, 63–64, 76–78; scale of, 64–65; use of public space during, 65–70; processions during, 71–76, divisions during, 78–79; emphasis on respectability during, 80–82; gender roles in, 82–88; oratorical traditions during, 88–99; representations of Africa in, 91; and depictions of slavery, 91–93; and interpretation of Civil War, 93–94; and record of black progress, 95–97; and expressions of black politics, 97–98; as vehicle for counter-memory, 99–104

Emancipation Proclamation, 8, 32, 55, 86, 89

Essence Festival, 311

Evans, Gen. C. A., 26

Every Saturday History Class (Atlanta, GA), 23

Farmville (VA), 86

Faulkner, William, 11

Fayette County (TN), 70

Felton, Rebecca Latimer, 40

Field, Henry, 189

Field, Mamie, 181

First African Baptist Church (Savannah, GA), 63, 292

First Bryan Baptist Church (Savannah, GA), 63

Fisher, Rev. Miles Mark, 252

Fisk University, 150, 151, 158

Flagler, Henry, 187, 188

Florida, University of, 46

Flower women (Charleston, SC), 213–214

Fonvielle, William, 269

Foote, Shelby, 1, 8

Fordice, Kirk (Gov. of Mississippi), 340

Forrest, Nathan Bedford, 3, 334

Fortier, Alce, 118

Fort Mill (SC), 281

Fort Sumter Hotel (Charleston, SC), 193
Fort Worth (TX), 56
Fourth of July celebrations, 59, 61–62, 66, 68, 69, 75, 82, 101
Francis Marion Hotel, 193
Frazier, E. Franklin, 232
Fredericksburg (VA), 67, 176, 315
Frost, Susan Pringle, 41, 205
Fuller, Blind Boy (Fulton Allen), 254
Fuller, Sara, 312

Gandy, John M., 158, 180
Garden Club of Virginia, 197
Garrett, William R., 119
Garrison, George P., 124, 134
Gatlinburg (TN), 221
Georgia Association of Black Elected Officials, 292
Georgia Federation of Women's Clubs, 32
Georgia Historic Preservation Office, 287
Gibbes Museum of Art, 219
Gilbert, Rev. Ralph Mark, 262
Gilchrist, Albert W., 46
Gilman, Charlotte Perkins, 31
Gilmore, James (Gov. of Virginia), 273, 337, 341
Gladstone (VA), 167
Glenn, Rev. Gerald O., 273
Golden Waves Debating Society, 77
Gone with the Wind, 184
Gorr, Louis, 299
Gould, Katherine Clemmons, 195
Grabarek, Wensell "Wense," 244
Granger, Gen. Gordon, 55
Green, Anna W., 177
Green, Gertrude, 174
Greenberg, Abraham, 250–251
Greene, Lorenzo, 151, 156

Greensboro (NC), 269
Greenville (MS), 312, 319
Griffith, D. W., 157
Griggs, Sutton, 152
Guinn, Dorothy C., 171
Gunner, Frances, 175
Gwynn, Bessie Taylor, 182

Haley, Alex, 295
Hamburg (SC) Riot, 69
Hamilton (VA), 63
Hamilton, India, 177
Hampton (VA), 138
Hampton University, 150
Harlem Renaissance, 225
Harleston, Edwin, 214
Harris, Joel Chandler, 20, 32
Harvard University, 152
Hayes, George Edmund, 150
Hayti. *See* Durham
Haywood, Emily Benbury, 52
Hemings, Sally, and Thomas Jefferson, 5
Henneman, John B., 127, 130
Henry, Patrick, 36
Heritage Preservation Association, 273, 341
Herndon, Dallas T., 112, 114, 120
Heyward, DuBose, 210–211, 215
Hinton, Mary Hilliard, 30, 38, 42
Historic Charleston Foundation, 208
Historic Savannah Foundation (HSF), 256, 257, 258, 260, 261, 287
Historical memory: concept of, 4–8; role of state in, 16–19
Hollywood Cemetery (Richmond, VA), 49
Holt, Curtis, 1
Home and Garden, 204
Hot Springs (AR), 189
Houston (TX), 70

Howard University, 150, 151, 154
Hughes, Langston, 182
Hunter, Charles N., 94, 100
Hurston, Zora Neale, 174
Hutty, Alfred, 207, 211

Inman Park (GA), 286
International Council of Women of
   the Darker Races (ICWDR), 148,
   149
Isaiah Davenport House (Savannah,
   GA), 256

Jackson, Alfred, 33–34
Jackson, Alphonse, Jr., 278
Jackson, Andrew, 14, 192
Jackson, Luther P., 151, 156, 157–
   162, 179, 280; *Virginia Negro Sol-
   diers and Seamen in the Revolution-
   ary War,* 160; *Negro Officeholders in
   Virginia, 1865–1895,* 160, 161
Jackson, Maynard, 292
Jackson, Thomas "Stonewall," 316
Jackson Highway Association, 196
Jacksonville (FL), 18, 66, 74, 82, 87,
   95, 193
James Island (SC), 281
Jamestown (VA), 21, 196, 291
Jamestown Tercentennial Exposition
   (1907), 30, 36
Jarvie, William, 190
Jeanes Foundation, Anna T., 173
Jefferson, Thomas, 36; and Sally
   Hemings, 5
Jefferson Davis Elementary School
   (New Orleans, LA), 320
Jenkins, Rev. Daniel J., 215
Jenkins Orphanage (Charleston, SC),
   215
John Canoe festival (NC), 80
Johnson, Clifton, 189

Johnson, Edward A., 146
Johnson, James Weldon, 57, 182
Johnson, Lyndon B., 274
Johnston, James Hugo, 156
Jones, Thomas G., 105
Journal of Negro History, 139, 145,
   155, 156, 157, 163, 174
Joseph Manigault House
   (Charleston, SC), 205, 209
Juneteenth, 55, 56, 57, 60, 68, 70, 315

King, Edward, 185
King, Martin Luther, Jr., 252, 315
King-Tisdell Cottage (Savannah,
   GA), 288
King, Wilma, 150
Kirkland, Rev. A., 227
Kohn, Robert D., 206
Knights of Pythias, 73, 77
Knoxville (TN), 76, 189
Ku Klux Klan, 248

La Crosse (VA), 167
Ladies' Confederate Monument As-
   sociation, 12, 13
Ladies' Hermitage Association, 13,
   33–34
Ladies Memorial Association (Co-
   lumbus, GA), 25
Laurens (SC), 2
Law, W. W., 262, 263, 287–89, 293,
   305, 308
Leary, Samuel Linton, 285
Lee, Richard Henry, 36
Lee, Robert E., 192, 316
Legerton, Clarence W., 211
Lexington (KY), 170
Lincoln, Abraham, 8, 62, 163
Lindsay, J. C., 91, 97
Litigation: and historical memory,
   332–335

Logan, Rayford, 156
Lomax, Michael L., 321
Lott, Sen. Trent, 340
Loudoun County (VA) Emancipation Association, 63–64
Louisiana State Museum, 116
Louisiana Education Association, 278
Loving, Mildred and Richard, 271
Lynchburg (VA), 68, 166

Maclean, Malcolm, 262
Madison, James, 36
Mallory, Angela S., 37
"Mammy" monument, proposed (Washington, D.C.), 33
Manning, J. F., 13
Marshall, John, 40
Marshall, Thurgood, 320
Martin Luther King, Jr., Center for Nonviolent Social Change, 303
Martin, Coleman C., 198
Mary Washington Monument Association, 14
Mask, James W., 176
Mason, George, 40
Mason, Lucy Randolph, 40
Matheus, John, 171
Matthew, Mrs Patrick, 31
Maxwell, Rev. L. B., 94
Maybank, Burnett Rhett, 219
McCallum, Jane Y., 41
McFadden, Ira Caldwell, 24
McKinley, William, 81
Mecklenburg County (VA), 80–81
Mecklenburg "Declaration of Independence," 131–133
Melrose (Natchez, MS), 325
Memorial Day (Confederate), 184; founding of, 26
Memorial Day (Union), 64, 69, 71, 85

Memphis (TN), 269, 302
Merchant, Mrs. W. C. H., 46
Merrick, John, 233, 254
Metropolitan Museum of Art (New York), 203
Mexia (TX), 70
Miami (FL), 228, 269
Miller, Kelly, 150, 163
Mills, Joseph N., 254
Mingledorff, Lee, 262
Minneapolis Institute of Art, 203
Minor, Ellen, 87
Minor, Kate Pleasants, 43
Mississippi Division of Tourism, 312
Mississippi Historical Society, 110, 120
Mississippi, University of, 2, 108, 115
Mitchell, John, Jr., 81, 228
Mitchell, Margaret, 184
Mitchiner, Reginald, 235
Moffitt, Evelyn E., 29, 135
Montgomery (AL), 92
Moore, Dr. Aaron McDuffie, 254
Moore, Juanita, 305
Moore, Leonard, 308
Morehouse College, 150
Morgan, Sarah B. C., 32, 40
Morgan College, 169
Morial, Ernest N., 320
Moses, William Jeremiah, 103
Mount Vernon Ladies' Association (MVLA), 42
Murphree, Albert A., 46
Murray, Pauli, 142, 143
Museum of the Confederacy, 298–300
Museums: and desegregation, 291–296; advent of new museumology, 296–299; revised exhibits, 299–301; African American history museums, 301–304

Musgrove, Ronnie (Gov. of Mississippi), 341

Napier, Nettie L., 148
Nashville (TN), 65, 228, 236
Natchez (MS), 225, 308, 310; and tourism, 322–324; African Americans and tourism in, 324–327
Natchez Association for the Preservation of African-American Culture, 324
Natchez Garden Club, 324
Natchez Museum of Afro-American History and Culture, 325
Natchez National Historic Park, 325
Natchez Trace Parkway, 197
National Afro-American Museum and Cultural Center, 300
National Association for the Advancement of Colored People (NAACP), 252, 262, 273, 281, 287, 337, 341
National Association of Colored Women (NACW), 147, 148, 149
National Civil Rights Museum, 302, 305
National Education Association, 277
National Historic Preservation Act, 286
National Negro Business League, 75, 78
National Park Service, 292
National Register of Historic Places, 285, 286, 287
National Urban League, 248, 281
National Voting Rights Museum, 302
National Woman's Party, 41
Negro Heritage Trail Tour, 308
Negro History Bulletin, 164
Negro History Week: origins of, 162–165; adoption of, 165–166; activities during, 167–173; role of women teachers during, 173–175; response to, 175–177; assessments of, 177–182
Negro Society for Historical Research, 146, 147
New Bern (NC), 95
Newcomb, James, 56, 88
New Orleans, 221, 225, 240, 269, 308, 311, 312, 329
Nineteenth Amendment, 51
Nineteenth of June Organization, 70
Nixon, Richard M., 279
Norfolk (VA), 8, 69, 76, 84, 93, 96
North Carolina Booklet, 39, 135
North Carolina College for Negroes, 227, 233
North Carolina Historical Commission, 110, 114, 121, 131
North Carolina Historical Review, 135
North Carolina Leaflets, 120
North Carolina Mutual, 232, 243, 252, 252, 254
North Carolina Supreme Court, 68
Northeast Mississippi Confederate Veteran Association, 19

Oak Alley (Vacherie, LA), 327
Ocala (FL), 76, 77, 83, 84, 86, 91
Odd Fellows of Captolo, 77
Odenheimer, Cordelia Powell, 33
Oglethorpe, James, 258
Oglethorpe (GA) Light Infantry Association, 19
Oldham, Carvie, 248
O'Neal, William, 247
Order of the Crown of America, 24
Order of the First Families of Virginia, 24

Order of Good Samaritans, 63
Order of the Knights of the Golden Shoe Society, 24
Owen, Thomas M., 124, 125, 126
Oxford (NC), 68
Oxford (GA) Women's Club, 23

P. G. T. Beauregard Elementary School (St. Bernard Parish, LA), 320
Packard, Nina, 39
Page, Thomas Nelson, 16
Palm Beach (FL), 187
Pan-Africanism, 102
Parks, Rosa, 304
Partisan politics: and contemporary historical debates, 337–342
Paul, Rep. Ron, 340
Pearson, Josephine, 39
Penn Normal Industrial and Agricultural School, 211
Pensacola (FL), 12
Perdue, Sonny (Gov. of Georgia), 339
Perry, Ben, 245
Phillips, Ulrich B., 127, 172, 178
Phillis Wheatley Elementary School (Louisville, KY), 321, 322
Pijeaux, Lawrence Jr., 303
Pinter, Harold, 4
Pittman, W. Sidney, 252
Plumb, J. H., 11
Pollard, Lizzie, 30
Porgy, 210, 212, 215
Portsmouth (VA), 280, 308
Preservation Society of Charleston, 206, 219
Pringle, Ernest H., 205
Prosser, Gabriel, 271, 336
Public space, and historical memory: 6–7, 229–230, 263–269, 270–272, 284–291, 313–315, 316-317, 328–330, 342–344
Public Works Administration, 213
Purcellville (VA), 63

Raleigh (NC), 94, 96
Raleigh News and Observer, 339
Ralph Mark Gilbert Civil Rights Museum, 292, 302
Randolph, Janet Henderson Weaver, 39
Rauers, John J., 257
Red, Bull City (George Washington), 254
Reed, Ralph, 338
Reparations for slavery movement, 332–33
Reynolds, John Hugh, 112
Rhoads, Joseph J., 153
Richardson, Tamah, 139, 145, 182
Richardson, Willis, 169
Richmond (VA), 1, 6, 8, 66–67, 68, 73, 77, 85, 93, 228, 269, 310, 315, 316, 317
Richmond County (VA), 176
Riley, Franklin L., 108, 115, 120, 124
Rittenberry, Alma, 196
Roanoke (VA), 84, 166, 175–76
Robert E. Lee Elementary School (Birmingham, AL), 320
Robinson, Dorothy Redus, 277
Rome (GA), 78
Rosewood (FL), 333, 334
Rowen, Carl T., 182
Rowland, Dunbar, 119, 120
Royal Knights of King David, 252
Rutherford, Laura Cobb, 37
Rutherford, Mildred, 39

Saint Augustine (FL), 187, 188, 189, 221, 309

Saint Joseph's AME Church (Hayti, NC), 232, 252, 285
Saint Paul CME Church (Savannah, GA), 260
Saint Philip's Church (Charleston, SC), 204
Saint Philip's Junior College, 150
Saint Phillip Monumental Church (Savannah, GA), 260
Salley, Alexander S., 125–126, 198
San Antonio (TX), 55–56, 60, 78, 88, 330
Sass, Herbert, 183, 203
Saturday Evening Post, 183
Savage, Sherman, 151
Savannah (GA), 68, 69, 71, 75, 77, 83, 85, 87, 91, 97, 231, 240, 302: urban renewal in, 255–269; preservation movement in, 256–258; renewal in black neighborhoods of, 258–263; African American historic preservation movement in, 287–291
Savannah Evening Press, 259
Savannah Neighborhood Action Conference, 290
Schomburg, Arthur, 147
School desegregation, 274–284
Scions of the Cavaliers, 24
Scriven County (GA), 77
Selma (AL), 3, 302, 311, 334
Shaw University, 58
Shepard, Dr. James Edward, 227, 233
Sherman, V. O., 87
Simons, Albert, 206, 207
Sims, William Gilmore, 128
Sixteenth Street Baptist Church (Birmingham, AL), 302, 311
Smith, Alice Ravenel Huger, 67, 202, 214
Smith, C. Alphonso, 131

Smith, Henry Louis, 47
Smith, Lucy Harth, 170, 174
Smith, T. C., 208
Smithsonian Institution, 17
Smythe, Hugh H., 156
Snell, Arthur V., 199
Society for the Preservation of Old Dwellings (SPOD), 205
Society for the Preservation of Spirituals (SPS), 216–218
Sons of the American Revolution (SAR), 19–20, 21
Sons of Confederate Veterans, 124, 273, 334–35, 339, 340
South Carolina Historical Society, 198
Southern Christian Leadership Conference, 263
Southern Good Roads, 191, 195
Southern Historical Association, 19
Southern identity, 1–3, 11
Southern League, 340
Southern Party of Virginia, 1
"Southern Road to Freedom," 324–25
Southern States Industrial Council, 282
Southwestern Historical Quarterly, 133–134
Spanish-American War, 71
Spartanburg (SC), 78
Spaulding, Charles C., 254
Spaulding, Janie Marie, 254
Stanley, Thomas B., 291, 307
Statesboro (GA), 190
Steward, O. M., 91
Steward, Theophilus G., 82
Stewart, John S., 241
Still, William, 59
Stoddard, Albert, 257
Stone Mountain (GA), 48

Stoney, Thomas P., 199
Street vendors (Charleston, SC), 218–219
Styles, Rev. W. H., 97
Suffolk (VA), 144
Summerville, Rev. C. C., 91
Supreme Court: on desegregation, 274–75, 292
Sutton, George W., Jr., 191
Sykes, N. A., 179

Talbert, Mary B., 148
Tapia, Brenda, 280
Taylor, Alrutheus A., 156
Taylor, Bride Neill, 133–34
Taylor, Calvin, 272
Taylor, Eugenia, 87
Tennessee Department of Archives and History, 111
Tennessee State College, 151, 169
Terrell, Mary Church, 64
Terry, Sonny, 254
Texas Library and Historical Commission, 52, 125
Texas State Federation of Women's Clubs, 52, 125
Texas State Historical Association, 52, 133
Textbook revision: in Virginia, 282–283
Thomas, David Y., 105
Thomas "Stonewall" Jackson House, 300–301, 328
Tillman, Benjamin, 142
Tourism: and southern identity, 183–226, 307–313; during nineteenth century, 185–190; impact of automobile on, 190–193, 194–196; during first half of twentieth century, 221–226; during late twentieth century, 307–315

Trenholm, H. Councill, 164
Trent, William P., 117, 128, 131
Trice, Richard, 254
Trice, Willie, 254
Trinity College (Duke University), 115
Troup Ward (Savannah, GA), 260
Truth, Sojourner, 172, 174, 175
Tubman, Harriet, 172, 174, 175
Tucker, Samuel, 1
Tulsa (OK), 333
Turner, Alice L., 166, 175
Turner, Nat, 182

Ullman, William, 196
United Confederate Veterans (UCV), 13, 19, 21, 46, 124, 128–29
United Daughters of the Confederacy (UDC), 21, 24, 36, 125, 128–29, 131, 196; education campaign of, 45, 166, 275; fund-raising by, 49
United Daughters of Lincoln, 83
Universal Negro Improvement Association, 102
Urban renewal: and African American memory, 227–269, 284–291. *See also* Durham; Savannah

Van Noppen, Charles, 132
Vardaman, James K., 2, 142
Verner, Elizabeth O'Neill, 207, 210, 211, 214
Vesey, Denmark, 202
Virginia Conservation and Economic Development Commission, 197
Virginia Council of Social Studies, 283
Virginia Military Institute, 300
Virginia State Board of Education, 283

Virginia State College, 158, 168, 180
Virginia Teachers' Association, 159, 161, 278
Virginia, University of, 40, 131
Virginia Voters' League, 161
Voorhees Industrial School, 158

Waco (TX), 96, 103
Waldheim, Kurt, 5
Walker, Maggie, 228
Wallace, George C. (Gov. of Alabama), 283, 311
Walton County (GA), 270
Warner, E. E., 86
Washington, Booker T., 155, 182, 232, 254
Washington, D.C., 74
Washington, George, 61
Washington, Margaret, 148
Washington and Lee University, 46–47
Watson, E. J., 198
Webber, Marie L., 198
Wednesday Club (Galveston, TX), 23
Weeks, Stephen B., 130
Welty, Eudora, 7
Wesley, Charles, 151, 153, 156
West Virginia State College, 154–155
Wheatley, Phillis, 175
Wheeler, John, 241
White Rock Baptist Church (Hayti, NC), 232, 251–52, 285
White women, commemorative activities of: 12–54; proliferation of clubs for, 22–24; and influence of ideal of "republican motherhood," 24–25; and revision of Victorian

mourning rituals, 25–27; and ideology of civilization, 28–33; and gendered spaces, 33–36, 41–44; and uses of the past, 38–41; use of public influence, 45–47; and fundraising, 47–49; decline of influence, 49–53
Wilder, Douglas (Gov. of Virginia), 337
Wiley, E. L., 167
Wiley, Joseph L., 91
William Johnson House, 325
Williams, Frances L., 84
Williams, George Washington, 72
Williams, Hosea, 263
Williams, Rev. R. S., 93
Williamsburg, 225
Williamson, Mrs. Chalmers Meek, 24
Wilmington (NC), 193, 333
Wilson (NC), 281
Wilson, Joseph T., 76, 96
Wister, Owen, 223
Women of the Confederacy monument (Jacksonville, FL), 18
Women's Relief Corps, 85
Woodbury, Rosa, 38
Woodson, Carter G., 151, 152, 153, 162, 280, 283, 288, 290; *African Myths Together with Proverbs*, 164; *The Negro in Our History*, 164
Woodson, Jonathan M., 22
Woodville (GA), 77
Woodward, C. Vann, 11
World War I, 71
Wright, Ethel, 87
Wright, John, 227
Wright, Rev. R. R., 93, 96
Wright, Richard, 324